THE Black Parenting BOOK

Linda Villarosa is the editor of *Body & Soul: The Black Women's Guide to Physical Health and Emotional Well-Being* and the coauthor of *Finding Our Way: The Teen Girls' Survival Guide*

Allison Abner is the coauthor of *Finding Our Way: The Teen Girls' Survival Guide*

THE Black Parenting BOOK

Anne C. Beal, M.D., M.P.H.,
Linda Villarosa,
and Allison Abner

BROADWAY BOOKS NEW YORK

Broadway Books titles may be purchased for business or promotional use or for special sales. For information, please write to: Special Markets Department, Random House, Inc., 1540 Broadway, New York, NY 10036.

Library of Congress Cataloging-in-Publication Data
Beal, Anne C.
The black parenting book : caring for our children in the first five years / Anne C. Beal, Linda Villarosa, and Allison Abner. —1st ed.
p. cm.
Includes index.
ISBN 0-7679-0196-7 (pbk.)
1. Child rearing—United States. 2. Afro-American parents. 3. Parent and child—United States. I. Villarosa, Linda. II. Abner, Allison, 1959– . III. Title.
HQ769.B3455 1998
649'.1'08996073—dc21
98-28120
CIP

FIRST EDITION

DESIGNED BY RENATO STANISIC

Illustrations by Arleen Frasca
Charts and graphs prepared by Jeff Ward

00 01 02 03 10 9 8 7 6 5 4

To our families

Contents

Acknowledgments

The three of us want to graciously thank all of the people who committed to this project and helped us bring it to fruition: Barbara Lowenstein and Madeleine Morel, our invaluable agents, who got this project off the ground and made it happen. Daisy Alpert, for her enthusiasm and good spirit—and for being the superglue who pulled together all the elements and details. Janet Goldstein, for having the insight to see the value of such a book and for helping us make sense of it. Tracy Behar and Angela Casey, who helped us make it to the finish. Sabiyha Prince, for being such a diligent and talented interviewer and researcher. Your participation was a wonderful contribution to our book. Desiree Vester, who despite several other obligations, always came through with incredible research on black children. Regina Cash, for interviews that were difficult to come by, and Melinda Goodman, for her valuable research. Pam Toussaint, Ziba Kashef, and Ann Brown for pitching in on writing and reporting. All the parents of young children who agreed to be interviewed and photographed for this book—we appreciate your time, honesty, and courage. The many experts on child health and development who offered their time and often hard-to-come-by information.

Anne

My first thanks go to my children. You sustain me and were the inspiration for so many wonderful things, including this project. I can't begin to say how much I love you.

Special thanks to my family and friends. You have been there through my darkest days and have shared my joys and successes. My sister Lisa, I look at the girls and think about us. What a long way we've come! My sister/girlfriends, thanks for sharing life's journey. To my coauthors, Linda and Allison, thank you for your support through this process—it's been great! And to my husband. You joined me after I started the journey through parenthood. You have taken on the role of parent and partner with amazing ease and manage to make me laugh on a daily basis. Thank you for your love and support—and for sharing your computer :-)

Linda

Thanks loads to: First and foremost to my parents and my sister for giving me a strong foundation and continued love and support. To my friends, Jacqui and Michelle, who help me be the person and the parent I want to be. To the rest of my friends, who really are family, too. To my former colleagues at *Essence*, for allowing me to grow as a person and a mother. To Lorry and Miguel, the greatest fathers. To my coauthor, Anne, for being smart and good, and to Allison, a wonderful cowriter and caring, attentive friend. And, finally, to Vickie and Kali, I bless the day each of you came into my life.

Allison

I send special thanks to: My father, who gave me a strong sense of identity and a wonderful example. I know you're with me. My mother for teaching me what it means to be a mother and supporting me inexhaustibly through this project, and the rest of my life. My brother for being my friend and confidant, and for introducing Miles to *Star Wars*. Linda for partnering once again. Your generosity and amazing talents have made me the luckiest coauthor I know. Sabiyha, my girl, for being such a reliable and special friend to me. And, best for last, my husband, Mark, for being such a good partner in the journey through parenthood. And my baby, Miles, for being the funny, beautiful, articulate, intense whirlwind that you are.

Fifteen Ways to Be a Better Parent

"Let's write a book for us." This was the first thing the three of us thought of when we conceived of the idea of a resource for African-American parents that would provide not only essential medical and developmental information but also practical tips and shared stories from other parents around the country. We understood intimately the need for parents with young children to have a single sourcebook at hand that would offer easy-to-digest advice from child development experts as well as honest discussions of challenges that are unique to black families. We had each longed for and looked for such a book, and when we couldn't find it, we decided to create it ourselves.

At the time, writing a book specifically for African-American parents was of special interest to all of us, and we each had our own specific issues to contend with. Linda, then the executive editor of *Essence,* was a working mother who had to balance a highly rewarding but demanding career with the daily responsibilities of parenting. As a lesbian parent of a biracial, bilingual daughter, Linda seemingly had the most challenges out of the three of us, but as it turned out, she actually had the most support because her family and extended community of friends were eager to pitch in on the child care. Of all our children, Linda's daughter, Kali, has had the most diverse—not to mention exciting—upbringing, including visiting her father's family in Peru, being cared for by an array of black, white, Latino, gay, and straight "uncles" and "aunties," and playing with an equally mixed group of children who live right on her block. Linda and her partner, Vickie, have maintained a stable and loving environment for their daughter, and Linda shares many stories from her special point of view that all of us can relate to.

When Linda saw the need for a parenting column in *Essence,* Dr. Anne Beal seemed to materialize at just the right moment. Her experience as a divorced mother of two preschool girls (Naima and Djavan), as a pediatrician helping African-American families from a variety of backgrounds, and as a researcher at one of the nation's most renowned medical schools made her the perfect candidate for the column, called "Doctor's in the House," and, as it turns out, an excellent collaborator for *The Black Parenting Book.* Anne was undergoing her own series of life challenges: beginning a new career, starting life in a new city, getting remarried, and blending a new family. By sharing her personal stories, Anne believed parents would get a fresh perspective, knowing that an acclaimed expert on babies, who also holds a medical degree, still makes mistakes and faces the same dilemmas as all parents.

During the writing of this book, Allison also was no stranger to family stresses. She moved from a racially mixed neighborhood in downtown Manhattan to a predominately white suburb, lived and worked in a nine-month home renovation, and coped with the death of her father. As a work-at-home mother, she contended with meeting the needs of her husband and toddler, Miles, while trying to carve out enough time in the day for work, household chores, and downtime. Like Linda and Anne, Allison wanted to impart her stories to other parents who are learning through experience how to parent with patience, love, and lots of room for improvement.

What all three of us have learned through trial and error is that no one person or book has all the answers. In fact, we aren't interested in providing all the answers but rather in sharing with you what we have found to be helpful in establishing loving, trusting, and healthy relationships with our own young children. Like you, we know that parenthood is not an exact science and can never be perfected, only improved. In order to do this, we prepared a list of what we consider to be some—but definitely not all—of the most important ways that we can become better parents.

1. Be a good example. Unlike most other animals, humans don't function primarily on instinct. We learn by watching those we are closest to, imitating their behavior and values, and then experimenting until we master the skills or practices ourselves. As parents, we aren't always aware that we influence our children's behavior by our actions—more so than by our words. How you spend your time, how you express your emotions or creativity, and how you involve yourself in your spiritual and local community are absorbed by your child. One of the best gifts you can give your child is to be a good example, in which you embody and live by your family's values and beliefs. (For more on this topic, refer to Chapter 5 on discipline, Chapter 8 on spirituality, Chapter 11 on learning and play.)

2. Respect your child as a person. Many of us were brought up in authoritarian families where respect meant "do what I say and do it now!" Stating an opinion was considered "back talk," trying to be understood was "sass," and both could get you a swift switch on the backside. Researchers now know that children raised in families where parents place reasonable demands, set clear and firm limits, and allow children to participate in household rules grow up to have better relationships with their parents, feel more assertive, and exercise better problem-solving skills than children from authoritarian homes. One of the fundamental differences is a parent's respect—for the child's opinion, physical space, and contribution to the family. Examine your views of children and how they should be treated and ask yourself if this is how you would want to be treated as an adult. If the answer is "no," then consider other ways to exercise your parental role. (For more on this topic, see Chapter 5 on discipline and Chapter 12 on stress.)

Taking a humorous approach can help ease parenting struggles.

3. Keep a sense of humor. Whenever possible, take the opportunity to step outside of yourself to see what's funny, even in not-so-funny situations. Sometimes showing your child how ridiculous something is can be more effective than scolding (for example, if she wants to go outside in sneakers instead of rain boots, remind her that she'll get cold, wet "raisin" toes). Children are masters at finding the silly and the absurd in most things. So take the opportunity to join in and let out some tension with a good laugh.

4. Take time for yourself. Single parents, stay-home parents, and working parents take note! We all need a break at least once a week to spend time with our friends or by ourselves doing something we really enjoy. Reading, going to a movie, eating out, taking a mineral bath, or whatever you find life affirming or fun should be part of your weekly schedule. And don't leave out your partner all of the time. Relationships have been known to suffer because parents spend too much of their free time on chores and other family obligations. So book a baby-sitter and do what *you* want.

5. Plan for the future. Sadly, most of us are too stressed and often too strapped to do much planning for the future. We live day to day, sometimes even moment to moment. However, setting personal and family goals is a key means to reduce stress in your life. While everyone needs room for spontaneity, there are areas that require careful planning to assure you accomplish what you need to for your family.

Not all of your goals need to be financial; spiritual, social, and educational ones are just as valid and important. However, most goals also carry a price tag (for example, paying for private school or donating money to your church). Many of us avoid planning because we realize that it often involves sacrifice and delayed gratification—a great lesson for your child to learn! Planning takes discipline and a clear vision, but the rewards are enormous.

6. Have reasonable expectations for your child. Your relationship with your child is in part determined by your expectations for her behavior and abilities. Being aware of what is developmentally appropriate behavior or understanding your child's personality can help you avoid friction and appreciate what your child *can* do. Often our fear, frustration, or insecurity leads us to compare our children to others, wondering "Is my child normal?" or "Keisha's child doesn't have tantrums, why does mine?" or "What's my child's problem?" Instead of comparing, observe your child and keep track of her behavior patterns. Knowing and understanding your child's unique qualities and quirks will improve your relationship now and forever.

7. Help your child think for herself. The goal of parenting is to care for and guide your child until the day comes when she is an independent adult. Being independent requires good judgment and problem-solving skills, tools that we begin providing for our children from the start. Giving a child guidance and setting clear limits helps her establish her own internal voice of reason that tells her, "Don't put the screwdriver in the light socket because it's very dangerous and I'll get hurt." Parents do their children a disservice by not explaining clearly the reason behind their rules. "Because I said so" or "Because I'm your father" will establish your authority, but it won't help your child learn. Whenever possible, explain the consequences of your child's behavior and, as she gets older, ask her to recall why certain rules are necessary to follow. You'll begin to see that, through consistency and repetition, your guidance pays off.

8. Remember what's important. Most family fights can be avoided if we keep in mind what is most important. Maintaining family ties with respect, dignity, love, and clear limits is what matters most in parenting. Children who learn to compromise and let go of petty fights and concerns have fewer conflicts inside and outside the home. So when you find yourself locked in a struggle, ask yourself, "What's important and how can this be resolved so we can all get what we want?"

9. Lean on your friends and family. Being a parent takes tremendous energy and reserves, especially when your children are under school age. Therefore, having the comfort and support of family and friends is crucial in your daily life. Without an emotional support network, parents feel overwhelmed, burdened, and alone. Connecting, swapping stories, and venting with those who know and love us (especially if they're parents, too) renews us. We feel understood and validated, and we are often able to see our way clearly through a difficult situation.

10. Forgive your parenting mistakes. Just about every parent has to survive parental guilt, that awful feeling when you know you've hurt your child in some way. As our own parents had hoped, we see that being a parent requires making mistakes, being hated, and making difficult decisions. We also see that most of the time we do our best for our children but, regardless of our best efforts, sometimes we fail them. Acknowledging your wrong is the first step in doing what's right and learning from what didn't work. It's also a way to demonstrate to your child that when you hurt someone you love, you can make amends and rebuild trust. Even if you feel you've failed your child profoundly, it's never too late to be a better parent.

11. Spend individual time with your child. The best way to improve or maintain your relationship with your child is to spend time alone with him. Every day or once a week, plan an activity that you both enjoy or explore activities together. If possible, each parent should set a regular date with each child. He will feel special and important knowing that you want to be with him. This time will also allow you to talk privately about family issues or other topics important to you and your child.

12. Talk to your child. Studies of parents and infants show that the more we speak to our children in a loving way, the more we boost their IQs. Talking teaches children new words, concepts, and complex ideas, and activates brain activity that affects intelligence. So chat away about what you're cooking for dinner, what you did at work, or what your life was like when you were her age.

13. Read and sing to your child. Talking, reading, and singing teach our children about language, rhythm, and tone. While having fun, children also learn about our culture, are introduced to concepts like counting, and learn to love learning. Although reading to a child often and early is one of the best ways to boost school performance in later years, many of our children are not read to as part of their daily routine. So get started: Reading at least one book a day will go a long way in your child's future.

14. Help your child foster relationships with others. For the first few years, even when you are away, you will remain the center of your child's universe. A parent holds the most esteemed place in a child's heart, and through that close relationship a child feels free to branch out into other meaningful bonds with family members, caregivers, teachers, and peers. From these other relationships, she will acquire important social skills (like resolving conflicts and following directions outside the home) and become exposed to ideas and subjects she may not learn at home. She will also come to see herself as someone separate from you who has her own likes and dislikes, makes her own choice of friends, and pursues interests outside of your relationship.

15. Find the child in yourself. By the time we reach adulthood, much of our sense of wonder, our creativity, and our ability to have uninhibited fun is gone. When we tap into that part of ourselves, we discover that our most true, free, and happy selves have been buried for years. Having children can help us return to those days of making mud pies, puddle jumping, and fantasy. Why not join in on the fun with your child, rediscovering a cookie, making bubble beards, or following a favorite story character in make-believe? We could all use a break from adulthood every once in a while.

As black parents, we know how important having the support of family, friends, and our community is in raising our children. We hope this book will become part of your support network and will open new avenues for you and your children. We welcome any comments or suggestions addressed to us in care of the publisher.

Good reading and good luck,
Anne, Linda, and Allison

Chapter

1

Healthy Baby (The First Year)

This chapter starts where your baby's life begins—in the delivery room or birthing center. From the first checkup to the nine-month doctor visit, your infant will undergo various tests, receive a number of shots, and hit several physical and cognitive milestones. It will be important and reassuring for you, as a new parent, to know what to expect.

Ten Ways We Can Give Our Babies Great Starts

Welcoming a new baby into your family requires more than just buying a stroller, crib, and cute clothes. Babies demand an enormous amount of care and patience and are entirely dependent on us to meet their needs. The following are ten of the most important things we believe you can do to help your child be happy and healthy, and to thrive.

1. *Breast-feed your baby, if possible.* There is no formula or food in the world that can replace breast milk. It is the single most nutritious food for a baby. Plus, it boosts the immune system to protect against colds, ear infections, and diarrhea. And the closeness it provides for you and your baby cannot be replaced. (See more about breast-feeding in Chapter 7.)

2. *Do not smoke.* If you or anyone in your household smokes, you are putting your baby at risk for a number of ailments, including asthma, respiratory infections, and SIDS (Sudden Infant Death Syndrome or crib death—see more about SIDS on p. 12). Furthermore, smoking while breast-feeding can pass along many harmful chemicals through your breast milk. These reasons—along with concerns for your own health—should be enough incentive to quit.

3. *Do not hit, shake, push, grab, or otherwise hurt your baby.* Whether or not you believe in spanking as a form of punishment, hitting your baby is abusive. Thousands of infants each year are killed or permanently injured by shaken baby syndrome, which occurs when a caregiver shakes an infant to stop him from crying. Your baby is too young to understand rules, to know the difference between right and wrong, or to purposely try to work your nerves. If you find yourself getting frustrated, losing your temper, or frightening your child, take a break. Put your baby in a safe place (like his crib) and leave the room. Call for help and have someone else take over for a while. (See Chapter 5 for more on disciplining and shaken baby syndrome.)

4. *Get your baby vaccinated on time.* There is no more effective way to protect your child from life-threatening or harmful diseases than to have her immunized. Many African-American parents have fears about the effects of vaccines on their small children or have a general mistrust of the health care system. While these misgivings are understandable, when they are weighed against the benefits, the clear winner is vaccinating. (See pp. 13–14 for a discussion of vaccinations.)

5. *Expect your baby to cry.* Think of your baby as a completely helpless being whose main form of communication is crying. Babies' cries are biologically programmed to unnerve us, so that we're motivated to find a reason for the crying and address that need to stop the crying. And if you can't get your baby to hush, it does't mean you are an incompetent parent. There might not be anything more to do than hold her. As your baby grows, she'll find other ways to communicate her needs, but until then, comfort your baby when she cries and try to find the reason for the tears. (See Chapter 6 for more on crying.)

6. *Show your baby love. There is no such thing as spoiling an infant.* African-American relatives are famous for telling new parents they are spoiling their children by picking them up "too much" or calming them when they cry. Don't listen. Babies come in cute and cuddly packages because they're meant to be held, smiled at, and comforted. Studies show that babies who are worn in baby carriers or held a great deal gain weight, are healthier, happier, and cry less.

7. *Choose a competent primary health care provider for your baby.* Finding a physician for your child may take some time, but it will pay off in the end. As African Americans, we are more likely to have low-birth-weight babies, and infants with anemia or lead poisoning. This means it's critical that our babies get the care they need as soon as they are born. If we are vigilant about their health and health care, our children are more likely to stay within healthy height and weight percentiles, reach milestones on time, and have fewer health problems throughout their lives.

8. *Carefully choose a child care provider.* Even if you will be your child's primary caretaker, you will need extra help. Family members tend to be the best first choice, but they aren't always available. If you, like most African-American parents, work or find that you need more help, be sure to use the same rigorous process in choosing a professional baby-sitter or day care facility that you would in making any important decision: research, get references, interview at least once, have your sitter spend time with your child in your presence, and be willing to pay for good care. Your child is a vulnerable, dependent person who deserves to be taken care of by someone who will respect her, likes to be with her, and wants to see her thrive. (See Chapter 10 for more on choosing child care.)

9. *Get a bedtime routine established early.* Unfortunately, almost one-quarter of African-American children aren't getting enough sleep. Healthy sleep patterns contribute to good behavior, better learning and school performance, and higher IQs! By setting up a regular bedtime routine while your child is still an infant (some time after four months), you will help him learn how to fall asleep on his own, sleep through the night, and have fewer sleep problems later in life. (See Chapter 6 for more on sleep.)

10. *Have fun.* The more you smile at your baby, the more she will smile at you. New research shows that babies learn best when they are being loved, smiled at, and talked to in "parentese" (baby talk that parents instinctively use with their children). Children who are talked to, sung to, and cuddled often grow up with a stronger self-esteem and higher intelligence and are better socially adjusted than those who aren't. Learning to appreciate your baby's achievements, enjoying her company, and sharing her desire to play will help establish a closer parent-child bond. (For more ideas on play and activities see Chapter 11.)

At Birth: Milestones

The Apgar Test

Right after delivery, your baby will be assessed by an Apgar test. This test helps the delivery nurse or physician determine the newborn's general condition and overall responsiveness. Your child's heart rate, respiration, muscle tone, reflexes, and color are checked and scored one minute after birth and again at five minutes. An overall score of 10 means that your baby's condition is excellent; a lower score may mean that your child needs some extra assistance adapting to her new environment. If, for example, the one-minute score for your child's respiration is low—indicating that his breath is slow and irregular—the delivery staff may place an oxygen mask over his mouth to deepen his breathing and improve his five-minute score.

Most healthy babies' overall scores fall between 8 and 10. If your child's score is lower—say because she was premature or stressed during delivery—the Apgar test

Apgar Scoring System

Score	0	1	2
Heart rate	Absent	Less than 100/min	More than 100/min
Respiratory effort	Absent	Slow irregular	Good, crying
Muscle tone	Limp	Some flexion of extremities	Active motion
Reflex irritability (in response to catheter in nose)	Absent	Grimace	Grimace and cough or sneeze
Color	Blue, pale	Body pink, extremities blue	Completely pink

Each sign is evaluated individually and scored from 0 to 2 at both one and five minutes of life. The final score at each time is the sum of the individual scores. From Apgar: *Curr Res Anesthesiol* 32:260, 1953.

will help the staff identify and treat any problem right away. (However, it's important to note that there isn't a strong association between a low Apgar score and ongoing physical or neurological problems. The test is only useful as an initial assessment after delivery.)

Newborn Visit

Soon after birth, in the delivery room or nursery, your newborn will be weighed, measured, and given additional treatments. You may be feeling tired while you are in the hospital, but now's a good time to ask some basic questions about breast-feeding (or bottle-feeding, depending on your plans), baby care basics and your own well-being. Below are some of the tests and treatments to expect:

- *Vitamin K shot.* Because all newborn babies are deficient in this vitamin, which promotes normal blood clotting, your baby will need a vitamin K shot after birth to prevent excessive bleeding.
- *Antibiotic eye cream.* To avoid eye infections that can be contracted during passage through the birth canal, antibiotic eyedrops or silver nitrate ointment will be given to your new baby.
- *Umbilical cord care.* The stump of the umbilical cord, which was clamped at birth, will be cleaned with alcohol to help the cord heal and stave off infection. In some hospitals they paint the cord with an antibacterial dye or other medication.
- *Blood tests.* A blood sample will be taken (by pricking your baby's heel) to test

whether she has a number of illnesses such as phenylketonuria (PKU), a serious condition that can cause mental retardation, or hypothyroidism, which can also lead to retardation. Depending on the laws in your state, the blood sample may also be checked for sickle-cell anemia, a condition that is more common in African Americans. (States vary on HIV testing. Some are testing anonymously, so it's best to ask.) The PKU test is best done after the first 24 hours; if not, the test should be done within three weeks of birth.

- *Hepatitis B.* At the hospital, your baby may receive her first vaccine against Hepatitis B, a viral illness that affects the liver. It will be administered shortly after birth (if not now, then at one of the first visits to your health care provider), and later your baby will be given two more doses.

Nursing

Moms who decide to breast-feed (and you should if you can) should make the first attempt as soon as possible (within an hour or so after birth) when the baby is still alert and active. When you put your baby to your breast, she will most likely lick it and then, with some coaxing, grab the nipple and begin to suckle for several minutes. Some babies take more time getting the hang of it, especially if they are sleepy. That's why you shouldn't wait more than an hour after birth to start breast-feeding. In fact, it's best to inquire in advance about the hospital's procedure on nursing.

You shouldn't be discouraged if breast-feeding is difficult at first. Remember that your baby is new to the world and you may be new to motherhood (and you're both probably tired and overwhelmed), so it might take a little time and practice for the two of you to be in sync. Don't give up, and don't be afraid to ask for help. A nurse or lactation consultant can give you some pointers while you're in the hospital. Afterward, your pediatrician or obstetrician can help you or refer you to a lactation consultant. (For more detailed information on breast-feeding, see Chapter 7.)

Breast-feeding in those first few hours causes the uterus to contract, which helps prevent uterine bleeding. Plus, the yellowish fluid that your breast produces within the first few days after birth (known as colostrum) is rich with protein and antibodies that boost your child's immunity and help protect her from infection.

Your Baby's Health Care: The First Year

During the first year, your baby will need to make a number of visits to your pediatrician. It's vital for your child's well being that you stick to the basic schedule of visits:

First Week
One Month
Two Months
Four Months
Six Months
Nine Months

At each visit your health care provider will give your child a complete physical exam. She will measure weight, length, and head size and mark them on a graph to evaluate growth. Your provider will also discuss certain developmental milestones, such as your baby's first real smile (look for this at about two months), and she will receive the vaccines listed below. (See a discussion of vaccinations on pp. 13–14.)

The First Week

The first week of your baby's life signals a major adjustment in your life. You'll be trying to heal your body—especially if you needed a C-section or episiotomy—and, at the same time, care for a newborn. As a new parent, you may be feeling overwhelmed and tired and maybe frustrated as you learn to deal with your baby's needs by trial and error. You'll also be getting used to a new sound in your home: crying.

During this time, you may be wondering if your baby is getting enough to eat. She'll need breast milk or formula at least every three to four hours, but many babies like to eat every one to two hours. The best way to gauge her hunger is to pay attention to her cues. Your pediatrician will check her weight gain (remember that newborns generally lose weight after delivery but gain it back in the first week) and give you advice about feeding. Also, six or more wet diapers and three to four stools per day will let you know that your baby is getting enough to eat.

As far as your needs go, try to conserve your energy and rest when the baby sleeps. Ask for help from family and friends, but try to be firm and put a stop to any unwanted or annoying advice. Make it a point to share your feelings and concerns with someone you trust. If you start to feel overwhelmed by well-meaning visitors or too many phone calls, take some time for yourself.

Choosing a Pediatrician

One of your first and most important acts as a parent will be selecting your child's pediatrician. (Ideally, you should take care of this task before your baby is born.) There are a lot of questions to consider, and as a black parent you may want a pediatrician who is not only well trained and accessible but who also understands your culture and traditions.

To find a good pediatrician, ask your obstetrician/gynecologist for two or three referrals and quiz other mothers about who they take their children to and why. Call first to find out whether the doctors accept your insurance plan, then arrange to meet each one.

Here's what you'll want to consider when choosing a pediatrician before your baby is born—and after:

1. Accessibility

- *Is the office convenient for you?* (Remember, you're going to be carrying a baby and all of her "stuff" with you to each appointment.) Can you get there by public transportation? Is there parking?
- *What are the office hours?* Is the office open early in the morning? After 6 P.M.? On weekends?
- *How does the pediatrician handle emergencies?* Where is the emergency room she or he uses?
- *Is there a long wait?* Your time is as valuable as the doctor's, so take note of waiting time when you visit.
- *How does the doctor manage referrals to specialists?* Do the specialists have to be affiliated with a particular hospital or health care plan?

2. Communication

- *How comfortable are you with the doctor?* As a new parent, you'll have lots of questions and concerns, so it's very important that you choose a pediatrician you can talk to.
- *How comfortable is the doctor with you?* Does she spend time with you and patiently answer your questions? Or is the visit hurried and her answers short?
- *Are other staff members accessible to you?* Nurses and physician's assistants can be very helpful and informative.
- *How does the doctor handle questions you may have between visits?* Is there an answering service? Who staffs it? These are critical questions for black parents since our higher rates of low-birth-weight babies mean our infants often have "special needs" and need extra attention.

3. Competence

- ***Is she gentle and skilled as a physician?*** **You may not think you'll be able to judge this, but watch her carefully as she examines your child and trust your gut reaction.**
- ***Have patients lodged complaints against this doctor?*** **Your state's licensing board may provide this information.**
- ***Which hospital is she affiliated with?*** **Make sure the hospital has a good reputation; teaching hospitals are generally the best.**
- ***Is she highly regarded by other medical professionals?*** **Ask your ob-gyn about her reputation or talk to the staff of the hospital she's affiliated with.**

4. Race and Gender

- ***Would you prefer a black doctor? A woman?*** **Think about your comfort level, because it's critical that you can communicate with your pediatrician.**
- ***Is the doctor—regardless of race—aware that our children may have different needs?*** **Is she up on the latest findings about African-American infants and children? Does she have other black patients?**
- ***Consider this:*** **If the doctor and her staff come highly recommended, you can talk to her comfortably, she respects you and is accessible, she has knowledge of some of the specific needs of black patients or is at least sensitive to them, her office hours and location are convenient, and she seems competent and skilled, those factors may be more important than race and gender.**

But if you feel strongly about finding a black pediatrician seek a referral from your ob-gyn, other black physicians, or call the National Medical Association at (202) 347–1895 for the name of a physician in your area.

Health Care: First-Week Visit. Now that new mothers are often discharged within 48 hours of childbirth, families need more health supervision than in the past. So it's important to make this first appointment a few days after getting home.

At this visit, your pediatrician will take a complete medical history and examine and measure your child. If your baby didn't receive a vaccine against Hepatitis B, she may get it now. Use this first visit as an opportunity to express any concerns about your baby and to ask even the most basic questions. It's also a good time to talk about the kind of relationship you would like to have with your health care provider.

Caring for Colic

Most people have heard horror stories about infants with colic. Lots of crying, fussy babies, late nights pacing the floor, and no real effective treatments—this sounds like every parent's nightmare.

Colic is characterized by long bouts of crying that don't stop even after the baby has been fed, changed, and rocked. While a certain amount of crying is normal, infants with colic can cry for hours. In general, if your baby cries for more than three hours per day, at least three times per week, she has colic. Many parents describe their colicky infants as being fretful, especially toward the end of the day, and/or having a lot of gas and appearing uncomfortable.

No one can explain why colic occurs. Since colicky babies seem to have a lot of gas and abdominal pain, some parents have focused on relieving gas to stop the fuss. There are several products available to reduce gas, but none really helps. Other parents have tried different types of formula, and many are marketed to parents as being easier to digest and helpful for colicky babies. Again, no formula has been consistently found to help with colic. Other babies with colic seem to be sensitive to their environments and are easily startled or overwhelmed by stimuli. By the end of the day, these kids have a "melt down" and seem to soothe themselves by having a crying fit.

The good news is that your infant will definitely outgrow her colic. Most babies learn to calm themselves and cry less at around three months of age. Until that time, here are some things you can do:

- Swaddle your baby in a blanket.
- Walk with your baby or keep her next to you in a baby carrier.
- Place your baby in a swing.
- Take your baby for a ride. A lot of babies calm down when in a car.
- Let the vacuum cleaner run. The "white noise" calms some infants.
- Put your baby on top of the dryer. This mimics the sound and motion of being in a car.
- Rub your baby's belly.
- Put your baby down and let her cry it out.
- Give yourself a break and let someone else take over for a while.
- Keep repeating to yourself that nothing is wrong with your baby and that she will outgrow this phase.

One-Week Milestones. Your baby will be sleeping frequently during this period (but, unfortunately, probably not through the night), so it's important to take advantage of his waking time to encourage development and establish the parent-infant bond. Be creative: Talk and sing to him, smile at him, rock and cuddle him.

MOVEMENT: He moves his arms and legs, but these are not purposeful movements.

SIGHT: He likes staring at your face and follows it with his eyes.

HEARING: He responds to sound by blinking, crying, quieting, changing respiration, or being startled.

One Month

At this point, you're probably feeling a little more confident as a parent. You can probably understand your baby's cries (you may have realized, for example, that your child—like many—has a fussy period at the end of the day) and you have learned to comfort her through touch, soothing sounds, or a smile. Feeding has probably gotten more routine, and you've also gotten to know your child's stool patterns very well.

Nonetheless, you may still have feelings of stress and inadequacy. Continue to rest, ask for help, and take time for yourself. If you have other children, try to give individual attention to each sibling. It's also a good idea to join a parenting group or get together with other parents of newborns to share experiences and tips.

Health Care: One-Month Visit. At this visit, your pediatrician will examine and measure your child. She'll receive the second Hepatitis B vaccine if the first was given at birth. New parents often worry about constipation—which is rare in breast-fed babies—and diarrhea. You may want to ask specific questions about the color and consistency of your baby's stools to be sure everything is normal.

One-Month Milestones. Your baby will spend more time awake than she did at birth—an hour or longer balanced with three or four hours sleeping at a time. She will also begin to demonstrate advances in development.

MOVEMENT: Once-jerky arm and leg movements will now begin to smooth as your baby's nervous system develops. You may also notice that her hand grasp is getting stronger. She may lift her head momentarily when on her stomach.

SIGHT: Born with peripheral vision, your baby will slowly acquire the ability to focus, track objects, and recognize patterns. At one month, he should be able to

What You Must Know About SIDS

Sudden Infant Death Syndrome, or SIDS, is the term used when babies die in their sleep for unknown reasons. (You may also have heard it called "crib death.") This happens to approximately two to three newborns out of one thousand per year. Though there is no known cause of SIDS, several risk factors have been recognized. Babies are more likely to have SIDS if they were born prematurely, have a low birth weight, are male, are one of a multiple birth, have a family history of SIDS, sleep on their stomachs, or have a mother who smokes.

African-American babies are more susceptible to SIDS for several reasons. Black babies have a much higher rate of low birth weight, almost ten times higher than whites. Smoking is more common in our community, while breast-feeding—which decreases the risk of SIDS—is not.

Though there is no sure way of preventing SIDS, there are concrete ways to lower the risk:

- Place your baby on his back to sleep. The American Academy of Pediatrics (AAP) recommends this practice, especially during the first six months of life.
- Use firm bedding. Do not allow your baby to sleep on beanbag cushions, sheepskins, sofa cushions, adult pillows, or fluffy comforters, which have all been identified as hazardous for infants by the U.S. Consumer Product Safety Commission.
- Avoid overheating. Too much clothing, heavy bedding, and high room temperature have been associated with increased risk of SIDS. Dress your baby lightly, especially when she is ill.
- Breast-feed. Research has shown that breast-feeding has been linked to decreased risk of SIDS.
- Stop smoking. Mothers who smoke during and after pregnancy triple their babies' risk of SIDS. Also, don't allow others to smoke around your child.
- Maintain high health standards for your child. Keep up with doctor visits and immunizations. Notify your health care provider immediately if your infant demonstrates any breathing difficulties, such as prolonged pauses in breathing or episodes of turning blue.

focus on objects eight to twelve inches away (he especially likes your face) and will be more attentive to black-and-white patterns and bright colors.

HEARING: Though your baby will be sensitive to loud noises from birth, her hearing ability will mature remarkably during the first month. At one month, she will respond to human voices and recognize familiar sounds such as the ringing of a bell or music from a toy. She is easily soothed by the sound of your voice so continue singing and talking to her.

SMELL/TOUCH: Your baby will display sensitivity to different scents and textures. By the end of one month, he recognizes the smell of your breast milk and exhibits a preference for sweet smells over bitter ones and soft over rough sensations.

The Facts About Vaccines

Immunizations are a fundamental part of your child's health care. Vaccines provide protection against a host of illnesses, including measles, tetanus, whooping cough, and, most recently, chicken pox. Unfortunately, African-American children, for a variety of reasons including financial and distrust of health care providers, are more likely to not be adequately vaccinated.

One of the most recently reviewed immunizations is the polio vaccine. Because of the rare risk (1 in 1.4 million cases per year) that a parent or household member whose immune system is weak could contract paralytic polio from an immunized child, the Centers for Disease Control and the American Academy of Pediatrics recently recommended a new strategy for polio prevention. Instead of four doses of oral vaccine, which contain a type of live polio virus, the polio immunization schedule can include two doses of injected inactivated polio virus followed by two doses of oral vaccine. Because the inactivated virus cannot cause polio even in people with weak immune systems, the CDC estimates that the new guidelines will decrease cases caused by the vaccine by up to 75 percent. Nonetheless, some people remain worried about the last two doses. (If the immune system of someone in your household is compromised, discuss this vaccine issue thoroughly with your doctor.)

In the past, the DTP (diphtheria/tetanus/pertussis) vaccine sparked controversy. The vaccine was known to cause side effects such as high fevers and even brain damage in rare cases. In 1991, a safer version of the DTP vaccine, known as the DTaP vaccine, was introduced, which was much less likely to cause serious side effects. This newer formulation of the vaccine is now available for babies as young as six weeks old. ➢

In 1995, the chicken pox vaccine was included in the American Academy of Pediatrics list of recommended vaccines, but some parents were skeptical. The vaccine is not 100 percent effective, but it does prevent the disease in the majority (about 80 percent) of children. For those who aren't completely protected and catch chicken pox, the illness tends to be less severe, which is a key benefit for working parents who can't take a lot of time from work to care for sick children.

Because of an historically ingrained mistrust of doctors and the medical establishment—fueled by documented injustices—black parents may be especially wary of vaccines. Some parents have heard about the side effects of the DTP vaccine, but don't know about the newer version. Others fear vaccines because of the side effects and are concerned about their children. (And the side effects are real: The measles vaccine, for example, can cause a rash and fever. Ask your pediatrician for more details.)

But weighing the benefits against the risks, vaccines are truly advantageous and protect children against serious illnesses. In fact, the authors of this book have all had their children vaccinated. Think about the odds: One out of every hundred babies under age six who gets pertussis dies from it; three out of four require hospitalization. Four out of ten people who get tetanus die from it. Because of vaccines, smallpox has been completely eradicated and measles could be eradicated.

Parents who have concerns about vaccines should speak to their pediatricians, but keep in mind that nearly all doctors will encourage you to vaccinate your child. (For more information about vaccinations, see Resources.)

Two Months

At this point, you will be more comfortable being a parent, and you'll be settling into your new role. Your baby is probably communicating more with smiles, coos, and sounds. It's important to provide feedback by smiling back, singing, talking, and cuddling. Your schedule has probably gotten more regular—and you may even be getting a little more sleep.

If you have a mate, you should ideally be spending some time together alone. If you have other children, it's great to plan family activities together so they don't feel left out.

You may be going back to work, which means you'll have to think about child care. (See Chapter 10.) If you are heading back to your job, you may be feeling guilty about leaving the baby. Be sure to discuss these emotions with someone close to you.

Health Care: Two-Month Visit. At this visit, your pediatrician will perform a complete physical exam and check baby's length, weight, and head circumference and plot it on a standard chart. She will also evaluate your child's development as well as eating and sleeping patterns. Your baby will probably receive vaccines at this visit. (See the Appendix for immunization schedule.) Be sure to ask your health care provider about any side effects you should expect from the shots.

Two-Month Milestones. Each month, your infant will gain 1½ to 2 pounds, grow 1 to 1½ inches in length, and his head size will increase 1½ inch in diameter. The two soft spots on his head will remain open and flat. Infants are (finally!) sleeping through the night at this age.

MOVEMENT: Your baby will continue to display certain infant reflexes but these will fade as his movements become more deliberate. By this time, he will be able to briefly raise his head—and maybe his neck and upper chest, too—while lying down on his stomach. You may also notice that he has more head control while upright but still can't totally support his neck.

SIGHT: By two months, your baby will be better able to track objects, moving and focusing her eyes simultaneously. Your face is her favorite image.

HEARING/SPEECH: In response to your voice, your infant will coo and gurgle.

SOCIAL/EMOTIONAL: Your baby's smile will become more expressive as he learns to maintain eye contact and smile in response to your smile.

Checking Up on Your Checkup

Don't forget that four to six weeks after your child's birth, you need a postpartum checkup. At this visit, your ob-gyn will check your weight; blood pressure; and uterus, cervix, and vagina. It's a good time to ask about any concerns such as hormonal changes, problems with your breasts (e.g., engorgement), hemorrhoids, varicose veins, or if you're feeling blue. Now is also the time to discuss birth control. If you use a diaphragm, it may need to be refitted—after your cervix has recovered fully from labor and delivery. If you aren't breast-feeding and you use birth control pills, ask about your prescription.

Helping Your Baby's Development in the First Year

In the first few months, it will seem as if your baby does nothing but eat, sleep, and poop. However, long before she can smile, gurgle, or coo, she is learning about her environment, and there is a lot you can do to stimulate her development as she learns about the world around her in her first year.

- *Talk to your baby.* Your baby knew your voice before she was born. You'll find that, even at birth, the sound of your voice will help calm your baby. Babies learn to speak from their caregivers—nothing else can substitute, not even the television, as many people think. By the time your infant is six months old she will learn the basic sounds of your language. You'll also find your baby can read your emotions by looking at your face while hearing the tone of your voice. Although she cannot understand your words, you are definitely communicating with your infant and can let her know how much she is loved and cherished.
- *Read to your baby.* You can buy baby books, borrow baby books, or ask for them as gifts. It doesn't matter how you get them—just read to your baby! Your baby loves the sound of your voice so it's never too early to start reading to him. He also loves to look at bright pictures, touch the pages, and chew on the edges; expect that to be a part of your reading also. Reading to your child gives you time together that's quiet and calm, and lets him begin to realize that there are many interesting things such as animals and shapes that he can learn about in books. It also teaches him at an early age that reading is something you value. Children who grow up with books in their homes and who see their parents reading books, magazines, or newspapers are more likely to enjoy reading themselves and carry that joy of reading into their school-age years.
- *Sing to your baby.* Your baby loves your voice, and she loves music. There's no better way to combine them than by singing to her. Music will stimulate your baby and she will learn creativity and ways to express herself when she decides to play along by shaking a rattle or beating on a drum. Since music is such an important part of our culture, singing to your baby is a great way to introduce her to a rich part of her heritage. Babies enjoy simple songs such as lullabies but can also have fun with popular songs. Try teaching her a clapping game and singing "Rockin' Robin."
- *Laugh with your baby.* Being able to laugh is a crucial part of being a parent. Whether you're laughing from joy or "to keep from crying," share that with

your baby. Teach her about joy and sharing good times. Let her know that she makes you happy and that her happiness also gives you pleasure. As your baby gets older, you'll start to notice that certain sounds or faces you make will tickle her. Nothing is better than the first time you hear your baby give a good belly laugh—just get used to it because she'll be doing it for a long time.

- *Touch your baby.* Studies have shown that premature babies who get a lot of skin-to-skin contact do better and gain weight more quickly than those babies who aren't touched. A tender touch is a great way to soothe your baby and let her know she is loved. While nice soft clothing and pajamas are great, nothing beats the feel of skin. Learn about infant massage and use bathtime as a time to caress her and move her limbs. Letting your baby lie on Dad's chest is a great way for them to bond.
- *Encourage her to explore and experiment.* One of the pleasures of parenthood is seeing the world for the first time through your child's eyes. Things you take for granted will interest and delight your baby. Keys become rattles, pots become hats, and telephones are completely fascinating. When your baby is playing and trying new things, he is learning about his environment and trying to figure out how he can control the things around him. Some parents say their kids are "nosy" and get into everything. But that's your baby's way of exploring and learning and is a sign that he is curious and intelligent. Give him lots of chances to get around and get into things. When he makes a mess, just remind yourself that this is evidence of his intelligence.

Keeping your baby close encourages bonding.

- *Leave her on the floor.* Babies need exercise and can only reach their physical milestones if they have a chance to practice. Since pediatricians are now counseling patients to put their kids on their backs to sleep, infants are spending less time on their stomachs doing "baby push-ups." Give your baby some time on the floor so she can challenge herself and get some exercise. At two months she should be able to lift her head, by six months she should roll over in both directions, and by nine to twelve months she should be crawling. But she'll only learn to do these things if you let her spend time on the floor.

Four Months

As your baby becomes more social, encourage her by singing, talking, and playing interactive games like pat-a-cake. At this point, you should be establishing a bedtime routine and helping her find ways to console herself when she cries. Try giving her a pacifier, stuffed animal, blanket, or favorite toy at bedtime or when she gets upset. If she can control her neck and has good head control, try to introduce some solid food such as baby cereal at this time. Don't be surprised if you notice lots of drooling at this age.

Health Care: Four-Month Visit. Your health care provider will perform a complete physical and measure your child's length, weight, and head circumference and will plot these on a standard chart. She will also evaluate your child's development as well as eating and sleeping patterns. Your baby will probably receive vaccines at this visit. (See the Appendix for immunization schedule.) Now's a good time to ask the pediatrician about starting your baby on solid foods.

Four-Month Milestones. By four months your child's height should fall somewhere between 22 and 27 inches; weight should be between 11 and 18 pounds (note that height and weight tend to be greater for boys). Senses (vision, touch, hearing) are becoming more acute, and motor skills (playing with hands, putting objects in mouth) are improving now.

MOVEMENT: Now able to lift his head while being pulled up, your baby will also start to push up on his arms and kick his legs when on his stomach. He should also be able to support his head and neck. He can easily reach for objects and bring them to his mouth.

SIGHT: Your baby's range of vision is now several feet. She should show interest in complex shapes and patterns.

LANGUAGE: Baby notices the unique way you talk and distinctive sounds you make and really responds to your voice. He'll also start to make vowel sounds like *oooh* and *ahhh* at this stage.

SOCIAL/EMOTIONAL: Your baby will clearly recognize you and will smile and want to play when you come close.

What About Me? How You May Be Feeling

With all of the attention focused on your newborn, you may forget to pay attention to how you feel. But it's very important to avoid neglecting your feelings—some of which may not be positive. Don't be shocked if you experience any of the following emotions; all are perfectly normal. (However, if you feel depressed for more than a couple of weeks or you start to feel hopeless or aggressive toward your baby, seek counseling.)

- ***You don't feel an immediate bond with the baby.*** **This is not unusual and nothing to feel bad about. Right after the baby is born, you're probably exhausted and overwhelmed. If you've had an episiotomy or C-section you may be in pain and perhaps on painkillers. Give yourself time to recover.**
- ***You feel like you don't know what you're doing.*** **Parenting takes practice . . . and you'll have plenty of time for that. Ask hospital personnel, your parents, and friends who have children for help. If you can afford it, consider a doula, a woman trained to provide support and information to new parents. Call the Doulas of North America at (800) 941–1315 for information.**
- ***You miss being pregnant.*** **For nine months, you were the center of attention, but once the baby came, all eyes shifted to the little one. Ask for what you need—be it a leg massage, a break, a nap, help cleaning, a sympathetic ear.**
- ***You don't feel well.*** **Your body—and your hormones—will take time to bounce back. Plus, because of night feedings, you'll be sleep deprived all the time. Be patient; you'll be feeling better soon. Exercise helps, too.**
- ***You need time to yourself.*** **Don't believe the hype: Motherhood doesn't have to be a full-time job. Instead, think of: job sharing. Enlist your mate, friends, and family members to help out so you can have some time for you.**
- ***Your hair falls out.*** **Normally, the average person sheds about one hundred hairs per day. But during pregnancy, hormonal changes keep your hair from shedding. After pregnancy (or sometimes after breast-feeding has ceased), those hairs will fall out, so you may notice your hair coming out in clumps—especially around your hairline. Don't worry, though, you won't go bald; this is usually just a three-month ordeal. During this phase, be kind to your hair. Switch styles if necessary (braids and weaves will only exacerbate the hairline problem) and try to avoid harsh chemicals such as relaxers and dyes.**
- ***You love your baby more than you ever thought you could love another human being.*** **After you've recovered from the shock of having a baby, the intensity of the parent-child bond can be startling . . . and wonderful.**

Six Months

Your baby will be much more social at this age, but also more discriminating about whom she interacts with. She will be rolling over and able to sit up. Over the next few months she will become much more mobile, so you'll need to begin baby-proofing your house to make it safe for her to explore. She should also be eating solid foods that include a variety of cereals, fruits, vegetables, and juices. (See Chapter 7 for more information on feeding and nutrition.)

Health Care: Six-Month Visit. Your health care provider will perform a complete physical and measure your baby's length, weight, and head circumference against standard charts. She will also evaluate your child's development as well as eating and sleeping patterns. Your baby will probably receive vaccines at this visit. (See the Appendix for immunization schedule.) He may get his first tooth around this time, so ask about dental care and managing teething pain.

Six-Month Milestones. At this stage, your child will recognize family members, and it will be clear that you are her favorite. She will watch you as you move around the room and will cry to get you to pick her up. This signals a normal developing attachment to you and other close caregivers. Between four and six months of age, your baby's length should increase by about 2 inches, his weight by 1 to 1½ pounds per month.

MOVEMENT: Your baby will begin to sit up, first by leaning on her arms, then without. She may also be able to stand with help. She can manipulate objects, moving them from hand to hand, and roll over.

SIGHT: Baby can see further away and can distinguish between different colors. He can track an object, such as a ball rolled across the floor, as it moves.

LANGUAGE: Your baby responds to his own name and babbles chains of consonants. He understands and expresses emotion through tone of voice.

COGNITIVE: Your baby will experiment with her ability to make things happen, like making a sound by banging an object.

SOCIAL/EMOTIONAL: You'll notice dramatic changes in your baby's personality as she more actively responds to your attention and enjoys play. She will also respond to her name.

Nine Months

As your baby becomes more and more independent, it's increasingly important to child-proof your home and create a safe environment for him. With independence comes protest. That little baby whom you used to be able to totally control now has his own opinions—which he generally expresses by crying, shaking his head, or clamping his mouth shut when he doesn't want to eat. You may mourn the passing of his earlier months when you could hold him without his crawling away or cuddle him without his wiggling. He may also be feeling insecure (another response to independence), and you may notice he protests vigorously when you leave but enjoys his independence and will ignore you when you return.

Health Care: Nine-Month Visit. Your pediatrician will perform a complete physical and measure your baby's length, weight, and head circumference against standard charts. She will also evaluate your child's development as well as eating and sleeping patterns. At this visit, ask your health care provider about your baby's sleep schedule. At this age, most babies are on a schedule which helps you organize your day as well as keep your baby happy.

Nine-Month Milestones. Your child will grow rapidly during this time, but keep checking the growth charts to make sure she is within the normal range.

MOVEMENT: By this time, your baby will sit up without assistance and begin to use his arms and legs to get around by scooting on his bottom, crawling, or even cruising alongside furniture in preparation to walk. He may be able to pull himself to stand.

HAND AND FINGER SKILLS: As she reaches out to grasp objects in her path, your nine-month-old will use the thumb and first or second finger (the "pincer" grasp). She may also be able to feed herself and begin to drink from a cup.

LANGUAGE: Your child's coos and gurgles will turn into recognizable syllables or words such as "ma-ma" and "bye-bye." He also responds to simple requests, like "no."

COGNITIVE: Inanimate objects (toys, spoons, plastic containers) will be a source of endless fascination as your baby shakes, bangs, throws, and drops them. Beginning at nine months, she'll also learn that objects exist even when she doesn't see them (a concept known as *object permanence*), so peek-a-boo can become a fun game rather than something that startles her.

SOCIAL/EMOTIONAL: During this peak period of separation anxiety, your nine-month-old may become shy around strangers and cry when you leave.

What If My Child Misses Milestones?

Watching your baby develop and grow is one of the most rewarding parts of early parenthood. But as you read and hear more about children's milestones, you may start to worry if your child doesn't hit one of those milestones on time. Don't fret—yet. Each child matures at his or her own pace. Children also have different areas of strength and weakness. While one six-month-old may begin babbling early, another will sit up sooner than most.

Missing milestones does matter, however, when it signals a medical or developmental problem. If by six months your child does not respond to sound or doesn't seem to enjoy being around people, for example, there may be a hearing or behavioral difficulty. If you notice something out of the ordinary or suspect your baby has some developmental delay, contact your pediatrician immediately. Early intervention can sometimes correct an otherwise troubling situation.

In most cases, missed milestones are probably not a sign of a problem but simply your child's individual developmental course. The best way to ensure that your child develops appropriately is to follow your pediatrician's recommended schedule for checkups and spend as much time interacting with and watching your child as possible. Research shows that infants who receive sufficient attention from their parents fare the best in childhood and later in life. Infants develop most rapidly in the care of loved ones who spend a lot of time talking with them.

RESOURCES

Recommended Reading for Parents

Mama's Little Baby: The Black Woman's Guide to Pregnancy, Childbirth, Baby's First Year, Dennis Brown, M.D., and Pamela A. Toussaint (E.P. Dutton, 1997). Here is a babycare book with special emphasis on black parenting issues.

Mayo Clinic Complete Book of Pregnancy and Baby's First Year, Robert V. Johnson (William Morrow, 1994). This is a comprehensive, accessible guide with tremendously useful medical information.

Now That Baby Is Home: From Infant to Toddler, William Sears and Martha Sears (Mass Market, 1998). From the renowned experts on babies, the latest book focuses on the first two years.

What to Expect the First Year, Arlene Eisenberg, Heidi E. Murkoff, and Sandee E. Hathaway, B.S.N. (Workman Publishing, 1989). This book answers parents' questions during a baby's first year, including development and medical issues.

Recommended Reading for Children

All About Me, Debbie MacKinnon and Anthea Sieveking (Barron's Educational Series, 1994). This is a multicultural photo book of children pointing out body parts.

Here Are My Hands, Bill Martin, John Archambault, and Ted Rand (Henry Holt, 1991). This is a multiethnic exploration of body parts and how they work.

Organizations

American Medical Association, 515 N. State St., Chicago, IL 60610, (312) 464–5000. Call for a referral for a pediatrician in your area.
Website: www.ama-assn.org

National Medical Association, 1012 10th St., NW, Washington, D.C. 20001, (202) 347–1895. The NMA provides referrals to consumers for African-American physicians.
Website: www.natmed.org

Chapter

2

Healthy Toddler (Ages One and Two)

The little baby you've just learned how to care for is now growing into a separate person. And it shows. He still needs you but wants to explore his new world by himself. These divided desires are the source of his greatest angst. At one year, he is thrilled to bits that he can stand up and possibly walk. He spends several months reveling in his new accomplishment, and it is about as much fun for you as it is for him. As he gets older, nearing two, he is struggling so hard to mature he is often frustrated and needs you there for comfort and reassurance. The happy one-year-old can become a demanding toddler, testing the boundaries of what is, and what isn't, appropriate behavior. The so-called "terrible twos" can be trying for many parents and can start well before two years.

Experts, and many parents, believe that the eighteen-month-to-two-year period is crucial to a child's behavioral development. Here is where discipline comes in, moms and dads. At two, the toddler is learning how to walk and talk, and think with more confidence. You can delight in their efforts—if you are forewarned about their mood swings and equip yourself to handle them effectively. Otherwise, you'll find yourself involved in more and more power struggles.

Your two-year-old is more sociable than before and has probably made friends with children in day care or play groups who she plays with (or attacks!). New friends also mean exposure to common childhood illnesses and since the toddler's immune system is still immature, she is less able to fight off infections.

Beyond your child's increased exposure to illness, your main challenge will be keeping up with his intellectual, social, and psychological changes. The key is being aware of the changes that will occur as your toddler moves from one stage of growth to the next and being ready for them. Then the two of you will have a much more enjoyable time together.

Your Child's Health Care: The First and Second Year

As your child continues to grow and develop, it remains critical that you make and keep all of her visits to the health care provider.

One Year
Fifteen Months
Eighteen Months
Two Years

One Year

At one year, your baby can stand and may be walking or at least trying to. His newfound locomotion will prove challenging to you, as you race behind him trying to avert bumps and bruises and keep his life—and yours—in order. He will test your ability to set limits—and your patience—as he struggles for autonomy. Your goal will be to let go and allow him to explore his ever-widening world, while still keeping him from getting hurt or destroying your home.

Health Care: One-Year Visit. Your health care provider will perform a physical examination and measure your child's height, weight, and head circumference to plot on a standard growth chart. Vaccines against chicken pox (varicella) and mumps, measles, and rubella (MMR) can be given. Your child *may* also be tested for exposure to tuberculosis and lead, and will definitely be tested for anemia. (For more on lead and anemia, which affect our children disproportionately, see Chapter 15.)

Now that your child is probably in contact with more children, get tips from your doctor about how to deal with viruses that cause colds and flu. (These are covered in more detail in Chapter 15.)

New Vaccination Heads Up!

Rotavirus causes vomiting and diarrhea and is very common in children under two years old. Infections by the virus account for over 500,000 visits to physicians each year with over 100 deaths in the United States. Like other viral illnesses, there are no effective antibiotics against rotavirus. Fortunately, a vaccine has been developed that will soon be available in the United States. This vaccine has been tested in countries where diarrheal illnesses are a major cause of death in infants and young children. Studies have found the vaccine is safe to administer and prevents or diminishes the severity of rotavirus infection.

The vaccine has been deemed safe by the Food and Drug Administration (FDA) and must be licensed for use before being released. The vaccine will be given by mouth and will be added to the immunization schedule at two, four, and six months. Look for announcements or discuss this vaccine with your pediatrician.

One-Year Milestones

MOVEMENT: Learning how to move is the one-year-old's primary task. Most babies will be walking unaided by fourteen months, and many will be running—however strange they may look! Your one-year-old can now throw a ball with an underhand toss. Her fine motor skills are improving because of her new ability to focus on smaller objects. She will have mastered her pincer grasp (thumb and forefinger) and will want to grab everything in sight as practice.

To Help:

- Teach her about "in" and "out." Offer plastic container with lids and objects to put in them.
- Roll a ball back and forth to her.
- Teach her how to climb stairs by walking with her; she'll be going up long before she can manage coming down.
- Give her objects of various textures to feel.

COGNITIVE (PERCEPTION): As the one-year-old explores objects with his feet, eyes, hands, and mouth, he begins to develop an understanding of how things work. Once he discovers how an object opens, closes, shakes, bounces, or turns, he will repeat the function over and over in order to master it. He is gaining a greater understanding of object permanence—the fact that things don't disappear forever when they go out of sight. He will have a vocabulary of about three words which will expand as he's forming simple, two-word sentences by age two. You may not always know what he's talking about, but he understands more than he can express.

To Help:

- Give your child "free" space to play in by making your home child safe. (For a detailed discussion on child-proofing, see Chapter 14.)
- Stimulate his senses by offering everyday items or toys of various textures, colors, and shapes for him to examine.
- Offer favorite toys such as: toy telephones, push and pull toys, balls, blocks, board books, pots and pans, and straddle toys. Make sure they are simple and sturdy.
- Help nurture her curiosity by offering toys and objects that open and close such as a box or an old eyeglass case.
- Play peek-a-boo games to help her understand object permanence.

SOCIAL/EMOTIONAL: The one-year-old is not a social diva. Though she may stare at, smell, grab, or even kiss other infants, she is only mildly interested in interacting with them. She is more interested in interacting with you and other adults who come into her life on a regular basis. She wants your attention and will experiment with ways of getting it when she wants it. Interestingly, she may show concern when another child hurts herself—or when she hurts another child—but this kindness isn't to be taken too seriously. Often, she doesn't understand the connection between events or actions and resulting feelings.

Emotionally, she may begin to experience the dreaded separation anxiety (again). It is the biggest emotional issue for the second year of life, and usually hits its peak at around eighteen months. Other than that, the one-year-old is generally fearless and will try anything just to "see what happens." Know that she is trying to balance her strong sense of relief at seeing you with her new desire for independence. Give her the space she needs to sort out these new, intense emotions.

To Help:

- Talk to your baby and wait until she responds to you in whatever way she can—be it in babbling, smiles, or body movements.
- Be understanding when your child seems indifferent toward you—even if she cried her heart out when you were leaving her.

SPEECH: A toddler's happy babbling is not to be ignored or quieted but encouraged. The unintelligible babbling of your infant has grown into sounds with more intonation and even a few simple words by the time she's a year old. During the second year, her vocabulary will expand, and she'll speak in simple two-word phrases by age two. A one-year-old should be able to obey simple commands.

To Help:

- Talk to your toddler instead of trying to teach him how to talk. You are the primary person he will learn language from, not other children or television, as many parents assume. Take time to chat with him about anything and everything in his world.
- Communicate with your child using gestures and facial expressions when you talk. This will aid his language development.
- Listen to his attempts to talk, and be responsive. This will tell him that there is satisfaction and enjoyment to be gained from using language.

- Sing to your child. It teaches him another use for language and is enjoyable for both parents and babies.

Fifteen Months

Your fifteen-month-old, a whirlwind of activity and curiosity, is probably keeping very busy—and keeping you busy. Children this age require constant attention as they walk—or run—from place to place, curious about every little thing. They love to touch everything, too, including (probably to your embarrassment) their genitals. Toddlers also begin to display a new emotion: frustration. Your child may become angry when his independence is curbed or when his rudimentary communication skills don't allow him to make you understand what he wants. Expect screaming, falling-down tantrums, and perhaps episodes of breath-holding.

Push toys help toddlers perfect their walking skills.

Your goal is to continue to help him find his way in the world without getting hurt and to help him navigate his emotions. Show him plenty of respect and affection. In the midst of "toddler chaos" don't neglect yourself or other family members.

Health Care: Fifteen-Month Visit. Your health care provider will evaluate your child's growth, hearing, vision, development, and general health. Immunizations: MMR and varicella, if not administered at twelve months; and possibly vaccines against polio, diptheria, pertussis, tetanus (DTP or DTaP) and H. influenza type B. Your provider may also examine your toddler's feet and observe her walking and gait. At this visit, you may want to ask for advice about discipline and limit setting, especially with difficult situations such as biting or other aggressive behaviors that are common in toddlers.

Fifteen-Month Milestones

MOVEMENT: Your fifteen-month-old will be getting into everything. It will seem as if she has been sitting for the past year and waiting to touch, feel, and taste everything she has been watching. She will try to run everywhere, climb on the furniture, climb up stairs, and explore all the places in your home. Safety is an extremely important issue at this age so it is critical your home be completely child-proofed and made safe. Your child's curiosity will make her want to explore the world around her, and now that she can walk, she is ready to *go!*

To Help:

- Make sure your home is completely child-proofed. You'll need a safety zone, a safe room or area where your child can play while you are doing other things.
- Help her explore. Take her on outings and walks. Keep it simple. Trips to the park or store are as interesting as trips to the museum.
- Since he has developed his fine motor skills and can begin to use a cup and spoon, let him feed himself. Just be patient with the mess.
- When your toddler is getting into something he shouldn't, distract him with another interesting activity or object.

COGNITIVE (PERCEPTION): Everything your child does these days feeds his curiosity and increases his understanding of things around him. He will constantly want to try new things, touch them, put them in his mouth. You may catch him imitating you. One minute he may pretend he is cooking with a pot, the next he may decide it makes a better hat. This is the time your child has been waiting for—when he can finally get up, move himself, and explore all the interesting things there are to get into. Your child will begin to know right from wrong. You will often catch her looking at you before she does something she isn't supposed to; usually, she will go ahead and do it anyway. She's beginning to understand what doesn't make you happy, but still is not aware of the consequences of her actions.

To Help:

- Give her toys that let her use her imagination. Building blocks are good.

- She is now ready for more complex toys that allow her to fit pieces together. Simple puzzles and blocks with various shapes will let her apply her growing understanding of how things work.
- Offer her toys to help her imitate adult activities, such as cooking utensils, play vacuums, baby tools, or pretend computers.

SOCIAL/EMOTIONAL: Your child will start to develop some social skills at this age. She will begin to play with other children, but expect plenty of conflicts since sharing is a foreign concept to her. Although your child thinks she's independent, it will be your job to curtail some of her activities. This will definitely lead to conflicts which can result in tantrums, screaming, and crying fits. Do not give in to these tactics and try not to let them get you angry. When your child is having a fit in the middle of the supermarket, you'll notice that the only people who seem bothered do not have children. Other parents will simply smile and think "Yes, mine acted the same way at that age."

To Help:

- Have him spend time with the entire family. Let him sit with the family during meals.
- Respect his shyness even when he withdraws from family members and close friends. Let him sort out his feelings and warm up to people on his own.
- Maintain a regular bedtime and nap schedule so he doesn't become overtired and cranky.
- Give him plenty of affection and let him see others sharing affection.
- When he is having a hard time or acting out, help him label his emotions and encourage him to express his feelings verbally.

SPEECH: Your child's vocabulary is rapidly expanding at this age. She will repeat everything she hears and begin to use more and more words. Your child understands much more than she can express and may get very frustrated when she cannot make herself understood.

To Help:

- Talk to your child all the time. Name objects, places, colors, animals.
- Give him picture books and have him point to things you name in the books.
- Watch what you say in front of your child unless you want to hear certain words repeated.

- Play games or sing songs that involve body parts such as "This old man . . ." or "Head, shoulders, knees, and toes"
- Read to him at least once a day.

Eighteen Months

As your child continues to assert her independence, you may find that she seems defiant and aggressive. "No" is a now a large part of your child's vocabulary. The two of you may be walking happily down the street when all of a sudden she pitches a fit, her legs collapse, and she refuses to go on. She may eat a bowl of cereal one day and throw it against the wall the next.

Take a deep breath and try not to think of this as a negative period. Instead, understand that her behavior reflects an emerging sense of her own identity. You can cut down on power struggles by trying to be consistent and patient—and don't forget your sense of humor. Use transitions, set limits, and show her respect.

Though her often frustrating behavior may be the dominant development, she's also more and more fun to play with and to be with—when she's in a good mood. You'll also notice her emerging competence—she can do more things, say more words, and understand you better.

Health Care: Eighteen-Month Visit. Your health care provider will evaluate your child's growth, hearing, vision, development, and general health. Immunizations: He will need the DTP (or DTaP) and polio vaccines if they weren't given at the fifteen-month visit. At this point, your child should have received all of his vaccines and will not require any more until he reaches four to six years. You might again ask for advice about discipline and limit setting.

Eighteen-Month Milestones

MOVEMENT: Now that walking is old hat, the eighteen-month old focuses on his running and climbing abilities. A favorite position is the squat, which shows off his improved sense of balance. He will be able to get himself from sitting to a standing position without help. The next physical task for most eighteen-month-olds will be learning to do two movements at the same time, such as pulling a toy while walking or turning his head to look at something while walking. He will be frustrated walking with you, because he cannot keep up and may be afraid of being separated from you. He may be able to shuffle-kick a ball, but is not yet coordinated enough to catch. His fine motor skills are continuing to improve and he may now be able to feed himself with a spoon held in his fist, hold a baby cup with both hands, and scribble.

To Help:

- Bring a baby back-carrier or stroller on outings with your toddler, even though he can walk. He moves much more slowly than you, so you need to be able to carry him if he—or you—becomes frustrated.
- Offer crayons, clay, sand, water, and other objects to aid learning about physical properties of different items and to exercise the hands and fingers. However, make sure these are nontoxic, since putting things in his mouth is still your child's favorite way to explore.
- Help your child experiment with sound and rhythm by introducing toy musical instruments and tambourines, pots, and pans.
- Consider investing in a special pushcart that allows baby to stand up by holding on to the handles and walk supported while pushing the cart.
- Find ways to give your child quiet times in between periods of active play without putting him to bed. This will help him rest without actually having to nap and will serve you well in places where quietness is preferred (e.g., in church, the doctor's waiting room, or the library). You could look at a book together, or draw a picture, or play with a quiet toy, for example.

COGNITIVE (PERCEPTION): The development of thoughtfulness is a mark of the eighteen-month-old. She will begin to think before she acts. Often, this will involve talking to herself when she is about to do something she is unsure about. This new leap in her cognitive growth may convince her that she can do almost everything herself—the result of which is often frustration. On the other hand, eighteen-month-olds sometimes giggle wildly with happiness when something they tried to do gets done, even if a grown-up had to help out a little.

To Help:

- Continually affirm your toddler and remind her how beloved and special she is. This will help her feel secure during those times when her eager exploration of the world lets her down.
- Offer toys that help her learn how smaller things fit into larger things or

how shapes fit together. Large, wooden puzzles with five or fewer pieces are a good choice. Or, you can use plastic containers of different sizes.
- Read a picture book with her and make simple requests such as "Find the dog." Sturdy pop-up books or those with "things to feel" on their pages are good book options for this age.

SOCIAL: She will show much more interest in actually playing with other toddlers than she did at one year, though she is still not a big socialite. There is no point in teaching sharing at this point; just try to distract her with another toy or object if she has a conflict with another toddler. She is still testing the effect she has on others and will often seem to be stubborn and hardheaded. Right now, she sees other toddlers as nice objects to have around to poke, pull, and pinch. Often, she will be startled by any reaction other children make in response to her actions.

On the other hand, she may obey your simple commands and will show interest in helping you with adult tasks. How well she interacts with you, your mate, and the other adults in her life will set the stage for her interactions with other children later.

To Help:

- Show your child acceptance, respect, and affection, and you will lay the foundation for a positive self-image and satisfying social encounters. Learn how to enjoy your child as much as possible; it will help you both through the difficult times.
- Allow her to help you with everyday tasks such as dishwashing, laundry, or dusting.
- Correct unacceptable behavior by being firm but loving. There should be no reward for or giving in to temper tantrums. (For more on discipline, see Chapter 5.)

EMOTIONAL: Separation anxiety is in full swing at around eighteen months. Your child may holler and scream when you leave the room, accept a quick hug from you when you return, and then push you away. He may repeat this pattern again and again. He may also become joined at the hip with a blanket, ribbon, or stuffed animal, which he uses to give comfort when you're not there. These comforting companions are called transition objects and help make separating easier. Clearly, learning how to be close to you and away from you is the beginning of an important emotional growth step for the toddler, one that actually continues into adulthood. Fears also tend to emerge now: of bedtime, of the toilet, of large animals, of water, of almost anything. Some will be rational, some will not. Toddlers this age also pick up on parents' fears and internalize them. Parental anger will be a new and scary encounter for the toddler.

To Help:

- Stop yourself from responding angrily to your child when he misbehaves. Count to three, and remember that what he is going through is quite natural and beyond his control right now. Speak to him firmly but calmly.
- Don't ridicule your child about his security object, whether it's a bear or a raggedy piece of material. This object means a lot to him now and helps him to cope with his fears and anxieties.
- Help bedtime go more smoothly by making sure daytime separation is handled well. Make sure your baby is comfortable and familiar with his sitter or caretaker, especially if you are away from him overnight, and be sure to spend a good amount of time with your child before you go.
- Allow your child to express his fears, and show him understanding. Assure him there is nothing to be afraid of but that you will help protect him from the thing he fears. Be careful not to emphasize that you too are afraid (of bugs or heights, for example). Fear is infectious.

SPEECH: Your eighteen-month-old has a better understanding of language and will show an increased interest in talking. She will often use one- and two-word sentences to communicate but will also use noises and body motions, such as pointing, to let you know what's up. She can probably say numbers but doesn't understand real counting. One of her favorite games may be pointing to an object in a book and naming it. "No!," which is used often by the eighteen-month-old, can also mean yes.

To Help:

- Try modeling or incorporating what the child says into a longer sentence, and then repeating it back to the child. For example, the child says "No more" when he's eaten all of his lunch, and you reply, "That's right because you ate all of your sandwich."
- Sing or recite nursery rhymes to help your child learn language by singing

along. (If those rhymes and songs are a distant memory from your childhood, get a tape or CD.)

- Remember not to push or correct the child who is struggling to get words out. Many speech therapists believe that a normal period of stammering may be exacerbated by too much correction. Listen, encourage, and praise your child for his efforts at learning this new form of communication.

Two Years

The two-year-old is spirited, funny, and eager to try new things. Though he still may not be a big talker, his communication skills are growing as he masters more and more words. He's also more social, though the concept of sharing may still be just out of his grasp. He can do more things such as brush his teeth, do "pretend" chores, and read his books. It is rewarding, amusing, and amazing to watch his developments.

The power struggles are probably continuing. If he refuses to obey you, remember that he isn't rejecting your standards but is curious as to how you'll react to his behavior. That's why it's important to have simple, consistent rules that you communicate clearly.

Though your child yearns for independence, he may also seem clingy. Children often develop fears at this age; he may be afraid of monsters hiding under the bed or being sucked down the drain with the tub water.

Health Care: Two-Year Visit. Your health care provider will evaluate your child's growth, hearing, vision, development, and general health. She will also check your child for anemia and lead poisoning. You may want to talk to your pediatrician about how your child's speech is developing and also inquire about toilet training. (For a more detailed discussion of toilet training, see Chapter 4.) You should take your child to see a dentist when she is two years old. She'll need to have her teeth checked every six months after that.

Two-Year Milestones

MOVEMENT: The two-year-old's body movements are much more coordinated than they were just six months ago. She is more sure of her movements and wants to use her entire body to the max. She would now rather walk than be carried (thank goodness!) and will experiment with walking sideways and backwards, and up and down stairs unaided while holding the handrail, pausing on each step. Two-year-olds also begin to routinely climb out of their cribs, indicating that it's probably time for a junior bed. She will want to dress herself, though she still needs your help. Her agile fingers can now turn the pages of a book one at a time. A preference for right- or left-handedness will probably show itself now.

To Help:

- Bring your toddler outdoors to play as much as possible. She will love running around in a park, learning about grass, wind, twigs, and dirt and will also enjoy a playground as long as it has equipment suited to her age.
- Use soft balls to help her learn how to catch and throw (but don't let her put them in her mouth).
- Introduce finger painting to help your child learn a rudimentary form of drawing. First she learns how to create shapes with her finger; later, she will become adept at drawing with a crayon, paintbrush, and pen. Also, let her scribble with a nontoxic crayon.
- Offer toys with large parts that screw on and off or require winding, to help exercise finger coordination.
- An old-fashioned swing made from a tire on a rope will offer your child endless hours of swinging fun and will teach her about gravity, weight, and balance.

COGNITIVE: Two-year-olds love to sort and categorize objects into groups in their minds and in their play. This sorting is the beginning of concept development. He is creating a picture in his mind when you say "cats," so he'll remember what visual image to call up whenever he hears it. This process becomes more sophisticated as the child grows and begins to understand and categorize feelings and other more abstract ideas. He may ascribe human characteristics to inanimate objects, such as, "that wall hurt me." The two-year-old has learned the lay of the land in his home or apartment. He feels secure in his ability to find things easily. (Moving to another home at this point could be quite disconcerting, so prepare him well in advance.) He can probably name most of his body parts and can remember familiar places and people.

He also has some concept of morning and night based on the things that happen in his life at those times, such as Daddy feeds him breakfast and takes him to the sitter, and Mommy comes home at night and gives him a bath. Two-year-olds will begin to show the use of judgment as they progress to the age of three.

To Help:

- Be open to your child's questions and offer simple answers she can understand and learn from.
- Expose her to as many different experiences as possible to help her intellect.
- Don't force her to do things she is not ready for, like reading. You cannot speed up intellectual growth in a child this age unless she is mentally and emotionally prepared.

SOCIAL: If there were a motto for age two it would be: "Hey, it's about me!" She still thinks she is the center of the universe and wants everyone's attention all the time. Needless to say, this attitude isn't well suited for social settings, and she must learn how to behave in more appropriate ways in order to survive preschool—and life. She will show more of an interest in playing with other toddlers, but since children her own age won't give her the attention she seeks, she will prefer "talking" to and mesmerizing the nearest smiling adult. Some two-year-olds can be negative, controlling, and indecisive. ("No" is sometimes quickly followed by "yes.") The problem is that she very much wants to make decisions but isn't equipped with enough information or experience to make good ones. This often results in frustration and temper tantrums that further inhibit her social acceptance. Furthermore, since she is still focused on herself and doesn't yet understand that other children have feelings, you'll have to keep an eye on her during group play—bearing in mind that it's best for young children to work out their own differences.

To Help:

- Learn how to deal with tantrums. You have three main goals: to protect the child from her own rage; to teach her that this behavior won't get her what she wants; and to comfort her.
- Determine how you will discipline your child. Enforce it and be consistent. (Read more about discipline in Chapter 5.)
- If your child seems ready, arrange for her to play with another toddler so

she can practice her social skills. Be there throughout to help facilitate play. Try to have enough toys so each child has choices.

EMOTIONAL: There's a truism that goes like this: If you can deal with the emotional ups and downs of a two-year-old, you'll be able to handle his emotional fluctuations during his teen years. At both stages, he wants to be grown up and do his own thing, but he also needs your guidance to feel emotionally stable. Toilet training may be another emotional hot seat (pun intended) for your two-year-old. This is a weird new feeling for him, allowing a bowel movement to "escape," to fall into a bowl of water and be flushed away forever. Also remember that he wants to be more in control of his life right now and this bowel movement control issue may seem like the ultimate lack of control to him. He may resist compliance just because he knows you desire a particular result. (See more on toilet training in Chapter 4.)

The eighteen-month-old's initial fears can become full blown in the two-year-old. The nature of the fear may change and get more involved as the child grows up. As a baby it was the dark, as a toddler it is the monster in the closet, as a young child it may be the men in the television set. The two-year-old realizes that he is living in a big world and isn't sure that he will be protected from everything and everyone he thinks might harm him—which is actually true. A fearful child of two needs to know that his parent is his greatest human protector. There will be enough time later to teach him about things he should genuinely fear (like the stranger who wants to snatch him, and so on).

To Help:

- Acknowledge her fears and help to dismantle them. Gradually begin talking with her about the positive aspects of whatever it is she's afraid of, be it dogs, nighttime, or water.
- Give the child time and space to come to terms with her fears. Don't get anxious or angry if she persists in her fear for a while, even after you feel you've "explained it away."
- Offer solace at bedtime in the form of hugs, stuffed animals, night-lights, soothing music, and the comfort of bedtime prayers. This is a great opportunity to talk about God's love and protection.

SPEECH: A two-year-old has a large vocabulary, but uses fewer words than he actually knows. He is still processing the meaning of words, even of those that he uses. When he feels comfortable, he may suddenly amaze you with a burst of eloquence. Three- and four-word sentences become commonplace as the child nears age three. Though you may think he's ready for the debate team, strangers will still be unable to understand most of what your child is saying.

To Help:

- Avoid speaking to your child in baby talk. Remember that she will imitate the way you speak. A two-year-old can understand much more than she can say, so don't be afraid to use more sophisticated language to describe and explain things.
- Don't make your toddler perform by commanding her to recite the numbers or the alphabet for every new visitor who comes through your home. This rarely, if ever, works, and can inhibit her experimentation with language.
- Encourage your toddler to tell you things: about his day, his shoes, or his teddy bear—anything to get him to form sentences, use descriptive words, and practice speaking to another person.

RESOURCES

Recommended Reading for Parents

The Hip Mama Survival Guide, Ariel Gore (Hyperion, 1998). This book contains advice from a single mother, with special sections on toddlers, immunizations, and diapering.

Touchpoints, T. Berry Brazelton, M.D. (Addison Wesley Publishing, 1992). In this book, a famous pediatrician provides advice on parenting challenges, family relationships, and developmental milestones through the third year.

What to Expect the Toddler Years, Arlene Eisenberg, Heidi E. Murkoff, and Sandee E. Hathaway, B.S.N. (Workman Publishing, 1994). This is an extensive reference book for parents of one- and two-year-olds.

Recommended Reading for Children

Germs, Germs, Germs, Bobbi Katz and Steve Bjorkman (Scholastic Press, 1996). This rhyming story teaches about germs inside and outside the body and about hygiene.

Healthy Me, Angela Royston and Edwina Riddell (Barron's Educational Series, 1995). Children will learn about how the body recovers from minor infections and injuries (colds and scrapes) and about the importance of doctor checkups.

Organizations

The American Academy of Pediatrics, 141 Northwest Point Blvd., P.O. Box 927, Elk Grove Village, IL 60009–0927, (800) 336–5475. Write or call for brochures on child health and immunizations, among many other topics, and for a pediatrician referral in your area.

Office of Minority Health Resource Network, 514 10th St. NW, Washington, D.C. 20013–7337, (800) 444–6472. This agency provides educational material and a newsletter focusing on minority health issues. Will locate organizations, community programs, or experts in your area.

Chapter

3

Healthy Preschooler (Ages Three to Five)

Much of your preschooler's development will be in the areas of speech, social skills, and cognitive abilities. She can now express herself with more sophisticated language, play happily with other children, and use reasoning to figure things out. A large part of your task over these next three years is to enhance these abilities, keep your child healthy, and prepare him to thrive in a school setting.

Your Child's Health Care: The Fourth and Fifth Years

During the preschool years, your child will only need to visit your health care provider annually—around her birthday—unless something is wrong. As always, make sure to keep up with the visits listed below, which are very important for monitoring your child's development and good health. And don't forget to have her teeth checked every six months.

Three Years
Four Years
Five Years

Three Years

As your child reaches age three, you may be relieved that he has moved out of the twos. Your three-year-old, while still unpredictable, is more in control of his world and better able to communicate his wants and needs than he was a year or even six months ago. This probably means that he's more agreeable, although most children still have occasional tantrums. Your child's improved speech and locomotion also help him participate more easily in family activities. He should also have a good sense of what "wait" means and be able to negotiate. Be sure to continue giving him choices—where to go, what to wear, what books to read.

Your child will also be more aware of how he fits into the world. He may want to discuss the color of his skin and how his shade is alike or different from that of friends and family members. He may also notice gender and say things like "I am a boy."

At this age, your child is eager to learn, so try to provide plenty of stimulating opportunities for exploration. Talk to him, answer his questions, and encourage him to come up with answers of his own. He may be ready for preschool if he isn't attending one already, which makes this a good time to find a school that suits your needs.

Health Care: Three-Year Visit. As before, your child's height and weight will be measured and plotted on a standard chart at this doctor's visit. Generally, no vaccinations are needed at age three. However, if you live in a large city or an overcrowded area, consider getting your child tested for tuberculosis. Ask your pediatrician or check with the board of health in your state for guidelines. Your toddler should have an annual blood test for lead exposure and iron-deficiency anemia. (For more on lead and anemia, see Chapter 15.) Also, as children are newly potty trained—or working on it—their wiping habits may be poor, causing genital irritations, particularly in girls. (If you need help, now's a good time to ask questions about toilet training.) You may want to have a discussion with your pediatrician about how to explain gender differences and the notion that some areas of the body are private. Because your child is in frequent contact with other children, ask about preventing viruses and infections—and what to do when they occur.

Three-Year Milestones

MOVEMENT: Running, jumping, and hopping are easy now, and your preschooler should have good posture and be pretty agile. In the third year, expect your child to be comfortable riding a tricycle, going up and down stairs, moving forward and backward, and kicking and throwing a ball (though not necessarily catching it yet). She'll also hone her fine motor skills such as drawing with a crayon or pencil and properly using a fork and spoon.

To Help:

- Take her to a park or playground where she can run around.
- Allow her to play in snow and water (supervised) so she can learn about texture and temperature.
- Play ball with her to help hand-eye coordination. (Try those baseball mitts with Velcro in the palm.)
- Use puzzles, pegboards, and tool kits to help strengthen hand muscles.

COGNITIVE: Questioning everything in detail is typical of the three-year-old's new fascination with the world. Your child wants to know "why" everything is the way it is, though he only understands the simplest answers to his questions. He will enjoy identifying things as "the same" and "different," "small" and "big," "up" and "down," "inside" and "outside." He will begin to develop a sense of time: He'll be able to tell you what time he gets up and goes to bed and that he went shopping "a whole week ago." He can tell you how old he is, though he doesn't really understand how long a year is. He may also notice differences in gender and race.

To Help:

- Encourage climbing so your child can learn about space and direction.
- Provide things for him to touch and examine so he can understand form. Interlocking building blocks, clay, or moldable toys are great choices.
- Take turns playing guessing games and games where your child keeps his eyes closed and has to touch, taste, or smell something to determine what it is.
- Answer his questions about race and gender in a simple, straightforward way. Do your best to explain where babies come from and use correct terms for body parts. Talk about race, hair texture, and skin color in honest, positive ways: "Yes, your skin is darker than Zach's. People have many different colors of skin, and they are all beautiful."

SOCIAL: Friendships with other children her age will become more enjoyable and important to the three-year-old. She will play *with* another child now, often in various games of make-believe such as "dress up" or "house." She will slowly begin to be more sensitive to the feelings of others, less competitive, and more willing to share—though she will need your help with this. She will look to you for guidance on how to deal appropriately with frustration and anger. Your child will begin to show a strong identification with his or her own gender at this age and will exhibit the behaviors associated with that gender (such as wanting to wear only dresses or wanting to watch football with guys). Also, don't be surprised if she or he latches onto behaviors and clothes of the opposite gender! A three-year-old may playfully imitate an adult's expressive or flirty behavior but is usually quite unaware of any sexual suggestion behind the actions.

To Help:

- Encourage her to express anger in nonaggressive ways; let her do something physical (running around or dancing an angry dance). And when she gets mad, tell her that you understand how she feels and give her the vocabulary to express and label her emotions.

- Teach her the "do unto others" principle and tell her to apologize to others when she hurts them.
- Play make-believe or "house" with him when you can—it offers numerous opportunities to teach him various roles with in the family and how to be a contributing member.

EMOTIONAL: Creating imaginary friends and clinging to a security object (teddy bear, blanket, ribbon, etc.) are common and normal behaviors of the three-year-old. Often, he is emotionally insecure and feels like he has no control over this big world he is discovering. His parents are the first people he will try to control via strong pronouncements, tantrums, and other irritating behaviors. He may also not want to be separated from you, especially in new situations. Dreams and nightmares begin to emerge. Imaginary friends may help him cope with emotions and explore different roles. He may drift back and forth from fantasy to reality, talking to an imaginary friend in one moment and then asking you to explain things the next.

To Help:

- Though her controlling behavior and continued tantrums may be trying, remind yourself that your three-year-old is not just being a pain, she may be looking for help. With these actions, three-year-olds are actually begging for you to give them boundaries and steady routines to reassure them that their world has some predictability and order.
- Limit television viewing—three-year-olds cannot distinguish well between what's real and what's not. A TV show depicting a parent dying or being turned into something by a magic wand (as in many popular children's stories) can be very upsetting for a child this age. Also, negative depictions of African-Americans, which are, of course, common on TV, can begin to sink in. Spend time with your child when watching television; he needs your guidance to help figure things out.
- Point out the feelings of other children when they are crying, laughing, or angry and talk to your child about it. This will help him label and understand feelings in himself and others.

SPEECH: Your preschooler wants to gain some control over her world through the use of language. A three-year-old is just beginning to understand the "if . . .

A Word About St-St-St-Stuttering

Occasional stuttering is normal for a preschooler. Nine times out of ten, it is not a sign that your child is ill or that he will have long-term speech problems. Often stuttering is caused by anxiety, overexcitedness, or a general inability of a small child to speak as quickly as he thinks. Help your child relax when he's talking if he stutters. Lovingly encourage him to slow down or say, "Think of what you want to say first." *Do not* command, "Stop stuttering!" or "Hurry up!" This will worsen the stammering and make the child feel inadequate. Build his self-esteem by praising him for things he's done well and the stuttering should stop before kindergarten. If, however, it is severe and persists for more than three months, keep track of when it occurs and consult your pediatrician. Speech therapy can help eradicate the problem. For more information on stuttering or to find a local support group, contact the National Stuttering Project, (800) 364–1677. On the Internet, visit the Stuttering Homepage which offers links to many other organizations and a section for children. You can find it by typing "stuttering" as a keyword on a search engine such as Yahoo or Excite.

then" concept (for instance, "if I touch the stove, then I will hurt my hand"). Speaking in short sentences and imitating adult speech patterns are typical. She knows hundreds of words now and can clearly ask for what she wants. She may not be able to tell a coherent story yet, and you can also expect normal mispronunciations and lisping. She chatters to herself quite a bit as she thinks about new words and learns how to use them.

To Help:

- Read to her, even if it seems she's not that interested. Let her "read" parts of books. For example, you say, "The cow goes . . ." and she answers, "moo."
- As she is playing, help her learn to express herself. For instance, if she rides a tricycle, teach her the meaning of "slow," "fast," "turn," etc. while she's riding.
- Sing to her.

Four Years

The four-year-old, with her abundant energy and boundless curiosity, continues to want to enlarge her world and increase her independence. She should be much more self-sufficient, able to dress and undress herself and use the toilet—though she may need a diaper at night. At this age, she begins to understand the feelings of others and recognize emotions such as joy, sadness, anger, and fear in herself and others. Though she is able to play alone for stretches of time, she probably likes to be with other children and has formed some friendships with peers. She can also follow rules, understand limits, and respond to praise.

Depending on her personality, your four-year-old may be very talkative and enjoy telling stories, real and imaginary. She'll probably be asking plenty of questions, especially about her body and perhaps about race and skin color. Do your best to answer her queries simply and honestly.

Health Care: Four-Year Visit. Your child's height and weight will be measured and plotted on a chart during this visit. He should also have his annual blood test for iron deficiency anemia and lead exposure. In preparation for school, your health care provider will test your child's vision and hearing, and he will give immunizations according to the guidelines listed in the Appendix. If you haven't already done so, discuss how to prevent viruses and infections that your child may contract because of frequent contact with her peers.

Four-Year Milestones

MOVEMENT: Pumping himself on a swing, skipping, running like an athlete, and even turning somersaults characterize new physical capabilities. He is so eager to test his new adult-like agility that he will try things he doesn't yet have the judgment to accomplish safely. You will need to monitor him and give him clear boundaries, especially when in water. Fine motor skills are almost fully developed. He can draw a recognizable picture, print some letters, dress himself (including buttons and zips), use a table knife properly (if taught), and tie his shoes.

To Help:

- Take him on walks, even if just around the block. Point out natural objects and talk about nature; rocks are often a big hit with four-year-olds.
- Play hopscotch, jump rope, and games like Twister to further strengthen his agility and flexibility.
- Teach him how to swim if you haven't already.
- Help him build things with interlocking blocks.

- Encourage him to make things using paper, paste, and safety scissors so he can fine tune his finger and hand coordination while using his imagination.
- Encourage him to move his body to music.

COGNITIVE: A four-year-old's general concept of time has improved. She can now tell you things she did "last summer," or "a month ago," and she understands days, weeks, months, and even seasons. She also understands "behind" and "in front of," knows the names of several colors and shapes, and can count at least ten objects. She can tell you her first and last names. Her questions are now more difficult to answer, such as, "Why do people die?" and "Where do babies come from?" and "Why is my skin this color?"

To Help:

- Provide her with books specifically written for children to help answer some of her many questions about life. This is a great time to use black and multicultural books to discuss race, ethnicity, and skin color.
- Take her places—the museum, the zoo, a photographer's studio, a construction site, an airport, or a mechanic's garage.
- Introduce her to age-appropriate card and board games that require her to use reasoning, strategy, and counting skills.
- Begin to teach her about money.
- Limit her play with video games and the hours (if any) that she watches TV; encourage more person-to-person interaction.

SOCIAL: Playmates and "best friends" are plentiful and vitally important in the four-year-old's life. Through these new friends, she will be exposed to the values and lifestyles that are different from the ones she's learning at home. As a result, your child will begin to question and challenge what you've taught her. This is when "talking back" takes on a new meaning. Fantasy games that involve guns and shooting may abound, even if you forbid it, because of TV and peer play.

To Help:

- Arrange play times in your home with his playmates. Your child will feel proud to show off his new friends to you, and it gives you a chance to see who your child is hanging out with.
- Use children's videos to *help* teach and entertain him. Carefully monitor what your child watches on television.

- Explain the morals or values behind why you want her to behave a certain way. Let your child know why it's important to tell the truth, for example, and to treat other people kindly.
- When disciplining your child, understand the difference between "bad behavior" and "bad child" and make sure he does, too. Always make it clear that it's the behavior that's bad, not your child.
- Give your child simple responsibilities and chores in the home and praise her when they are well done.
- Encourage him to help other children.

Peer Pressure Starts Early

As your child begins to spend more time in the company of other children, he will be influenced by their values, behaviors, and habits. He will learn what's considered "cool" in music, clothes, toys, food, sports, television shows, slang, attitudes, and a host of other things. He will discover that some of these "cool" behaviors and opinions are different from those he has been taught at home. While some of what rubs off on your child will be positive, some of it will be less desirable. This is not to be taken lightly, even at the preschool age. Drs. Darlene and Derek Hopson, authors of *Different and Wonderful: Raising Black Children in a Race-Conscious Society* (Fireside Books, 1992), note that peer pressure is one of the most powerful influences on a child. "For black youth, the peer group is more than just a group of kids. They rely on one another to authenticate and affirm their identity," say the Hopsons.

One way to reduce the influence of negative peer pressure is to build your child's self-image by affirming her uniqueness as a black child. This includes being careful about the comments you make at home about light and dark skin, nappy hair, black achievement, and even "CP time." These behaviors contribute to—or take away from—a black child's developing self-image. When he doesn't feel worthwhile at home, he will look to his peer group for validation, which may not always be positive.

The best thing parents can do is get involved. "Early in your child's life, show an interest in who his friends are," advise the Hopsons. It's also wise to meet the parents. If you have a problem with one of his friends, don't forbid the friendship. Tell your child why you object to the friend's behavior and remind him that he must not slip into his habits. Explaining the reasons behind your concerns and admonitions creates cooperation instead of rebellion.

- Teach common courtesies such as "please," "thank you," and "excuse me," and be sure to use them yourself.

EMOTIONAL: Patting another child when he gets hurt and other expressions of sensitivity are nice additions to the four-year-old's emotional repertoire. He is learning that the feelings of others are important, and he is exercising his conscience. He is more confident and expressive when talking to adults. He now knows the difference between fantasy and reality, though he may still switch back and forth. Four-year-olds are very curious about the body, genitals, and sexuality (they may have shown this curiosity at three), and may engage in "playing doctor" with other children.

To Help:

- Pause when reading a bedtime story and ask your child, "How do you think (the character) feels about that?" and "How would you feel if that happened to you?" referring to whatever is going on in the story. This will help introduce him to empathy and abstract thinking.
- Ask her to show you how it feels to be afraid, happy, sad, excited, etc., so she can recognize and define her feelings.
- Instill a standard of modesty in your child. For example, say "We don't touch other people's private parts or let others touch ours."

SPEECH: Telling a story in *all* its detail is the four-year-old's favorite thing to do. Her English pronunciation should be good now, with the exception of *f, v, s, z, sh, l, th,* and *r,* which she should perfect by about age six. The four-year-old is experimenting with the effect of what she says has on others. She may say "I'll kill you!" or "I hate you!" or even use an expletive to express her anger. She will also ask "Why?" incessantly. Four-year-olds generally ask "why?" to understand, whereas at three she may have just wanted your attention.

To Help:

- Be patient and attentive to your child's long-winded stories. When he senses you're growing weary, he may begin to stutter or start a series of the "um, uh's."
- Be patient with the constant "whys." After a couple of answers, redirect the conversation by asking your child the question "Why do you think?"
- Use silly-rhymey speech, books, or audio or video tapes to teach things to a four-year-old; she'll love it, and it'll help her retain the information.

- Express disapproval for his use of profane language, and stop using it yourself. Don't shout as you correct him; he probably doesn't understand what the words mean. Plus, the more emotionally you react, the more you'll hear the bad words. When he uses profanity, ask him to use other words to tell you why he's upset.
- Encourage him to express his likes and dislikes.

Five Years

Now that your child is turning five, much of your attention will be focused on getting her ready to start school. (If your child's fifth birthday falls in autumn, you'll need to decide whether she's ready to start kindergarten, or if you should wait a year; see p. 55.) As school approaches, it will be important for your child to understand rules, how to get along with others, and how to control her impulses. She'll also need prepa-

Don't Hold It

Though preschoolers may no longer be in diapers and have fewer rashes, "pee pee" accidents and constipation may be a problem. Preschoolers are often "too busy to go" or are "holding" their urine or stool because they don't want to stop playing and go to the bathroom. To avoid this, make a game of using the bathroom. Try telling the child it's her job to let the urine or bowel movement out when it wants to come out (preschoolers love having "jobs"). Another suggestion is to set a timer to ring every two hours to remind your child that it's time to "go." This relieves the parent of being the bad guy.

You'll also need to watch for skin irritations, inflammation near the genitals, and infections that can arise from urine leakage and poor wiping, especially in girls. Many kids this age tend to pull their pants up before they are "done," or don't wipe themselves very well. A soak in a warm bathtub every day should quell most minor irritations. Apply zinc oxide ointment to the affected area, if daily baths don't help. If your child complains of pain when urinating, she may have a urinary tract infection. See your health care provider if your child has any problems with urination or bowel movements. You can help by increasing the amount of water your child drinks, making sure he is emptying his bladder, monitoring him for daily bowel movements, and keeping his genital area clean.

ration for separating from you when she enters a new situation—obviously less of a problem for children who've been in day care—and interacting with both her peers and authorities.

With school comes increased independence, which means it's critical she understands rules about safety. While you don't want to make your child afraid and overly cautious, she must understand how to be safe in the playground, on the street, in cars, and on her bicycle, and how to deal with strangers (see p. 56). It's up to you to teach her to negotiate potential danger without being constantly fearful.

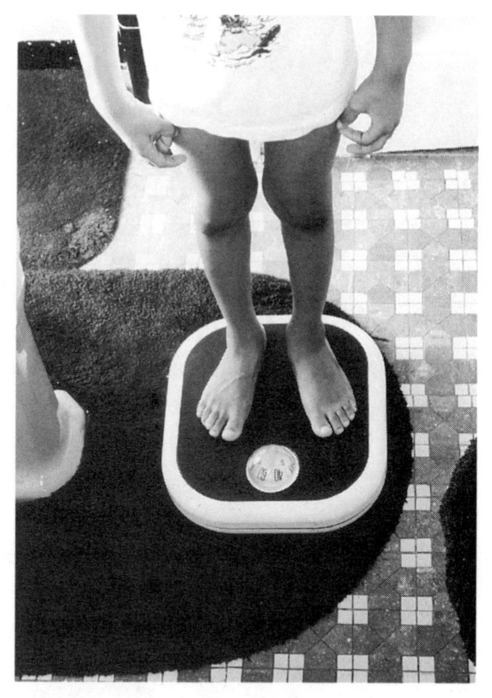

Keep an eye on your child's height and weight and discuss the results with your health care provider.

Health Care: Five-Year Visit. At this visit, your health care provider will measure your child's height and weight, and plot it on a chart. If your child didn't have hearing and vision tests and immunizations at the last visit, he'll need them now. He should have his annual blood test for iron deficiency anemia and lead exposure.

During this visit, you may want to have a discussion about your child's growth. This is the age when many parents begin to worry about their child's height and weight. Will she be taller than everyone in her class? Will he be big enough to play football? A parent's hopes for a child are all mixed up in anxieties about the child's growth.

Your height and build, and that of your mate, will strongly affect your child's size, but that's about your only guidepost at this stage. Height and weight at puberty are much more accurate predictors of what your child's final adult height and weight will be.

Five-Year Milestones

MOVEMENT: Agility and fine motor skills continue to improve. Holding a pencil or a fork in an adult manner is easier now, and he can wash his own hands, brush his teeth, and dress himself.

Here's Looking at You, Kid: Eye Exams

It is essential to have your child's eyes checked before you send him to school. If your child is working hard just to see, he probably isn't learning well. At worst he could be mistakenly labeled "slow" or learning disabled. Poor eyesight can also trigger distracted behavior—if a child can't see, it's hard to pay attention, and this can be mistaken as hyperactivity or attention deficit disorder.

Don't rely on your preschooler to tell you if she is having trouble seeing things clearly—she doesn't know how "clearly" is supposed to look. She may think fuzzy vision is quite normal. Signs of possible vision trouble include squinting, tearing, or tilting the head to see better.

At your child's annual physical exam, your pediatrician will do a basic test for visual acuity using an eye chart (or "E" chart). She or he will examine the eyes and check for crossed-eyes and other abnormalities. A complete vision test is best performed by an ophthalmologist or optometrist specializing in children. An ophthalmologist is a medical doctor who specializes in detecting and treating eye diseases and is licensed to perform eye surgery, while an optometrist examines the eye for visual defects and prescribes corrective lenses. Optometrists refer patients to ophthalmologists if they detect problems that cannot be corrected by lenses. If your child's eyesight is worse than 20/30 and can be corrected with lenses, see an optometrist. If, however, he has signs of any other visual impairment such as crossed eyes, you should see an ophthalmologist.

The eye doctor will check your child's eyes for color vision, examine the contour of the eyeball and retina, test for glaucoma, and fit her for glasses, if necessary. Make sure your child is comfortable in her glasses for several months before school begins.

Contact the National Optometric Association at (812) 855–4475 for additional guidelines on children's eyecare.

To Help:

- Prepare your five-year-old for school sports and gym class by exposing her to team games and athletic activities. She should have some kind of regular exercise activity for at least thirty minutes each day. Whether it's Little League, soccer, or taking regular walks with you, make it fun.

COGNITIVE: The five-year-old is beginning to understand the difference between what's real and what's not, though she may still think there are little people in the television set. Her attention span is about twenty minutes. She can count more than ten objects and can write a few numbers, though she may not be able to identify them. She remains very curious about the world.

To Help:

- Teach him to think ahead by allowing him to pick his clothes for the next day. It's best to give him two choices, i.e., "either this shirt or that one." Also, he can help you prepare his lunch and pack his schoolbag the night before.
- Play Simon Says so your child can learn how to focus on verbal instructions; don't always match your actions with your commands, to see if he's listening carefully.
- Stop in the middle of a familiar bedtime story and ask your child to tell you what happens next. This helps him think about logical progression.

SOCIAL: Five-year-olds are often preoccupied with who likes who and who doesn't, especially as they are exposed to new friends in school settings. Friends and enemies have a fast turnover. In his peer group, your child may be a leader sometimes and a follower at other times.

Is Your Child Ready for Kindergarten?

These questions can help you decide if your child is ready for kindergarten. Can he:

- **Interact well with other children, even those who are a few years older than he is?**
- **Share and take turns with other children?**
- **Follow directions?**
- **Identify a range of colors?**
- **Say or sing the alphabet?**
- **Draw a circle, square, or a stick-figure person without help?**
- **Execute basic manners ("please," "thank you," etc.)?**
- **Communicate sufficiently?**
- **Handle small responsibilities?**
- **Handle himself in the bathroom without assistance?**
- **Manage without you for several hours?**

Never Talk to Strangers?

In our often dangerous world, parents walk a fine line between keeping our children safe and making them timid and fearful. That's especially true when figuring out what to tell your child about dealing with people they don't know. How do you encourage your child to be friendly and personable, while teaching her about "stranger danger"?

To help, follow these guidelines:

- ***Practice prevention.*** **Make sure you've thoroughly checked out your child's caregivers and anyone else who'll be looking after her. Most people who abuse children are close to the children's family.**
- ***Use positive language.*** **When explaining why a child shouldn't get into a car with someone she doesn't know, say "I want you to be safe" rather than "Someone will hurt you."**
- ***Let her know that her body is her own.*** **Teach her that she can decide who touches her and who doesn't. And you, too, should respect her boundaries.**
- ***Encourage her to speak up.*** **First, let her know that you want her to express her feelings to you, which calls for you to be an attentive listener. And explain to her that it's OK to say "no" to an adult if she feels uncomfortable or unsafe, even if it's a family member.**
- ***Discuss instincts.*** **In some situations it's OK—and good—for her to think, "I don't like this person," or "he's frightening me"—and leave. It's important that she trust her gut and judgment about danger.**
- ***Enroll her in a self-defense class at a community center or local college.*** **It will be fun and instructive; make sure it is meant for children.**

To Help:

- Teach cooperation by assigning simple tasks that must be done by two, your child and her playmate or a sibling.
- Let your child help you in the kitchen so she learns cooperation, patience, and the steps involved in making something from start to finish. For instance, she could snap the ends off of green beans or shuck corn.

EMOTIONAL: The ability to share more easily and handle frustration with less trauma characterizes most five-year-olds. Girls tend to handle conflict in less aggressive ways than boys. Also, as your child learns to manage life's ups and downs, don't be surprised if she's laughing one minute, crying the next, and then laughing all over again.

To Help:

- Teach your child to feel good about asking for help instead of whining or pouting. When she needs assistance, encourage her to say, "Can you help me?" Then answer, "Yes. What would you like me to do?"
- When a problem arises, help your child find a solution by himself. Ask questions like, "What's the problem?" "What are some things we can do about it?" "Which idea is best?" Be sure to congratulate him when he solves his dilemma.

SPEECH: Your child should be able to tell you what day it is, should know the days of the week in order, and should show interest in learning how to tell time. He tells and understands jokes and can engage in more adult conversation.

To Help:

- Laugh *with* your child. Encourage him to express humor through the telling of a joke, a funny story, or even creating a mini comedy routine.
- Use everyday words to help him learn the more difficult letter combinations, such as "th" and "sh."
- Teach him about family structure: aunts, uncles, sisters, grandparents, etc. by using family photos to explain the relationships.
- Introduce analogies, such as "hat-head," "shoe-foot." Ask your child to identify how the two go together (you will probably need props to help him understand this). This is a difficult game and takes patience and diligence.
- Make conversation with your child daily. Comment and ask questions that encourage her to tell more.

RESOURCES

Recommended Reading for Parents

Caring for Your Baby and Young Child, Steven P. Shelov, M.D., F.A.A.P., ed. (Bantam, 1993). Here is a complete reference for parents of children birth to five years, with extensive medical and developmental information for each age group.

Dr. Spock's Baby and Child Care, Benjamin Spock, M.D., and Michael Rothenberg, M.D. (Pocket Books, 1992). This is a classic sourcebook for parents, with a special section on preschoolers.

Recommended Reading for Children

Dinosaurs Alive and Well!: A Guide to Good Health, Vol. 1, Laurene Krasny Brown and Marc Brown (Little, Brown and Company, 1992). This book provides children with interesting and useful ways to maintain good health.

It's Up to Me, JoAnne Nelson and Diana Magnuson (Wright Group, 1995). This book helps kids make healthy choices around such issues as nutrition and smoking.

Organizations

The National Black Child Development Institute, 1023 15th St., NW, Suite 600, Washington, D.C. 20005, (800) 556–2234, (202) 387–1281. NBCDI provides information and resources regarding young African-American children's health and education with over forty affiliates nationwide. Call for local program or educational information.

Chapter

4

Every Body: Skin, Hair, Eyes, Teeth, Clothes, and Toilet Training

As black adults, we keep entire personal care companies in business, spending $618 million and $262 million a year on hair and skin-care products, respectively. What about our children? How much time and money should we spend to keep our babies' skin and hair healthy? The answer, thankfully, is very little. In this chapter we will provide suggestions and resources for easy day-to-day body care for your child, offer ways to approach potty training, and tell you how to talk to your child about her body.

Body Care: Birth to One Year

Your Baby's Hair and Scalp

A newborn's hair is usually fine and soft and often has a slight curl. It's not very well rooted in the scalp and falls out easily. Your baby will probably not be born with "kinky" hair, even if both parents have it. During the first year of life, your baby's hair will continually fall out and his permanent hair will begin to grow in at around six months. At that point, you'll be able to see its genetically programmed texture—which can be anything from coarse, tight curls, to wavy, loose ones. Just because you and your mate have a certain type of hair doesn't mean that the baby's permanent hair texture or hair color will be the same as either one of yours. Hair texture and color are determined by the gene mixture the baby received when conceived. Often, a recessive or "hidden" gene that was present in both parents shows up in their baby. For example, no living members of either of your families may have red hair, but if both of you possess that recessive gene, your baby could end up a redhead.

Regardless of the color or the texture of the hair, you may notice that your newborn's scalp looks greasy and scaly. Though this doesn't occur in all babies, cradle cap, as this condition is commonly known, is a condition of the scalp called seborrheic dermatitis. It really isn't a big problem, but it can look bad and can spread to the face, ears, neck, and other parts of the body. Although it can cause your baby to lose his hair, it should disappear within the first few months with proper care. (For suggestions on treating cradle cap, see p. 62.)

Your baby's hair may also appear patchy and sparse—which is exaggerated by the loss of hair around the sides and back of his head. This hair falls out because the baby spends so much time lying down or sleeping, thereby placing pressure on those

"I was so focused on my daughter's bald spot because my own hair was falling out as well." —Linda's Story

I was thrilled when my daughter, Kali, was born with a full head of thick black hair. I imagined her as a three-year-old sitting between my legs while I pulled her long, thick hair into three braids as my mother and grandmother had done for me.

At about month three, Kali's sleeping habits changed. Now before she fell asleep, during one of her several daytime naps and before bedtime, she'd close her eyes and toss her head vigorously from side to side for a few minutes, then relax and settle into sleep. Eventually, all that rubbing created a bald spot on the back of her head. It started out small, but in a few weeks it began to get larger. I couldn't let Kali sleep on her stomach because of the risk of SIDS, and she didn't like sleeping on her side.

I knew I was being neurotic, but that bald spot really started to bother me. I tried to comb some of the other hair over it, similar to the way older men create a severe side part and drag a few strands over their bald spots. But, of course, that was silly and didn't work. I also pointed the bald spot out all the time, and made nervous jokes about it. Vickie and I said that if it got worse we were going to start filling it in with shoe polish or use our hair to create a weave. Mostly, Kali wore a lot of hats.

I think that I was so focused on the bald spot because my own hair was also falling out, and that's what was really getting to me. During pregnancy, my hair had been extremely thick, and now it had become thin around the hairline and on top. My comb was full of hair, and I could see my scalp in places. I was starting to look more like Ben Franklin than myself. Apparently, during pregnancy hormonal changes prevent the normal shedding of the hair, and after pregnancy different hormones cause the hair to make up for lost time. Though I knew the shedding would stop, I hated how it looked.

When Kali was about seven months old and could lift her head, our pediatrician assured us that it was safe for her to sleep on her stomach. Once she switched from her back, little by little, her bald spot filled in. At the same time, I weaned her from breast-feeding, which triggered a new round of hormonal changes in me. And soon, I noticed that my brush had less hair, and my hair was starting to fill in.

areas of his head. Alternate the side you place the baby on when you put him down to sleep—one day right, one day left—to minimize early bald patches. If this doesn't help, don't worry. It is only his fine baby hair and will not affect the growth of permanent hair, which starts to come in at around six months. You will also notice that when he begins to sit and crawl and spends less time lying down, his bald spots disappear.

Hair Care

- *To wash the hair*, use a gentle no-tears formula baby shampoo once or twice per week. Shampoos formulated for black children such as those mentioned on page 78 may make thick hair more manageable. Hold the baby along your forearm, in what is called the football hold, or place him in a small tub or sink with his head and neck firmly supported. Wet the scalp first, then pour a small amount of shampoo directly on the head. Massage into a lather with your fingertips. To rinse, pour small cups of lukewarm water over the baby's head, pouring from the front to the back of the head so the water doesn't fall on his face. Pat dry with a washcloth. You can massage a small amount of mineral oil into the scalp if he needs it.
- *To style the hair,* use a wide-toothed comb or very soft brush to avoid pulling out too much hair. Most infants have very fine hair that is easy to break, so it is best to go "au natural" and leave your child's hair in a cute little afro. However, if you want to use hair accessories, make sure they are small and lightweight and don't pull your infant's hair. Barrettes, cotton ribbons, small baubles, or coated bands are fine for baby hairstyles. If you're using a headband, make sure it isn't too tight. (Note: most headbands pull on the same parts of the head where your baby loses the most hair.)
- *To treat cradle cap* (seborrheic dermatitis), massage a small amount of olive oil or unscented mineral oil into the baby's scalp before shampooing. Use a comb, toothbrush, or washcloth to gently loosen the flakes. (Don't worry, this doesn't hurt any more than combing or brushing.) Then shampoo the scalp (with a gentle baby shampoo, of course), rubbing gently to wash away the scaly residue. Once the cradle cap is gone, you will have to shampoo your baby's hair frequently to keep his scalp clear. In cases of severe cradle cap, where the scales don't respond to your treatment or become thick and crusty, your pedia-

trician can recommend a medicated baby shampoo. Though hats look cute, a baby with severe cradle cap should go without one as much as possible to keep the scalp open to the air. If the problem spreads to the face and neck, your pediatrician will prescribe a special ointment to use.

Your Baby's Skin

In the womb, the baby is covered by vernix, which is a cheesy-looking substance that keeps the skin protected while in the amniotic fluid. You may have seen some of this on your baby at birth, especially if he was premature. Once his skin is washed, it may peel and develop cracks at the joints, particularly at the wrists and ankles.

As far as skin color, you may be surprised at how light your baby is. Newborns of just about every shade are born very light and have pinkish skin. This is because the red blood vessels show through the baby's thin skin. The baby's true skin color will appear gradually during the first year. It can be difficult to predict what your child's color will be, but you can follow what the old folks say and check the tops of the ears and base of the nails to determine your baby's eventual skin color.

Birthmarks. Your baby may have birthmarks on his body at birth. He may also develop others as he goes through infancy. Most of them are nothing to worry about and will disappear during childhood. It's best to routinely scan your baby's skin at bathtime or when changing her diaper and point out anything you find to your pediatrician during checkups. Here's what you may see:

- *Newborn jaundice* is a yellowing of the skin that occurs in most infants. It is caused by high bilirubin levels in the blood. In the first few days of life, your child will begin to eat and will pass bilirubin in his stool. During the time before his feeding pattern is established, his bilirubin levels rise and he will appear more yellow. Jaundice occurs more frequently in breast-fed babies, because it takes three to four days for Mom to produce adequate amounts of milk. Just continue putting your baby to your breast, and he will get enough milk to help pass the bilirubin. Babies will become more and more jaundiced until about day five of life and then it should start to clear. If you notice that your child's jaundice is getting worse or hasn't disappeared fourteen days after birth, contact your pediatrician.
- *Fine body hair* (lanugo) can be seen on the back, shoulders, and ears of many

newborns. It is more common in premature infants. No treatment is needed. These hairs fall out by themselves and are usually gone by one month.

- *Mongolian spots* are common in black children. They are flat, dark-colored marks that look like bruises but aren't painful. They vary in size and are usually found on the baby's back and bottom but can appear anyplace on the body. They are not harmful to the baby and most disappear by late childhood but can remain into adulthood.
- *Angel kisses and stork's bites* (macular hemangiomas) are pale pink to red flat marks present at birth. Caused by a collection of blood vessels under the skin, "angel kisses" are found on the eyelids, nose, and upper lip while "stork bites" are found at the nape of the neck. These marks usually disappear in the first few months, although 25 percent of stork bites persist into adulthood.
- *Cafe au lait* spots are irregularly shaped, flat marks that are usually light brownish in color—about the shade of "coffee with milk," as its French name suggests—though they can also be dark brown in our children. These marks appear in varying sizes and may darken as your child grows to adulthood. More than a few large spots on a baby can indicate the presence of a genetic disorder called neurofibromatosis, so be sure to mention them to your pediatrician.
- *Moles* are dark spots on the skin caused by a collection of melanocytes, the cells that produce melanin. Some children are born with these, while most others develop them as they grow older. The vast majority are benign, but anyone (adults and children) with a mole should check it frequently for changes to make sure it has not become cancerous. The shape, size, regularity of borders, and rate of growth of the mole will determine whether it should be removed or left alone. Always point out moles or marks to your doctor. She may choose to remove an abnormal-looking mole as a precaution or send your child to a pediatric dermatologist for another opinion.
- *Strawberry hemangiomas* are red marks that appear anyplace on the body and vary in size from very small to palm-sized. They are caused by a collection of blood vessels under the skin. Most start out as red or skin-toned flat marks that begin to grow and become raised and lumpy during the first few weeks of life. The marks increase in size during the first year, then stop growing and begin to slowly flatten and fade. Most disappear by five years but some can re-

main until late childhood. No treatment or surgery is usually necessary since they go away on their own. However, if the hemangiomas are located on the eyelids or nose, they can impair vision or breathing as they grow. You should discuss treatment options with your pediatrician if they are causing problems.

Rash Decisions. Several types of rashes can appear on your baby's body. They can be a reaction to several irritants, including friction from clothing and diapers; soiled diapers; allergic reaction to food, clothing, soaps, detergents; overheating; or a change in hormonal levels. Most rashes don't require any special attention, but those that do are generally easy to remedy.

- *Erythema toxicum* is a rash common in newborns. It looks like small red splotches with white dots in the center that may resemble pimples. The cause of this rash is unknown but no treatment is necessary since it resolves in the first couple of weeks.
- *Milia* are tiny white bumps found mainly on the nose but can also be on the cheeks, chin, and forehead. They are caused by blocked pores that are not infected and should be left alone. Like many newborn rashes, these also go away without treatment and are gone by two months.
- *Pustular melanosis* is a newborn rash that is more common in black infants. It is present at birth and consists of superficial pus-filled bumps that burst leaving dark brown marks. Although the rash can be anywhere on the body it is most commonly found on the neck, forehead, and back. There is no treatment for this condition, and the darker marks will disappear by three to four months.
- *Newborn acne* is caused by the mother's hormones in the baby's blood. It usually begins at about one month and looks like teenage acne with small pimples on the face and oily skin. There are no treatments for this. Anti-acne medications are too strong and should never be used on baby's sensitive skin. Just keep your baby's face clean, wash with water, and the skin will get better as the mother's hormone levels in the baby's body drop.
- *Diaper rash* happens to most infants at one time or another. Babies have a tendency to get rashes in their diaper area because the warm, dark, moist environment provides a breeding ground for bacteria and fungus. It often appears

Leave It Alone:
Caution About Home Remedies for Baby's Skin

Many parents will hear advice from well-meaning grandmothers and great aunts on how to treat various skin rashes on newborns. These treatments vary from using baking soda, toothpaste, alcohol, or even harsh acne medicine to dry and clear up rashes. Whatever remedy your friends and family suggest, always check with your pediatrician first. While everyone pictures her newborn with clear, bronze skin, the reality is that babies usually have a bout with one rash or another. If left alone, they usually go away quickly. Using home or over-the-counter remedies to treat these rashes is dangerous and can often cause other problems without helping the rash. If your baby develops a rash, follow your pediatrician's advice.

as a red, irritated rash on the baby's genitals, bottom, and thighs. Unchecked, "normal" diaper rash can sometimes develop into a yeast infection.

To prevent diaper rash, change the baby as soon as you see that she is wet or has had a bowel movement. Try different brands of disposable diapers or cloth diapers, which are softer and more breathable than disposables. To treat diaper rash, clean area thoroughly with a washcloth or cotton balls and warm water; avoid excessive use of soap and commercial baby wipes. A great way to stop diaper rash in its tracks is to allow her bottom half to air dry after bathing and between diaper changes. When your baby doesn't have a rash, applying ointments with each diaper change is not necessary. If your baby has diaper rash, use ointments that contain zinc oxide such as Desitin. These really stick to the skin and form a protective barrier so skin doesn't get further irritated. *Do not* try to wash the ointment off between changes. Because these ointments are so sticky, trying to remove them will only cause more irritation. If these measures don't help or if the rash is spreading, consult your pediatrician. Babies can also get fungal diaper rashes that require medicated creams for treatment.

- *Eczema* (atopic dermatitis) can begin in the newborn period. It usually starts on the cheeks in the first few months of life with a dry rash that can become irritated and cracked. Eczema is hereditary and is generally present with asthma and allergies. As the rash progresses it can be found anyplace on the body.

Eczema is treated by keeping the skin moistened with hypoallergenic lotions such as Aveeno or Eucerin. You can also use the "old time" moisturizer—Crisco in a can. It is made of vegetable oil which doesn't irritate skin. Avoid harsh soaps and detergents. Use only hypoallergenic products, or nondrying soaps such as Dove. Finally, your doctor may recommend a steroid ointment such as hydrocortisone to soothe the irritated skin.

- *Drool face* is not an official or medical term, but it describes the rash that develops when your baby's drool gets all over her face and causes irritation. You will often see it around the mouths and on the cheeks of infants who suck on pacifiers. The best treatment is to wipe the saliva off her face and apply an ointment such as A&D or petroleum jelly to protect her skin. If excessive drooling has caused a rash in the folds of your baby's neck, treat it by washing with water and letting it dry thoroughly. The excess moisture can also lead to a fungal rash in your baby's neck, so consult your doctor if the rash hasn't improved.
- *Prickly heat rash* is caused by the baby being overheated and occurs in both the summer and winter. This common rash is usually a result of overdressing the baby, a constant tendency of anxious new parents. A baby's immature sweat ducts cannot yet handle the excess sweat, so the moisture gets trapped beneath the skin. This rash will not bother your infant but he may be irritable because of the heat. To avoid heat rash, keep him in a cool room or, if

Umbilical Cord Care: An Important Part of Caring for Your Newborn

You should clean your infant's umbilical cord with alcohol-soaked cotton balls or Q-tip swabs two to three times per day, focusing on the moist portions at the base. The cord should fall off by two weeks leaving a small moist area in the belly button. Continue cleaning the area with alcohol until the belly button has completely dried. If the area hasn't dried one week after the cord falls off, you should have your pediatrician look at it. She may need to apply some medicine to help the cord finish drying and healing. If, at any time, your baby develops redness or swelling around the cord, or you see pus coming from the cord, contact your pediatrician immediately.

outdoors, in a shady place and remove some or all of his clothing so he doesn't get overheated. If he does develop heat rash you can give him a lukewarm sponge bath, dry him thoroughly, and apply powder to absorb excess moisture. Heat rash usually subsides within a few days.

General Skin and Body Care

- *Washing and Bathing.* You should give your newborn sponge baths and clean her umbilical stump with alcohol until it falls off and heals. After that, she should be bathed in a baby tub. Infants do not require daily baths like adults because they don't sweat or get dirty like we do. The only part of their bodies that gets dirty is the diaper area which should be cleaned with each diaper change. You can bathe your baby two to three times per week, and can limit soap to the diaper area. Use only hypoallergenic products made especially for infants, and don't use bubble bath. After a bath, pat your baby dry with a towel.
- *Moisturizing.* It's best to moisturize the skin after bathing so you can apply lotions that "lock in" moisture. (Moisturizers won't keep a newborn's skin from peeling, but they will keep her skin soft.) Apply lotions that are hypoallergenic and made for use on babies' sensitive skin. Although a lot of baby products smell good, the perfumes they contain can irritate your infant's skin, so stick with lotions that have no perfumes or dyes.
- *Powdering.* Powders are used to keep baby's skin dry and smelling sweet, but they have a few drawbacks. Talcum powder, which is great for keeping the diaper area dry, can cause severe respiratory problems if accidentally inhaled by your baby. And cornstarch, which is safer for the lungs, can cause fungal and yeast infections when used on moist areas. Powder is not necessary, but if you want to use it, the best solution is to use talc for the diaper area, where it's less likely to be inhaled, and cornstarch for the neck and body area, where it won't cause a fungal infection. Fortunately, a new alternative will be on the market soon called "dustless" baby powder. This rice-based powder is compact and applied with a sponge (like powder foundation) rather than sprinkled, so it's unlikely that your baby will inhale it.

Be Gentle with Genitals

What's the best way to keep your baby's genitals clean? Make sure her bottom and genital areas are thoroughly cleaned at each diaper change. This means paying attention to the creases in the genital area as well as the genitals themselves. Give newborns a good wipe with a few wet cotton balls, or use a moistened washcloth or baby wipe for older babies. Wipe the baby's front first, then lift both legs at the ankles and wipe her bottom.

Cleaning boys: If your son was circumcised, wait until the glans, or head, of his penis has healed before you give him a full bath. Clean his penis and scrotum with soap and water, making sure to wipe all the nooks and crannies. If your son is not circumcised, you should *not* attempt to retract the tight foreskin of his penis in order to clean under it. It is attached to the glans and you can tear it. The foreskin will naturally separate from the glans by the time he is about three years old. At that point, it can be easily retracted and cleaned. Some newborn boys will appear to have enlarged testicles due to fluid that collects in the scrotum. The fluid will eventually be absorbed, and the scrotum will be normal by about one year. If not, you should contact your pediatrician. Two things to be aware of while washing your baby boy's genitals: He may have an erection or may urinate while you are cleaning him. Both functions are normal. To avoid a "christening" by your son, just put the washcloth over the penis until he is finished urinating. After cleaning, pat your son's genitals dry.

Cleaning girls: A newborn baby girl may have a white, sticky, or bloody vaginal discharge, and her vagina may also appear swollen due to her mother's hormones. The discharge is caused by the hormones and their effects on her uterus and vaginal lining and should disappear within the first few weeks of life. Don't go crazy trying to clean all of the discharge out. To clean her genitals, spread the outer folds of the vagina, called the labia, and wipe the baby from front to back with a damp or lightly soaped washcloth. Be careful: Too much soap may irritate the baby's vagina. Rinse the cloth, squeeze out excess water, and wipe the area again with the opposite side of the cloth. Pat the area dry with a towel.

Throw Some Shade? Straight Talk About Sunburn. Do black babies get sunburned? The answer is yes. Don't be fooled into thinking your baby's beautiful brown skin is immune to sun damage, which is responsible for 90 percent of skin cancers.

Since sunscreens are not recommended for babies under six months of age, the only prevention is to avoid bringing a young baby out into direct sunlight.

Go outside with your baby first thing in the morning or in the late afternoon to avoid the sun's strongest rays. Make sure your stroller has a cover that can provide some shade. Use it even on sunny winter days and hot, cloudy days, as cold and clouds do not prevent sunburn.

Babies six months old or older can and should wear a sunscreen with an SPF of at least 15. Look for products that are PABA-free (para-aminobenzoic-acid) as this ingredient can trigger allergic reactions. Products that are hypoallergenic and fragrance-free are also good choices, especially if your baby seems to have sensitive skin. The sunscreen should be waterproof so it doesn't wash off if the baby gets wet. Remember to put it on her nose and on the tops of her ears, feet, and shoulders. Limit sun exposure to about one hour, even with sunscreen.

Your baby should also wear a hat in the sun. A lightweight cotton hat will block some of the sun while keeping the baby's head cool. Choose a light color to reflect the sun instead of absorbing it the way a denim or dark-colored hat would.

If your baby does get sunburned, remove her from the sun immediately and apply cool compresses to the burned skin. Do *not* use any lotions, creams, or salves such as hydrocortisone, Noxzema, or baby oil on a baby younger than one year. These products are harmful and too harsh.

Your Baby's Ears

This may come as a surprise to Q-tip lovers, but cotton swabs should *not* be stuck inside your baby's ear canal for *any* reason. Swabs are for cleaning the outer ear only, and it says so very clearly on the package directions. Swirling the swab around inside the ear canal might take out a little wax but it will also push the rest of it further down, and embed it in the ear canal. This can cause damage to your baby's eardrum, pain, and even a loss of hearing. Wax works by trapping dust and particles that enter the ear and will fall out without your assistance. Remember the rule: Nothing bigger than your elbow goes in the ears!

You can also use a damp washcloth placed over your fingertip or a cotton ball to clean your baby's outer ear—and leave the inner part of the ear alone. Mothers with

Piercing Questions

To pierce or not to pierce your little girl's—or boy's—ears, that is the question for many black parents. Parents should wait until the child is at least six months old before having her ears pierced. At that age she has had three tetanus shots, and her earlobes have grown so the earrings can be put in a more accurate position. Waiting until your child is one year may be even better. Any earlier and you risk piercing holes that may not be in the center of her earlobes (a condition many adult women who were pierced as babies find aggravating).

When getting your child's ears pierced, make sure sterile instruments are used. Blood-borne infections such as HIV and hepatitis can be transmitted with unclean instruments so take great care when choosing who will do the job. Many pediatricians pierce ears or can recommend a place where your baby's ears can be safely pierced.

The type of metal used in baby's first earrings is also important. Surgical stainless steel earrings are best. You can also use earrings made of precious metals such as gold but be careful of allergies to nickel. Gold earrings contain trace amounts of nickel which can cause a reaction if your baby is allergic to nickel.

Posts and small hoop earrings with a self-closure are good choices. Hoops should not be large enough for the baby to fit her finger in and pull down. If you choose earrings with posts, make sure they are shortened posts designed for babies and children. Posts used for piercing have a sharp point that can scratch your baby's skin, while children's posts are shorter with a rounded tip and are less likely to cause scratches.

long fingernails: Be very careful, because you risk damaging your baby's ear when you clean it. You should never stick your nails in his ears.

Your Baby's Mouth and Teeth

During your baby's first year, he will be growing and developing faster than he will at any other point in his life, and his teeth are no exception. Although some babies seem unbothered by oral infections or new teeth, many babies can be made quite miserable. Here are some things you might see in your baby's mouth:

- *Epstein pearls* are small, white cysts on the roof of the mouth. These are caused by the collection of fluids and cells and aren't cause for alarm. They appear at birth and should soon disappear without treatment.

- *Thrush,* another common oral condition found in babies, is a mild fungal infection that affects the mouth and tongue. Thrush looks like white, cottage-cheeselike patches that can be confused with milk residue. Don't try to wipe these patches off, or you'll cause bleeding. The baby will feel some discomfort in her mouth, especially when sucking. If you see signs of thrush, call your doctor. It will require treatment with an antifungal medicine. If you're breast-feeding, you may also need to be treated to avoid a relapse in your baby. If you are bottle feeding, sterilize your baby's nipples by boiling them.

Note: Avoid giving your baby a bottle with juice or milk at bedtime, because the sugars from these drinks remain on your baby's teeth as she sleeps, causing tooth decay. If you want to give your baby a bottle to go to sleep, put water in the bottle or give her milk and wipe her gums and teeth clean afterward. Some dentists recommend, at the very least, having your baby take a few sips of water after a milk bottle.

Something to Chew On: What to Do About Teething. At about six months of age, you'll probably experience the thrill you've been waiting for—or the period you've been dreading—your baby will begin to sprout his first teeth. The lower middle teeth usually appear first, followed by the upper middle teeth. The rest of the lower and upper lateral teeth should begin to appear between the sixth and eleventh months, though it's perfectly normal if none of his teeth come in until after age one. (Sometimes, one or two stubborn teeth don't appear until near age two.) Interestingly, girls' teeth have been shown to erupt a bit faster than boys'. Of course, there are a few babies who are born with teeth. Your pediatrician will tell you what to do if this happens.

The teething period is uncomfortable for babies, so you may notice your baby cries more during this period. You'll also notice he drools a lot and chews on his fingers or toys. Your baby may also experience slight diarrhea and a low-grade fever during the initial teething period. However, the fact that your baby is teething does not mean he will be constantly inconsolable. If he develops a high fever or begins to play with his ears, you should see your pediatrician. Neither of these signs is associated with teething, and your infant may have another illness that requires treatment.

To soothe a teether, try the following:

- *Frozen teething rings, bagels, or teething crackers are all helpful in eliminating teething pain.* Babies will naturally want to bite to relieve the soreness as new teeth push on the surface of the gum. Hard, frozen items will numb the area and provide temporary relief. Try putting the teething ring in the refrigerator if your baby finds frozen rings too cold.
- *Offer lots of rubber teething toys.* These, of course, should be safe (babies shouldn't be able to bite off small pieces that they can choke on). These toys come in an assortment of rings, soft and spikey balls, or even keys, are flexible enough to chew and generally entertaining enough to play with.
- *Some babies prefer a wet or frozen washcloth.* They are soft and easy to carry in a diaper bag or purse, and help to keep your baby's mouth clean.
- *Talk to your pediatrician about pain relievers.* Some doctors will suggest using a mild pain reliever, such as acetaminophen (Tylenol).
- *Wipe saliva from your baby's face often to avoid skin rash.* If necessary, apply A&D or petroleum jelly to her chin and cheeks to protect them from a rash.
- *Clean your baby's teeth with a piece of gauze or washcloth after a meal or bottle.* Don't bother with toothpaste or baking soda.

When Teeth Appear. The following is a list of when, roughly, to expect your child's teeth to arrive. A description of each tooth is followed by the age of your child. Your child's pattern may vary slightly from this chart:

Should Your Baby Take Fluoride Drops?

Since the 1950s doctors and dentists have recommended that young children have enough fluoride in their diets to help prevent tooth decay (a very small amount of fluoride provides ample protection while too much can cause white spots to appear on permanent teeth). Most communities add fluoride to tap water, but your child will not receive any if he is breast-feeding. Most doctors do not think fluoride drops are necessary for infants or for children taking formula. However, if you are breast-feeding or if you do not live in a community with fluoridated water, ask your child's pediatrician if she recommends fluoride drops.

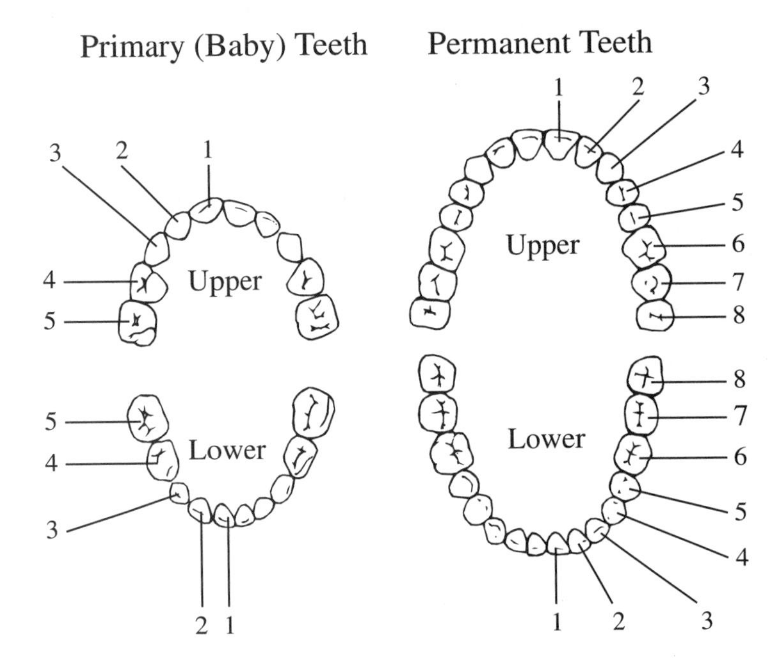

PRIMARY (BABY) TEETH: UPPER

1. Central incisors (front teeth): 8 to 12 months
2. Lateral incisors (side teeth): 9 to 13 months
3. Cuspids (long, pointed teeth next to incisors): 16 to 22 months
4. First molars (large teeth at back of the mouth): 13 to 19 months
5. Second molars: 25 to 33 months

PRIMARY (BABY) TEETH: LOWER

1. Central incisors: 6 to 10 months
2. Lateral incisors: 10 to 16 months
3. Cuspids: 17 to 23 months
4. First molars: 14 to 18 months
5. Second molars: 23 to 31 months

PERMANENT TEETH: UPPER

1. Central incisors: 5 to 7 years
2. Lateral incisors: 7 to 9 years

3. Cuspids: 11 to 12 years

4. First bicuspids: 10 to 12 years

5. Second bicuspids: 10 to 12 years

6. First molars: 10 to 11 years

7. Second molars: 10 to 12 years

8. Third molars: 17 to 22 years

PERMANENT TEETH: LOWER

1. Central incisors: 5 to 7 years

2. Lateral incisors: 7 to 8 years

3. Cuspids: 9 to 10 years

4. First bicuspids: 10 to 12 years

5. Second bicuspids: 11 to 12 years

6. First molars: 10 to 12 years

7. Second molars: 11 to 13 years

8. Third molars: 17 to 22 years

Your Baby's Nails

Your newborn baby's fingernails may be so long and sharp, she could be a danger to unsuspecting adults who try to play with her. Though long nails may look pretty, practically speaking, they are a hazard to you and your baby. Babies do not yet understand their hands are under their control. This is why babies often scratch themselves—and you—unconsciously. And dirt trapped under a baby's long nails ends up where her hands usually go—in her mouth.

For these reasons, you should keep your baby's fingernails short and rounded. Since a baby's nails grow very rapidly, you need to cut or file them every other day. (A good time for nail care: while she's sleeping, taking a bottle, bathing, or otherwise distracted.) Toenails do not grow as quickly as fingernails and don't need to be cut as frequently. The toenails of some newborns appear ingrown. Ask your pediatrician to look at them and advise you on the best way to care for them.

How to do it: Hold the finger or toe between your thumb and index finger and rub the emery board across the nail edge until it is even with the baby's fingertip, creating a rounded edge. If you are cutting your baby's nails, use either baby clippers or scissors. Begin cutting each nail at the end, cutting off a section before moving to the middle and far side of the nail. If you attempt to cut the entire nail at once, it could be painful for your baby. File any sharp edges after cutting.

Your Baby's Eyes

Most newborns do not have very good vision. Infants can see movement and bright colors and will look at close objects that resemble faces. When you first hold him in your arms he may look everywhere but at you. As his vision improves, you'll see him making eye contact and looking at your face by the time he is one month old. He may appear "cross-eyed" from time to time, but this should improve and completely disappear by the time he is two months. When your baby is first born, his eyes can be any color. You'll notice his eyes getting darker as he gets older, becoming their permanent color by the time he is six months.

Taking care of your child's eyes is very easy because not much needs to be done. When he is born, he will have medicine put in his eyes to prevent infections. This medicine can cause a reaction that creates a sticky discharge in his eyes. If you notice this, simply clean his eyes with warm water and a cotton ball and the discharge will disappear in a few days.

As he grows older and you take him outside, make sure his eyes are protected from the sun. You can start by having him wear hats with a brim that shade his face from the sun. As he gets older—about six months—you can give him a pair of sunglasses to protect his eyes. Most children love to wear their glasses (maybe they feel grown up). Just make sure the lenses filter out UV (ultraviolet) light. Otherwise, there is very little you need to do for his daily care. Your doctor will examine his eyes, ask you about his visual development, and make sure his vision is normal at your regular checkups. Here are some common things that can affect babies' eyes and should be brought to your doctor's attention:

- *Conjunctivitis,* or pinkeye, is an inflammation of the lining of the eye. It can be caused by chemicals (like the medicine that is put in a newborn's eyes), germs, or allergies. If your child develops pink, glassy eyes, or you notice discharge or crusting of his eyes, you should take him to see his doctor. When conjunctivitis is due to an eye infection, your child will require an antibiotic that must be prescribed by your doctor.

Newborns can also catch germs from their mothers' vaginal canals during birth. Conjunctivitis can be caused by chlamydia, which is an extremely common sexually transmitted disease. This infection must be treated because it causes both conjunctivitis and pneumonia in newborns. So don't be surprised, or offended, if you take your child to the doctor for pinkeye and she asks if you've ever had a sexually transmitted disease. She's just making sure your child receives the right antibiotic to treat his eye infection.

- *Lacrimal duct obstruction* is a blockage of the duct that drains tears from your child's eyes. If there is a blockage of the lacrimal duct, the tears will not be drained to his nose but will overflow, running out of his eye instead. If your child's eyes are always overflowing with tears you should point this out to your pediatrician. Lacrimal duct obstruction is very common in infants and your pediatrician can show you how to apply warm compresses and massage the duct to help open it, while making sure he does not develop an eye infection. Most obstructed lacrimal ducts will open with your treatments, but if your child's haven't improved by the time he is one year, he may require a simple surgical procedure to repair the problem and should see an ophthalmologist.
- *Strabismus* is the medical term for crossed eyes. Although infants will be cross-eyed from time to time, you should be concerned if your child's eyes never straighten. This needs to be treated immediately because a child with crossed eyes will start to use only one eye and the vision in the other will deteriorate. Your child will need to see a pediatric ophthalmologist and treatment usually involves some combination of surgery, glasses, medicine, and eye patches.

Body Care: Ages One to Five

Your Child's Hair and Scalp

Hair Care. Your grandmother may have shook her finger at you (or maybe she's shaking it now) saying, "Don't you cut that child's hair. It'll never grow," or "It'll cause speech problems." We black folks have always been superstitious about cutting small children's hair even though, in reality, trimming it won't stunt its growth. To ensure healthy hair in adulthood, proper care must start early on.

Sisters may remember back to those painful days sitting between our mother's legs having our hair combed and braided. Although we were accused of being "tender headed" when we winced at every knot, our mothers may have been a little heavy with the comb and light on the detangler. Now parents know that taking it easy on children's hair helps keep it strong and healthy, and also keeps tempers from flaring.

- *Washing and shampooing.* Wash your child's hair at least once a week. Massage the scalp with your fingertips to lift any loose dirt and oil. Choose shampoos and conditioners made specifically for our children; adult products can be too harsh and can irritate the eyes and/or skin. There are a number of hair products on the market targeted to black children, including ProLine's "Just for Me," Dark & Lovely's "Beautiful Beginnings," and "Dream Kids" from African Pride. Many of these shampoos and conditioners contain ingredients to help detangle or soften thick hair.
- *Combing.* The best way to comb thick hair is to spray on a leave-in conditioner or detangler after washing, says Barbara Winston, owner of Los Angeles–based Clairvoyance salon. Then part the hair into sections. "I usually make four sections for my daughter's hair," says Winston. "Comb and brush the hair section by section. As you continue to do this the hair will get softer."
- *Cutting hair.* Start your child off right by trimming her hair every six to eight weeks. You can do this yourself as soon as the hair starts to grow. Take your daughter to her first beauty salon visit around age four or five, your son to the barber shop at about age two, when he's able to sit still. "Contrary to what we've been told through the family grapevine, cutting your toddler's hair actually encourages hair growth," says Winston.
- *Styling.* For the most part, black parents who choose to relax their daughters' hair begin the process too early. Winston advises parents not to relax a child's fragile hair until age twelve or thirteen. Doing so earlier can cause hair damage, making it dry and brittle and causing the ends to break and split. "I see so many mothers bringing in their daughters with hair damaged from relaxing too early," says Winston. "Even the relaxers made for kids are too harsh. They still contain chemicals that alter the makeup of the hair."
- *Hot combing.* If you want to straighten your child's hair, hot combing is suggested as an alternative, but, says Winston, it too should be kept to a minimum.

A hot comb is a metal comb that is heated (either by plugging it in or heating it on a stove the old-fashioned way), and then combed through well-conditioned hair from the scalp to the tips. Because of the excessive heat from hot combs, they can be dangerous for squirmy children or inexperienced parents, and if used often, can damage fine hair. Here are some hot combing suggestions:

* *Only comb for special occasions.* If you comb weekly, consider an alternative hairstyle for your child (see below).
* *Be careful.* Use a paper towel to test the comb. If the comb burns the paper, it'll burn the hair.
* *You may want to buy a professional "hot comb oven,"* which avoids placing the comb on direct fire and controls the heat better. These are available at most beauty supply stores for about $50.
* *Don't load the scalp and hair down with globs of grease.* "Use about a half a dime's worth and distribute it throughout the hair," advises Winston. Try lotions and oils made especially for pressing, such as Luster's Pressing Lotion.
* *Have your child hold her ear down when you do that area* so as not to burn her.

• *Braiding and more.* Braiding your young daughter's (or son's) hair is fine as long as you don't do it too tightly, a mistake many parents make in an attempt to make it look "neater." While many women feel braiding promotes hair growth, it can actually cause damage if done incorrectly. Tight braiding can cause a condition called *traction alopecia,* hair loss attributed to pulling on the hair during braiding. "We see this scalp condition a lot," notes Berkeley, California, dermatologist Dr. Greta Clarke. "It's a progressive condition that starts with childhood. You may notice a lot of adults, mostly women, with less hair around the temple and by the ears. It's from too tight braiding as a child." The Pediatric Report's *Child Health Newsletter* notes such hair loss can be reversible, but tight braiding over prolonged periods of time can result in permanent damage to the hair follicle and permanent hair loss. "Those tight tiny braids may look cute," says Winston, "but then years later I get women wondering why their hairline is thinning or hair doesn't grow."

You may want to have your child's hair twisted (a loose braiding technique) or locked. "It's best to have a professional do these styles," advises Winston.

"They can be tricky to get right." Remember with locking, if you want to change the style or comb the hair out you must have the locks cut out.

Most cities have salons that cater to natural black hair. If you live in New York, check out Lock Chops Natural Hair and Khamet Kinks, both in Manhattan; in L.A. visit Oh, My Nappy Hair.

Braiding is a great style for young children, but don't braid too tightly.

Heads Up: Common Scalp Problems. As your child grows and becomes more active he'll undoubtedly spend more time with other children. That means he may contract minor scalp disorders commonly passed between children. Here are some common problems:

- *Head lice* is a condition common in day care settings and schools because it is easily passed from child to child. You will probably first notice the tiny, oval eggs, or nits, attached to the hair and your child's scalp may be very itchy. You should discuss the best treatments with your doctor, as some can be toxic, especially for children less than one year. Treatments that can be purchased over the counter include RID and NIX. These products are applied to the hair and left on for ten minutes to kill the lice. After rinsing, you will have to comb through your child's hairs with an extremely fine-toothed comb that is usually included with these kits. If this isn't done, the eggs will not be removed and could hatch and reinfest your child with head lice. This entire process should be repeated one week later to make sure any surviving lice or eggs have been removed.

  After you have treated your child's hair and scalp, you will need to wash all of his hats, combs, brushes, clothes, and sheets to make sure all lice and their eggs have been killed. You should also check all members of the family

"One day one of my daughter's white classmates said she wanted to have hair like hers so she could wear it in braids and have beads, too." **—ANNE'S STORY**

I have two little girls, so hair is a major issue in our house. As they have gotten older, I've become more and more concerned that they grow up feeling good about their hair. Even though I grew up during the days of Black Power and big afros, I remember not liking my hair because it was so thick, which for me meant nappy and difficult to manage. So I wanted my girls to have styles that they would associate with beauty and feeling good, rather than with struggle and feeling ugly.

With these concerns in mind, I undertook a personal campaign to instill an appreciation of beauty that included all types of people, and all types of hair. I pointed out attractive women of all colors and with various hair textures and styles on the street or in magazines. I told my girls they were beautiful and that their hair was nice, soft, and thick. I made a point to minimize their contact with dolls and videos that glamorized women with long, flowing, Rapunzel-like hair. And I tried to be gentle when combing their hair so they wouldn't associate its upkeep with pain.

Despite these efforts, I came home one evening to find my girls playing with stockings on their heads pretending they were princesses with long, flowing hair. I felt betrayed by a world that tells our little girls that beautiful is something they will never be because girls with curly hair will never have long, flowing hair without chemically altering it. And I felt I had failed my children because I was unable to protect them from that lesson.

Eventually, I got over my disappointment and continued my campaign to instill my girls with an appreciation for their own beauty. When they were old enough to sit still I began to put cornrows in their hair and decorated them with beads. The girls loved choosing the decorations in their hair, and loved the sound their hair made as they moved. I was heartened when one of my daughter's white classmates said she wanted to have hair like hers so she could wear it in braids and have beads. I then realized that while we are often surrounded with Eurocentric images and standards of beauty, when given a chance, children are willing to appreciate beauty in all its forms.

While my children still play "princess" with stockings on their heads, they also play "African Princess" and wrap themselves in towels. And they love having their hair braided, cornrowed, and decorated. When I finish doing their hair I tell them to look in the mirror, and they often ask, "Mommy, don't you think I look beautiful?" And I always tell them yes.

to make sure they haven't been infected too. To prevent lice infestation, do not let your child share hats, combs, or brushes with other children in day care and school. If your child has been infected notify your day care center or school because he probably got it from another child there whose parent has not yet noticed the lice. All children in the center will have to be examined and treated or else your child could get reinfected.

- *Tinea capitis,* or ringworm of the scalp, is a fungal infection that is more common among African-American children and may be misdiagnosed as dandruff. Symptoms include itching, scaling, and flaking of the scalp. If it goes untreated, it can progress to pus-filled sores and loss of hair in patches. Treatment will involve taking an antifungal medication by mouth for at least one month, and your doctor may also give you an antifungal cream and shampoo.

Your Child's Skin

After the first year, most children have overcome the myriad of skin ailments that affect infants, such as acne and most diaper rashes. However, just because your child is no longer a newborn doesn't mean his skin doesn't need the same gentle attention during his toddler and preschool years. In fact, this is the age when parents can begin teaching children how to care for their own bodies and begin good habits that will last them a lifetime.

General Skin and Body Care

- *Washing and bathing.* Many parents of toddlers and preschoolers are content to wash their children only a few times a week, making sure that their children are diligent about hand-washing and wiping themselves after using the bathroom. Still other parents swear by a warm bath as part of the bedtime routine that helps their children sleep well. Besides, they say, it gets rid of the caked mud and sand that simple handwashing can't. As long as your child's skin isn't dry and irritated, a daily bath is fine.

  Toddlers will usually think of bathtime as playtime, so make a game out of it. Give him a special sponge all his own. Show him how to wash his face first, then arms, legs, and so on. You'll probably have to go over the same areas yourself with a washcloth, because a child won't do a thorough job just yet.

Soap your child's hands and show him how to spread the soap over his body and arms; then make a game of rinsing all the suds off.

Toddlers are eager to do things themselves, so keep a close eye on them in the bathroom. Make sure your child doesn't turn on the hot water while in the tub or get soap or shampoo in her eyes. Drape a towel or put a specially designed cover over the taps and faucets in the bath to protect against falls or bangs.

Starting at about age eighteen months, a child can learn to wash her hands. Make sure she can reach the sink by putting a stool in the bathroom for her to use. Point out which is the hot tap and which is the cold, and tell her not to use the hot. Show her how to suds up, wash between her fingers and under her nails, and rinse off. Make it clear that hands should be washed after using the toilet. Start this at the same time you begin potty training. Also make sure your child washes hands before meals and after playing with pets.

- *Moisturizing.* Apply lotion right after the bath to seal in the moisture. If your child was prone to rashes as a baby, she probably has sensitive skin, so be careful with the products you use and follow the guidelines below:
  * Avoid deodorant soaps, high-alkaline soaps, and soaps with perfumes and dyes.
  * Look for soaps with built-in moisturizers or cold cream, such as Dove, Caress, or Tone.
  * Limit use of Vaseline. Vaseline and lotions with heavy oils can clog pores and cause inflammation of the follicles (or breakouts). If you like baby oil, choose a "light" version and use sparingly.
  * Avoid using perfumed lotions, which can irritate the skin. Make sure to select "fragrance-free" products.

Common Skin Infections. The following is a list of some skin infections your toddler or preschooler may contract, along with common remedies:

- *Ringworm* is a fungal infection that can occur anyplace on the body. It is commonly found in young children and appears as small, round patches on the skin. The patches usually have scaly or dry edges with a clear center and look like ring-shaped marks. This rash does not itch or cause your child discomfort. It can be treated with over-the-counter antifungal creams that contain clotrimazole (e.g., Lotrimin). The old-fashioned remedy of washing the skin with bleach does not work and can be dangerous. If your child's rash does not get better with the cream, have your doctor look at it. It may require a stronger medicine, or it may be something other than ringworm.

- *Impetigo* is a common bacterial infection of the skin and occurs when there has been a break or minor injury of the skin that gets infected. The infection causes small blisters that break and form small honey-colored crusts on the skin. Children with chicken pox sometimes get this skin infection on top of their chicken pox, but it can occur with any break in the skin. You will need an antibiotic ointment to treat this infection, and your doctor may decide to give your child antibiotics by mouth. Until it has been treated, this infection is extremely contagious so wash your hands after applying the medicine and do not let your child share towels or washcloths with anyone.
- *Scabies* is caused by small insects or mites that burrow under the skin and lay their eggs. The insects then die, but their eggs and bodies cause an extremely itchy rash of red, irritated bumps. Scabies can be located anyplace on the body, and is often found between the fingers because of scratching. Do not try to treat this yourself. Your doctor must prescribe a lotion to treat this infection, and the type of lotion depends on the age of your child. Treatment occurs after bathing. You will apply the lotion all over your child's body and let it stay on overnight. Then wash it off in the morning. All clothing and bed sheets must be washed, and all members of the family examined to see if they have been infected as well.
- *Eczema* is an extremely common skin condition among children and tends to run in the family along with asthma and seasonal allergies. Eczema often starts in infancy but can also begin later in life. The rash causes dry and itchy skin with thick patches, usually on the inside of the elbows and behind the knees in older children. Most cases of eczema can be managed by keeping your child's skin well hydrated. You should also limit the number of times you bathe your child, and when you do, use moisturizing soaps that are for sensitive skin—Dove and Aveeno are good choices. After bathing, apply hydrating moisturizers that are gentle on the skin and do not contain perfumes or dyes. Aveeno, Eucerin, Keri

Lotion, and Lubriderm are good choices. Crisco in a can is also an excellent moisturizer. It is made of vegetable oil so is less likely to cause a reaction, has no perfumes or dyes, is easy to apply, and is much less expensive than other hydrating creams and lotions. You should also avoid using products that may irritate your child's skin. Harsh soaps and detergents should be replaced with hypoallergenic products. If these measures don't work, speak with your doctor. She can recommend steroid ointments but will need to instruct you on their proper use.

Toilet Training: Do We Expect Too Much Too Soon?

Most parents feel a sense of pride and accomplishment when their child begins using the toilet regularly. "Whew," we say, believing that we have traded in the expense and mess of our children wearing diapers for a clean, painless alternative. In some cases this is true. However, for many families, toilet training can be a prolonged process that lasts much longer and causes more conflict than parents had hoped. To help parents understand the entire process of toilet training, we have spelled out the best methods to use and addressed many questions parents have. There are many ways to encourage children to develop good habits, but parents must understand toilet training takes time, patience, and learning from both sides.

Give your child plenty of praise to encourage toilet training success.

When to Begin

The "best" age to begin toilet training is truly up to your child. There are many signs of readiness. However, just because your child is physically and cognitively ready doesn't mean she is emotionally ready to give up diapers and become a "big girl." Think of the courage it takes for you to begin a new job, move to a new home, or learn a new task. Then you will begin to understand what an important milestone toilet training is for small children.

Although parents could begin toilet training when a child learns to walk (and gains muscle control over the lower half of her body), starting at this time is impractical. Some children begin walking as early as nine months. That is clearly too young to understand the concept of having to "go." Unfortunately, in a desire to rid themselves of the expense and mess of diapers, many parents push their children to begin using the toilet too early. This results in frequent accidents, feelings of failure and frustration, and lengthens the amount of time it takes for a child to be fully trained. Parents would do better to wait until their child shows most or all of these signs:

- Pulls at a dirty diaper indicating that she wants to be changed.
- Shows signs of having a bowel movement or urinating (strains face, squats, or makes noise).
- Can tell you beforehand that he is going to have a bowel movement or urinate.
- Goes to a special area to have a bowel movement or urinate.
- Understands the concept of "clean" and "dirty."
- Has long periods of being dry during the day.
- Is having bowel movements at regular times of the day.
- Can follow simple commands, like "go to the bathroom and sit on the potty."
- Shows interest or signs of wanting to use the toilet like a "big boy" or daddy.

Most children don't begin to demonstrate a true readiness for toilet training until sometime after two years old. After this age, and once a child shows he's ready, toilet training and daytime dryness can take up to six months. Nighttime dryness may take much longer.

How to Begin

1. Purchase a potty or child-sized toilet seat to put over the regular seat. If you can, bring your child with you to pick it out, casually explaining what it's for. It's important that she feel it is her special item. You will also need a small stool.

2. Next, suggest to your child that she sit on the seat a few times, to try it out. You might make a game of dropping small bits of toilet paper into the toilet and letting her practice using the flush handle a few times.

3. Begin toilet training with control of her bowel movements. If she seems okay with sitting in the childseat, suggest she sit on it in her training pants or diapers when she feels a bowel movement coming. Try it at the time of day she usually has a bowel movement. Start slowly. If you're too aggressive and make this a steady routine too quickly, she's likely to rebel. Have a book or a toy handy to help her stay on the seat longer. Praise her if she potties; encourage her if she doesn't.

4. Begin establishing urine control by asking her if she wants to urinate. If she says yes, take her to the toilet and have her sit on the seat and urinate into her training pants or the potty. A mother can demonstrate sitting on the toilet and urinating for both sons and daughters. A father or adult male can do the stand-up demonstration for a boy either right from the beginning or later. Toilet training can be tricky, so go slowly and be calm. If she urinates or does a BM, change her right there in the bathroom and show her that it goes into the toilet. Talk to her and explain each step.

5. After a meal, remove her training pants and allow her to be bottomless or in "big girl" panties for a while. Let her know, nonchalantly, that she can sit on the toilet if she wants to. If she does, hooray! Offer praise and congratulations, hugs and kisses! She must feel a sense of pride and accomplishment in using the potty and should feel this is something she wants to do for herself and to please you.

6. Once your child has used the toilet a few times, be consistent about taking her. Just after waking up, just after meals, before bath, and before a nap or bedtime are good times to start a routine. Always take her when she asks to go, since she is not able to "hold it" very well.

7. Keep a chart or calendar with stickers. Each time she uses the toilet, place a sticker on the chart to show her progress. Be sure her day care providers reinforce your efforts.

8. When not at home, carry a portable potty in case of emergency. Be sure to use the bathroom before and after extended car rides. And bring an extra change of clothes along for the first few months, just in case.

Do's and Don'ts of Toilet Training

Do

- *Wait if your child indicates he's not ready.* If he insists on using diapers still, refuses to use the toilet, or has frequent accidents, put off training for another couple of months. If he shows resistance one day but not the next, take it easy and let him set the pace.
- *Always praise him.* Show your approval for his having used the toilet, or taking another big step (keeping his underwear dry all day, for instance).

- *Expect accidents.* They are bound to happen as he is learning, so be prepared to take them in stride.

Don't

- *Punish, shame, humiliate, or force your child.* Don't enter this process with the mistaken belief that "tough love" will work. Only he has control over his bladder and bowels, so you cannot win with this method. Besides, associating negative emotions with toilet training will frustrate him and prolong the process. Be calm, compassionate, and encouraging throughout and you'll have much more favorable results.

The Birds and the Bees for Beginners

It's never too early to begin teaching our children about sexuality. Don't worry about sounding like a biology instructor; just stick to the very basics. Here are a few things to keep in mind as you talk to your child:

- *Name body parts correctly.* The words "penis" and "vagina" should be as normal to your child as "arm." Using words like "wee wee" or "pee pee" not only confuses children but highlights your own discomfort.
- *Touching his own genitals is normal.* Children's sexual organs, like their mouths and hands, are sensitive to touch. As they grow and explore, they will begin touching their genitals. This is a healthy, normal part of development and a way for your child to get to know her body. While it may feel good to her, it does not mean she is getting sexually aroused like an adult would. (See the next page for inappropriate behavior and warning signs of sexual abuse.) Try not to act shocked or disgusted if you notice your child touching herself. She might start to believe that her genitals or touching them is "dirty"—and that could later affect how she feels about herself sexually. Try to treat it as no big deal. When your child is about age two you can begin explaining that the genitals and bottom are private, and touching them should also be done in private. Though your child won't understand immediately, she'll catch on soon.
- *Establish privacy after age three.* Most child development experts believe that children begin associating naked bodies with sexual stimulation at age three (although not consciously). Therefore, to avoid discomfort and to establish sexual boundaries, they recommend adults cover up when their children are

Her Body Is Hers

Teaching your child about her body should include a lesson in sexual abuse. While you want her to understand how to protect herself from unwanted sexual advances, you don't want her to be afraid of all strangers. The most important lesson a young child can learn is that her body is hers and she has the right to tell anyone, including any adult, not to touch her. You can also help her by:

- ***Respecting her desire to not give you or anyone else a kiss*** **(it's best to ask for a kiss, rather than demand one).**
- ***Keeping communication open.*** **The more you share about your child's day—where she was and with whom—the more likely it is you'll know if something is wrong.**
- ***Explaining "OK" and "not OK" touches.*** **OK is a hug or kiss on the cheek when she wants one. Not OK is any unwanted hug, kiss, touch, tickle. An adult touching her genitals is never OK, and she can yell, cry, or use phrases like, "No, stop touching me." Tell her to tell you immediately if an adult asks, forces her, or tries to touch her genitals, or asks her to touch his.**
- ***Discussing that not-OK touches can come from strangers or people they already know.*** **Not allowing your child to accept gifts or favors from people outside the family unless you approve will help him ward off ploys from a stranger. But molestation often occurs with someone the child already knows, like a family member, teacher, or member of the community. It's important to teach your child to be aware of any uncomfortable situations or feelings and to act on them.**
- ***Keeping in mind that abusers can also be children as young as eight or nine years old.*** **So when having these discussions don't focus on adults or strangers, focus on giving her the courage to say "No" in any situation she finds uncomfortable.**

If you have reason to believe your child has been sexually abused, look for the following signs. But understand that sexual molestation can be hard to detect because there is often no physical evidence. Here are some behaviors and signs that should make you suspicious:

- ***If your child tells you.*** **Believe your child if she tells you she has been molested. Although children have rich fantasy lives, it's highly unlikely they will fabricate a fantasy of sexual abuse, especially if they have had no other sexual exposure. Report the abuse to either the police or an agency that specializes in child sexual abuse, and have your child examined by a doctor.**
- ***Vaginal or rectal bleeding, swelling, sores, pain, or itching.*** **If your child has any infections or STD, this is clear evidence that abuse may have occurred. Check clothing, especially underpants, for tears or stains. ➢**

- ***Unusual sexual behaviors,*** **such as interest or knowledge of explicit sexual practices, like oral sex. Frequent and/or unusual sex play (playing sexually coercive games, forcing others to undress, repeatedly putting objects in genital openings, playing sex games with strange children, frequently undressing in public).**
- ***Aggressive or disturbed behavior.*** **This includes infantile behavior (bedwetting, thumb-sucking, excessive crying), loss of appetite, very aggressive play or tantrums, recurrent nightmares, and not speaking.**
- ***Fear or intense dislike of a particular person or situation.*** **This may be especially noticeable when the child is left alone with a particular person or in a particular place.**

If you believe your child has been sexually molested, contact the Incest Helpline at (212) 227–3000 or the National Center for Missing and Exploited Children at (800) THE–LOST.

around three years old. At around five, your child may begin to demand privacy on his own. So to protect his feelings, avoid confusion, and establish appropriate boundaries, it's best to be dressed in front of him after he turns three.

- *Explain what inappropriate behavior is.* For some of us, getting caught at playing "doctor" used to mean a scolding or worse. But child development experts note that engaging in some kind of sexual experimentation is normal for preschoolers. If you find your child and her friends engaged in a game of "doctor," gently tell the kids to get dressed and play another game. If your child is exploring with a much older child, demonstrating knowledge of overt sexual acts, or playing a sexually violent game, it should be discussed with the older child's parent and, later, with your child.
- *Let her learn by example.* Letting your child see you in a loving and affectionate relationship is the foundation for your child's healthy sexual development.
- *Get a book.* When your child is ready to learn how babies are made (somewhere between ages three and five), get a book at the library or bookstore to help you through the tough parts. When talking about sex, be straightforward and not embarrassed. This will help your child feel comfortable communicating concerns or questions he has both now and later.

YOUR CHILD'S TEETH

Dental care should start as soon as your child's first tooth appears in order to help insure healthy permanent teeth. Children should be introduced to the joys of toothbrushing at about age two. By the time your child reaches age three, the basic routine of tooth care should be well established, though you'll need to remind him until age six to eight.

Here's a rule of thumb: If your child can't tie his shoelace, he doesn't have the manual dexterity to brush his teeth. When he's ready, choose a toothbrush with soft bristles and an easy-grip handle. Let him select the color or style of brush he wants as long as it's one that's recommended for his age group. Replace your child's toothbrush every three or four months.

Basic Toothbrushing

If you're doing the brushing, sit your child sideways on your knee, holding him still with one hand while you brush his teeth with the other. (This can be awkward, so experiment and create your own groove.) Only a small dot of toothpaste is necessary. Most toothpastes contain fluoride, which strengthens tooth enamel. But too much fluoride can cause a condition known as dental fluorosis in which the developing adult teeth become discolored with bright white spots. Consider purchasing a nonfluoride children's toothpaste that's safe to swallow (many are sold at health food stores).

Hold the brush at a 45-degree angle to the gums. Using circular strokes, brush the outer portion of the upper teeth, then the lower. Position the toothbrush vertically and use an up-and-down motion to clean the inside surface of the top and bottom teeth. Scrub the tops of all teeth, and remember to brush the tongue.

Have your child take turns brushing his teeth with opposite hands. He'll reach his teeth at different angles and will apply different

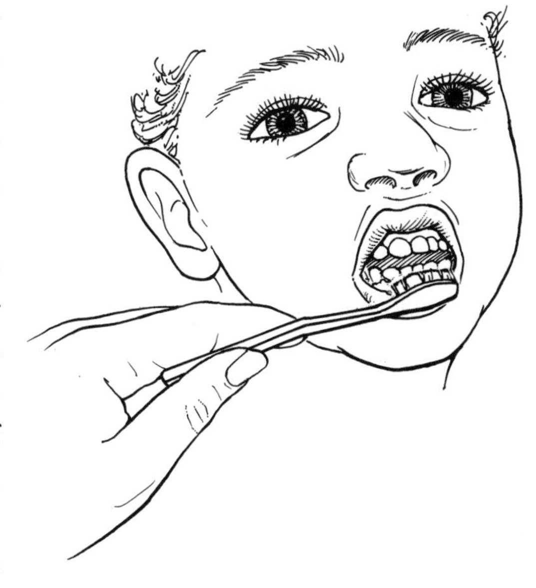

Brush your child's front teeth with toothbrush at a 45-degree angle.

pressure with each hand. Brush for at least three minutes (using a kitchen timer is helpful). Start with brushing in the morning and at bedtime, though you should encourage your child to brush after all meals and snacks. When he's finished brushing, have your child spit and rinse.

If you suspect your child isn't brushing well, you may want to try "disclosing" tablets, which tint areas of the teeth that have not been brushed thoroughly. The tablets, which are harmless, can be purchased over the counter at drug stores. After finding the areas that your child misses, help him reach the teeth he is unable to brush.

Going to the Dentist

The National Institute of Dental Research recommends that a child first visit the dentist around age two or after all the primary (baby) teeth have emerged (see chart on p. 74). Dental visits should then take place every six months. There are a few reasons why you should take your child to the dentist before age two or three: if your child chips or injures a tooth or if teeth show signs of discoloration, which may be a sign of early tooth decay.

Look for a dentist who is comfortable with children. If your child is absolutely terrified of the dentist but needs dental work, consider finding a pediatric dentist, known as a pedodontist, who can use anesthetics if necessary. Prepare your child for his first visit by reading her a book on dental visits for kids. Try not to make your child scared of the dentist—but don't mislead her either by saying it won't hurt. Let her know that she may feel discomfort. Ask your dentist to explain the instruments to your child; most know how to put children at ease. If possible, find out the terminology your dentist uses when talking to kids, such as calling the drill "Mr. Buzz," so you can talk with your child about her visit and what's going to be done. Stay calm and comforting.

New York dentist Dr. Eric Gothelf notes that children are often more brave than their parents. "A parent should comfort the child, but excessive patting and cooing during a procedure can be distracting to both the child and the dentist. The child may sense the parent's fear and get even more scared."

Note: While you're at the dentist's office, ask about sealants. Once permanent teeth start arriving, some dentists recommend using a protective sealant to cover the cavity-prone back teeth. A sealant is a clear or pale-colored plastic liquid that is applied to the biting surface of molars—and hardened under a special light. According to the American Academy of Pediatric Dentistry, sealing "dramatically reduces the risk of tooth decay," especially when the sealant is used on six- and twelve-year molars (when most decay occurs) and back teeth with pitted surfaces that are hard to keep clean. A sealant can be applied in a single office visit and is painless. Sealants cost significantly less than fillings and last for about five years.

Healthy Teeth Begin with a Good Diet

Diet is very important in developing and maintaining healthy teeth. Follow these tips:

- *Cut the sugar.* Sugary foods produce acids in the mouth that damage the enamel coating of the teeth. Get in the habit of giving your child fruit or yogurt as treats instead of sweets to avoid encouraging a sweet tooth.
- *Watch the juice.* While some juices can be good source of nutrients, too much fruit juice can cause tooth decay, even among children who eat very little candy. Eight ounces a day is sufficient.
- *Stay away from sticky foods.* Raisins, dried fruit, gum, caramel, and other candy get stuck in the teeth and promote tooth decay. If your child does have an occasional sticky food, be sure to brush immediately afterward.
- *Don't forget calcium.* One way to help your child maintain healthy teeth is to make sure he gets enough calcium in his diet. Children ages one to ten need 800 mg of calcium a day, the equivalent to two eight-ounce glasses of milk. A piece of cheese eaten at the end of a meal adds calcium to your child's diet and helps counteract the acid that erodes teeth.

Your Child's Clothes

At eighteen months, toddlers can manage fastenings and by age two and a half, they can close a button in a loose buttonhole and put on pants, T-shirts, and sweatshirts. By age three children may be able to dress themselves, though it will seem like it takes an eternity for them to get their clothes on. By age four, most children can dress and undress completely. Like using the toilet or helping with household chores, getting dressed is another step on your child's road to independence. Here are some helpful hints in teaching your child to dress herself:

- Lay out your child's clothes in such a way that she can slide them on easily. For example, drape a cardigan on the back of a chair so she can sit down and slide her arms into the sleeves.
- Teach your child to button from the bottom up.
- Buy clothing with Velcro fastenings, which are easier for a child to manage. (But be careful that they're not positioned where they might chafe a child's skin.)
- Attach a ring to the end of zippers. It'll be easier for tiny hands to grasp.
- Explain to your child that the label always goes at the back of pull-on sweaters and shirts.
- Buy overalls with sliding buckles so they can be adjusted for the best fit.
- Choose dresses with fastenings at the front—ones that close in the back are too hard for toddlers to manage.
- Show girls how to get tights on by rolling them up before putting their feet in and then pulling them up.
- Avoid pants with difficult fastenings—especially since boys are usually slower at being potty trained. Elastic waists are easiest, but if he has trousers with zippers, show him how to pull the zipper away from him as he closes it to prevent getting his penis caught!
- Avoid very fitted clothes; they don't leave much room for growth.

Clothes for Our Kids

If you're tired of pale pinks and baby blues and would like to dress your child in clothes that are a little (or a lot) more jazzy, here are a few places to check out that sell ethnically inspired items for our little ones.

Fannie Lou Kids (610–971–0442) offers clothing in newborn to size seven via mail order. While they sell items for both boys and girls, Matrice Johnson, owner and main designer, says the line features mix and match unisex outfits, great if you're planning on having more children. Prices range from $3 for socks to $15–$65 for outfits. One snazzy five-piece outfit comes with a jacket, jumper, vest, pants, and skirt. Another big seller is unisex mud cloth vests. Each piece is designed with the com-

"We found a solution that satisfied my need to keep Miles's teeth clean and healthy, and made him feel independent and competent." **—Allison's Story**

When I first started brushing Miles's teeth, I made a few key mistakes. One was putting too much toothpaste on the brush. Not only did he just suck it off because of the flavor, but he also demanded more to keep the brush in his mouth. Another was to let him brush his own teeth, which was really nothing more than an occasional swipe of the front teeth. And the last was to try to take the brush away from him to do a more thorough job. This resulted in screaming and clamping his jaw shut.

I soon decided the strong-arm approach wasn't working and we had to make this a more playful part of the bedtime routine. After reading that children who swallow too much fluoride toothpaste can get permanent white spots on their adult teeth, I went to the health food store and bought ingestable, nonfluoride toothpaste that he could use until he understood the concept of spitting out. Then I bought two new toothbrushes, a baby-size one with Sesame Street characters for him to use and another slightly bigger brush so that I could brush his teeth, along with some children's fluoridated toothpaste.

That night I tried my new method: I gave Miles his own baby toothbrush and edible toothpaste to use but mostly just hold, while I put a tiny dab of flouride toothpaste on the bigger brush and brushed his teeth. Though our brushes clashed a few times, and Miles wanted to trade, it worked. Miles could brush his teeth his way—or at least hold his own toothbrush—and I could brush them the proper way until he learned how. He even learned how to spit out and rinse from watching me. I was happy we found a solution that satisfied my need to keep his teeth clean and healthy, and made Miles feel independent and competent.

pany's signature technique of mixing African prints with denim, corduroy, and cotton. Call for a free catalogue.

Kinte Kids, Inc. (770–995–1390) is another mail-order catalogue that sells clothes designed for African-American children. Their line, says president/CEO Odette Russell, is "culturally educational." Sportswear items such as T-shirts and sweatpants feature original artwork with the saying, "I'm a Kinte Kid" on the back. On the front is kinte-patterned artwork in the shape of the African continent, featuring an animal, such as a friendly lion. The animal characters have been spun off into a coloring book. One nice feature: Each piece of clothing has a child-friendly hang

"After Zandreal chose a cute red-and-white pair of glasses, she noticed that other children actually admired how she looked."
—Regina Blakely, mother of Zandreal, age 5; Decatur, Georgia

Zandreal was about four when I noticed her eyes were crossing. She had to really strain hard to look at something, and when her eyes would cross, I'd say, "Can you see, Zandreal?" She'd say yes, but it was clear that she was having trouble. So that's when I took her to the eye doctor.

During the eye testing she became a little nervous when they gave her an eyewash to dilate the eyes, but after that she was fine. The doctor explained that she was putting too much strain on her eyes which was causing them to cross. The remedy: glasses. If she wore them continuously, her eyes would stop crossing.

At first Zandreal was not pleased, afraid that other kids would pick on her. But after she chose a cute red-and-white pair, she noticed that other children actually admired how she looked. Now she's even got a best girlfriend whose eyes are worse than hers and who has to wear thick glasses with bifocals. The two of them get along real well, like two peas in a pod. So now she has no problem.

tag explaining African and African-American culture. "This is an alternative to Barney, Bart Simpson, the Gap, and Guess," says Russell.

JC Penney's "Influences" catalogue targets African-Americans and includes toddler sizes. Call 800–222–6161 for a catalogue.

Baby Needs New Shoes

Shoes can be a fabulous fashion statement, but for small children they should be practical. To begin with, babies who aren't walking don't even need shoes yet. Their tootsies can be adequately covered with antiskid socks or soft moccasins. Walking children need flexible and supportive shoes. Sneakers, which are all the rage in kiddie fashions, may not be the best shoe choice. The rubber soles catch on the floor and can cause trips and falls.

When buying shoes, follow these suggestions for practical tips and a good fit:

- *Save your money.* Before you plop down lots of cash for designer sneakers, remember that during the second and third years of her life, your child's shoe size can change three to four times a year. In fact, it isn't unusual for a preschooler to jump four sizes in a year. Most children will do just as well in a good pair of $5.99 sneakers as they will in an expensive designer brand. Inexpensive shoes won't make your child's feet flat—arches don't "fall." Hand-me-down shoes are a good bet if they are in good condition. Be sure they fit properly and the soles aren't worn down.

- *Say no to heels.* Save your child the pain of shoes with heels. They can cause tripping and falling in youngsters.
- *Get a good fit.* The right fit is essential in a child's shoe. Don't go solely by the shoe-measuring device found in many shoe stores; it can be off by 1½ inch, depending on the type of shoe your child is trying on. To check for a correct fit, have your child stand in the shoes and ask him to kick his heel against the floor. The front of the shoe should be about ½ inch (the width of an index finger) longer than his big toe. If you can grasp a small piece of shoe at the widest portion of the foot, the width is correct. The heel area should be snug and the shoe should not flop up and down when your child walks. Make sure the top of the shoe is high enough so that it doesn't exert pressure on the toenails and top of the foot. A well-fitting shoe should have maximum flexibility where the foot flexes, not in the middle. If your child's feet continually slip out of low-cut shoes, high-top sneakers may be the answer. Also note that wide toes in shoes are roomier and allow a child's toes to fan out. Remember, shoes with Velcro closures are easy for small children to fasten—a plus when teaching them how to dress by themselves.

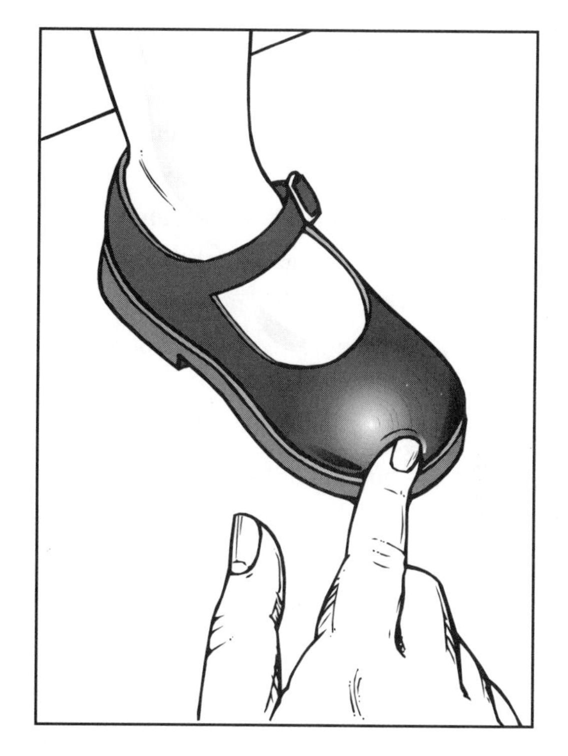

For correct fit, the front of your child's shoe should be about ½ inch longer than the big toe.

What's Wrong with That Walk?

So you've checked everything twice and bought the shoes only to find your child is walking funny in them? You may notice that your child is either bowlegged or knock-kneed. Most toddlers have some kind of curving to their legs which will straighten as they grow and walk more. If you have concerns about the shape of your child's legs, ask your pediatrician to examine them. She'll be able to tell you if the curving is within normal limits, and can send you to a pediatric orthopedist if there is a problem. The old-fashioned practice of using shoes with bars between them is no longer in use, so don't worry that treatments will mean putting your child in what many parents say look like shackles for their toddlers.

Some children begin walking on their toes during the beginning stages of walking, but stop once they learn to run (running stretches the Achilles tendon). If toe walking is accompanied by a weak arm or leg, or you notice a marked difference in your child's ability to use one of her legs, bring it to the attention of your child's pediatrician.

RESOURCES

Recommended Reading for Parents

The American Medical Association Family Medical Guide, 3rd edition, Charles B. Clayman, M.D. (Random House, 1994). This is a fully illustrated comprehensive guide to identifying and dealing with a myriad of medical issues, including rashes and skin infections.

Good Health for African American Kids, Barbara M. Dixon (Crown, 1996). This book offers guidelines for raising healthy African-American children. It includes sections on allergies, dentist visits, doctor visits, and talking to your child about sex.

Having Your Baby, Hilda Hutcherson, M.D. (Ballantine Books, 1997). The last two chapters of this book address the basics of newborn care.

Raising Healthy Kids: A Book of Child Care and Natural Family Health, Michio Kushi (Avery Publishing Group, 1994). This book gives natural and dietary solutions for many childhood ailments including skin disorders, rashes, and insect bites.

The Second Year of Life, Nina R. Lief (Walker and Co., 1991). This book continues where *The First Year of Life* left off. It includes sections on basic body care, toilet training, and sexual identity.

What to Expect During the Toddler Years, Arlene Eisenberg, Heidi E. Murkoff, and Sandee E. Hathaway, B.S.N. (Workman Publishing, 1996). This book explains what to expect as your child develops mentally and physically. It covers such issues as "resisting baths," toilet training, and sexual abuse.

Recommended Reading for Children

Being with You This Way, W. Nicola-Lisa and Michael Bryant (Lee & Low Books, 1994). This book is a celebration of all the different ways people look.

Contemplating Your Belly Button, Jun Nanao (Kane-Miller Book Publishers, 1995). This teaches children about where their belly buttons came from. It shows a baby in the mother's womb, the birth, the doctor cutting the cord, and breast-feeding.

Cornrows, Camille Yarbrough, illustrated by Carole Byard (Paper Star, 1979). Mama and Grandma braid children's hair into all different African patterns while teaching their children about the history and culture of the African-American past.

I Like Me! Deborah Connor Coker, illustrated by Keaf Holliday (Essence Books for Children, 1996). A little girl has pride in herself and her body.

Look at You, Baby Face! Madeline Carter (Western Publishing Co., 1995). This book has great big photos of faces made by all kinds of babies.

Nappy Hair, Carolivia Herron, illustrated by Joe Cepeda (Alfred A. Knopf, 1997). This wonderful and funny picture book is written in the traditional African-American "call and response" style. It tells a joyous story about a little girl who has beautiful, thick, "nappy hair."

Pretty Brown Face, Andrea and Brian Pinkney (Harcourt Brace & Co., 1997). A toddler learns from his daddy about all the wonders of his "pretty brown face."

See Me Grow, Head to Toe! Nanette VanWright Mellage, illustrated by Keaf Holliday (Golden Books Publishing, 1996). Written in cooperation with Essence Communications, this is a young child's book about how babies grow.

When I Look in the Mirror, Sopoeia Greywolf (A and B Books and Publishers, 1993). This picture book encourages a positive self-image through celebrating all the shades of African-American children.

Why Do We Laugh?, Susan Jacoby, ed. (DK Publishing, 1997). This book, with its cheerful, multiracial photographs, answers lots of questions that children ask about the human body, such as "Why do we have eyebrows?"

Organizations

American Academy of Dermatology, 930 N. Meacham Rd., Schaumburg, IL 60173, (888) 462–DERM, (847) 330–0230.

Website:www.aad.org

Call for referrals for a dermatologist in your area and for pamphlets on skin disorders, such as eczema.

American Dental Association, 211 E. Chicago Ave., Chicago, IL 60611, (800) 621–8099.

Website: www.ada.org

This organization provides consumers with general information and answers questions about specific products through their Public Information Department. Although the ADA does not provide referrals, they will direct consumers to state dental boards.

American Academy of Pediatric Dentistry, 211 E. Chicago Ave., Chicago, IL 60611, (312) 337–2169.

Website: www.aapd.org

This organization provides referrals to dentists who specialize in treating children. They also answer parents' questions and provide pamphlets about proper care of children's teeth.

National Medical Association, 1012 10th Street, NW, Washington, D.C. 20001, (202) 347–1895. The NMA provides referrals to consumers for African-American physicians, including dermotologists.

Chapter

5

Ain't Misbehavin': Discipline and Parenting

Stern, strict discipline has long been an accepted way of parenting in our community. This legacy stems from the past, when an undisciplined child could—literally—lose his or her life. Emmett Till's lynching in 1955 for allegedly talking "fresh" to a white girl sent shock waves through black America, confirming everyone's worst fears about the price of falling out of line. Life-threatening incidents such as this and countless others since slavery forced black parents to be exceptionally strict and even harsh with their children, demanding that they obey rules for their own protection.

Because even seemingly small incidents could mean the difference between life and death, African-American parents didn't have the luxury of explaining the whats and whys of their rules. Children who didn't obey were usually physically punished, no questions asked.

Times have changed, but has our parenting style? By and large, our children don't face the same kinds of risks our parents and grandparents did, so does strict, harsh discipline still make sense? Are parents who attempt to reason with their children, and who spend time explaining why certain behavior is unacceptable instead of administering a good, old-fashioned "whipping," adopting "white" parenting styles and spoiling their children?

This chapter will explore some of our attitudes about parenting and discipline and demonstrate through studies and advice from experts ways that you can discipline your child to get the behavior you want. Keep in mind that there is no magic method and that all parenting takes patience. Our goal is to give you choices so you can choose the styles that work best for you as you move toward your ultimate goal: to raise a safe, happy, respectful, emotionally healthy child.

Our Job as Parents

Parenting, as you've probably already figured out, is a full-time job—whether or not you have full-time hours to devote to it. Not only are we required to meet every physical need of our children when they're babies, but as they mature, they require a tremendous amount of emotional care, guidance, and affection. "Children are a part of us," explains Morgan State University psychology professor Henrietta Hestick, Ph.D. "We are a large tree, and our young children are our branches and get all their sustenance from us." According to Hestick, our primary function is to provide nurturing, love, protection, guidance, understanding, and flexibility in order to raise healthy, productive adults who can make positive contributions to society. No wonder we're tired!

As black parents our role is more complex. "Black parents have to raise their children with an understanding of how society really is," says Bryan Nichols, Ph.D., clinical psychologist and instructor in the Effective Black Parenting Program at the Center for Improvement of Child Caring in California. "While there are no great differences between black and white children's behavior, there are much greater consequences for more minor infractions if a black child doesn't adhere to society's standards." That leaves black parents to face a strange juggling act: Though we disagree with society's double standards, we must still find ways to help our children succeed within these limitations—and eventually work to change those standards.

The Four Walls Parenting Quad

Parenting is the structure by which we raise our children and it is made up of four walls: discipline, limit-setting, consistency, and love. When balanced and used together, they help us develop our children's behavior, self-control, and ability to make good decisions. Here's a brief description of each wall and how it benefits our kids:

Discipline. In the minds of many—and many of us—discipline is synonymous with rigidity, toughness, punishment, and anger. (The image that comes to mind is Louis Gossett, Jr., as the never-smiling, unbending drill sergeant barking orders in the movie *An Officer and a Gentleman*!) In reality, discipline actually means to teach and as parents, we definitely should think of it that way. With small children, our role is to show them how to respond in different situations, to guide them toward the right choices and help them learn to think for themselves.

Limit-setting. This means laying down the ground rules and establishing consequences for your child's conduct. Setting these boundaries helps your child learn concepts like "right and wrong" and that other people have feelings. Children may test and protest limits many times before they actually learn to live within them. This is completely normal and repetition is part of how children learn. It is also how they gain a sense of security, because they know that when they can't exercise self-control, you'll be there to help them.

Consistency. This is the broken-record concept. You will find yourself repeating phrases your mother said to you, like "I'm not going to tell you again," when in fact you will probably have to remind your child many more times not to touch that plant, or to hold your hand while outside. Being consistent also provides your child with a sense of comfort, as youngsters thrive on knowing what comes next, and will often test you just to make sure you react the same every time.

Love. This is the most important of all four components in parenting, because more than any other, your child needs to feel a special bond with you. As the foundation for healthy parenting, love will help you to act in your child's best interests (despite her protests), and help her to understand that you are close by to support and comfort her.

Understanding Discipline

With discipline, your main goal should be teaching, not punishing. While we each have our own rules and beliefs, basically, there are four identified parenting styles:

Authoritarian. This style of parenting is based on many rules with few explanations and no challenge to the authority of the parents. Parents who favor this style also don't use a lot of praise when the child behaves well because she's "supposed to do it anyway." This style tends to create children and adults with a strong sense of order but who struggle to think for themselves and to express their emotions.

Lax. The lax parent usually demands little to nothing from her child. There are few clear limits set and children often receive praise and rewards when they may not be warranted. These children often go on to lead chaotic lives; they also lack direction and are generally insecure.

Abusive/Neglectful. This is really a nonparenting style, in which the parent doesn't assume proper responsibility for the child. The child is left to fend for himself before he has the judgment and maturity to make decisions. These children are considered abused and, unless helped, often lack the social skills needed to succeed.

Authoritative. This term was coined by University of Berkeley researcher Diana Baumrind, as she tried to describe the parenting style that worked best with subjects of her studies. Authoritative parents demand responsible behavior from their children by setting high yet reasonable standards according to their children's personality and development. These parents set firm rules but were open to their children's opinions about the rules. Family values and morals are discussed as the basis for the family rules (except in obvious cases in which safety is an issue), and children are expected to behave responsibly (for instance, cleaning up after play, pitching in on family chores). At the crux of this style are parental love, support, and commitment. Research shows that children raised with this style tend to be creative, competent, and experimental as well as responsible.

Fussy babies need comforting not scolding.

As a whole, black parents tend toward the authoritarian style of parenting, but many parents are integrating positive discipline techniques into their parenting styles. "Black parents are accused of causing everything that's wrong in society," says Nichols. "I like to remind parents that they are already doing a lot of things right, but just need to add things." Like Nichols, Hestick sees ways that African-American parents can improve on their disciplining techniques with the addition of "new tools." "Children these days are exposed to so much," explains Hestick. "Given that, parents need to communicate with their kids in a much more sophisticated manner than their parents did." Both suggest that we move more toward the authoritative model of parenting.

Don't Shake

You should never, ever shake your baby. Shaken baby syndrome describes the injuries that result when an infant is shaken vigorously, usually when the baby won't stop crying. Since infants have weak neck muscles and relatively large heads, shaking an infant causes the brain to "rattle" within the skull. This causes brain injuries that can result in serious consequences, including death.

Our babies are programmed to cry to have their needs met. And that sound is programmed to get on our nerves so that we'll meet those needs. Unfortunately, some people are less tolerant of hearing a baby's cry, and some babies have temperaments that make them cry a lot. If you feel your self getting frustrated with your child, put him down and walk away. No baby ever cried himself to death, but some have been shaken to death.

Shaken baby syndrome does not happen when you bounce your baby in your lap, during a rough car ride, or by falling while learning to walk. So you shouldn't be afraid to touch and play with your baby. Another important fact to note: Studies show that fathers and/or boyfriends are twice as likely to cause shaken baby syndrome, followed by female babysitters, and then mothers. Also, baby boys are twice as likely to be victims than are baby girls.

To prevent shaken baby syndrome:

- Make sure your baby's caretakers don't have quick tempers and are patient.
- Try to have more than one adult around your infant. People are less likely to become violent while another adult is watching. The other adult can also provide some relief to the caretaker.
- Recognize when you are angry or frustrated and find someone else to help you. Or put your baby in a safe place such as his crib and walk away.
- If you feel like you're going to lose it, count to ten and take deep breaths.
- Let your baby cry, but check on him every few minutes to make sure he is OK.

How to Discipline

As you move toward the authoritative model, you will need to find new ways to discipline your child. In the Effective Black Parenting Program, Nichols teaches parents seven-step strategies for praising and reprimanding their child. Mirror images, Nichols's strategies are simple and effective ways to guide children toward the behavior you want.

When **praising** your child:

1. *Look at her.* Eye contact lets your child know you're sincere and that you are giving her your full attention.

2. *Get close.* Bring yourself down to her eye level, if possible, but at least get close enough to touch.

3. *Show physical affection.* A kiss, a rub on the back or head, or a hug accompanying praising words make a loving impression on a child.

Appropriate Discipline for Your Child's Age

The following are some guidelines to help you understand what your child understands in the way of discipline. Keep in mind that understanding rules, knowing right from wrong, and being honest are developed after many years of consistent parenting and don't actually begin to take shape until after age three or four.

0–Age 1: While you will no doubt run into situations that call for setting limits and rules, babies don't understand the concept of rules and consequences yet. Don't use punishment; instead use words in the positive, which give direction and clear explanation. Babies aren't able to be intentionally mean, hurtful, or "naughty," but their natural curiosity and impulses can take over. They need your judgment and guidance to steer them away from harm and into an interesting activity. You will find yourself repeating rules many times until you see even small progress. Be patient.

Age 1–3: Children this age are delighted to know that their actions can produce reactions, although they don't yet understand that biting and hitting aren't ways to greet others. Tone of voice and clear words help children this age learn what is appropriate behavior. Consequences, such as removing children from a situation, can also help them learn what will happen if they continue unwanted behavior. Some children begin to display aggressive behavior at this age in the form of tantrums or losing control (see p. 116 for more on tantrums). This is a natural part of development and is more an expression of inner tension than outward anger. This is the age at which clear and consistent limits are crucial to avoid conflicts and power struggles, because children test over and over to be sure what the rules and consequences are. You will continue to repeat rules many times before they are followed. Praise positive behavior as a way to encourage what you want.

Age 3–5: Children this age are more able to express their feelings, reason, and understand explanations for rules. When a child misbehaves, using time-outs or revoking privileges of certain toys can be very effective. Explain what you expect from your child ("I expect you to keep your food in your bowl, not throw it.") and then describe the consequences if it occurs ("If you throw food, you'll have to clean it up and have a time out.") Children are much more likely to follow rules more carefully at this stage (or try to sneak if you're not around), but you will still have to repeat your expectations and rules often. If you can, find out why your child is misbehaving, because often she has a perfectly good reason (in her own mind) that might not occur to you.

4. *Smile.* This is one of the most powerful nonverbal ways of showing your approval.
5. *Use positive words.* Your words greatly impact how a child feels about herself. Use pleasant phrases, such as "Wow, what a great drawing" and "I'm so proud of you," while avoiding critical comments, like "Finally you did what I asked" or "You're smarter than I thought." Be upbeat and excited about your child's accomplishment, and this will add to his feelings of pride.
6. *Praise behavior, not your child.* This means don't tell your daughter she's "a good girl" for brushing her teeth. This will lead her to believe she's only good when she's doing what you want, and "bad" when she's misbehaving. Your child should feel she's always good, whether she's misbehaving or not. Instead, tell her that what she's just done, hung up her coat or used the potty, is wonderful.
7. *Do it within five seconds.* Immediacy is crucial. The sooner you praise your child after she has completed the act, the better. Because children have very little sense of time, it's important to get to them immediately so they will remember what they did and be more likely to repeat the same behavior next time.

When **reprimanding** your child:
1. *Look at him.* As with praise, looking at your child, rather than yelling from across the room, lets him know you're serious and you're paying attention.
2. *Get close.* This helps assure that he has heard and understood you.
3. *Show facial disapproval.* Young children learn about anger, disappointment, and other emotions by associating them with our facial expressions. Frowning or having a stern look will bring your point home.
4. *Use a disapproving gesture.* Point, put your hands on your hips, hold up your hand, or do whatever comes naturally to show that you don't like the behavior without hurting your child.
5. *Make a brief statement about the behavior.* Nothing will lose your child's attention faster than a lecture. By using short statements—not questions like "Didn't I just tell you not to do that?" or "What did I just say?"—you will be most effective. Try "Stop that or I'll have to take it away" or "No hitting."
6. *Remain calm and serious.* Without being either too extreme (yelling) or too polite (pleading), convey your disapproval and what you want to happen. Use what Nichols calls the Clint Eastwood style: firm, not loud, and very direct.

Testing the Temperament

No two children (or people for that matter) are exactly alike, and parents who have more than one child understand this completely. One of the many ways children differ from one another is that each has a different temperament. Established in infancy, temperament consists of three major areas: energy level, adaptability, and frustration tolerance. Minor areas of temperament are sensitivity, regularity (such as with sleeping and eating schedules), and distractibility.

Knowing where your child fits in each of these categories (and where you fit) can improve your relationship with your child because you can adjust your parenting style and expectations accordingly. While there are no good or bad temperament traits, some may be considered problematic until both you and your child learn how to deal with them positively.

An article in *Parenting* on-line magazine, by Ginny Graves, outlined the five basic temperament categories that begin to emerge around six months but become fully recognizable after the first year, with tips for parents:

- ***The yo-yo* is generally active and hard to settle down (especially when learning new skills), has a hard time with even small changes unless she's in control, and has irregular schedules (with eating and sleeping, for example).**
  ***Your best bet:* Let her burn off energy, help her find ways to calm herself (she may need some hugs from you), and stick with a routine. Don't force her to eat when she's not hungry, and try not to confine her to a high chair for very long. Give her plenty of space and time to learn skills her way.**
- ***The whirlwind* is like a cyclone of emotion, with very high highs and low lows. He wants to be in control and finds it difficult to move on to the next activity.**
  ***Your best bet:* Allow your child to express himself strongly and try not to overreact. Help him find ways to calm down (maybe a favorite blanket or stuffed toy), establish a routine he can count on, and give transition warnings to prepare him for what's coming next.**
- ***The tiptoer* doesn't like to jump into anything without completely checking it out. She may say "no" to any situation that's new until she gets used to it, in large part because she's incredibly sensitive—to fabrics, foods, and too many people.**
  ***Your best bet:* Don't force her to do anything uncomfortable and respect her sensitivities. She's not just making them up. Help her by giving her plenty of space and time to get used to people, allow her to make decisions in her own time, and buy her food and clothing that she can tolerate.**
- ***The footdragger* tends to be quiet and deliberate, taking his time with tasks.**

He has a hard time with change and a low frustration level.
Your best bet: **Encourage him to use his quiet time constructively (buy books, puzzles, art supplies), set a routine, and give warnings about changes or transitions. Give him space to learn skills on his own time without pressure.**

- ***The trooper*** **is generally easygoing and calm and can handle spontaneous changes.**
  Your best bet: **Don't overlook her needs just because she doesn't require a lot of attention, and teach her how to express her wants when others assume she's "fine."**

If you'd like more information about your child's temperament, Preventive Ounce, a research group in Oakland, provides free on-line assessments. You can get a free evaluation of your child's temperament on-line at http://www.preventiveoz.org

7. *Do it within five seconds.* Immediate action is more likely to get results. If too much time passes, a child may forget what he did and not understand why he's being chastised.

The Well-Behaved Child: Fifteen Ways to Get Results

The following section covers what we consider to be the most effective ways to apply some of the information mentioned above to everyday situations. With time and repetition (a component of consistency), your child will incorporate these methods into his own behavior and you will have less correcting to do. Remember, however, that above and beyond these suggestions, your own behavior—how you treat others, how much you value yourself, and what you actually *do*—is the best way to model the behavior you want.

1. *Baby-proof the house.* This is critical during the first three years of your child's life. Young children don't understand the meaning of danger or the value of precious objects. At the same time, they are innately curious and exploratory, and when they are young, their main way of gathering information is through taste, touch, and sight. When your son grabs your priceless vase from atop a table and watches it crash, he has no sense of the danger he faces *or* how much the vase means to you. His mind is processing the sound the vase makes when it hits the floor, all the shiny pieces that have just appeared, and that objects fall when they aren't attached or resting. And this information is extremely valuable when it's learned in a safe environment; babies use it to expand their knowledge of the world. Limiting your child's world by expecting him to learn what's off limits and continually punishing him—either by spankings, "no's," or constant admonishment—will squash his natural curiosity and his motivation to learn or try new things. This, in turn, will limit his desire and ability to accomplish new goals.

The best way to keep children safe while teaching them about danger is to protect them and their surroundings. Eventually your child will learn what's OK and not OK to touch, but until he's old enough to really understand, why not put your valuables out of reach and create a safe environment where he can explore? You'll feel better too.

2. *Find distractions.* This is one of the best ways to avoid an escalating power struggle. A typical scenario goes like this: Your toddler takes something she's not supposed to have out of your purse, like lipstick. You tell her to give it back, but she refuses and is intent on taking the cap off and putting the lipstick on like Mommy does. If you snatch it from her, she's sure to cry. If you demand it back from her, she'll probably ignore you and continue to prove to you she's independent enough to do it anyway. But if you find something appropriate to trade with her, like a favorite toy, or pick her up and play pat-a-cake while quietly taking the lipstick away, she's less likely to protest. You will have accomplished your goal and avoided a tantrum or hurt and angry feelings. Other distraction tactics:

- Sing a song.
- Remove her from the trouble spot by saying, "Hey, I know something fun we could do."
- Use a stuffed toy to play a game.

3. *Fight the bad with the good.* Be sure to put the focus on what your child is doing right instead of what he is doing wrong. This is a very effective way to give your child positive reinforcement while boosting his self-esteem. For instance, if your child is pulling your hair for fun, get him to stop by telling him it hurts and showing him a more gentle way to touch. Every time you see him use that gentle touch, tell him how good it feels and how proud you are that he's learning so well. If you ask him to help you pick up his toys and he does, praise him for being a good listener. Small children thrive on their own accomplishments, so if you go out of your way to praise rather than criticize, you'll help him feel good about himself and encourage him to do more for your praise.

As you praise your child, choose your words carefully. Here are some brief guidelines:

- *Remember: There are no good or bad girls or boys.* Praise the "good" deed, and correct the "bad" one.
- *Try not to overdo it.* Every action a child makes doesn't call for a cheerleader. Pick effective times to use praise or else the praise becomes meaningless. Your child will look for praise when he doesn't deserve it or will only be motivated by other people's wishes.
- *Avoid using praise as a bribe.* If you get locked into a battle and promise a gold star or special sticker if your child takes a bath, you're sending the wrong message. Praise is meant to help children feel good when they do something for the right reasons (such as picking up their toys so nobody gets hurt), not just to get gifts or prizes.

4. *Let children work out their differences themselves.* How many times have you watched two small children engage in a nonviolent argument, over a toy for instance, and resolve it without anyone stepping in? Probably not very often because parents generally don't give kids a chance to work things out by themselves. But recent studies show that when a child takes a toy from another child, the owner of the toy almost always gets it back without too much aggression, if parents don't interfere. This hands-off approach, of course, only applies when there is no danger of either child getting hurt; if an argument turns into a hitting or biting brawl, both children need separation and a break.

5. *Explain what feelings mean.* Discussing and exploring emotions is key to raising a healthy, well-behaved child. From the early months, babies learn about different emotions from their parents' facial expressions, exaggerated smiles and frowns that mirror their babies' moods. As children get older, they learn to attach words to their feelings. But they don't really begin to grasp the difference between happy, sad, and mad until they are old enough to speak. It's important to help your children recognize their feelings early on so they won't be overwhelmed, frightened, or frustrated by them, and so you can avoid clashes. Here are a few great ways to help children understand their emotions:

- *Name feelings as they come up.* If you see your daughter bouncing on her tiptoes and singing, you can say, "You look really happy right now." Likewise, if she's angry about not getting her way, you can acknowledge her feelings by saying, "I know you're really frustrated/angry/mad that you can't have that right now."
- *Look at picture books.* Show her pictures of characters expressing their emotions and ask her to help you identify how the characters feel. Then explain each emotion by noting tears, smiles, frowns, etc.
- *Play the happy, sad, mad game.* By using your own facial expressions you can help her figure out what you're feeling. Then let her pick the feelings and show you.

6. *Teach your child to problem-solve.* As your child gets older, try giving her tools to help her think for herself. Myrna Shure, Ph.D., author of *Raising a Thinking Child* (Pocket Books, 1994) and *Raising a Thinking Child Workbook,* has developed a method called ICSP ("I Can Solve a Problem") to teach children as young as four years old how to solve problems for themselves by getting them to come up with solutions on their own. Problem-solving cuts down on frustration levels and gives your child a sense of independence, which is usually what's at stake when she challenges you. Here are the steps:

- There's a problem, for example, Aisha took a toy from Michael. Michael runs and tells Mommy.
- Mom presents Aisha with the problem by saying, "Michael tells me you took his toy. What happened?"
- Mom listens to Aisha's explanation and asks more questions, such as "Why did you take the toy from Michael while he was playing with it?"
- This gives Mom new information, such as that Aisha was playing with it first when Michael snatched it, or they had agreed to share but Michael took too long with the toy.
- Mom helps Aisha understand how she made Michael feel by saying, "How do you think Michael feels when you take his toys like that?"
- After hearing Aisha's answer, Mom helps her understand the consequences of her actions by asking, "What happened when you took his toy?"
- Aisha may say he cried and told. Mom then helps Aisha understand her own feelings by asking, "And how did that make you feel?"

- When Aisha answers, Mom asks her to think of a different way to get Michael to give her the toy.
- With each answer, Mom asks Aisha, "And what do you think might happen then?" If it's a positive solution, Aisha will problem solve to get the results she wants without negative consequences for anybody.
- Mom praises Aisha for coming up with such good ideas.

After reading about ICSP above, you may be thinking "oh come on," but think again. Although her method may make you feel like "Dr. Freud," Dr. Shure has twenty years of experience with ICPS, and she insists that it's more effective and its benefits last longer than those of spanking or yelling.

7. *Do something zany.* Sometimes you just can't get your child to pay attention or cooperate no matter how much you ask. Before you get too annoyed and stressed and the two of you start to tangle, try taking a sharp left turn and do something off the wall. In other words, take "distraction" to a new level. For example, if your baby's fussing at the diaper-changing table, put a sock on your hand and make a puppet. (Or put it on your head!) Or if your preschooler is pouting about not getting another bowl of ice cream, pick him up and start dancing. Not only will you be able to maintain control over the situation, you'll both have a lot more fun.

8. *Don't take your child's behavior personally.* Much of parenting requires self-control and patience and the ability to take your child's behavior in stride. For black parents this can be tough, considering the challenges we face outside the home that we are forced to dismiss. By the time we get home, many of us take *everything* personally! Although there is no easy answer to dealing with aggressive or negative behavior (except to address it firmly according to your household rules), understand that it's a normal part of childhood, and that your child isn't trying to hurt you.

9. *Provide choices, unless there aren't any.* As parents, we become so used to making decisions for our children we sometimes forget that they have their own preferences. Letting your child decide—within limits—which shirt to wear, which juice to drink, or which book to read helps him feel he has some control over his world. A child who feels like he has a partnership with you is less likely to throw a tantrum. For example, many children fight about getting dressed. If you ask your child which pair of pants he wants to wear and hold out two for him to choose

Tempering Tantrums

Imagine if you had all the feelings you do now, but no words to explain them. This is how young children feel before they are able to speak well. Throughout the day, these feelings build and are released in spurts we know as tantrums. And your child is more likely to have one if he's sleepy, hungry, off-schedule, sick, or made to sit still.

Although tantrums are a normal part of early childhood (they begin between one and three years old and end at about age four), many parents react to them with anger or worry. Many African-American parents think tantrums are a challenge to their parental authority. But for the sake of our children's healthy development, we need to let our children "get it all out" at a young age when we can still help them identify what they're feeling. Otherwise, they will learn to keep their emotions bottled up—only to be released in more dangerous ways. Once children learn to speak and identify their feelings, their tantrums decrease. In the meantime, remember that tantrums are never easy to deal with. But as the parent, you must keep your cool.

Try applying these suggestions the next time your child explodes, but know that there will be times when none of these methods works:

- ***Stay calm.* Your child is out of control and though it may be hard to believe, she's looking to you for help. The calmer you are, the sooner the tantrum will subside. But if you get angry and yell, she'll do the same.**
- ***Try distractions.* Immediately try to get him interested in something else, like a toy or song, before the tantrum gets full blown.**
- ***Ignore it.* As long as her outburst doesn't put her in danger of hurting herself or someone else, try to ignore the behavior until she's calmed down.**
- ***If you can't ignore it, be understanding.* Put yourself in his shoes by remembering times in your life when you've gotten very, very frustrated. Think about what you wanted most: to vent your feelings with someone who would be sympathetic and caring. You can even say to your child, "I understand you're angry because I wouldn't buy you that toy." That helps him identify what he's feeling and lets him know you understand him. If you can, calm him by picking him up and giving him a warm hug. After a tantrum, children crave reassurance.**
- ***Don't give in.* If your child isn't too hysterical, try asking why she's upset. If it's because she wanted candy and you don't allow it, for instance, don't give in just to stop the tantrum, even if you're in public. Tell her you understand her feelings but stay firm. If she has a tantrum in a public place, pick her up and get her out of there as soon as you can.**

from, he's more likely to cooperate, because he's part of the decision-making process.

When it comes to more critical situations, such as whether or not to take medicine, there is no choice. But you can still give him the option of using water or juice to wash it down. Other times, when there are no options, you can explain why there isn't a choice—"no playing with knives, because they'll cut you"—and be prepared for some disappointment.

10. *Give a countdown for transitions.* Transitions between activities often provoke tantrums and because small children love routines and consistency, it's important to give them time to prepare for change. Countdowns and good-byes work amazingly well in helping young children move from one activity to the next. Depending on your child's temperament, you may have to use this technique for both large and small events.

Keeping a cool head can help your child work through a tantrum.

Here are some suggestions for easing transitions:

- *Give your child a two-minute warning before changing locations or activities.* You can either set a timer or look at a clock, but try to stick as close to your time limit as possible so that your child will come to know how long two or five minutes is.
- *Say good-bye.* Once the time limit is up, you can tell your child to say good-bye to her toys, friends, the park, or whatever she was doing and think of a way to help her look forward to the next event. Saying goodnight to family, dolls, and toys can help your child let go of the day and go to bed more easily. If your child has picked up a toy in the store and is having a hard time putting it back, let her examine it for a minute and then tell her it's time to say bye-bye to the toy. You'll be surprised how many times this works.

11. *Don't let "no" make you crazy.* Many African-American parents feel that when their children tell them "no" they aren't showing proper respect. "Don't tell me no when I tell you to do something" is a phrase many of us heard growing up, and we knew our parents meant it. But toddlers don't understand the concepts of defiance and "talking back" the same way older kids and teenagers do. When she says "no" she means "I don't want to" or "Do I have to?" Rather than punishing her or engaging in a power struggle, take a deep breath, ignore the "no's" and guide her toward the action or behavior you want her to take. And do yourself another favor: Teach her the word "yes."

12. *Ignore unwanted behavior that isn't dangerous.* Much of the time children will do whatever it takes—good or bad—to get your attention. And any parent who has ever been stressed or busy knows how small children can pick the worst times to act out. One way to deal effectively with some of these small problems is to do your best to ignore the behavior as it's happening. Here's how:

- *Identify the behavior you want changed and when it happens.* Does she always whine for candy in the supermarket? Or scream until you get off the phone? Either avoid those situations or talk to her before they happen and tell her how you expect her to behave.
- *Be conscious of your previous response and try a new one.* You may have tried to placate your whiner to get her to stop, or chastised your screamer, or just given her a stern look. These are all reactions that your child picks up on, and she will repeat her behavior in order to get your attention. Instead, try to resist the urge to say or do anything, no matter how loud she becomes, and no matter how many people are around.
- *Act as if it isn't happening.* At first this may aggravate her even more, but if you continue to ignore the behavior each time it occurs, she'll eventually see it's not going to get your attention.
- *Praise her for correct behavior.* When she asks you, without whining, if she can have a candy bar, praise her for being a big girl while reminding her of the "no candy" rule. Or tell her how proud you are of her for playing quietly until you got off the phone. She may fall into old habits again, but use this method and it should help her behavior the next time around.

13. *Try not to set too many rules.* Even if you decide upon a strict parenting style, be aware that the rules you set should be appropriate for your child's age. Babies and very young children don't understand rules and need to be guided away from harm toward safety. Children don't even begin to understand the meaning of rules until around age two or three, and, even then, their impulses are so great they can't always be expected to follow them. In general the rule about rules is that the more you have, the more opportunities there will be for your child to break them. This doesn't mean you shouldn't set any rules or limits, it just means that you should limit rules to the most important ones until your child is old enough to understand them.

14. *Use time-outs effectively.* Time-outs aren't just for white families; they can be an effective way to calm your child when she gets out of control. While some parents use time-outs as punishment, it's best to use them as a way to help your child shift gears from unpleasant behavior into a more quiet state. Children, especially preschoolers, need help bringing themselves down before they get overly excited. When you see your child spinning out of control, try these tips:

- *Stay cool.* This is the key to getting your child under control and behaving the way you want. Yelling will only make it worse.
- *Take your child away from the activity.* You could take him to another part of the room or into his bedroom. Anywhere works as long as it allows him enough quiet to take a break.
- *Let him go once he's calm.* A time-out can be as short as thirty seconds.
- *Try not to use time-outs as punishments.* They are really meant as chill time, not as a temporary prison sentence.
- *Tell him what a good job he's done when he's behaving well.* Once he's calm, give him a hug and kiss and let him go back to what he was doing before he started misbehaving.

Of course, there are times when you're the one who needs a time-out, when all you want to do is scream or lash out. Before you lose it, it's usually best to separate. Place your child somewhere safe, a crib or playpen, and then go into another room where you can take a few deep breaths and let your blood pressure return to normal. This will protect both of you from doing something you'll regret. Call a friend, take a quick shower, or lie down and meditate until you feel you are able to return to your child and calmly handle the situation. If you're having a particularly difficult day, let your child know and explain what you would like to happen. If you still find you can't

"Have time-outs worked every time? No. Have I been frustrated? Yes."
—Anne's Story

As a pediatrician, I have always counseled parents to use "time-outs" to discipline children and steered them away from hitting or spanking. However, when my daughters were born, I learned that in the real world, using time-outs rather than hitting requires a great deal of time and energy from a parent. It's harder than I thought.

First, I found that my children didn't begin to understand the concept until they reached age two. Trying to get them to sit down and take some time to calm themselves didn't really work before then. What *did* work was holding them when they were crying and upset and telling them to take a deep breath to calm themselves. When things got out of hand and they had tantrums or were really testing their limits, I put them in their playpen and told them they had to stay there until they had calmed themselves. "You're getting a time-out!" I would say.

My oldest child quickly learned that if she wanted to get out of "jail," she had to calm herself and listen to her mother. But my youngest would cry and holler and carry on, taking forever to get herself together.

What I liked about using the playpen was that I knew they were safe and I could leave the room—to give myself a time-out. However, it became a problem when they were big enough to climb out, or when I needed to discipline them outside our home. By the time they were two, they had learned how to calm themselves and better understood the time-out concept. This is when time-outs began to work and make sense.

The conventional wisdom says that the length of the time-out depends on the age of the child: two years = two minutes, three years = three minutes, and so on, but I gave them as much time as they needed to get themselves together, and it was different for each child. Now that they are four and five, I use time-outs not only as a way to calm them, but also to give them time to think about why they are being punished.

Have time-outs worked every time? No. Have I been frustrated? Yes. Have there been times when I slipped up and popped them on the butt? Yes. But now that they're older, I can really see they know how to control themselves and understand how to behave in a way that is considerate and respectful of others. I like to think that all the talking and reasoning is bearing fruit as my daughters grow older and become thoughtful young girls.

cope, call a friend or relative to come and relieve you for a while. Or call the National Family Violence Helpline at (800) 222–2000.

15. *Give lots of hugs, kisses, and reassurance.* Like most African-American parents, you work, so most of your free time is spent cooking, cleaning, going to the doctor, shopping, paying bills—the list seems endless. The amount of time and energy it takes to run a home and raise a family can be so overwhelming that it's easy to forget how important it is to take time with your child. Those times when your child seems clingy, overly frustrated, is acting out or feeling anxious, he's probably in need of reassurance. It's surprising how something so small as a hug or a kiss can produce great results. It lets your child know you haven't forgotten about him, that despite your harried pace you love him, and that he's not the reason for your stress. Hugging also helps you, because it forces you to slow down, calm down, and connect with your child.

Taking the Trauma Out of "Good-bye" (and "Hello")

Separation is one of the biggest challenges for both children and parents. Working mothers are especially vulnerable to feeling guilty for "abandoning" their teary-eyed children. But working or not, all of us must experience the pain of separation from our children whether we leave them with a sitter or simply say goodnight. Separation anxiety is a natural stage of a child's emotional development.

Newborns have very little concept of where they end and you begin, and therefore don't understand the idea of separation until about six months. At the same time, six-month-old babies are just beginning to grasp the idea that when you two separate you don't just disappear, but are actually somewhere else. When babies fully understand this concept, called "object permanence," they will reach for a ball you have shown them hidden behind your back. A baby who now knows that you are somewhere else will miss you and want you with him. And since your baby has no real understanding of time, he will wonder when you will return. All of these developmental factors come together at around nine months when your baby will begin to show signs of separation anxiety, marked by excessive crying, clinging, and acting out just before and after you leave.

Toddlers, whose hallmark of development is independence and exploration, also experience a fear of separation. They are beginning to understand how vast (and

Are the Twos Really So Terrible?

Think back to when you were a teenager. If you were like most, you probably had power struggles with your parents, wanted to do things your own way, and began making your own decisions about your likes and dislikes—however much they clashed with those of your family. Now think about any two-year-old child. The similarities are striking enough that many experts call the twos the *first* adolescence. But are the twos really so bad?

According to Dr. Jay Belsky, Distinguished Professor of Human Development at Pennsylvania State University, who conducted research with sixty-nine families and their two-year-old boys, "A few bad apples have given every other two-year-old a bad reputation." His studies revealed that most parents don't have problems with their children's behavior at this stage, which is marked by children "stepping out of infancy to assert themselves, take control over their bodies, and decide what they want." Using his favorite word, "no," is a short and effective tool for him to achieve this new independence.

Belsky's study showed that only 20 percent of parents had a difficult time with their two-year-olds, and these families tended to have high levels of stress anyway, and therefore lacked the emotional resources to effectively discipline their children. Additionally, parents with very strict or authoritarian styles tended to have problems at this stage as well.

Rather than struggling over authority with a two-year-old, Belsky suggests you acknowledge her wishes. "What most kids want when they say 'no' is for you to hear them, not necessarily go along with them." Just saying "I understand you don't want to do this" and then giving a short explanation as to why and what you are going to do can cut down on the number of battles. "Saying you understand how your child feels isn't the same as giving in to his desires," says Belsky.

Two is also the age when children begin to bit, hit, throw things, and basically act out their aggressive impulses, actions that are understandably troubling to many parents. But this behavior is normal, too, and a part of human development. Parents need to understand that although your child can sometimes act out of anger, he still can't grasp that he's hurting you or even stop his own impulses. Here are some ways to help your two-year-old's aggressive urges:

- ***Be patient and firm.***
- ***Talk to him.* Explain which behavior you find unacceptable (like hitting), why (because it hurts), what you'd like him to do instead (touch gently, or punch**

a pillow if he's angry), and that if he continues he'll have to be removed from the situation. You'll need to repeat this process many times until your child really gets the concept of hurting someone else, and understands that your rules apply to many different circumstances.

- ***Praise him when he shows the correct behavior.***

Power struggles and constant "no's" aren't always fun to deal with, but this behavior will pass quickly. In the meantime, support your child's assertiveness while channeling it in a positive direction, appreciate his struggle for independence, and keep a sense of humor.

sometimes scary) the world is. While they need to satisfy their curiosity, they also need the security of your presence. In this "rubberband method" of exploring, children will go away to investigate and return after a couple of minutes to check in, sit on your lap, or get a hug, all of which gives them the courage to continue their discovery.

Fortunately, as children mature they also learn through experience that you will return. Time, or at least the sequence of predictable events, becomes a clear marker for when you will come back. Both of these new developments generally mean that separation is easier, though not always painless, especially in the case of family transitions. (See Chapter 12.)

If your child hasn't shown any real difficulty with transitions, you may be one of the lucky ones—at least for now. Some children who have gotten through infancy without much anxiety still may experience separation anxiety later. Often children who are highly sensitive to their surroundings or have difficulty with transitions in general may be more likely to have separation anxiety. Although separation may never be fun, there are ways to make parting less sorrowful:

- *Face your own separation anxieties.* Children are masters at sensing our discomfort, even when we think we're masking it. Think first of what your own feelings of separation are (such as guilt about working, guilt about enjoying time alone, fear of abandoning your child, fear of "damaging" your child). If there are reasonable explanations for your decisions or ways to resolve your feelings, your sense of security will be more clearly communicated to your child. And remember that many of these issues will need to be revisited throughout parenthood.
- *All separations are hard for small children at first.* Have faith that the most

Don't Spank!

According to a 1994 Gallup poll, only 68 percent of parents approve of spanking, compared with a 1964 survey in which 94 percent approved. And recent studies show that as a child grows older and continues to be spanked, the greater the chance that spanking will escalate into greater violence because the child will hit back. Despite these facts, black parents—women especially—are more likely to spank children compared with our white counterparts. Regardless, we're taking a hard line, and one that many folks won't agree with: Don't ever spank your child. Here are all the reasons we believe you shouldn't spank your child:

- ***Spanking teaches children to use violence to solve their problems.*** **Parents often spank when they are frustrated or irritated and trying to get a child to do something they want. And since we teach through our actions, this sends a message that when you're angry, frustrated, or bigger than someone is, physical pain is the way to get what you want. If parents who spank were to iron out their problems with other adults in the same manner, they would be breaking the law. So why should it be OK to do the same to a small person—not to mention your own child?**
- ***Spanking really doesn't work.*** **Several studies reveal that spanking is less effective in helping teach proper behavior to children than discipline without spanking. The results point out that parents who started spanking their children before age one spanked their four-year-old children just as often as parents who began spanking later. In other words, children who get spanked aren't learning the proper behavior or parents would have to spank them less for the same problem. And in a 1995 study funded by the National Institute of Child Health and Human Development, parents who used physical punishment had children who were more unruly than those who didn't hit.**
- ***Love and affection are more effective than pain and fear.*** **Children who are spanked generally feel angry, resentful, humiliated, fearful, and helpless. These feelings don't foster healthy self-esteem, nor do they help your child learn respectful behavior.**
- ***Spanking is dangerous.*** **For babies, it can lead to shaken baby syndrome, a deadly problem that can cause brain damage or death. If you are very angry and out of control, you can injure or—at very worst—kill your baby. It's better to not get in the hitting habit at all.**
- ***Other methods of discipline work better.*** **Spanking may have immediate results, but it doesn't help your child learn to think. If you have tried all the**

methods mentioned earlier in this chapter and still feel the urge to hit, try clapping your hands together, or hitting your knee or a table. The loud sound alone may startle your child and you will have avoided hurting her.

- ***Spanking will negatively affect your child later in life.*** **The Family Research Laboratory at the University of New Hampshire has found that the amount of physical punishment people receive as children directly affects their level of income. This means the more a person was physically punished as a child, the less he earns as an adult. What's more, children who are spanked often are at risk for using violence with their siblings, their spouses, and with someone outside the family when they get older. These children are also more likely to face depression, criminal behavior, and impaired learning compared to those who aren't spanked.**

difficult period is brief, and that after time your child will grow accustomed to the routine, and even rely on it.

- *Stick to a routine.* This is the key to easing your child's fears. When she knows what to expect—that you will return after her nap and snack at day care, for instance—she is less likely to be fearful when you drop her off. Likewise, have a set routine for drop-offs and pick-ups. A ritual of a familiar phrase ("I love you" or "Daddy will be thinking of you all day"), song, or activity before you leave can help your child settle into her new environment or say good-bye when it's time for her to go.
- *Respect your child's feelings.* Your child's response to separation can cause frustration. Resist any urge to reprimand your child. It will only make her more fearful and upset. Reassurance is the only way to ease your child's fears, so be patient and loving. Enlist the support of your child's caregiver in helping you comfort your child. She can distract your child, or involve her in a special activity.
- *Make coming home less stressful.* Reuniting at the end of the day is especially hard for parents, who feel pressured to both decompress from the end of the day and reconnect with their children. Take a few moments to focus on yourself and bring your day to an end. Then you can focus on your child.
- *Share your day.* Encourage your child to share the day's events by talking

about your own highlights of the day. Ask lots of questions about her friends, teachers, and activities and listen carefully.

- *Have lots of cuddle time.* Having your child sit on your lap or hugging and kissing can reassure your child and help you both relax. Giving your child emotional and physical attention is a vital part of gaining your child's cooperation and helping your child to feel content enough to play alone while you attend to other family matters.
- *Keep it simple.* Don't overload yourself with too many chores when you get home. Get your child to pitch in with the few chores you do have, such as cooking dinner or picking up, as a way to spend time together. After completing the essentials, take a break until after you put your child to bed.

RESOURCES

Recommended Reading for Parents

Becoming the Parent You Want to Be: A Sourcebook of Strategies for the First Five Years, Laura Davis and Janis Keyser (Broadway Books, 1997). Cheerful, culturally inclusive, and often funny, this sourcebook includes a section called "The Problem with Spanking."

Good Behavior Made Easy: 1,200 Solutions to Your Child's Problems from Birth to Twelve Years Old, Stephen W. Garber, Ph.D., Marianne Daniels Garber, and Robyn Freedman Spizman, Ph.D. (Great Pond Publishing, 1992). This book includes problem/solutions sheets, readiness tests, and motivational charts. It's easy to use with lots of ideas for how to work with your child in a positive way.

The Moral Intelligence of Children: How to Raise a Moral Child, Robert Coles, Ph.D. (Random House, 1997). The book's premise is that the most important skill a child must learn is to be a kind person. The author is the Pulitzer Prize–winning author of *The Spiritual Life of Children.*

Parenting the Strong-Willed Child: A Self-Guided Program for Children Who Are Often Disruptive, Rex Forehand and Nicholas Long, Ph.D. (Contemporary Books, 1996). This program helps improve a child's behavior while encouraging a better family relationship.

Raising Black Children, James P. Comer, M.D. and Alvin F. Poussaint, M.D. (Plume, 1992). As the cover says, "Two leading psychiatrists confront the educational, social, and emotional problems facing Black children today." This is one of the few books that confronts racism in America as a major obstacle to the health and safety of black children. These two authors are respected experts who answer many of the most common questions asked by black parents.

Raising Your Spirited Child, Mary Sheedy Kurcinka (HarperPerennial, 1991). This book looks at how parents can evaluate and live with a child who is "more intense, sensitive, perceptive, persistent, or energetic" than the average child.

Ready, Set, Cooperate, Marlene Barron (John Wiley & Sons, 1996). The author is the head of the West Side Montessori School in New York City. The book provides instructions for sixty playful activities that encourage your child to get along with others.

Smart Parenting, Peter Favoro, M.D. (Contemporary Books, 1995). This book gives stories of real-life problems and shows how they were resolved. Favoro coaches caregivers on how to help children "survive and thrive in a difficult and demanding world." He includes sections on building confidence, self-esteem, a sense of responsibility, and social skills.

Teaching Your Child the Language of Social Success, Marshall P. Duke, Ph.D., Stephen Nowicki, Jr., Ph.D., and Elisabeth A. Martin, M.Ed. (Peachtree Publishers, Ltd., 1996). This book helps caregivers recognize and understand their children's nonverbal language. It explains how children can be encouraged to use their nonverbal language in ways that will become the basis for having satisfying relationships and social success throughout their lives.

Touchpoints, T. Berry Brazelton, M.D. (Addison-Wesley Publishing, 1992). Starting with pregnancy and continuing through childhood, this book lays out issues and questions concerning all stages of childrearing. It also shows ways that aggressive children can learn to control their own behavior and shows parents how to "reorganize" when they make mistakes.

Twenty Teachable Virtues, Barbara C. Unell and Jerry L. Wyckoff, Ph.D. (Berkley Publishing Group, 1995). Some of the virtues this book focuses on are empathy, fairness, humor, respect, patience, honesty, resourcefulness, self-discipline, responsibility, self-motivation, peacemaking, cooperation, and loyalty. The authors believe it's important to start teaching these virtues as early as possible.

Why Children Misbehave and What to Do About It, Christine Adams, Ph.D., and Ernest Fruge, Ph.D. (New Harbinger Publications, Inc., 1996). The authors teach parenting methods that send messages of love and respect for oneself and others. Children learn how to "do the right thing." The book includes lots of photographs of children in various situations, attitudes, and moods that you will recognize.

Organizations

Center for Anti-Corporal Punishment, (215) 579–4865. This is an organization that promotes the concept that it is never OK to hit a child.

Center for Improvement of Childcaring, 11331 Ventura Blvd., Suite 103, Studio City, CA 91604–3147, (818) 980–0903. This organization has the "Effective Black Parenting Program" for instructors who help teach parenting skills to African-American parents.

Family Communications, Inc., 4802 5th Ave., Pittsburgh, PA 15213, (412) 687–2990. Family Communications, Inc., produces materials to facilitate communication between parents and children. Its booklet series topics include moving, going to school, discipline, separation, divorce, and death. For one free booklet, indicate your choice of subject matter and send a self-addressed, stamped, business-size envelope.

Family Resources Warm Line, (800) 641–4546. This hotline provides answers to nonmedical, nonlegal childrearing questions and concerns about children from birth to twelve years old. They have a counselor on hand to give advice from 9 A.M. to 9 P.M. weekdays and from 1 P.M. to 5 P.M. on Saturdays and Sundays. They also give referrals for emergencies.

Fatherhood Project (FP), Families and Work Institute, 330 7th Ave., 14th floor, New York, NY 10001, (212) 268–4846.

Website: www.fatherhood project.org

The Fatherhood Project encourages the participation of males in childrearing by operating a national clearinghouse on fatherhood. It includes information about programs and resources in areas of employment, law, education, health, adolescent fathers, and social services. Referrals to programs that deal with the father's role in parenting are available upon request.

National Committee to Prevent Child Abuse, 332 S. Michigan Ave., Suite 1600, Chicago, IL 60604, (800) CHILDREN, (800) 55–NCPCA, or (312) 663–3520.

Website: www.childabuse.org

This organization runs a program called "Healthy Families America" for new parents which focuses on parenting skills, child development, child health, and other aspects of family functioning. They also publish material on parenting and child abuse prevention.

Parent Training and Children's Social Skills Program, UCLA Neuropsychiatric Institute, 300 UCLA Medical Plaza, Los Angeles, CA, 90024, (310) 825–0142. This is a program run out of UCLA offering individual counseling and parenting classes for parents of children ages two through twelve.

Parents Anonymous (PA), 520 Lafayette Park Pl., Suite 316, Los Angeles, CA, 90045. PA is a self-help program for parents under stress and for abused children. There are no fees, and no one is required to reveal his or her name. Group members support and encourage one another in searching out positive alternatives to the abusive behavior in their lives. To locate a PA group in your area, call toll-free outside California (800) 421–0353.

Parents United/Daughters and Sons United, 232 E. Gish Rd., 1st floor, San Jose, CA 95112, (408) 280–5055. Parents United is a national self-help organization with many local groups throughout the United States. It provides assistance to families dealing with child sexual abuse and also sponsors self-help groups for adults who were sexually abused as children.

Parents Without Partners, Inc. (PWP), 8807 Colesville Rd., Silver Spring, MD, 20910, (800) 637–7974, (301) 588–9354.

Website: www.parentswithoutpartners.org

PWP has activities and mutual help groups for single parents and their children in all fifty states, Canada, and overseas. Bibliographies, resource lists, and information about a PWP group in your area are available.

Chapter

6

Baby, Go to Sleep

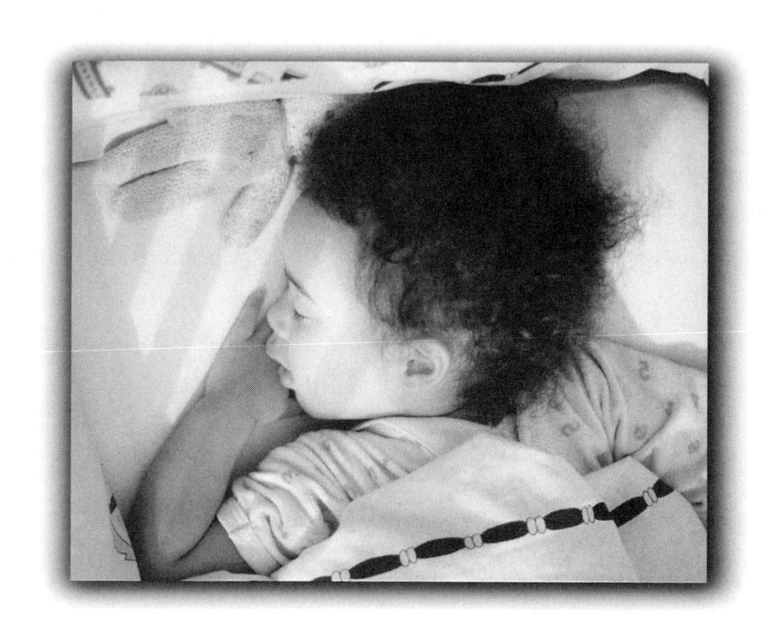

According to a 1994 report from the National Center for Health Statistics, over 25 percent of African-American children have an irregular or late bedtime (defined as after 10 P.M. for children under twelve). This means that more than one in four of our children isn't getting enough sleep and starts the day at a big disadvantage. This chapter will discuss why sleep is important and how to get your young child to learn to be a good sleeper, and will answer commonly asked questions about sleep problems.

Why Our Children Need to Sleep

There are more theories about getting your child to sleep than there are hours in the night. But we want to stress something more critical: You must make sure your child gets *enough* sleep. Often parents don't realize how important it is for their babies to sleep well until a problem develops and both baby and parents are at their wit's end.

Sleeping is part of our natural biological rhythms that cycle every day along with eating, physical activity, change in body temperature, and the secretion of hormones. Finding a balance of these rhythms helps us feel contented. When we're out of balance, our whole system, and life, is thrown off, an especially difficult situation for young children who need regularity in order to thrive. When children are thrown off balance because they haven't gotten enough sleep or their bedtimes are irregular, the effects can greatly alter their behavior. A study at the University of Indiana on young children in a Head Start program noted that children whose bedtimes varied from night to night exhibited the most severe behavior problems when compared to their peers, including other children who had late, though regular, bedtimes. Sleep deprivation in both adults and children can cause irritability, fatigue, inability to concentrate, and, worse for our children, an inability to learn. In fact, a 1983 Canadian study showed that school-age children with "superior" IQ scores slept thirty to forty minutes longer than children of average IQ. This study and hundreds more indicate that with enough sleep, most children can spend their waking hours alert, happy, relatively calm, and ready to learn.

How Do We Get Our Children to Sleep?

To get children into good sleep patterns, it's best to start a routine for both daytime and evening. Routines are like cues because they help babies and children know what's coming next so they can prepare for the transition. For infants, nursing or bottle-feeding

Sleep Stages

During the night, we go through various stages of sleep. While scientists don't know exactly how each stage benefits us, they know that we need deep sleep and several hours of REM sleep each night to survive.

Stage 1: During this light sleep stage we are easily awakened. Sometimes we feel we are daydreaming and not really asleep.

Stage 2: Our brains are still quite active during this stage, although we are definitely asleep. We spend about half our night's sleep in this stage.

Stages 3 and 4: These deep sleep states are called "restorative sleep" because during these stages brain activity slows, and we feel good when we wake up. We spend 25 percent of the night in stages 3 and 4, and they occur early in the night. Growth hormones are secreted during these stages.

REM: This is the dream state, called REM for rapid eye movement, because our eyes move quickly behind our lids during this stage. Adults spend about 20 percent of sleep time in this state (newborns spend 50 percent), which occurs late at night.

is usually the transition to napping, and for older children a meal or snack followed by quiet time means it's time for bed. Routines can also include such small details as turning on a night-light, closing all closet doors, a kiss, and an "I love you." For some children, if a parent forgets any of these steps, the child is thrown off and unable to sleep, another indication of how much children rely on consistency to feel secure.

Getting a child to bed is one thing, but getting her to sleep is another. The issue of how to get a child to actually sleep has been both confusing and even controversial, with experts arguing over which method works best. To help, we have put together a review of methods by several experts for you to see for yourself what works best. Each method takes time and patience—which may be in short supply if your child isn't getting much rest, and you're starting to feel sleep-deprived yourself. Take a deep breath and remember that, ultimately, finding the right method involves lots of trial and error, based on your individual circumstances and your child's temperament and age.

The following is a chart that shows how much sleep children and adults typically need every day.

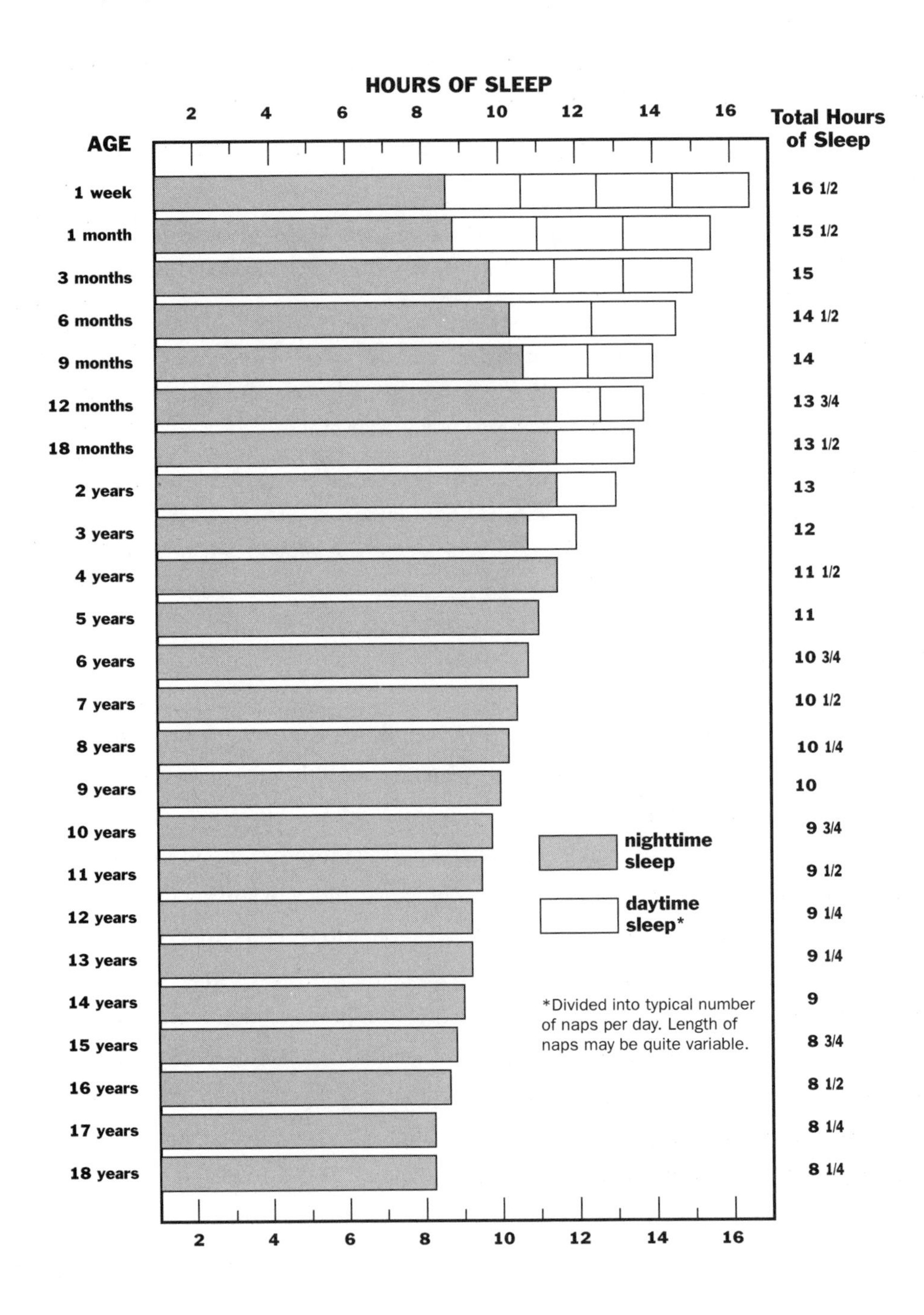

Richard Ferber, M.D., author of *Solve Your Child's Sleep Problems* (Fireside Books, 1985)

Ferber is such a well-known sleep expert that every year thousands of children get "Ferberized" through his method of nighttime sleep training. His research has shown that children who have been rocked or held or in other ways "helped" to sleep have learned to associate these activities with falling asleep and cannot fall asleep on their own. When these children, who have fallen asleep in their parent's arms, wake up in the middle of the night they cannot go back to sleep without their parent's help. Zombies from lack of sleep, lots of desperate parents use Ferber's method to teach children how to put themselves to sleep at bedtime and back to sleep in the middle of the night. While Ferber's is the leading (though not the only or necessarily the best) "cry it out" method, don't try it with a baby under five or six months old. Here's how Ferberizing works:

1. Agree with your partner that you will follow the method. Because Ferberizing involves hearing your child cry—sometimes very loudly, sometimes for hours—you or you and your partner have to agree that you'll give it a good try for a couple of days. (Big hint: Alert the neighbors so they don't give you dirty looks the next morning or call 911.)

2. Go through your child's normal bedtime routine, except for the rocking or patting. Put your child in the bed awake without a bottle, and, ideally, without a pacifier either.

3. Decide ahead of time how long you can stand to hear your child cry before going in. Time seems to stop for many parents when they hear their children cry, so be realistic. Start with one to five minutes.

4. When your child begins to cry, wait the allotted time before going in to comfort her. When you do go in, stay for only a couple of minutes. Do not pick her up, but reassure her that you love her and that it's time for her to go to sleep. Leave the room.

5. Extend the length of time before you go in by another one to five minutes. So if you went in after five minutes, wait another ten after this first visit before going in again.

6. Go in again briefly, to reassure her, tell her to sleep, and leave.

7. Extend the length of time by yet another one to five minutes. So, if you went in the last time after she'd cried for ten minutes, this time don't go in again for another

"It took a couple of bouts of 'Ferberizing' before Nate began to go down reliably but he was not psychologically harmed at all by our decision to use the method."
—MARTHA SOUTHGATE, MOTHER OF NATE, AGE 2; BROOKLYN, NEW YORK

I distinctly remember the moment I decided that it was time to help my son Nate learn to sleep through the night and to wean him from nighttime nursing. He was about six months old and had been up three times to nurse the night before. Early in the morning, he sat in our bed, looking adorable as always, fresh-faced and ready to start the day. And I was so tired that I wanted to kill him. I was furious with him for interrupting my sleep yet again. I had reached the end of my rope.

Some parents take much longer to reach the end of theirs; some don't get as resentful as I did; others feel resentment and swallow it. But that morning, I knew that if we didn't get Nate to start sleeping through the night regularly soon, I was only going to get angrier and it would ultimately poison our relationship. I got Richard Ferber's book that afternoon.

The first night was really tough. Nate protested, by crying vigorously—for forty-five minutes. The next night, one of the toughest, he cried for over an hour as my husband, Jeff, shuttled in and out of the room with words of reassurance for him. I was almost in tears myself, watching the clock, waiting for the five- and ten-minute periods we'd agreed on to inch by. But I kept saying to myself and to Jeff (who found it even more difficult than I did) that this is how he'll learn to go to sleep on his own—a skill he'll need for the rest of his life.

I kept telling myself that this was the only way I was going to keep from being angry at him all the time and that our needs would be better met when we were all getting sufficient sleep. I was also reassured by the fact that during the day, Nate was his usual, chipper, charming self—apparently unharmed by the night's difficulties.

After about a week, when he began to go to sleep on his own without protest, he was even in better spirits than usual because he was getting sufficient sleep at night. I would still have periods of feeling guilty when I spoke to a friend who hadn't used Ferber's method or read in some periodicals about how this tactic was teaching my child that his cries wouldn't be answered. Such a message could not be further from what we hoped to accomplish.

In retrospect, I know that we did the right thing for our family and that we in no way broke Nate's spirit. It took a couple of bouts of "Ferberizing" before Nate began to go down reliably but he was not psychologically harmed at all by our decision to

use this method. Now he goes to bed easily most nights with the help of our established routine of bath, bedtime stories and songs, and then lights out. And he sleeps through the night most nights. We learned an important lesson here: Setting limits isn't only for the daytime. Our family is much happier and healthier for having set them at night as well.

fifteen minutes. Hereafter you can go in every fifteen minutes until she falls asleep. If your child gets more agitated when you visit, or you find she's calming down, don't go in.

Use this method every night for a week, extending the first visit by one to five minutes every night and all other visits by the same interval. So night two the first visit would be after ten minutes of crying, then fifteen, then twenty. On day three the first visit would be after fifteen minutes of crying, etc. The point isn't how many minutes, but just to extend the time between visits. Try this method for naps but allow only one hour of crying. If after this time your child hasn't fallen asleep, forget about the nap and try the method again at bedtime (without a nap, your child will probably need an earlier bedtime, too).

Ferber Pros: It's heartwrenching to listen to the crying, but many parents swear it works, often after only a couple of days. Each day, they say, gets easier, and each time their kids get out of their sleep routine, retraining is easier than the first time. They like this method better than just "cold turkey" where children are expected to cry until they fall asleep without any visits. Satisfied parents report that everyone sleeps more and is in a much better mood.

Ferber Cons: Many parents find it impossible not to respond to their child's crying. This method may be especially difficult for a single parent who doesn't have the support of a family member or for a household with other small children. Ferber's method also doesn't take into account the different maturation levels of babies and young children, and that some babies take longer to learn how to fall asleep than others. Emotionally, it may feel rigid, unnatural, and even mean. Plus, despite all the folks who swear by Ferber, it's really a Western thing. The vast majority of parents throughout the diaspora—and the world—have never heard of Ferber, and their babies make it through the days and nights just fine.

William Sears, M.D., author of *Nighttime Parenting: How to Get Your Baby and Child to Sleep* (Plume, 1987)

Sears is a well-known pediatrician who emphasizes parent-child bonding. He believes that letting children cry it out at bedtime goes against a parent's natural instincts and that it shouldn't be done. His philosophy, summed up as "family bed," is basically the polar opposite of Ferber's. "When cries are not responded to, a baby may fall back to sleep on his own," Sears writes in his book, "but this is a sign of withdrawal following the disappointment of not being listened to."

Sears's methods for getting young children to sleep include:

- *Establishing a nighttime routine, but not one that relies on schedules or strict bedtimes.* Nurse, rock, play music, or do whatever it takes to help your young child fall asleep.
- *Sharing a family bed.* This is the crux of the Sears method. If your baby wakes in the night, you can pat or nurse him back to sleep right in the bed. If that doesn't work, you can try "playing asleep" so that he will know that nighttime is for sleeping. Sears believes that sharing a bed adds to family closeness, which can be especially important for working parents who feel they don't spend enough time with their children. For those parents who can't get enough rest with a squirmy child or if there's not enough room in the bed, Sears suggests putting a mattress, sleeping bag, or cot next to the bed. As for age ranges, Sears believes co-sleeping should last as long as parents and children are happy with the arrangement. Once your child wants to sleep in his own bed, and many eventually do, your child may still want to spend an occasional night in your bed.

Sears Pros: Sharing a family bed allows parents to feel closer and more bonded to their children, especially when they're very young. It's great for breast-feeding, because mother doesn't have to get up. She can roll over, feed baby without fully waking, and then go right back to sleep. Plus, many parents admit that their children spend some nights, if not most, sleeping in their beds anyway. The family bed is com-

Strange Bedfellows? Does Sharing Your Bed Help or Hurt?

Throughout history, families have shared sleeping spaces and beds. Separate bedrooms for parents and children are a relatively new arrangement, a product of the amount of space available to families mostly in the West. Now some researchers are beginning to question whether separate sleeping setups are the best idea.

In a 1996 article in the journal *World Health,* Dr. James McKenna, an anthropologist, researched the benefits of co-sleeping and found several. For one, babies enjoy sleeping next to their mothers for warmth, to be comforted, and to be nursed. According to studies McKenna cites, babies who sleep next to their mothers also cry less and sleep more. Plus, parents who sleep with their children become very attuned to them, because they're near. (Contrary to popular worry, it's rare and nearly impossible to roll over and crush or smother your baby.) And babies who sleep with their parents may have lower rates of sudden infant death syndrome: In Japan, where SIDS rates are among the lowest in the world, sharing a bed is a common practice.

On the other side of the debate, a 1991 study at the University of Massachusetts Medical School of parents and their two- and three-year-old children found that children who were co-sleeping had high levels of sleep problems such as difficulty getting to sleep and night waking. Furthermore, studies in New Zealand in 1996 showed that those infants who shared a bed with mothers who smoked had a four times greater risk of SIDS than babies who didn't sleep with smoking mothers.

In conclusion, each family is different and, ultimately, the decision is yours and yours alone. Given the facts, it seems that while it may be beneficial for your baby to sleep with you when he's very young—say within the first year if you don't smoke (and you shouldn't, especially in bed!)—children tend to sleep better alone after infancy.

mon in the West Indies, Africa, and in many families in the United States, especially in single-parent families. So this method may already fit some parents' lifestyles.

Sears Cons: Sears is not a sleep researcher, and much of his advice is simplistic. For example, many babies don't fall back to sleep with just a pat on the back or a game of pretend sleep, but need more vigorous rocking. And this method assumes everyone is getting a good night's sleep, when thousands of parents are living, exhausted proof that too many bodies in the bed equals not enough sleep for anyone. (See above, "Strange Bedfellows? Does Sharing Your Bed Help or Hurt?") What's more, many parents don't want their children in their beds for a number of reasons, including spending time alone or together with your partner. And finally, there has been no evidence to prove that a child who is well loved and attended to during the day is harmed by learning to fall asleep at night on his or her own.

Marc Weissbluth, author of *Healthy Sleep Habits, Happy Child* (Fawcett Columbine Books, 1987)

Weissbluth's advice is based on his experience as a pediatrician and a child sleep researcher. In his book, he explains that sleep is part of our development, and it changes as we grow. Like Ferber, he encourages parents to teach their children to fall asleep on their own but tailors methods to fit a baby's age. He offers the following tips:

- Birth to four months: During the first week of life, a baby sleeps up to eighteen hours in short stretches (two to three hours at a time). After a few weeks, she may begin to sleep up to four hours at a time, unless she's colicky. Generally, babies don't follow any real sleep pattern until about six weeks when night sleep becomes the longest stretch, about six hours.

  After three months, you can let her cry for longer periods. Weissbluth suggests five to twenty minutes, as long as you can stand it, or however long you think it may take for your baby to fall asleep. Overtired babies cry longer and harder, some babies cry in protest, others cry as a transition into sleep. If she doesn't fall asleep after twenty minutes, pick her up and comfort her. All babies mature at different rates, so this may not work until a few weeks later.
- Four to twelve months: Babies at this age are sleeping much more regularly and for longer periods. Now is the time to allow your baby to fall asleep on his own and to soothe himself when he wakes. Weissbluth suggests the following pattern to help children fall asleep during the first year:

  *Once he's really awake and ready for the start of the day, consider putting him down for his first nap within three hours of waking.

  *Begin naptime and bedtime routines, but make sure they don't cut into his sleep time.

  *Try to have your baby sleep for at least one solid hour without your help. This means putting him down and leaving the room for as long as it takes him to sleep for an hour, regardless of how long he cries. Going in to check on him can teach him that if he stays up and cries long enough, you'll come in to be with him.

*Expect him to take another nap two to three hours after the morning nap, sometime in the afternoon before 3 P.M. This nap should also be at least an hour long. If he doesn't get to sleep before 3 P.M. and doesn't seem like he's likely to, skip this nap and put him to bed earlier.

Weissbluth Pros: Weissbluth is a well-respected and experienced sleep researcher and parent who has studied which methods are most effective in teaching children to sleep. He devotes an entire chapter to colicky babies and gives much-needed advice about how parents can help more challenging babies learn to sleep. He also deals with feelings when teaching their children to sleep, such as guilt, confusion, or anger. He explains that many of these feelings have more to do with parenting than with sleep and reminds us how vital sleeping is to raising a healthy child.

Weissbluth Cons: Unless parents start very early with his advice, they may find his cold-turkey method too difficult. And working parents who rely on day care providers to monitor their child's sleep during the day may discover that it's hard to make sure their children are getting enough naptime.

Personally, as a mom and a doctor, I say let your baby sleep either with you or in the bassinet next to you for the first few months—especially for those midnight breast-feeding sessions. Very early on your baby should learn to soothe himself when you put him down to sleep. A bedtime routine really helps him go down on his own. By the time kids are four months, I tell my patients to put their children in their own beds and let them go to sleep on their own. If not, Ferber is the next step. I advise a "Ferber" for wimps approach—three-minute intervals. My patients say it works!

Q & A: Answers to Our Children's Sleep Problems

The following section tries to answer some of parents' most commonly asked sleep questions. Whether you follow these suggestions or not, our main philosophy is try anything that gets results and doesn't emotionally or physically harm your child.

Baby

Q: How do I survive on the little sleep I've gotten? How do I get more?

A: How many new parents have come home from the hospital only to discover

Sleepy Head Signs

Here are some of the signs you can look for when deciding whether your child is sleepy or not. Many children have their own unique signs, too.

- **Rubbing eyes**
- **Yawning**
- **Putting head down or lying down on the floor**
- **Seeming full of energy and running around aimlessly**
- **Throwing, ripping, or messing things intentionally**
- **Talking loudly or screaming**
- **Throwing tantrums and crying a lot**
- **Insisting on clasping an object**
- **Staring off into space**
- **Being intentionally disobedient, defiant, or uncooperative**
- **Saying "my bed"**

that their quiet little baby is actually a screaming maniac? A lot. Think about it from a biological standpoint: Until a few months of age a baby's brain and nervous system aren't developed enough to fall into regular sleep patterns. Some lucky parents find their babies begin sleeping longer than most right from the start. But most of us have to get through the first three to five months working our lives, schedules, and nerves around the baby's needs. Sleep deprivation makes parenting difficult, and almost impossible for a single parent. Here are a few hints to help you get some sleep:

- *Steal sleep when your baby does.* You'll need the rest for those times when you'll be up in the middle of the night.
- *Unplug the phone.* You can talk when you wake up.
- *Learn to live with a messy house.* Rather than trying to clean or pick up while your baby's sleeping, get some rest. Choose one hour or one day for clean up.
- *Ask for help.* If you need a solid few hours of rest, ask your partner, relative, or friend—or hire a baby-sitter—to come in and relieve you.

Q: What is the best sleep position for my baby?

A: Because of the risk of Sudden Infant Death Syndrome (SIDS), you *must* put your baby on her back. This is the best way to prevent this deadly problem. (For more on SIDS, see Chapter 1.)

Q: My baby insists that I hold him all the time, even during naps. What do I do?

A: Many babies want to be held all the time and cry when put down for long periods. Experts call them "high-needs" babies, and they also tend to be quite social, which makes sense. Don't worry, it's probably not something you did, so don't let friends and relatives blame you and say you're "spoiling him."

While your baby is still small, you can accommodate him by wearing him either in a baby carrier or baby sling, or by holding him while he sleeps. A baby carrier makes it easier because it frees up your hands so you can do other things while he naps. However, sleep researchers warn that most babies who sleep while being held generally sleep lightly without falling into the deeper (and necessary) REM sleep. So when they awaken, they may be even more tired than before. If you find this to be true, try putting your baby down just as he's getting ready to drift off to sleep, allow him to cry for a bit, and see if he goes to sleep. If not, you may want to put him in his bed after he's already asleep but only until he is four months old. After four months, he should go to sleep on his own.

Q: I like having my eighteen-month-old sleep in my bed. Is that a problem?

A: Not necessarily, and advocates of family bed would say "no" definitively. (See section on family beds, p. 138.) However, it might be wise to take an honest look at your own motivations and consider whether you should come up with other ways to both bond with your child and get your needs met. Are you:

- Working long hours and want to spend time with your child when you get home?
- Having problems with your partner, and you get the affection and attention you need from your baby?
- Lonely or afraid to be alone and want company?
- Scared your child is "mad" at you and don't want him to cry?
- Using the baby to ease your own feelings of abandonment?

Q: Should I put my baby on a sleep schedule?

A: Some parents absolutely swear by putting their children on schedules from day

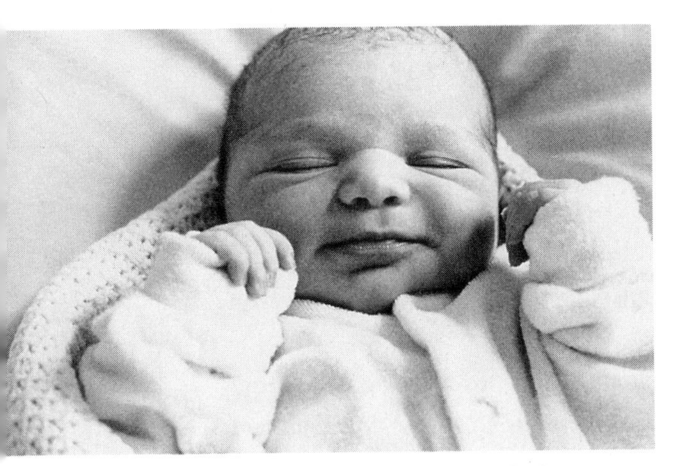

To facilitate sleep, start bedtime routines as soon as baby comes home.

one. They believe that regulating their baby's day helps them sleep and eat better and puts them in a better mood. However, while putting your baby on any kind of rigid schedule may be convenient for you, it might not be best for your baby. For one, babies don't eat or sleep on regular schedules naturally because their biological clocks aren't set until they are about nine months old. To deprive them of food or sleep (which parents who put their babies on schedules often do to stay "on time") is unfair and unwise. And schedules don't teach your baby how to fall asleep on her own.

Rather than schedule, think routine. Routines are wonderful and necessary and can begin as soon as baby returns from the hospital. Unlike schedules, which rely on set hours and clock watching, routines are flexible and regular and revolve around baby's needs. For instance, a schedule requires feeding strictly at 9 A.M., while a routine allows for feeding after the first nap or when your baby expresses hunger. Working and single parents (and especially single working parents!) find routines are more practical than schedules, because most people's lives are less predictable than they were decades ago, when the idea of scheduling babies became popular.

Q: My baby sleeps through the night but occasionally wakes up. What should I do?

A: No child ever sleeps through the night without waking up at all. It's just that some children have learned how to put themselves back to sleep. Until your child learns how, she'll need your help going back to sleep. In this case, you have two choices: You can teach your child how to fall asleep alone (using one of the methods mentioned earlier in this chapter), or you can help her by rocking her, for example, until you decide it's time for her to learn on her own. Expect a lot of crying, but also expect results.

If your child is already a good sleeper but is now waking at night, consider the reason. Is she teething? Might she have an ear infection or other illness? Has your

"I can still remember my first eight-hour sleep in as many months; it felt like heaven."
—LINDA'S STORY

After Kali was born, we were definitely a family-bed family. Kali slept either in bed with Vickie and me or was in and out of our bed for the first several months. It worked fine for a while, and it really made nursing much easier. But during the day, I was exhausted almost all the time. I fought it, but I felt bone tired from waking up two or three times for night feedings.

Eventually, as the months went by and Kali got bigger, our double bed felt like it was getting smaller and smaller. I started complaining that we needed a bigger bed. "I don't see why we can't get a queen-size bed," I whined. Vickie, however, finally said, "Listen, I think it's time to get Kali her own crib." I argued that it was too soon—Kali was only five months—and that we should keep her in our room and in and out of our bed a bit longer, for *her* sake. But eventually, I had to face facts: It wasn't for her sake that I liked her close by . . . it was for mine. I enjoyed having her warm body between us and I liked waking up and finding her in our bed. I also had to admit that I was holding on to her more tightly because I was getting ready to go back to work full-time and had started feeling a bit of separation anxiety.

Once I owned up to my feelings, it was easier to move Kali into her own crib in an adjoining room. She took the move in stride, and once we stopped the nighttime feedings, she slept longer without tears. At about eight months, we moved her into her own bedroom. After one night of modified Ferberizing—forty-five minutes of crying—she began sleeping through most nights. I can still remember my first eight-hour sleep in as many months; it felt like heaven.

routine changed in some way? Is the family going through some kind of emotional upheaval such as a breakup, move, or a death? Any of these scenarios could be triggering night waking.

Toddler

Q: My child has a really strong personality and puts up such a fuss about going to bed that I usually ignore the hour and get him to sleep when he's really tired. Is this all right?

A: We all get beaten down by our children's protests, especially when they're little and cute and we're exhausted. It seems easier at the time to give in and let him

Sleep Myths

Myth: When children wake up at night, the best way to get them back to sleep is with a bottle.

Fact: While nursing an infant back to sleep is OK, giving a baby a bottle to return to sleep isn't always a great idea. For one, a child who cannot go back to sleep without a bottle is learning to use food as a pacifier. As part of his nightly routine, a bottle is fine as a snack before bed, but babies with teeth should have their teeth brushed before going down to prevent cavities caused by the high levels of natural sugar present in milk. And never let your child suck on a bottle while he's lying down, as it is associated with ear infections. After your baby is several months old, it's best to find a method for getting him back to sleep that works for you without relying on milk or any other food.

Myth: Your child will get a good night's sleep if you keep her up late so she sleeps longer.

Fact: The longer you keep a sleepy child awake, the harder it is to get her to sleep. Stimulating hormones like adrenaline race through her system to keep her awake, and they build up the longer she's awake. A better idea: Set a regular bedtime and routine, one that coincides with the time of evening that she naturally gets sleepy—usually between 6:30 to 9 P.M. for most babies and small children.

Myth: Giving a child solid foods at night before bed helps him sleep longer.

Fact: How many times have friends and relatives encouraged you to stuff your baby with food before bed so that he doesn't wake up hungry in the middle of the night? Relax. There is no evidence that filling a baby or child up with food before bed helps him to sleep better. Offering a before-bedtime snack or bottle is fine if he's up for it (do not put cereal or other food in a bottle with milk or juice). However, most babies eat often and in small amounts, and until they weigh about 10 pounds, will probably awaken for night feeds anyway. After that, most babies can wait until morning to eat again.

Myth: Keep naps short or baby won't sleep well at night.

Fact: Generally it's not a good idea to wake your child from a nap. If she's sleeping it's because her body needs the rest. So let her sleep. Though it may seem hard to grasp at first, the better rested baby is during the day, the easier it'll be for her to fall asleep at night.

have his way, but in the end it doesn't pay. As a parent, it's your job to set limits, so you must stick by the sleep routine you've established, most critically because of the impact it has on your child's behavior and performance.

Many children don't like to go to bed because they feel they're missing out on all the fun. Nonetheless, you need to draw a firm line. Even if he refuses to sleep, put him in bed and tell him it's time. Your serious tone of voice and matter-of-fact manner will get the message across. If this method doesn't work the first time, he'll get the message if you remain consistent and firm. Use a bedtime routine to help him transition and let him know what's coming—bedtime.

Q: When should my child move from a crib into a regular bed? And how do I keep her in it when she does?

A: Unless you have good reason to move your child into a regular bed from the crib, such as a new baby on the way, there's really no rush. In fact, unless you feel your child is ready to handle the freedom of a "big kid" bed, it could cause a lot of headaches trying to get her to stay put in her bed. And some children need a lot of reassurance when going through transitions like switching beds, so be careful not to rush into something you think would be exciting only to find that she's not so hot on the idea. Here are some tips:

- *Wait until your child is two-and-a-half- to three-years-old before switching.* At this age she'll be able to handle her new privilege.
- *If you have to move her into a bed, buy a new one long before she actually needs to sleep in it.* If you can, put it in her room and let her slowly get used to the idea. First let her read on it, then take naps on it, and eventually sleep through the night on it.
- *If you have moved her into a new bed, and she loves the pop-out-of-bed game, try either closing the door or buying a childproof gate to put at the door so she can't come join you or—worse—get out of bed and into something dangerous.*
- *If you're switching because your child keeps climbing out of her crib, try putting a mesh net cover over the top, instead of moving her to a bed.* These dome-shaped, transparent covers that attach with Velcro allow baby to stand without getting out. You can find them in baby stores or catalogues. (FYI, these also keep pets out of the crib.)

"Miles has learned how good it feels to go to sleep." **—ALLISON'S STORY**

I was lucky to learn about the importance of sleep from a mother-infant group I started attending when Miles was just a month old. Our group leader, a therapist with years of training and experience in infant and toddler behavior, told us that when our children were three months we could start teaching them to go to sleep on their own. After a couple of months of experimenting with a modified Ferber method (Ferberizing is not recommended for babies under five or six months), Mark and I got Miles to fall asleep by himself. Except for an occasional bout of teething or an ear infection, Miles was very regular with his bedtime routine and didn't protest.

That is until he started to talk, at around eighteen months. He learned that he could stall my putting him in the crib for several minutes if he had a good excuse. The first ones seemed easy enough to handle, like "I'm thirsty" or "Milesy want a cracker." But he realized this only bought him about two minutes, so he began more dramatic measures.

Realizing how much attention—not to mention the extra privileges—he got when he was sick, he decided that every night some new part of his body was hurting and he needed medicine to fix it. Just before being put in his crib he'd point to his neck or jaw and say in his most adorable baby talk, "Hurting. Need Motrin." I was so happy that he was capable of expressing his pain that I fell for this for about a week. Then things got out of control. He was staying up thirty extra minutes by this point, drinking water, eating crackers, taking medicine, and now insisting that he had painful diaper rash that needed special ointment. Not only was he getting his way, but he was also becoming a hypochondriac, addicted to the attention he was getting for all his imaginary ailments!

This was the first real confrontation Miles and I had with limit testing, and he was better at it than I was. Once I realized his strategy, I began factoring into the routine a last snack, glass of water, check for diaper rash, and new-tooth check. I also tried to look at my own behavior just before his bedtime. I realized I was getting so involved in putting dinner on the table and returning phone calls I missed during the day that I wasn't giving him my full attention in the evening when he returned home from being out with his baby-sitter. So I made the decision to get him ready for bed and spend at least a half hour aside from the bedtime story and bath just talking and playing quietly. If Mark was home, he took over for me.

Not that the results were miraculous, because he still tries out new stall tactics

even today (his latest is "ten minutes, please Mommy"). But when I tell him he's going to be fine, and I put him down in his crib, he goes willingly. Now I know if something is really wrong—like he's getting sick—because that's the only time he asks to be comforted and sleep in our bed. At this point Miles has learned how good it feels to go to sleep.

Q: What can I do about my child's snoring?

A: If your baby or child snores, mention it to your pediatrician. While snoring doesn't necessarily signal a problem, some types of snoring might mean trouble. Here are some signs to look for:

- *His breathing is irregular during sleep* (for instance, taking a long pause between breaths or holding his breath).
- *He seems sleepy or acts overly tired even when he's had plenty of sleep.*
- *He breathes through his mouth rather than his nose.* While any sick child will probably do this for a short time, a child who regularly sleeps this way may be having problems.

Preschooler

Q: Does my child still need a nap?

A: If she's five years old or younger, the answer is probably yes. Because all children are different, the only way to really know is to see how she behaves when she doesn't have one. Is she tired around the time she'd normally have a nap and does she have a hard time making it all the way to her bedtime? If the answers are yes, then she's just like the overwhelming majority of toddler and preschoolers: She needs a nap now, but will probably be able to drop it by first grade.

Q: What's the difference between nightmares and night terrors, and how do I handle them?

A: During the toddler and preschool years, many children have their first nightmares. These are frightening to small children because they don't really understand the difference between dreams and reality. And even when they reach the age that they do, about two or three, the scary feelings and fears are still very strong.

Children who have nightmares need your love and support. They may even need the extra security of having you near if they can't get back to sleep. If your child has had a nightmare, gently reassure her and get her back to sleep. In the morning, try to talk with her about her dream to see if she's worried or frightened about anything and

"When I slowed down and made spending time with my children a goal, I found that the bedtime routine became more relaxed and fun." **—ANNE'S STORY**

When I was raising my daughters alone, I used to feel like there was never enough time in the day to do all that needed to be done. After working, there were errands, groceries, laundry, cleaning, and dinner, not to mention spending time with my girls. At the end of the workday I was always rushing home to make dinner and get the girls into bed so I could have a little time to myself. I realized that I was constantly rushed and frustrated, which left me little energy to enjoy my evenings or my children. I also found myself hurrying to get the girls into bed and this often led to fights and conflicts when they did not move fast enough for me.

As I became increasingly frustrated with this routine, I realized that I needed to find a way to decrease the stress I was experiencing. First, I decided that I would try to schedule my day so that I was home one to two hours before my girls' bedtime, and that this period would be devoted exclusively to them. While it was only a small portion of the day, it was important that I reserved this time for them and addressed their needs then. My friends and family learned not to interrupt this time, and when people did call, I told them I was busy with the children and would return their calls later in the evening.

After setting time aside to spend with my children, I started to feel more relaxed about our evenings together. When I viewed the evenings as a time to get the girls into bed so I could have some quiet time, it was just another task to be accomplished. But when I slowed down and made spending time with my children a goal, I found that the bedtime routine became more relaxed and fun. We would talk about our days, sing songs, say prayers, and reflect on the day's events. I also found that by slowing down and enjoying this time, I could get my children to bed much more easily. When we were rushing to get into bed, they resisted because they felt they had not spent enough time with me. Because I'd set some time aside, both of them could feel that they had been heard that day. And even though I now approach their bedtime routine—the bath, pajamas, songs, reading—in a more relaxed way, they know that it is leading to bedtime. They give me fewer fights about getting into bed, because they feel satisfied that we have spent some time together and are happier about going to bed.

to explain the difference between thoughts when she's awake and dreams when she's asleep. Because our waking hours can greatly influence our dreams, take note of any recent changes or problems she might have and see if you can ease her mind about them. For instance, if she's having a hard time at a new preschool, talk about how it feels to have to make new friendships and go to a new school.

Night terrors occur within the first four hours of falling asleep, and when she wakes up, she'll have no memories of what happened. Night terrors generally occur after some disruption in sleep habits (after a vacation or several nights of staying up late) and go away after a few days. They occur more frequently for children who have irregular bedtimes and are overtired. During night terrors, your child thrashes, screams, gets out of bed and runs, and is frightened, confused, or angry. As upsetting as it may be for parents to watch, night terrors can't be stopped and tend to worsen if you try. The key to dealing with night terrors is to make sure your child is safe, stay nearby, but leave your child alone. After several minutes the episode will pass. She will quickly fall back to sleep without any recollection of the event or any awareness that you were there. Sleep experts recommend regular bedtimes or earlier bedtimes as treatment in the case of infrequent terrors. However, frequent night terrors should be brought to the attention of your child's health care provider, who can refer you to a sleep disorder specialist. Some specialists will recommend a combination of therapies for frequent night terrors, such as counseling, medication, and sleep therapy.

RESOURCES

Bedtime Stories

There are many, many books that you can read aloud to children at bedtime. You will learn quickly which ones your child loves. Here are a few selected by the authors. Some of them are written for older children, but they are also fine for reading aloud.

AFRO-Bets Book of Black Heroes from A–Z: An Introduction to Important Black Achievers, Wade Hudson and Valerie Wilson Wesley (Just Us Books, 1993). This is a collection children are sure to enjoy.

Bo Rabbit Smart for True: Tall Tales from the Gullah, Priscilla Jaquith, ed., illustrated by Ed Young (Putnam/Philomel, 1995). This is a collection of folktales told in the Gullah dialect of South Carolina and Georgia. This edition of the 1981 title features two additional folktales.

Her Stories: African-American Folktales, Fairy Tales, and True Tales, Virginia Hamilton, illustrated by Leo and Diane Dillon (Blue Sky/Scholastic Press, 1995). This is a collection of narratives that capture the imagination, humor, and dreams of African-American women.

Jump Up & Say! A Collection of Black Storytelling, Linda and Clay Goss (Simon & Schuster, 1995). The poems, songs, and short stories in this book include new takes on old favorites.

The People Could Fly, Virginia Hamilton, illustrated by Leo and Diane Dillon (Alfred A. Knopf, 1985). This is a collection of twenty-four black folktales dramatically retold with spirit and poetry.

Tuck-Me-In Tales: Bedtime Stories from Around the World, Margaret MacDonald, illustrated by Yvonne Davis (August/LittleFolk, 1996). This is a collection of five traditional bedtime tales from several cultures with many illustrations.

When Birds Could Talk and Bats Could Sing: The Adventures of Bruh Sparrow, Sis Wren, and Their Friends, Martha Young (Blue Sky/Scholastic Press, 1996). This is a collection of African-American folktales.

Songs and Lullabies

Animal Crackers: A Delectable Collection of Pictures, Poems, and Lullabies for the Very Young, Jane Dyer (Little, Brown, 1996). This book of nursery rhymes, poems, and lullabies is arranged by subject.

How Sweet the Sound: African-American Songs for Children, Cheryl and Wade Hudson, illustrated by Floyd Cooper (Scholastic Press, 1995). This collection stretches from spirituals to Stevie Wonder tunes, including songs from Africa, work songs, gospels, jazz, blues, play songs, chants, soul, and popular music. This title is a companion to *Pass It On: African-American Poetry for Children.*

Once: A Lullaby, B. P. Nichol, illustrated by Anita Lobel (Morrow/Mulberry, 1992). This picture book has soothing bedtime lyrics.

Sleep, Baby, Sleep: Lullabies and Night Poems, Mary Harris Veeder (American Library Association, 1994). This is a collection of twenty-six lullabies, including old favorites and new songs with simple piano or guitar music. Also, it has a roundup of twenty-five "night poems"; poets include Nikki Giovanni.

Sleep, Sleep, Sleep: A Lullaby for Little Ones Around the World, Nancy Van Laan, illustrated by Holly Meade (Little, Brown and Company, 1994). This book is one long lullaby with a refrain on every page, which offers a phonetic spelling of "Good night, go to sleep, little one" spoken by parents in Norway, Bolivia, China, Chile, and Australia.

Organizations

American Sleep Disorders Association, 1610 14th St., NW, Suite 300, Rochester, MN 55901, (507) 287–6006. You can call or write to this organization to find out about a pediatric sleep clinic in your area.

National Sleep Foundation, 729 15th St. NW, Washington, D.C. 20005; (202) 347–3471. This is a nonprofit organization that provides educational and research programs related to healthy sleep habits.

Chapter

7

Let's Eat

As African-American parents, many of us have to change our thinking from our own childhoods when our mothers commanded that we clean our plates before leaving the table. This was a loving gesture made by concerned mothers who wanted to make sure they provided for their children. While our mothers may have had good intentions, experts agree that this is one rule of many from our parents' generation that needs to be put on a shelf. New research shows that the best way to raise a healthy eater is to provide nutritious food at regular mealtimes and leave the rest up to the kids. Hard to believe for some, but take a look at why this new approach works, as well as some other tips to help you set good eating habits for the rest of your child's life.

The Best Way to Feed Our Children

Eating is a very sensitive subject for parents. Because it represents nurturing, caring for, and raising children, some parents equate lots of food with lots of love. Eating can be a battleground. In our desire to see our kids grow, we may begin to struggle with our children about what, when, and how much to eat. To avoid food wars and to achieve what you really want—a healthy eating pattern for your child—follow these "Do's" and "Don'ts" from the nation's leading experts in child nutrition and health.

Do

- *Make breakfast the most important meal of the day.* This should be true for the entire family. No matter how young your child is, she needs to start her day out right. Studies from the National Center for Nutrition and Dietetics indicate that:
  - * Children who eat breakfast are more alert. Missing breakfast decreases attention span and ability to concentrate.
  - * Without breakfast, it's hard for children to eat enough throughout the day to obtain the nutrition they need to grow, learn, play, and stay healthy. They generally don't stay at the table long enough at other meals to make up for the lost calories, vitamins, and minerals missed at breakfast.
  - * Eating breakfast provides "brain food." School-age children perform better on tests and miss less school when they eat a morning meal.

  If you begin a breakfast routine during the early years, you'll be more likely to keep it in later years. Breakfast doesn't have to be elaborate, but it should contain a variety of grains, fruit or fruit juice, vegetables, and a dairy product. Here are some good, easy-to-prepare choices for toddlers and older children:

 * fruit with a yogurt dip
 * yogurt with granola or grain cereal
 * muffins made with bran, oats, or whole wheat and fruit or vegetables (like zucchini or sweet potatoes)
 * English muffin with cheese and tomatoes
 * scrambled egg with onions and green peppers
 * hot or cold cereal made with milk and mixed with dried fruit
 * any healthy "non-breakfast" foods like rice and beans, pizza, baked potato, soup, or chicken

- *Be a role model.* Small children love to imitate, so they will be more inclined to try a food they see you eating. This means building your family's diet around whole grains, fruits, and vegetables and preparing them in a low-fat, low-sugar, low-sodium way. (Check cookbook references in the Resources section at the end of the chapter.)
- *Allow your child to tell you when she's full and when she's hungry.* Teaching your child to listen to her body's cues is a loving act, because in the long run she'll learn to respect her body and use food in the proper way, as nourishment. People who are not taught how to do this can develop unhealthy eating habits later in life, like eating when full—which, obviously, can lead to obesity—or equating feeling full with being loved.
- *Be patient.* Feeding small children can be especially trying; one meal can drag on and on as you try to figure out how to get food into your child's mouth (and off the floors and walls!). Many parents complain about the amount of mess their kids make when they eat, but these messes are an important part of learning and accepting new foods and tastes. If you watch a baby try a new food, she examines it like it's something from outer space—touching, squishing, smearing, tasting, smelling, and then eating it—maybe. As they get older, children tend to develop eating quirks, like having only one food on their plate at a time or getting mad if foods "touch" on the plate. Learn to respect these quirks as you would any other idiosyncrasy. And if your child isn't eating a variety of foods, don't panic. It takes up to fifteen introductions until some kids acquire a taste for certain foods. As with adults, children have to learn to like different foods, and their tastes change over time. (Read more about introducing new foods on p. 167.)

- *Use mealtime to bond.* Mealtime should be a social time for the family. Try not to get in the habit of watching TV during dinner—which research shows we do more than any other ethnic group. Use meals as a time to talk and enjoy each other's company. Studies show that children from families that eat together several times a week perform better in school and are less likely to take drugs.

Don't

- *Struggle with your child over food.* Avoiding food struggles is key to getting your child to eat well. Here are two important steps to take:
  - Put yourself in his shoes. Imagine relying on someone else to feed you. How would it feel to have someone force you to eat something that doesn't taste good to you, or stuff you when you feel full? Respect your child's desire to decide for himself what and how much goes in his mouth. And don't worry, your child will not starve, though he may eat lightly or miss a meal every once in a while.
  - Teach him to eat by himself. Feeding your child finger foods and teaching him to eat with a spoon as early as possible—between nine and eighteen months—will help him achieve the independence he craves. Once he learns, let him take full control of his eating, regardless of whether or not you think he's eating enough.
- *Offer food rewards.* Starting on the slippery slope of bribing your child to eat what's "good" for him so he may be rewarded with what's "bad" for him will eventually come back to haunt you. Not only will he learn that desserts are more valued than dinner, but that he gets to eat sweets or chips if he's good. Think of all foods as equal as long as he's eating a balanced diet and growing at a normal rate. Some parents have done away with the idea of dessert all together, and instead serve one sweet but nutritious serving of fruit or a muffin with dinner.

Got Milk? Baby's First Year

During the first year, babies grow and change more than they do in any other year of their lives. To supplement the enormous amount of energy it takes to learn and grow, they need to consume an extraordinary amount of food, beginning with breast milk and/or formula and working up to cereals, fruits, vegetables, and, if you choose, meats. This section will examine the latest research into feeding your child during her first year.

Breast-Feeding: Why You Should Do It

For some of us, breast-feeding isn't a given. Over the past fifty years there have been conflicting recommendations about whether breast milk is best for newborns. "Space age" technology in the 1950s led many physicians to misinform mothers that fortified feeding formulas were actually better than breast milk. And today, manufacturers of formula still try to make it easy for women to begin using formula, as anyone who's left the maternity ward with plenty of free samples knows. Among some African-American mothers, being able to afford formula is considered a status symbol and a move away from "backward" or "country" ways.

However, none of these reasons in *any way* outweighs the tremendous benefits of breast milk to babies. Studies over the last couple of decades have just begun to list the good stuff in breast milk that is not found in formula or any other food. Experts have found:

- Children who were breast-fed have higher IQs.
- Breast milk boosts babies' immune systems, protecting them against illnesses even after they stop nursing.
- Mothers who breast-feed have a reduced risk of breast cancer, especially after nursing for one cumulative year (which means nursing, for example, six months with one baby and six with another).
- Breast-feeding strengthens the bond between mother and baby.
- Breast-feeding helps mothers lose weight more quickly.
- The hormones secreted during breast-feeding calm mothers.
- Breast-feeding helps establish healthy weight gain in babies and discourages a future tendency toward obesity.
- Breast-feeding is free, breast milk requires no warming, and you can breast-feed anywhere, anytime.

In short, breast milk is the food nature intended for babies to have because it provides what they need nutritionally and biologically. Even with all of this evidence, many women will still decide not to nurse their babies for the following reasons:

- They or their partners believe breasts are too sexual to use for breast-feeding.
- They don't want to be "tied down" to their babies.
- They tried and it didn't "work out."
- They think it hurts.

- They're afraid they don't have enough milk.
- Their breasts feel too big.

Unfortunately, our culture has eroticized breasts to such a degree that many women aren't able to enjoy nursing without feeling embarrassed. By demanding privacy and giving breast-feeding a chance for at least two weeks, most shy mothers will come to see how much they enjoy it.

This is also true of mothers who fear being "trapped" by nursing. A remedy for this is to begin pumping breast milk and enlisting the support of other family members and friends to help with feedings. Women who feel discouraged about breast-feeding often aren't given enough support from family, medical practitioners, or a lactation (breast-feeding) expert. Ninety-five percent of mothers who want to nurse can, provided they are aided during the first two weeks (see Resources). Finally, breasts full of milk do feel big and heavy (and they leak!), and breast-feeding can be uncomfortable at first. But if you try to find your groove—and think about the benefits to your little one—you will not only get used to breast-feeding, you'll probably also enjoy the experience.

If you decide not to nurse or have found you are one of the few who can't (women with illnesses such as HIV or who are taking certain medications are advised not to breast-feed), you shouldn't feel guilty about your decision. It's better to decide not to nurse your baby and feel comfortable with that decision than to nurse and feel resentful. Your decision will be what suits you and your baby best and will be reflected in the loving relationship you share.

Good Ideas for Breast-Feeding Mothers

1. *Check your positioning.* One of the best ways to make breast-feeding an enjoyable experience is to find a comfortable position for both you and the baby. Hunching, slouching to one side, or twisting baby's body away from her head can lead to tears and sore necks and backs for both of you. If you are not sure you're holding your nursing baby right, ask the doctor or nurses to observe you while you're still in the hospital. You can also check yourself using the illustrations that follow.

If baby doesn't latch on, tickle his chin or cheeks until he opens his mouth. If he latches on improperly (usually he is just sucking on your nipple and doesn't have as much of your areola as possible in his mouth) and has to try again, open his mouth by

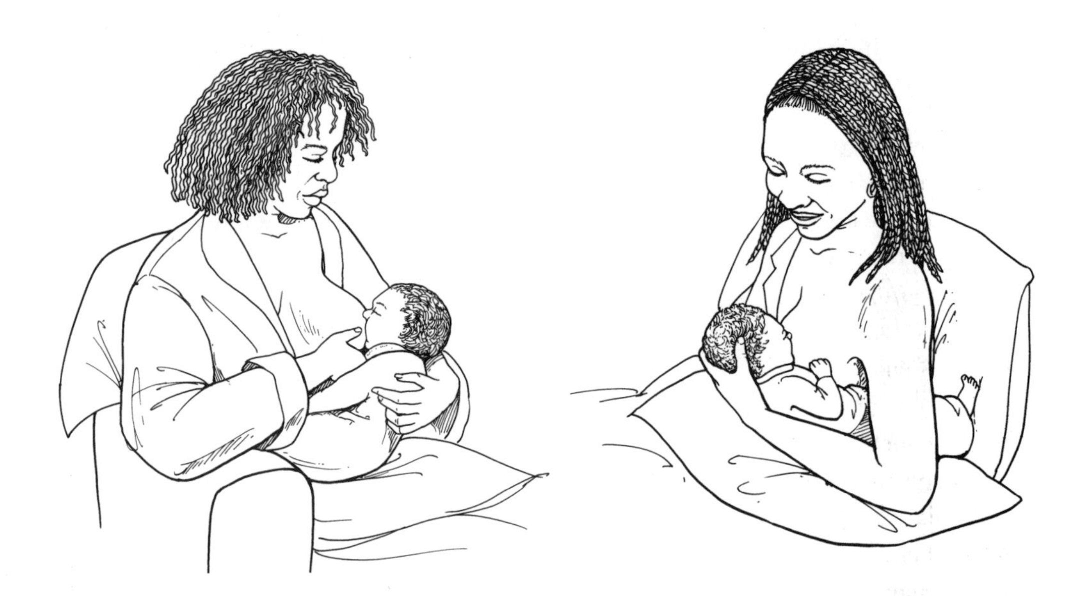

Above, left: Your back should be straight, even if you're sitting up in bed. Use pillows under your elbow, under the baby, and behind your back. You shouldn't feel strained. Your baby should be on his side with his entire body facing you so that his chest faces yours and his head and body are in a line. Hold his head on the top of your forearm, his back with the length of your forearm, and his bottom with your hand so that you are not leaning down and he isn't reaching up to meet your breast. Above, right: The football hold. While seated, place baby under the arm of the breast he will nurse. Hold his head; his body should be parallel to the pillow, feet upward.

To nurse while lying down, lie on your side with your body parallel to your baby's. Your baby should also be on his side facing you. This is a great position for those middle of the night feedings.

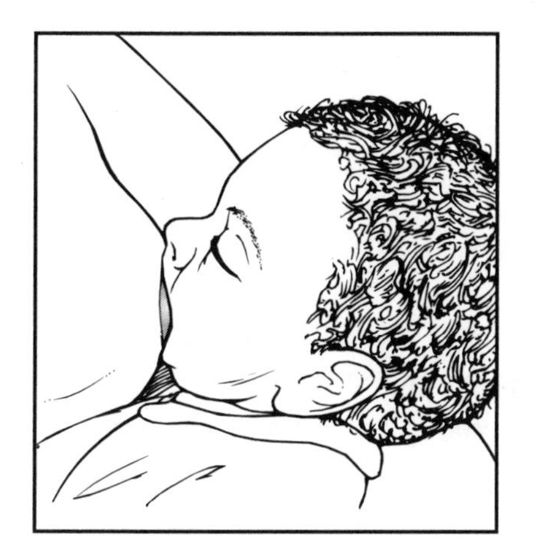

Latching on Correctly

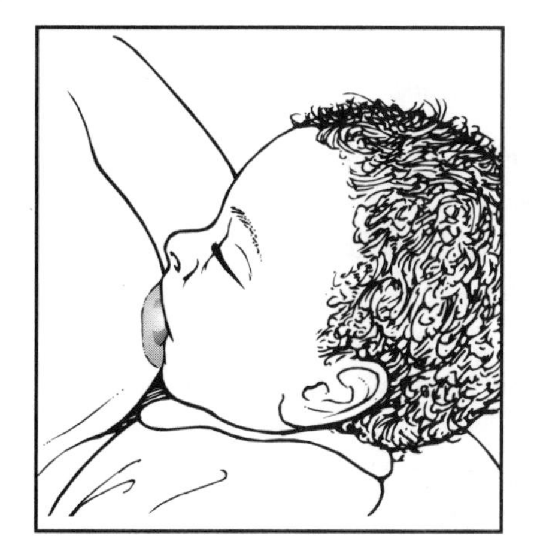

Latching on Incorrectly

With your thumb and forefinger forming a "C" around your areola (not your nipple), offer your breast to your baby by touching her lower lip. When she opens her mouth wide, put your whole areola and nipple in her mouth and pull her toward you, making sure she has your entire areola (the dark area surrounding the nipple) in her mouth. She is properly latched on if you have so much of your breast in her mouth that you think she can't breathe. She's sucking correctly if you can see her tongue below your nipple and hear her swallowing.

gently putting your finger into his mouth and break the suction of his suck. Your positions will change slightly every few weeks as your baby grows and you'll have to adjust by removing the pillows under him or moving his head to a different spot on your arm.

2. *Watch what you eat.* While you were pregnant you had to eat a healthy diet with lots of carbohydrates and protein. The nourishment that you get from continuing to eat these foods will also fortify your milk. However, be aware that what you eat could greatly affect your baby. You may begin to notice her becoming colicky (experiencing irritability or intestinal pain followed by gas), gassy, or rejecting your milk after you eat certain foods. Foods that you may want to avoid or greatly restrict are:

*Any foods you or her father are allergic to

*Any spicy foods, such as those containing hot pepper or garlic

"I liked to look down at Kali, happily sucking away, and think 'She's so healthy because of me.' " **—Linda's Story**

Kali came a month early and was very small, only 4 lbs., 13 oz. But early on, she was ready to make up for lost time: She was hungry all the time. The doctor encouraged me to feed her on demand, and so did my mother, my partner, and all of our friends. Their mantra was "She's got to eat!"

On demand meant every hour or two, even in the middle of the night. Kali would whimper softly and move her lips when she was hungry; she looked like a famine victim begging for sustenance. I felt for her, but eventually, I started to feel for me. During the day, I was the "milk slave," and it was no party waking up every hour or two during the night. (There was really no question that Kali would sleep in bed next to me; I was not getting out of the bed four or five times a night!) Plus, because she was feeding so often, my breasts hurt—I mean really hurt, especially when she first latched on. At one point, they were so raw and sore that the nipples bled.

Although I wholeheartedly believe in the benefits of breast-feeding, I thought seriously about giving it up. Maybe I could pump the milk and mix it with formula. Maybe I should just stop altogether. But then I gave myself a kick in the behind, remembering how important breast milk is for babies. I steeled myself against the pain. Each time she latched on, I would let out a soft yelp and then count; usually by the time I got to five, the worst of the pain had subsided.

After about two months, Kali was getting bigger and bigger, so she didn't need to be fed so often. And that helped my breasts heal. Breast-feeding stopped hurting; in fact, I began to enjoy it. I liked to look down at Kali, happily sucking away, and think "She's so healthy because of me." When it came time to wean Kali, I was surprised at the sense of loss I felt. For about a month after she switched over to formula, I missed the intimacy we had developed. Once I returned to work and dove back into my life the feeling subsided, but I will never forget that special time we shared.

*Vegetables that can cause gas, such as broccoli, cauliflower, cabbage, and brussels sprouts

*Cow's milk and milk products if you are allergic to milk protein

*Foods containing caffeine, such as coffee (although some practitioners agree that one cup a day is fine as long as you don't see any reaction from your baby, such as increased crying or inability to sleep), chocolate, and colas

*Excess alcohol (modest amounts such as one small glass of wine or beer are OK once in a while)

Of course, you should abstain from smoking cigarettes and taking any illegal drugs while you're breast-feeding. If you must take any over-the-counter or prescription drugs while nursing, discuss their safety with your health care provider.

3. *Make sure baby's getting enough milk—without worrying yourself to death.* It's difficult to measure the amount of milk breast-fed babies consume, so you may not be sure whether your baby is getting enough to eat. Some mothers panic, and are tempted to supplement breast milk with formula—though in most cases that's not necessary. If you answer yes to the following questions, you can be assured that your baby is eating well:

*Is she growing at a normal, healthy rate according to her pediatrician?

*Is she nursing frequently (ten to twelve times a day for a newborn, five to eight times for a three-month-old)?

*Does she have several wet, pale yellow diapers (generally ten times a day for a newborn)?

*Does she have regular bowel movements (normally eight to ten times a day in a newborn)?

*Does she look and act healthy and alert?

4. *Let the sun shine.* Breast milk is known to have low levels of vitamin D. And recent reports show that African-American babies who are breast-fed are more likely than others to suffer from problems related to lack of the vitamin. To help, make sure your child is exposed to the sun; twenty minutes per day of exposure on the face helps fight the problem.

5. *Pump and store.* Since most African-American mothers return to work soon after giving birth, pumping and storing breast milk is vital to continuing to breast-feed. Going back to work will require you to combine breast-feeding with giving baby breast milk out of a bottle, a routine you'll need to set up while you're still at home. To teach the baby to take a bottle:

*Begin offering breast milk in a bottle early, after the first few weeks of birth. Experiment with different types of nipples.

*Wait until the baby is hungry, but not starving, or she may be overwhelmed with frustration. Be encouraging, gentle, and ready to try again if she refuses.

*Have someone else give the baby the bottle. When she smells you and your milk but is offered a bottle, she will refuse it because she prefers Mom's breast.

*Once she's taking the bottle, give it to her at the same time every day, preferably the time of day you will be away.

*Bring your baby's caretaker up to speed about your feeding routine when the time comes.

While you are preparing your baby for bottle feedings, you'll also be pumping and storing your milk. When you do leave your baby for work during the day, pumping your milk can help you feel connected with him and can make the separation less traumatic. Here are some pumping tips to follow:

*Get support. When looking for a child care provider, be sure to find someone who supports your decision to breast-feed and takes the care to properly handle your expressed milk. It's best to overlap the end of your maternity leave with your new child care routine for at least a few days.

*Choose a pump that fits your budget and needs. Many working mothers rent high-end pumps used at hospitals from hospitals, hospital supply stores, or good pharmacies. Medela and Ameda, two of the more popular brands, rent from between $30 and $80 a month (much cheaper than purchasing them for a starting price of $1,000). They are comfortable, allow you to empty both breasts at once, and are affordable if used only for a short period. The downside: These machines are heavy and require an electrical outlet. Some women may prefer electric double pumps, which are less powerful than professional-grade pumps and cost about $280. Two brands to consider: Medela Pump In Style and White River 9050. You can also choose cheaper battery or electrical pumps, which are compact, inexpensive, and can come with two pumps. They run from $35 to $200. Look for Evenflo's Soft Touch Ultra and Medela's Mini Electric. However, they are slower than the higher-grade models mentioned above and can hurt during suctioning. The least expensive option: A manual pump, such as the Comfort Plus Kaneson Pump and the White River Breast Pump Kit, can be purchased for about $12 to $30. However, though they are lightweight and cheap, they are awkward, uncomfortable, and time consuming to use, better for relieving milk congestion than for collecting milk for bottle feeding. You can also express milk by hand without a pump.

**To pump, pick a private place*—office, bathroom, your car. Put up a picture of your baby to help the milk flow, and pump into a sterile bottle (boiled or washed in a dishwasher) that your baby will drink from later. While pumping, massage your breasts to be sure all the ducts empty. Clothes for nursing mothers or blouses that button in the front make pumping easier.

**Store your milk.* Once you have pumped, put a tight cap on the bottle and put it in a disposable bottle bag, write the date on the bottle or bag, and store the milk in a refrigerator or cooler if you aren't going to use it within one hour. Breast milk will keep in the refrigerator for forty-eight hours and in the freezer for two weeks.

**Keep milk at the back of the refrigerator where it's coldest.* When thawing milk, put it in the refrigerator or under hot running water. Do not thaw milk in the microwave or at room temperature. Never add fresh milk to an already used bottle, and don't refreeze thawed milk. If your baby doesn't finish all the milk in one feeding, discard it.

**Call for help and support.* If you are experiencing pain or difficulty, most problems can be handled easily and quickly with proper support, so always have your health care practitioner's number handy. Most pediatricians and obstetricians should be able to refer you to a lactation consultant or lactation expert in your area. Minor problems such as blocked ducts and nipple soreness should be addressed early so they don't lead to bigger problems later. A breast-feeding support group such as La Leche League (800-LA-LECHE) can also be a great source of information and put you in touch with other working and nursing mothers.

Weaning When It's Time

Although most pediatricians believe one year of breast-feeding is optimal, there is no set time when you should wean. You should try to breast-feed for at least six weeks to provide your baby with important nutrients and immune-boosting nourishment that has long lasting benefits. When it's time to quit nursing, you will know. Most mothers find that they begin weaning for several reasons:

- The baby loses interest in nursing, which usually happens as she begins to be mobile and more interested in her surroundings.
- The mother has to return to work and finds it too impractical to continue to pump and nurse.
- The mother loses interest in breast-feeding or feels it's time to quit. This can also be due to baby teething and biting while nursing.

It's normal to have mixed feelings about weaning. Some mothers are sad for the end of their child's infancy and the loss of such a close bond. Others are relieved and excited to see their children growing up and moving on to solid foods. When the time seems right for you and your baby to wean, here are some suggestions to make the transition easier:

- *Begin by substituting a bottle for one breast-feeding session a day.* Every week or so drop one feeding per day. If he's not hungry, think of another cuddly activity to do together, such as reading.
- *If possible, wean gradually so that your breast milk production slows down with the loss of each feeding.* This will help reduce pain from engorgement. Gradual weaning can take a few weeks, or longer depending on how long you hold on to the last feeding (generally the evening or nighttime feeding).
- *Help your baby get over the loss of a source of comfort by giving her another.* A favorite blanket, toy, or pillow can be a new calmer. Some babies take new interest in their thumbs or pacifiers or other habits like touching their hair. Encourage her to relax herself.

A Formula for Formula

Next to breast milk, infant formula is one of the most nutritious meals for babies. Though it doesn't contain the antibodies or provide the other hormonal benefits, iron-fortified formula is packed with vitamins and minerals similar to those in breast milk. Formula is really only useful during the first year, after which time your baby's growth slows considerably.

Finding a formula that suits your baby will probably require trial and error. You should ask your child's health care provider for advice and request samples of both dairy and soy formulas. Because some children are either allergic to dairy products or have lactose intolerance (which is more common among African-American chil-

CAUTION: Regular cow's milk is not a suitable food for children under one year of age. It is very difficult for babies to digest and doesn't contain adequate vitamins and minerals (such as iron) for them.

dren), soy often becomes the only choice, though it's somewhat harder to digest. (See section on food allergies, p. 169.) Even if you are breast-feeding, you may want to give your child formula every once in a while to get him used to it in anticipation of weaning, if you plan to do so before baby's first year. Be sure to discuss formula with your child's pediatrician if you are a nursing mother.

Since your baby is drinking from a bottle, it is much easier to know if she's getting enough formula. You can also monitor her bowel movements (look for eight to ten per day in a newborn), along with six wet diapers per day and healthy weight gain.

Introducing Other Foods

Most experts advise against giving solids before the age of four months, because babies cannot chew, swallow, or digest these foods well, and early introduction can lead to food allergies. The following is a chart from the American Dietetic Association to help you determine which foods are best to introduce and when:

AGE	FOOD
0–4 months	breast milk or iron-fortified formula
4–6 months	iron-fortified infant cereal
	strained vegetables
	strained fruits
6–9 months	fruit juice high in vitamin C
	strained meats
	plain toast or teething biscuit
9–12 months	chopped vegetables
	chopped fruit
	chopped meats
	bread and bread products

Many of us struggle between wanting to give our children the best and wanting to give them our time, which means that while some of us lovingly labor to provide home-cooked baby food, others prefer the convenience of food from a jar. Only you can decide where to compromise, but most children are satisfied with store-bought foods. However, be sure to read the labels carefully to avoid fillers such as tapioca or modified food starch. Avoid any ingredients you wouldn't add yourself, like sugar or salt. Though you may have to pay a little more, consider buying organic, pesticide-free baby food, which is free of chemical contaminants.

When your child begins eating food other than milk, let him enjoy the pleasures of eating. Let him sample different textures and smells; save learning table manners for when he's older, and simply use mealtime as a way to be with and learn from his family. There are a few easy steps to safely introduce your baby to solids:

- *Take it slow.* The first feedings should be at times when you can relax and spend some time with your child—usually the mornings or evenings.
- *Start with milk.* Offer the baby a few ounces of breast milk or formula so she isn't so ravenous, then try giving her a few small spoonfuls of cereal. If she doesn't eat much, give her a bottle for the rest of her meal.
- *Be careful to avoid choking.* A baby's sucking motion is still stronger than swallowing, and he can easily choke on a little bit of food. Put the food on a spoon and place it just in front of his teeth so he can taste it, suck it off if he likes it, or close his mouth if he doesn't. And don't be tempted to put cereal or other solids in a bottle. This can cause your baby to choke, because the motion used to suck milk from the bottle is different from that needed to eat even very diluted cereal. Babies need to learn how to develop their chewing and swallowing skills, so save the bottles for milk.
- *Introduce two to three new foods a week, but wait a few days between each food.* Keep track of what foods your baby likes, dislikes, or is allergic to. (See section on food allergies, p. 169.) Begin with vegetables like peas or carrots and then move to fruits. (Since children generally prefer sweet foods, it's better to let them develop a taste for vegetables before fruit.)
- *As your baby gets older, make foods interesting.* When he has graduated from rice cereal, try barley or rice cereal with bananas. As he's able to gum foods like bananas, cut them into tiny, bite-size pieces so he can develop his hand-

eye coordination and grasping skills. Babies love a challenge, so let him try drinking juice from a training cup at age nine to twelve months.

- *Prepare for a big mess.* Your baby will undoubtedly spend most of his meals touching, mashing, spreading, flinging, and smelling the food rather than actually eating it, because that's how babies learn and develop eating skills. Have bibs, splat mats (floor coverings that go under the high chair and can be wiped clean), and lots of washcloths, dishrags, and paper towels on hand to clean afterward. Experienced parents have mealtime just before bathtime.

Your baby should be able to sit up by six months, so investing in a high chair or infant booster seat is a must. It will keep him facing front and seated upright, a safe eating position.

Is Your Child Food Sensitive?

Food allergies are a common, often undiagnosed problem among children. If a child is allergic, her immune system perceives the offending food as a foreign body. Her body reacts as if she were fighting off a cold, causing symptoms to occur in her breathing, skin, digestive tract, or behavior. Here are some signs that your child might have a food allergy:

- *Breathing:* runny or stuffy nose, sneezing, wheezing, coughing, watery eyes after eating certain foods
- *Skin:* hives, dark circles under the eyes, puffy eyes, swollen lips, swollen or itchy hands and feet, small red bumpy rash especially on the face, swelling around the mouth
- *Digestive:* mucous diarrhea, constipation, vomiting, more spit-up than usual, bloated intestines, gas, diaper rash around the anus
- *Behavior:* crankiness, hyperactivity, increased crying or anxiety, nighttime wakings
- *Other symptoms:* headache, muscle and joint aches

In general, the easiest way to determine if your child has an intolerance or allergy is to keep track of what food she's eaten (a food diary is the best way because we all have faulty memories) along with how she reacts to it, and begin eliminating those foods that are problematic. Most children outgrow food allergies. Reintroduce those foods only after a four- to six-month break and watch for signs of allergy. If it's still a

Mealtime Musts for Parents

Here are a handful of suggestions that will protect your child from getting sick or choking:

- ***Always wash your hands with soap before a feeding.*** **This will cut down on the amount of bacteria he is exposed to.**
- ***Clean jars and can openers before serving baby's food.***
- ***Don't feed baby from the jar.*** **Put one serving in a bowl at a time with a separate spoon than the one you're feeding with. Saliva carries bacteria that will spoil the food more quickly, so throw away any uneaten portion rather than putting it back in the jar.**
- ***Don't keep open jars of food for more than two to three days.***
- ***Wash or peel all fruit and vegetables.*** **Even if you buy organic produce, other contaminants can be in the soil, so wash and brush every time.**
- ***Never serve your baby sushi or any other raw fish, which can contain parasites and bacteria.***
- ***Avoid stringy, gooey, pasty, or chunky foods.*** **Babies can easily choke on celery, peanut butter, and raw carrots.**
- ***Stay away from grapes, raisins, olives, hard candy, and nuts.*** **These are all the size of a baby's windpipe and big choking hazards. Either cut these foods lengthwise and crosswise into very small pieces or avoid them until your baby can handle them with a bigger windpipe and molars.**
- ***The American Academy of Pediatrics recommends buying jarred rather than fresh beets, turnips, carrots, and collard greens during your baby's first year.*** **In certain parts of the country, these fresh vegetables contain dangerously high levels of nitrates, which can cause anemia in infants. Baby food producers screen for this problem to make these vegetables safe to eat.**

problem, repeat the cycle. Because allergies can be hereditary, consider which foods you or your partner are sensitive to and introduce those with a cautious eye.

Note: Serious food allergies, including allergies to common foods like peanuts and shellfish, can be life-threatening even in small doses. People with a history of food allergies can have a severe reaction known as anaphylactic shock, in which the body reacts to an allergen with swollen airways and blood vessels. If your child has difficulty breathing, difficulty swallowing, or shows other severe reactions (vomiting, abdominal pain, increased pulse rate) within minutes of eating, get emergency help immediately by calling 911 or going to a hospital emergency room.

Food for the "High-Stepping" Years: Toddlers

Your baby has had her first birthday, and just as you're getting used to her eating habits and preferences, everything changes. For one, most babies are walking by this age, or "toddling," and though they're expending a lot of energy exploring new territory, their growth slows tremendously compared to the first year, and so do their appetites. You may notice your child eating less than you'd like and, as she grows more independent and is able to communicate more clearly, becoming more picky about food than when she was younger.

What Should Toddlers Eat?

What toddlers should eat and what toddlers want to eat are two completely different things. As they go out on foot into the world, opening drawers or inspecting grass, toddlers find it comforting to maintain a sense of security and familiarity through routines. At this point most parents understand the importance of scheduling regular mealtimes and snack times, which helps regulate children's lives and add to their sense of stability.

Kids, too, try to maintain their own sense of regularity, often by doing the same thing over and over and over—and this rings true at mealtime. Your child may think: "It's breakfast, so I'll have cereal just like I did yesterday and the day before." Though it may be comforting for the child, eating the same foods day in and day out isn't a nutritionally sound idea. To get around your child's food jag, try these suggestions:

- Offer a choice of two new foods at mealtime, when kids are hungry.
- Share some of your food with your kids as a way to introduce a new food.
- Make a new food look fun by cutting it into interesting shapes (for a sandwich), adding a little food coloring (to a pasta dish), or making a smiley face (with beans and cheese on a tortilla, for example).
- Have a stuffed animal friend try some new food first and say how good it is.

Eventually, as with adults, children crave certain foods until they lose interest

Foods to Watch Out For

These foods can trigger allergies: milk and dairy products, eggs, corn, chocolate, wheat, fish and shellfish, nuts and peanuts, berries, citrus fruits.

If your child has allergies, beware when serving prepared food or eating out, as many products contain these ingredients. For example, whey and other dairy products are found in many packaged foods, like gravies, margarine, and breads.

Another problem which causes intestinal problems such as gas or diarrhea is called lactose intolerance. This is not an allergy but is caused by the body's inability to digest the sugar in milk-lactose. Children often develop lactose intolerance as they grow older and get gas or diarrhea after drinking milk. Lactose intolerance is more common as people get older, and it affects as many as 75 percent of African-American adults. However, you don't have to eliminate dairy from your child's diet if he is lactose intolerant. According to experts, most children can be helped by drinking less cow's milk, using soy or rice milk, or simply switching to lactose-free milk. "Many parents will find that their children may not be able to digest large quantities of milk, but can handle some on their cereal or with a meal, or eat cheese and yogurt without a problem," says Sheah Rarback, MSRD, director of nutrition at Mailman's Center for Child Development in Miami.

and another takes its place. Our job is to introduce them to as many new foods as possible so they can feel "at home" with them and will be less likely to reject them just because they're new and different. Don't forget: Research shows that it can take up to fifteen introductions of one food before a child will eat it, so be patient.

As long as your toddler eats a balanced diet, he can keep his food preferences and hopefully add to them. A balanced diet for kids is similar to the food pyramid for adults.

Don't try to make sure your child gets exactly the right amount of each food group every day. Instead, try to look at her meals on a weekly basis. You will probably discover that vegetables aren't a big favorite at this age, even if she ate them in her first year. This is very typical of a toddler's taste buds. Some experts believe toddlers can do just fine drinking one pint of milk, two ounces of meat or one egg (vegetarians can substitute protein-rich meat substitutes or tofu), one ounce of juice or a piece of fruit, and a vitamin supplement to make up for the vegetables. Eventually, during the preschool years, kids bring vegetables back into their daily repertoire.

How Much Food Is Enough?

After the first year, many pediatricians note parents complain that their toddlers aren't eating enough. If you're worried about how much your toddler is eating, keep these points in mind:

- *Toddlers need less food than they did their first year:* one tablespoon per number of years is a serving, so that one serving of fruit for a two-year-old would be two tablespoons.
- *Toddlers are control freaks.* So much of being a toddler is learning how to be

The Beef with Meat

Many of us have changed our diets drastically compared to the way we ate as children. Some of us have cut meat out altogether. Unlike back in the days when breakfast was two eggs over easy with a side of bacon and grits, strict vegetarians are more likely to serve their children a bowl of oatmeal and raisins or other nonanimal substitutes. Vegetarians have the advantage of lowered cholesterol and saturated fat compared to the average meat eater, and children with a family history of heart disease can benefit from a meat-free diet.

Whether you decide to eliminate red meat, all animal meat and fish, or all animal products including dairy and eggs, discuss your decision with your child's primary care provider. She may put your child on vitamin supplements and suggest other ways for him to eat enough vitamin B-12, protein, and iron. Children have significant nutritional needs, so if you go the meat-free route, make sure that your child is receiving an adequate amount of calories, protein, vitamins, and minerals.

Whatever diet you choose, make sure your child has enough of the following:

- ***Calcium.* Sources include dairy products, fortified soy or rice milk, tofu, dark green leafy vegetables (spinach, kale, broccoli), almonds, oatmeal.**
- ***Iron.* Sources include enriched breads and cereals, seeds, nuts, raisins, prune juice, tofu, miso, green leafy vegetables, blackstrap molasses.**
- ***Protein.* Combining any of the following will provide your child with a complete protein: nuts and beans, beans and grains, grains and milk products, nuts and milk products, nuts and grains, and beans and milk products. Beans include black beans, black-eyed peas, chick peas, lentils, soybeans, and peanuts. Nuts include pumpkin seeds, sunflower seeds, and sesame seeds. Grains include wheat, oats, rice, and cornmeal. Milk products include milk, cheese, or yogurt.**

independent, and food is perhaps the easiest way for toddlers to assert themselves. Don't take it personally if your child doesn't want to eat the foods you choose. And don't you be a control freak, too—or mealtime won't be a very pleasant experience. Rejecting some foods and embracing others is normal and necessary behavior for your child, who is testing limits and learning to care for himself.

- *Toddlers are quirky.* Not only do they go on one-food binges, they also go through the "no" phase that irritates parents so much. "No" is one of the most powerful words in our language, a fact a toddler soon figures out. She may get so hung up on "no" that she turns down something she actually wants, or asks for something else only to refuse it. This is aggravating but normal behavior

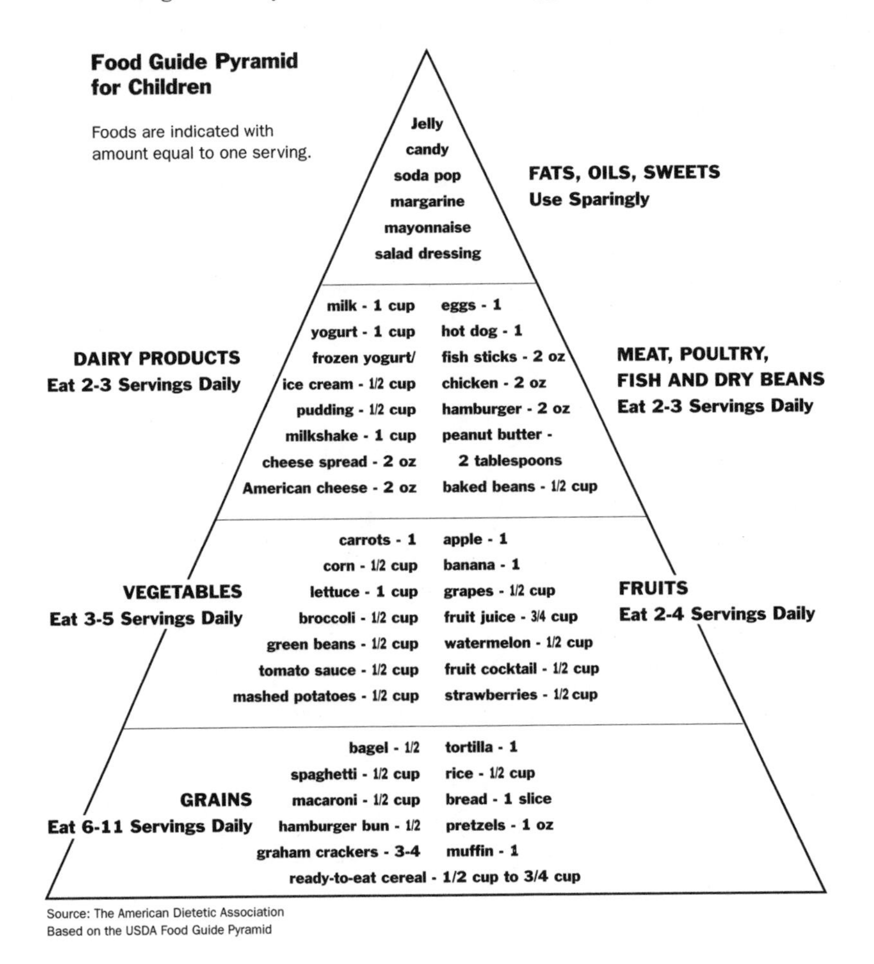

Source: The American Dietetic Association
Based on the USDA Food Guide Pyramid

and the easiest way to handle it is to offer alternatives, set limits on how many foods you offer in one sitting, and leave her alone. No healthy child ever starved herself voluntarily, so have faith that when she's hungry, she'll eat.

Don't Let Them Eat Cake? What You Need to Know About Sugar

Our children learn from our habits. So when they see us grab a candy bar instead of fruit to snack on, have our meals with soda instead of juice or water, or eat high-sugar cereal instead of whole-grain they, too, learn to crave sugar. Since obesity is a major health risk for black children (more than 25 percent of black children are obese), they will greatly benefit from eating less sugar.

Many health-conscious parents try to avoid using cane sugar at all and have switched to honey (but not for babies less than a year old because it is associated with botulism) and maple syrup, which have trace amounts of vitamins and minerals but are still high in calories, and blackstrap molasses, which is high in iron, potassium and calcium. These can be used in cereal, for baking, and in pancakes, but it's even better to get your child to appreciate the natural taste of food without sweeteners and to reach for fruit instead of sweets when his cravings hit.

To kick the sugar habit before it starts, follow these tips:

- *Look out for sugar.* When shopping for food, be sure to read labels. If sugar is one of the first ingredients on the package, the product is likely to be very high in calories and very low in nutrition. Food manufacturers have found ways to sweeten food without using cane sugar, so look out for these ingredients and try to avoid them where possible: corn syrup, sucrose, dextrose, fructose, sorbitol, and glucose.

  Don't feed your child any artificial sweeteners such as saccharin and aspartame, because of the controversy surrounding the effects of these products on humans. While the evidence is still inconclusive, some consumer advocates fear these sweeteners contain cancer-causing agents.
- *Learn how sugar affects your child.* The controversy over sugar's effect on children has both researchers and parents butting heads. While many parents can vouch for the change in behavior when their children eat sweets—running laps around the living room and then crashing into fits of inconsolable crying—some in the medical community continue to insist that there are no

"Though she is a picky eater, Briana is a healthy girl."
—Ruth Battle, mother of Briana, age 2; Englewood, New Jersey

At two years old, Briana is a very picky eater. She only eats a couple of foods, and doesn't like to try anything new. Sometimes, after two or three weeks of prodding, I can get her to try something new. And though I prefer that she eats three solid meals per day, she likes to snack.

I learned the hard way that it's a mistake to try to make Briana sit at the table until she finishes eating. She won't eat at all; she ends up crying and I end up with a mess. So I've made adjustments. I play airplane with her, or I take a bite of the food and say, "Oh, this is so good." If I do these things, she'll eat. The doctor also told me that it's OK to give her snacks throughout the day, so I do.

Though she is a picky eater, Briana is a healthy girl. And a big girl: She weighs 37 pounds. Some people say she's even too fat for her age, but I think she's fine. Besides, I talked to my sister about Briana's eating, and she reminded me that at Briana's age, I was a picky eater, too!

detectable changes in normal kids or kids with hyperactivity after they've eaten sugar. Given the contradictory evidence, parents are at a loss whether to let their children eat sugar or not and how much. But regardless of what research is able to prove, if you know how certain foods like sugar affect your child, take note and try to avoid them.

Easier Eating: Preschoolers

While they may still be somewhat picky, preschoolers are pretty low-maintenance eaters. They can wield a fork as well as adults and they may even be able to serve themselves a cold breakfast. Preschoolers' appetites also tend to resemble ours, with days of heavy eating alternated with light eating. Overall, they're natural-born cooks and great conversationalists at the dinner table.

Eating Like the Rest of Us

By this age meals are basically matter-of-fact. Unless you continue to make an issue of it, your preschooler is no longer interested in using food to show her

When to Throttle the Bottle

The American Academy of Pediatric Dentistry advises that children be off the bottle by their first birthday for two reasons. First, drinking from a bottle requires a sucking motion, which—over time—can cause front teeth to protrude. (Think about the cost of braces . . .) Second, many parents give their children bottles just before bed, which can give a child cavities. The natural sugars in milk, which are highly corrosive to teeth, settle into the crevices of the teeth throughout the night and can cause decay. Some experienced parents swear that taking a bottle away during a child's first year is much easier than trying to take it away later because of a child's strong attachment to sucking on the bottle for comfort.

Quitting the bottle is easier for some kids than others. If this is true for your toddler, then switching to a "sippy" cup full of milk at mealtimes or for a snack won't be a problem. However, most children hang on to their bottles well past the first year because of what the bottle means to them. It is a soother. The milk and sucking remind them of being close to Mommy, being nourished, and going to sleep.

Taking the bottle away without warning isn't a good idea. Instead, here are some strategies to ease away the bottle:

- *Brush your child's teeth at least twice a day, especially just before bed.*
- *Limit bottles to just before mealtimes or with meals.* Introduce milk in a cup and offer it several times a day with meals or when he might normally get the bottle. If he protests too much, put it away. Ideally, eliminate the number of bottles he has per day so that he gets down to just one. This may take several weeks, during which time you should keep offering milk in a cup. (During this process, be careful not to shortchange him: Your child should have 16 to 32 ounces of milk a day to meet his calcium requirements.)
- *Let him wean himself off the last bottle.* If you and your child are having trouble stopping the bottle, know that by the time most kids reach three, peer pressure can be enough to convince them that the bottle isn't cool. If not, you can try the "gold star" approach: The two of you set up a week to stop, and each day that passes that he doesn't take a bottle, he gets a gold star or some other reward. Books such as Sesame Street's *Bye Bye, Bottle* are a great way to help kids make the transition from bottle to cup. If you feel he's hanging on to his bottle longer than you'd like, discuss it with his health care provider. But rest assured: He won't go off to college with a bottle in his suitcase.

independence. She's independent in so many other ways that eating becomes a way to address hunger, not limits. And her physical development has enabled her to feed herself with a spoon or fork and hold a cup steadily, so getting the food to her mouth isn't the challenge it once was.

Nonetheless, your preschooler's food preferences might not have changed a great deal from when she was a toddler. Many parents still agonize over ways to vary their children's diets. Exposure to new foods from outside influences are the best remedy to this dilemma.

Toddlers and preschoolers love to help out in the kitchen.

These outside influences are most profound when your child spends time away from home. Day care and preschool gives children an opportunity to be around other children with their own particular food favorites. As making friends becomes more important to preschoolers, so will the desire to please and fit in, the beginning of peer pressure. Seeing her best friend munch on an apple can cause a child who usually turns up her nose at them to suddenly beg you to add apples to her lunch.

But peer pressure works both ways. Some parents may not be as health conscious as you and may allow their children to eat a lunch of chips and soda. If your child begins asking for foods that you want to limit, talk to her about why eating those foods may taste good but give her less energy than other foods that taste good, too. Then ask her to pick out a food she thinks would be better to eat for lunch. It can be fun to allow her to go to the supermarket with you and pick out food you can both agree on.

Television advertising also influences what kids want to eat. These ads have a way of making junk food look delicious and exciting to eat, and manufacturers are hoping that your child will hound you until you give in. This is a good argument for not watching TV while eating a meal and for sitting with your child when she's watching TV. Try to explain that the children in the commercials are acting and that eating cereal won't make them magical, or more popular, or turn them into superheroes. (See Chapter 11 on TV viewing.)

"I spend less time worrying about how much Miles eats and more about how to give him a balanced meal." **—ALLISON'S STORY**

Miles was an early walker, not quite nine months when he took his first steps. During this time he was growing at an incredibly fast rate, and it seemed he gained a pound and an inch every couple of weeks. Needless to say, he ate more than I did some days and was happy to try just about anything we put in front of him.

Then Miles hit one year. His growth didn't stop, of course, but it slowed down considerably. Now he was more interested in exploring cabinets and climbing furniture than he was in eating. The only time he would sit still was if *Sesame Street* came on. I began to notice that if he ate his breakfast during the show, he would usually finish his food. Otherwise, he would get antsy in his high chair or become fickle about what he wanted to eat. "Eggies," he'd say, but when I cooked them and put them on his tray his response was "No, applesauce," and so on until we came back to "eggies," which he had lost his appetite for by then.

I'm not a big fan of television, educational or not, but I found myself letting him watch *Sesame Street* through his breakfast. How convenient . . . for me. I felt satisfied that he had eaten a nutritious breakfast and that his morning nap wouldn't be interrupted by his waking up hungry. But the truth was, I was feeding him food he really didn't want, and I wasn't trusting his ability to determine for himself when he wanted to eat. Realizing my mistake, I started to tell him he could only watch TV *after* his meal.

Now we spend the morning meal together, talking about our plans for the day. While I prepare my coffee, I give him a packet of instant hot cereal and warm milk in a squeeze bottle and let him serve himself. He loves mixing and eating his own creations, and I love having that morning time with him. Even if he doesn't eat all or most of his food at breakfast, I know he'll eat more at lunch. These days I spend less time worrying about how much Miles eats and more about how to give him a balanced meal.

Teaching About Our Culture Through Food

Now that your preschooler is out of his high chair and sitting at the table (even if he's still in a booster seat or sitting on phone books) and is able to carry on a conversation, he can use mealtime to socialize with the rest of the family. Eating together is a wonderful way to help kids understand who they are and where they come from. First, he'll begin to see himself as a member of his family, someone worth listening and talking to. By hearing about other family members and talking about his own

Do Manners Matter?

We are a proud people and expect our children to act accordingly. Disapproving glances from stern relatives can make us feel embarrassed, like we're not giving our children "proper home training." While we can expect our children to follow basic rules from the start, like not throwing food or eating only in the kitchen, it will take some time before they are the models of proper etiquette.

Most preschoolers have learned how to behave at the dinner table from watching your example. Long gone, we hope, are the days when the bowl full of noodles became a hat. By now your child probably knows how to hold a spoon and fork (maybe a knife), drink from a cup, wipe her mouth with a napkin, and not to talk with her mouth full. But while some kids learn table manners easily and can follow them as young as four, others may not master them until six. When introducing rules, explain why you want her to follow them and why it's considered rude not to. But be patient if she can't remember all the rules all the time.

Quick Tips for Eating Out

With small children it's hard to cook three meals a day, every day, and there are days when it's easier to catch a meal on the run. Eating out can be just the answer as long as you do it healthfully. Here are some tips for eating away from home:

- *Pack a bag.* Before you leave, be sure to have diapers and wipes for those who still need them (wipes are always a good item to have with small children even if your child is out of diapers), books, portable toys, and a blanket or stuffed animal. These are good distractions before the food arrives and when she's finished with her meal and you aren't.
- *Plan to go at the right time.* The best time to go out is before she gets too hungry or too sleepy, so try to schedule around her actual mealtimes. Some families find breakfast out more pleasant than dinner, because it's at the beginning of the day rather than the end, when children are apt to lose it.
- *Choose a "child-friendly" restaurant.* This means restaurants that are equipped with high chairs, child-size portions, and experienced staff. Family-style restaurants tend to be casual (tile floors and paper napkins) with quick service, so you won't have to constantly say "the food will be here soon." Ask friends with small children which restaurants in your community are best or consult a guidebook with a section about kids. If you're not sure, call ahead and ask.
- *Know what to expect.* Don't expect her to sit and enjoy the scenery like an adult. And don't use an outing with your child as an opportunity to have a re-

laxing, romantic, or conversation-filled meal, or you will probably be disappointed. Most young kids can hardly sit still at home, and out at a new place with lots of new people, it's almost impossible not to explore. For this reason, eating out is easier with two people, so you can take turns getting up from the table to take little journeys around the restaurant while the other eats.

- ***Get situated.*** **Find a spot that will accommodate all of your "stuff," is easy to get in and out of, and where you won't interfere with other diners. Be sure to move all glasses, silverware, and dishes away from your child's reach and replace them with a book or crayons and pad. Outside seating is a great option, if it's available and comfortable. Infants can be held in a snugly, babies able to sit up can eat in a car seat placed in a booth (try turning a wooden high chair upside down and placing the car seat on top), toddlers can stay in strollers, and preschoolers can sit on booster seats.**
- ***Order quickly.*** **The best strategy is to get some food, any food, to the table fast, then order the main dishes. Babies just starting solids can eat sweet or baked potatoes plain, smashed bananas, cooked and smashed carrots, and smashed peaches or pears. Toddlers can eat bite-size pieces of hamburger, pork chops, bread, macaroni and cheese, or fruit; and preschoolers can eat small portions off your plate.**

experiences, he learns what values are important and how to interact socially in the world. Second, as food is an important part of our culture, learning about food and trying certain culturally specific dishes tells him where he came from. If, for example, your family makes coconut rice and curried chicken on Sundays, he can learn about life in the Caribbean. And when he gets old enough to help in the kitchen, he can begin to learn how to prepare food and one day pass his love of these foods on to his own children when that time comes.

In fact, helping in the kitchen is an activity that thrills most three-, four-, and five-year-olds. They feel responsible, helpful, and proud to be involved in such important household duties. And they love to smoosh, mix, and pour, chores they can handle without risk of injuries. Most preschoolers, if given the chance, are eager to pitch in, and when the final product hits the table, chances are they will eat what they helped to

Snack Attack: The Best Ten Snack Foods for Toddlers

These are great snacks to pack into small baggies to pull out later, or to stuff into a lunch bag if you're on the go. They give kids a nutritional boost during the day and most aren't too sugary:

- **Bite-size fruit, like grapes (cut lengthwise) or strawberries**
- **Raw veggies, such as baby carrots, red pepper strips, or broccoli**
- **Graham crackers, low-fat granola bars, or rice cakes**
- **Yogurt with fruit and granola**
- **Cheese squares or string cheese**
- **Muffins or oatmeal cookies**
- **Peanut butter squares**
- **Dried fruit like raisins, dried pineapple, or dried apple chips**
- **Hard-boiled eggs**
- **Dry cereal, like Cheerios**

make. Having them help with the salad, for instance, is a good way to get them to eat vegetables. Here are a couple of other hints for having kids help in the kitchen:

- Don't let him in the kitchen unless you're there to supervise.
- Always wash hands before cooking.
- Give him a sturdy stool to stand on, or bring a small table into the kitchen.
- Let him help with activities that don't put him at risk for getting cut or burned. Some good choices are:
  * ripping up lettuce
  * mixing frozen juice and water
  * pouring liquid into batter
  * putting sandwich meat on bread
  * helping to knead dough
  * stirring cold dishes
- Do not let him hold a knife, open the oven, work or go near the stove, work with glass or any other breakables, or work with or go near hot water or steam. Remember to turn all pot handles away from the outside of the stove while cooking. (For more on kitchen safety, turn to Chapter 14.)

RESOURCES

Recommended Reading for Parents

Allergies

The Allergy Self-Help Cookbook: Over 325 Natural Foods Recipes, Free of Wheat, Milk, Eggs, Corn, Yeast, Sugar, and Other Common Food Allergens, Marjorie Hunt Jones (Rodale Press, 1992). This allergy-free cookbook provides recipes for wheat-free breads, wholesome desserts, packable lunches, and quick-and-easy dinners.

Feeding Your Allergic Child: Happy Food for Happy Kids, Elisa Meyer (St. Martin's Press, 1997). For the parents of children allergic to wheat, dairy, corn, and eggs, this book provides delicious, nutritious, and fun recipes for foods kids love to eat.

Your Child's Food Allergies: Detecting and Testing Hyperactivity, Congestion, Irritability, and Other Symptoms Caused by Common Food Allergies, Jane McNicol (John Wiley & Sons, 1992). This book provides parents with a complete, step-by-step program for determining and eliminating a child's food allergies.

Breast-Feeding

Breastfeeding and the Working Mother, Diane Mason, Diane Ingersoll, and Kittie Frantz (St. Martin's Press, 1997). In addition to providing helpful tips and first-person anecdotes on breast-feeding and work, this book addresses legal rights, nursing dress and equipment, travel and meetings, and bringing baby to the job.

The Breastfeeding Answer Book, Nancy Mohrbacher (La Leche League International, 1997). This book addresses numerous breast-feeding concerns including milk storage guidelines, breast pump reviews, medicines to avoid, and help with such difficulties as mastitis and engorgement.

Having Your Baby: A Guide for African American Women, Hilda Hutcherson, M.D., and Margaret Williams (Ballantine Books, 1997). This book has a chapter on talking to African-American women about breast-feeding.

Cookbooks

African-American Child's Heritage Cookbook, Vanessa Roberts Parham (Sandcastle Publishers, 1994). This book provides recipes in African-American cookery and lessons in black culture.

Our Family Table: Recipes & Food Memories from African-American Life Models, Thelma Howard Williams (Tradery House, 1993). This book combines lessons in food preparation with a celebration of African-American heritage.

The Kids' Multicultural Cookbook: Food & Fun Around the World, Deanna F. Cook (Williamson Publishing, 1995). This book provides a medley of recipes, customs, activities, and games from Asia, Europe, Africa, the Americas, and the South Pacific.

A Taste of Heritage: The New African-American Cuisine, Joe Randall and Toni Tipton-Martin (Macmillan, 1998). This cookbook offers menu suggestions and three hundred innovative recipes.

Nutrition

Child of Mine: Feeding With Love and Good Sense, Ellyn Satter (Bull Publishing, 1991). This book, written by a registered dietician and licensed clinical social worker, presents practical and solidly researched information on child nutrition.

Food, Nutrition and the Young Child, Jeanette Brakhane Endres and Robert Rockwell (Merrill Publishing, 1993). This book helps parents provide sound nutrition for children from birth to age eight.

The Vegetarian Child: A Complete Guide for Parents, Lucy Moll (Perigee Books, 1997). This comprehensive guide covers nutrition issues for parents who have chosen vegetarianism for their children.

The Young Vegetarian's Companion, Jan Parr, illustrated by Sarah Durham (Franklin Watts, 1996). This book debunks myths about vegetarianism and provides basic facts about nutrition.

Recommended Reading for Children

Baby Bop's Foods, Mary Ann Dudko, illustrated by Margie Larsen (Lyrick Studios, 1994). This book depicts Barney's friend enjoying her favorite foods.

The Berenstain Bears and Too Much Junk Food, Stan and Jan Berenstain (Random House, 1985). This book depicts Mama Bear helping her family make healthful adjustments to their diets and fitness habits.

Bread and Jam for Frances, Russell Hoban and Lillian Hoban (HarperCollins, 1993). This is a gentle and amusing book aimed at picky eaters.

Bye Bye, Bottle, Ellen Weiss and Tom Cooke (Golden Books, 1991). This book helps little ones make the transition from bottle to cup.

Charlie the Chicken, Nick Denchfield, illustrated by Ant Parker (Red Wagon/ Harcourt Brace, 1997). This book depicts Charlie the Chicken eating healthy foods so that he may grow big and strong.

The Seven Silly Eaters, Mary Ann Hoberman, illustrated by Marla Frazee (Browndeer Press, 1997). This story depicts a large family of picky eaters.

Organizations

American Academy of Allergy and Immunology, 611 E. Wells St., Milwaukee, WI 53202, (800) 822–2762.

Website: www.aaaai.org

This is a referral and information line that provides physicians names in your area and general information on allergies and asthma.

American Dietetic Association, 216 W. Jackson Blvd., Suite 800, Chicago, IL 60606–6995, (800) 366–1655.

Website: www.eatright.org

You can call this consumer hotline to receive helpful nutrition brochures or to speak with a dietician regarding children's food needs.

La Leche League International, 1400 N. Meachan Rd., Schaumburg, IL 60173–4048, (847) 519–7730, fax: (847) 559–7730

Website: www.lalechleague.org

La Leche is an international, nonprofit organization dedicated to providing education, information, support, and encouragement to women who want to breast-feed.

The Food Allergy Network, 10400 Eaton Pl., Suite 107, Fairfax, VA 22030–2208, (703) 691–3179, fax: (703) 691–2713, e-mail: fan@worldweb.net

Website: www.foodallergy.com

This consumer-based group produces a newsletter and several publications related to food allergies.

The International Food Information Council Foundation, 1100 Connecticut Ave., NW, Suite 430, Washington, D.C. 20036, (202) 296–6540, fax: (202) 296–6547, e-mail: foodinfo@ific.health.org

Website: ificinfo.health.org

The mission of this organization is to promote the exchange of information on food safety and nutrition. This group also serves as a link between the scientific community, food manufacturers, health professionals, government officials, the news media, and the public.

The International Lactation Consultant Association, 4101 Lake Boone Trail, Raleigh, NC 27607, (919) 787–5181, fax: (919) 787–4916, e-mail: ilca@erols.com

Website: www.ilca.com

This organization provides information and support to breast-feeding women and families and can assist in the search for a lactation consultant.

Vegetarian Resource Group, P.O. Box 1463, Dept. IN, Baltimore, MD 21203, (410) 366–VEGE, e-mail: vrg@vrg.org

Website: www.vrg.org

The Vegetarian Resource Group is a nonprofit organization dedicated to educating the public on vegetarianism and interrelated issues of health, nutrition, ecology, ethics, and world hunger.

U.S. Food and Drug Administration, HFE, Room 16–18, Rockville, MD 20857, (800) 532–4440; in the D.C. area, (301) 827–4420.

Website: www.fda.gov

Their information line provides information on feeding your baby or young child.

Chapter

8

Spirituality and Family Traditions

Spirituality has been a guiding force in our community since the dawn of African civilization. Religion and its rituals have been a source of strength, a means of survival, and a way to pass on fundamental beliefs to future generations. This chapter will explore ways for you to introduce spirituality into your child's life and provide suggestions on celebrating the diverse traditions and holidays within the black community. And because one of our greatest assets as African Americans is diversity, we offer wonderful stories from parents of different faiths who discuss the ways they share spirituality and rituals with their young children.

In the Spirit

While some of us remain devoted to the religions we were raised with, others have found new ways to worship and pray, and still others are searching for alternative ways to nurture their spiritual selves. In fact, many new parents have found that having children forces them to think about their own spiritual beliefs and how to best pass them on to their children. Regardless of their particular religion or set of practices, most parents would agree that introducing the idea of a Higher Power, God, or Creator provides families with a set of values, goals, models of behavior, and a sense of community. "Spirituality gives children a grounding inside so that they feel connected to something greater than themselves," explains Ruby Burgess, Ph.D., Professor of Early and Multicultural Education at Winston-Salem State University in North Carolina. "It allows children to have a support system they can always call on and enables them to take risks, live out hopes, and set goals." Burgess believes that without that spiritual base, children will go on to find other sources of power and fulfillment that may ultimately let them down.

Burgess also stresses the importance of feeling part of a whole in developing self-esteem. With a strong sense of self, children are more likely to set and achieve goals, be thoughtful of others, and find meaning in their lives. "European values of spirituality are structured around the individual, whereas African values are supported by being part of a group," she says. Thus spirituality makes us look beyond our own needs to consider the greater good of the whole family, community, and universe. "These ties give us and our children strength, perseverance, and coping power," she adds.

Our Spiritual Children

Regardless of your spiritual beliefs or religious practices, you can begin to impart them to your child from the day she is born. Here are some ways you can bring spirituality into your child's life:

- *Decide what you believe.* This will probably be easier for those already involved in a structured religion, because religion provides many guidelines. If you are more comfortable formulating your own beliefs and practices, begin to think about what you believe and why. For example, you may believe in God, but think of it as a connection to everything and everyone. Or you may see God as an all-knowing, all-powerful man—or being. Knowing what you believe is extremely important as you share your ideas with your child, and so you can begin to formulate answers to that ever-popular question that children ask: Why?

Promote spirituality by reading the Bible to your child.

- *Devote time to your spiritual side.* By taking time to develop your spiritual side, you teach your child important lessons, such as allowing time for quiet contemplation, joyful celebration, and appreciation. You might take time every day, such as at dinner or bedtime, to pray together. Your prayers don't have to be elaborate. At mealtime, you might ask a different family member each night to give thanks for the food on the table and to pray that every person in the world has enough to eat. At bedtime, you can give thanks for being a family and offer special prayers to relatives and loved ones, especially those in need. Once a year you might go to a special place—a forest, seashore, or park—to make a connection with nature and all living things. Like many black families, you may want to take time once a week to worship as part of a church.
- *Find a community.* If you already have a place of worship, it will provide you with a set time and a place to reinforce your spirituality; like-minded friends

"Each person who came to Yetunwa's naming ceremony will have an influence on her life at some point."

—Oyabunmi Oyesegun, mother of Yetunwa Osakwe, age 1, Richmond, Virginia

I am Yoruba, and according to our faith, when a child is born, on the seventh day of her life [ninth for boys] we do a naming ceremony called Kamojade. The day before, there is a reading, to determine a child's purpose, her destiny, and which spirit will rule over her. My daughter was six days old on the day of her reading, and it was revealed that she was one of our ancestral mothers returned. So we named her Yetunwa Osakwe. Yetunwa means "mother returns" and Osakwe means "God agrees."

At the start of the naming ceremony the next day, my father, who is an Oba, or king, sprinkled water on Yetunwa, representing purity and freshness. Yetunwa slept through it, but generally if the baby screams out it's a good sign. Next my father presented her with salt, pepper, honey, gin, and coconut. The salt represents the spices of life, the different experiences the baby will have. The pepper is to introduce the child to any adversities that she may experience. The honey introduces the child to the sweetness and calm she may encounter in the days that remain. The gin represents African herbal medicine, and a kola nut or coconut represents the child's voice. My father dipped his finger in each and put it on her tongue to taste, then everybody else tasted a part of each, too. In doing that, each person present made a pledge to have an impact on Yetunwa's life as she grows up.

Afterward, everyone got a chance to hold Yetunwa and dance with her. The oldest male—my father—went first, followed by the rest of the men, followed by the oldest woman, and then the rest of the women. For a boy child, the oldest woman is the first to hold and dance with him. It was really a beautiful day. Each person who came to Yetunwa's naming ceremony will have an influence on her life at some point.

for guidance, study, and support; an opportunity to do good work for your community; and a place where your children can learn about religion. Some people aren't comfortable with organized religion but would like an opportunity to explore their spiritual side. Be creative: Find friends with like beliefs and come together. Try starting a discussion group to share ways to pass along spirituality to your children. Or start a reading group with other parents of preschool children to read spiritual books and discuss religion with your sons and daughters.

- *Practice what you preach*—so to speak. The most powerful teaching tool is behavior. Small children imitate as a way to learn the rules of culture and society. If they see you saying your prayers or meditating every day, they will understand that it's important to you that you take time for spirituality, and they will be more inclined to follow your lead than if they were just told to pray. Talking to children about what you're doing involves them in rituals more than if they just followed them without explanation. If at all possible, set an example for what you would like your child to do and explain or practice it in a fun and interesting way. For

"Every night we say a prayer, and then I ask each of my daughters to give thanks for something she has in her life." **—ANNE'S STORY**

Having children has made me think about a lot of life's issues, including spirituality. I've had to define what that means for me and decide what I want to impart to my children. Personally, I've found spirituality to be a great resource for me. Whenever I have encountered personal difficulties, I have often relied on an inner strength that comes from my faith. This is what I wanted to give to my children. I wanted them to have a source that they could tap into during difficult times, as well as a sense of ethics that would guide them through their lives.

As with other areas of parenting, I feel it is more important to live the lessons you want to teach than simply say them. But faced with the question of how to communicate this type of abstract thinking to very young children and to show that spirituality is part of my daily life and not just something I address one day a week, I decided to introduce a ritual—nightly prayers. Praying together would provide my children with a chance to reflect and give thanks.

Bedtime is a naturally quiet part of the day, and this has become a nice time we spend together. Every night we say a prayer, and then I ask each of my daughters to give thanks for something she has in her life. When they were younger, they usually gave thanks for their favorite toys or a favorite cartoon character. As they became older, they began to give thanks for important people in their lives. Any adult who is putting them to bed must also give thanks for something, which I hope serves as an example that a daily reflection is not just meant for children. I hope that they will continue to appreciate the people they love and to use the nightly prayer as a time for reflection throughout their lives.

instance, if the summer solstice is an important spiritual occurrence for your family, have your child draw a picture about it, or have your child tell a story about what it means to be a Muslim.

- *Be consistent.* Being a moral, spiritual person involves more than just saying blessings and going to church. Set an example by paying attention to important values like forgiveness, honesty, acceptance, generosity, kindness, compassion, sharing, and, most importantly, love.

Family Traditions Big and Small

In traditional African cultures, our ancestors celebrated births, performed rites of passage, gave thanks for a good harvest, and acknowledged other significant events, including death, together. Elders were responsible for passing those traditions down to the next generation, and many of them have survived in modern African nations and even in parts of the Americas to this day.

Celebrating holidays helps establish family.

Learning and participating in family traditions gives us and our children a strong sense of who we are, where we came from, and what we value about ourselves. Important events, like weddings and funerals, or celebrations, such as holidays and birthdays, bring us together and allow us to feel a part of a kinship network. For children, this is especially important because it gives them an understanding of their family's history and how they fit into it.

Let's Get Together: Family Reunions

African-American families have maintained the powerful tradition of family reunions for generations for many reasons. First, the ravages of slavery, which tore our families apart, left many of us longing to repair those lost ties. Second, the popularity of Alex Haley's groundbreaking book *Roots* sent many of us on a journey to locate and reconnect with branches of our family tree we may not have even known about. Finally, with our new mobile society, families can find themselves spread

"This past Kwanzaa was Marisha's fourth. She's learning the words now, and she can pronounce them much better, but we're still working on the meanings."
—MELVINA LEWIS, MOTHER OF MARISHA, AGE 3; MITCHELLVILLE, MARYLAND

Even before my daughter Marisha was born, I decided that observing Kwanzaa would be a good way to celebrate her heritage. She was born in September, so I started reading up in preparation for December.

That first year her father and I didn't do a big thing; we just acknowledged Kwanzaa and talked about the principles. The second year we exchanged gifts (although we didn't make them), one for each of the days of Kwanzaa. Marisha wasn't really into it; she was still too young. She would just bring out gifts and open them. I worked with her, though: I went over the dates on which Kwanzaa is observed, and helped her pronounce each of the principles. It's really hard to explain some of this to a child so young, but I bought her a book about Kwanzaa, which really helped.

The following year, when she was three, we let Marisha put out the Kwanzaa candle holder called a kinara and place the candles in it. She also brought out a bowl for each day. That third year we started celebrating with friends and family at a big celebration at my uncle's house. I was happy that she would get to learn more about sharing by seeing the family gathering together. And my family respects the decision that I have made to celebrate Kwanzaa instead of Christmas. I enjoyed introducing the principles to them at our Karamu ceremony; they were listed on a program that I designed and distributed. I explained to everyone the whole concept of Kwanzaa; I told them it's not a holiday, it's a celebration. My aunt prepared African-American dishes, we exchanged gifts, and we each explained what Kwanzaa or one of the principles meant to us. When it was Marisha's turn, she said, "I love Mommy and Daddy, and every day is Christmas when I get up."

This past Kwanzaa was Marisha's fourth. She's learning the words now, and she can pronounce them much better, but we're still working on the meanings.

across the country, and getting together at a reunion is a great way to affirm a sense of connection.

As a consequence of these and other factors, the past two decades have seen a nationwide explosion in African-American family reunions. While they take some planning and effort to be successful, these gatherings are a wonderful opportunity for children to learn about the importance of family in general and the uniqueness of their

"Attending church helps my children understand that there is a God, someone who is even bigger than their parents, that they have to answer to."
—ANDREA REID, MOTHER OF DREW, AGE 2, AND JASMINE, AGE 6; BOSTON, MASSACHUSETTS

I have been a Christian since I was thirteen, and my faith has really shaped who I am as an adult. I started building my children's faith at a very young age. This not only allows the children to stay in touch with God and explore their faith, it involves them in a community that includes people from all socioeconomic backgrounds. This is particularly important to me and my husband since our children attend a predominately white school in the suburbs near our home. By attending this church—located in an urban setting—our children have an opportunity to meet working-class African-American families who do not live in our community. When our daughter has birthday parties, for example, we are able to bring a diverse group of children together. To us this is another blessing that has come from our involvement with this church.

The church affects their behavior too. Attending church helps them understand that there is a God, someone who is even bigger than their parents, who they have to answer to. The world can be such a rough place, especially for African-American children. There are so many messages telling them they aren't worth anything and that they cannot succeed. The church gives my children a grounding in the belief that they are important to God and that they are special.

I'd like to share some advice and tips with other parents who are looking for a church to attend with their children:

- *Choose a church in which you feel comfortable.* This will make you more likely to attend regularly and make sure children are integrated into church activities.
- *Make sure the church has nursery services.* This is critical for families with young children. Nursery care lets parents enjoy the service while babies are looked after in another section of the church. Providing a nursery indicates the church has some commitment to parishioners.
- *Your church should have programs for children.* Adults shouldn't expect young children to sit through services without becoming bored and fidgety. Get them involved in a children's choir or other group for kids.
- *Engage children in community outreach.* I believe community involvement is very important not only as a moral issue, but because it gives your children an opportunity to work for community improvement. This creates meaningful experiences in a child's life and broadens the role of the church in their lives.

own individual families. Not only will they get the chance to meet members from various generations, but children will also learn about the family's special traditions, hear stories from older relatives of how life was "when I was your age," and gain a sense of pride from family accomplishments. Though it may take some time before very young children can appreciate family reunions, they can still have fun at the event. Here are some ideas to get your little one involved in the family festivities:

- *Babies:* Take a Polaroid photo of your baby at the reunion with her fellow baby relatives. She will gain instant gratification from the results and can keep it as a memento of the family occasion. Punch a hole through the photo and use it as an ornament to hang on the Christmas tree.
- *Toddlers:* Even the youngest dancers love to get their groove on. Parents can hold a tot dance contest or just pump up the volume as a way to bring them into the fun. You can also involve toddlers by including them in a family art project, such as drawing a family tree and attaching photos in the appropriate places or making a paper quilt with each member completing his or her own square and sewing them together with yarn.
- *Preschoolers:* Three-, four-, and five-year-olds are great helpers and can lend a hand in food preparation before the event and clean up during or afterward. For fun, this age group could pair up with older siblings or cousins for a family treasure hunt. Or, to help children learn about their family and get involved with family members they don't otherwise spend much time with, try this game suggested by Brown and Ninkovich, authors of *Family Reunion Handbook:* Devise a list of questions, such as who's the oldest and youngest, who plays on a soccer team, how many children did Grandma Bertha have, and who used to work on a fishing boat. Let the children mingle and ask questions. The ones who get the most answers correct can receive goody bags or special certificates. For more ideas check out the *Family Reunion Organizer* by Emma J. Wisdom (Post Oak Publications, 1992).

Traditions for Tots

To bring your child into the center of your family traditions and celebrations, we offer one or two examples of kid-centered activities for babies, toddlers, and preschoolers.

"With visions of Christopher Columbus in my head I sadly reflected on what would probably be a lifetime of unteaching much of what Mariama would learn about 'great' American figures." **—Sabiyha Prince, mother of Mariama, age 5; New York, New York**

My husband Steve and I were sitting in the kitchen one evening during the week of President's Day when our four-year-old daughter Mariama came in and proudly announced that she had learned a new song in school. We encouraged her performance—relishing the opportunity since she so rarely volunteers details of her daily school activities. She grinned sheepishly and shyly began her song. I forget the exact lyrics, but it was something about George Washington being great and being the father of our nation—the father of us all. She beamed, and I gave what may have been a half-hearted "very good." I fought the immediate desire to discredit Washington, not wanting to take anything away from her accomplishment. I took the time to gather my thoughts and was also curious about Steve's reaction.

After praising her effort, Steve told Mariama that although it is true George Washington was the first president of the United States, that didn't necessarily mean he was a good person. He told her that Washington enslaved African Americans, "people who look just like you and me," he said for emphasis, and that "he made them work hard so he could become rich." I added, "Some of the people you may learn about in school may have also done some bad things." With visions of Christopher Columbus in my head I reflected on what would probably be a lifetime of unteaching much of what Mariama would learn about "great" American figures.

She appeared puzzled and disappointed upon hearing the news. Usually very inquisitive, she didn't pursue the subject any further. We had talked about this before, so Mariama was aware of her ancestors' enslavement. But I still wondered what these ideas and events meant to her.

We knew such discussions would be inevitable, but Steve and I had a number of reservations about raising such complex issues with our preschooler. There is a danger in postponing such discussions—when some parents finally get around to tackling these tough issues, they find someone else has filled their children's head in the meantime. But we were concerned about the potential for this process to backfire and foster in our child feelings of racial shame or a victim's mentality. This is a particular concern of ours because most of Marima's classmates are white. Fortunately, however, Mariama is a smart, inquisitive child with a positive racial identity and a keen moral sense; she seems to be fine.

Baby's First Birthday Party. Most parents will agree that the first birthday party is mostly for the parents, but that doesn't mean your child can't have a great time and begin to learn the joys of a birthday celebration. Here are some ideas when you begin planning a party:

- *Keep it small.* Don't overwhelm yourself or your child by hosting a party with too many children or adults. It's enough to throw a party, let alone a party full of children who need lots of attention. Invite a few—meaning three or four at the most—of her young friends and their parents. Or you can stick to mostly adults—"aunties" and "uncles" and, of course, the relatives. She'll have the most fun with a few people she knows well; too many will overwhelm her.
- *Keep it simple.* Many one-year-olds can't walk yet, and if they do, aren't always surefooted. Plan for a couple of small activities, like finger painting or face painting, and play appropriate music—Sweet Honey in the Rock's "I Got Shoes" (Music for Little People, Redway, CA) is a good choice, for example. Serve finger food that small children won't choke on (diced fruit salad without grapes, or tuna salad finger sandwiches), juice in paper cups, and a small cake. Many parents buy or make carrot cakes (without nuts) because it's both sweet and has more nutritional value than most. Other good alternatives are a sweet potato pie or a fruit cobbler.
- *Pick a theme.* Having a theme will help you choose decorations and activities. Be sure to pick something that has meaning to your child. For instance, many one-year-olds love animals. You could have a jungle animal party and make up the children's faces like those animals from African jungles: elephants, lions, or gorillas.
- *Keep it short.* For the first birthday party, the shorter the better. Even if your child is having a ball, start to wrap things up after about an hour or two at most. More than likely, it will be time for an afternoon nap or bedtime anyway.
- *Take tons of pictures.* The cake-smeared faces and new toys will be best remembered by photos and videos. Be sure to get a photo album for the occasion and double sets to send to family and friends.

Toddler's Daily Affirmations. The smallest of traditions can add up to a lifetime of treasures. You can put this idea into practice by saying daily affirmations with your children. Like prayer, affirmations help us to be thankful, think positively about ourselves and our world, and help us strive to be better people. Books of affirmations have become popular recently, and two especially helpful ones for parents are *Guide My Feet: Prayers and Meditations for Our Children* by Marion Wright Edelman (HarperPerennial, 1995) and *Black Pearls for Parents: Meditations, Affirmations, and Inspirations for African-American Parents* by Eric Copage (Quill, 1995). *Black Pearls*

"I don't remember a thing about my early birthdays but love to look at the photos of the parties my mother threw. I hope Kali does the same." **—Linda's Story**

As Kali's first birthday approached, I began to feel more and more nervous. Vickie and I had been to a number of kiddie parties and had found them stressful. Lots of exhausted parents watching their out-of-control children run around wildly. Cake and ice cream on the walls. Sticky punch spilled on the floor. I didn't think we could hang.

However, we have lots and lots of friends and family, most of whom are very actively involved in Kali's life. So we knew we needed to get it together and find some way that everyone could celebrate her birthday and create photo opportunities since she was probably too young to remember it. We settled into the theory that "more is more" and decided to have two parties. The key—given what I mentioned above—was to make sure that they were low maintenance.

On the Sunday before her birthday, Kali's father invited all of his friends over for a traditional Peruvian brunch. They brought all the food and did all the cooking and cleaning, so we had a great time. And so did Kali, who was the only child and got lots of attention, hugs, and kisses.

On Tuesday, her actual birthday, we threw a small party with Kali's best friend, ten-month-old Sam; her baby-sitter, who brought her eleven-year-old son; my sister; two aunties; and Rebecca, our six-year-old neighbor. We kept it simple—pizza, cake, and ice cream. We took snaps of Kali's key moments: opening gifts, blowing out candles (with our help), hugging each person. We made color Xeroxes of the photos and used them as thank-you notes and put copies into a first-birthday scrapbook for her memories. I don't remember a thing about my early birthdays but love to look at the photos of the parties my mother threw. I hope Kali does the same.

"In a very emotional part of our family reunion, we had a formal celebration of the passing of our loved ones, some of whom we had never met." **—Laura Stone, mother of Alyse, age 4, and Brian Junior, age 1; Riverdale, New York**

Every year my husband's family holds a reunion. Family history is very important, and our children benefit from the opportunity to interact with their cousins, aunts, and other kin. Since our family is spread out, we don't get together much.

This year's reunion took place on Martha's Vineyard. The children had scheduled activities like kite-flying, bike riding, and a large outing to the beach. We also had a family portrait taken on the beach and in front of the family home.

In a very emotional part of our family reunion, we had a formal celebration of the passing of our loved ones, some of whom we had never met. We lit candles in remembrance of them, and someone from the immediate family of the person who died said something about the deceased. The children then said a prayer together—a little affirmation speech about the future, which they had practiced earlier. Two of Alyse's older cousins explained what they wanted for their future, and their mothers fashioned it into a poem or prayer. It was very memorable; I cried through the whole thing. My daughter still talks about the lighting of the candles.

I was very glad that my children got to hear about their granddaddy and grandmother. An aunt also told a story about Grandmother, who was small in stature but headstrong. She insisted on buying a mirror against the wishes of her husband, and that mirror remains in the Alabama house where my husband grew up. When we took the children to Alabama, I was able to show my daughter the mirror she had heard about at the celebration on Martha's Vineyard. That was something special she wouldn't have known if we hadn't attended the reunion. That was a very positive family tale for her to hear even at her young age.

The experience helped both children, but especially Alyse, understand the meaning and importance of family. Alyse learned that her family is more than just her mommy, daddy, and little brother.

for Parents has a theme, quotation, and topic of discussion for every day of the year. For example, one theme is Black Pride and the affirmation reminds parents that "On this day, I will take five minutes to discuss with my child a member of our family or a great man or woman of African descent."

You can use affirmations to begin the day, begin a meal, at the end of the day, to share together as a family, or to say privately with your child. Even if your toddler cannot understand the meaning behind all of the words, you can break down the basic concepts or pick simple affirmations.

Preschoolers' Black History Month. Black History Month is an excellent opportunity to begin a family tradition. Preschoolers are generally very vocal about people they admire, so what better time to honor their heroes and heroines than during Black History Month? Creating an art project, such as a book or collage, that features their favorite African Americans can be fun and educational. Here are some ideas:

- *Help your child pick some people (or one person) she admires.* It can be a family member, someone from the community, a historical figure, or a celebrity. Ask your child why she admires this person, and find ways to incorporate her answers into the project.
- *Get all the right supplies, including lots of magazines.*
- *Let your child direct the project.* Help him when he needs it, but don't criticize or take over even if he's doing something "wrong." Help him cut out images or apply materials, and don't worry about how neat or perfect it looks. What's important is for your child to have a sense of accomplishment and fun in honoring African Americans he respects.
- *Proudly display the finished product.* If your child has created a book, place it on a table so everyone can read it. If it's a poster collage, hang it in the kitchen or her bedroom.

RESOURCES

Recommended Reading for Parents

Acts of Faith: Daily Meditations for People of Color, Iyanla Vanzant (Fireside Books, 1993). Here is a collection of meditations by a leading Afrocentric, inspirational writer and public speaker.

The African-American Family Album, Dorothy and Thomas Hoobler (Oxford University Press, 1995). This is a historical photo album of African-American families.

Black Pearls, Eric V. Copage (William Morrow, 1993). This is a very popular book of daily inspirations for African-Americans.

Black Pearls for Parents, Eric V. Copage (Quill, 1995). "Meditations, Affirmations, and Inspirations for African-American Parents." These daily inspirational readings address topics of concern to African-American parents.

Black Pearls Journal, Eric V. Copage (William Morrow, 1995). This workbook is designed for readers who want to keep a written record of their own spiritual journeys. Families can use it to write about young children. Each page has a daily inspirational quote from the national bestseller *Black Pearls.*

Family Reunion Handbook: A Guide for Reunion Planners, Barbara Brown and Tom Ninkovich (Reunion Research, 1992). This book helps families plan events and activities.

Good News!: Sermons of Hope for Today's Families, Rev. Jeremiah A. Wright, Jr. (Judson Press, 1995). This is a collection of sermons for African-American families.

Guide My Feet: Prayers and Meditations for Our People, Marion Wright Edelman (HarperPerennial, 1995). Here are affirmations that children can easily understand and appreciate.

In the Company of My Sisters: Black Women and Self-Esteem, Julia A. Boyd (Plume, 1997). This is a bestselling spiritual, self-help book of inspirational quotes by black women.

It's Kwanzaa Time!, Linda and Clay Goss (G.P. Putnam's Sons, 1994). This book introduces Kwanzaa, explains the seven principles, and includes recipes, stories, games, clothes, and graphic designs.

Keys to Teaching Children About God, Iris M. Yob (Barron's Educational Series, 1996). This is a nondenominational introduction to the concept of one God. The book also addresses adult concerns about children's first questions about God or spirituality.

Mother Wit, Abena Safiyah Fousua (Abingdon Press, 1996). This is full of daily Afrocentric Christian meditations for women.

Nurturing Spirituality in Children, Peggy J. Jenkins, Ph.D. (Beyond Words Publishing, 1995). This book offers numerous visual experiences for children that will demonstrate spiritual principles and spiritual views of the world. This nondenominational book also teaches children about prayer, meditation, and more.

The Wisdom of the Elders, Robert Fleming (Ballantine Books, 1995). This collection of writings by such luminaries as Sojourner Truth, George Jackson, Paul Robeson, and others includes sections on youth, education, and family.

Recommended Reading for Children

A is for Africa, Ifeoma Onyefulu (Cobblehill Books/Dutton, 1993). This introduces children to various cultures, spiritualities, and customs of West Africa.

All Night, All Day: A Child's First Book of African-American Spirituals, Ashley Bryan and David Manning Thomas (Atheneum Publishers, 1991). Musical notation is included.

Celebrating Families, Rosmarie Hausherr (Scholastic Press, 1997). Multicultural, this book shows many kinds of families and family situations and circumstances.

Come Sunday, Nikki Grimes, illustrated by Michael Bryant (William B. Eerdmans Publishing Company, 1996). Presented as a set of four fun poems for children, this picture book tells the story of little Latosha "Sweet Pea" who goes to the Paradise Baptist Church.

Day by Day: A Muslim Bedtime Story and Coloring Book, Shahruzad Ali (Civilized Publications, Inc., 1996). This teaches Islamic values.

Day of Delight—A Jewish Sabbath in Ethiopia, Maxine Rose Schur, illustrated by J. Brian Pitney (Dial Books for Young Readers, 1994). This story is about the Ethiopian Jews in Africa.

Happy Christmas, Gemma, Sarah Hayes, illustrated by Jan O'Merod (Mulberry Books, 1992). This sweet story is told from the point of view of a boy whose baby sister is experiencing her first Christmas.

A House by the River, William Miller, illustrated by Cornelius Van Wright and Ying-Hwa Hu (Lee & Low Books, 1997). Belinda, an African-American girl living with her widowed mother, learns the true meaning of "family."

In Praise of Our Fathers and Mothers: A Black Family Treasury by Outstanding Authors and Artists, Wade and Cheryl Willis Hudson, eds. (Just Us Books, 1996). This is a collection of inspirational and educational essays, stories, poetry, interviews, photographs, and illustrations.

Irene and Jennie and the Christmas Masquerade: The Johnkankus, Irene Smalls-Hector, illustrated by Melodye Rosales (Little, Brown and Company, 1996). This is a colorfully illustrated book about African-American children at Christmas time.

Jafta and the Wedding, Hugh Lewin, illustrated by Lisa Kopper (Carolrhoda Books, 1983). These four charming stories set in South Africa introduce children to Zulu families and culture.

Jumping the Broom, Courtni C. Wright, illustrated by Gersham Griffith (Holiday House, 1994). This is a story about an African-American wedding ceremony during the time of slavery.

Juneteenth Jamboree, Carole B. Weatherford, illustrated by Yvonne Buchanan (Lee & Low Books, 1995). This is a story about the traditional African-American holiday that celebrates the day slavery was eradicated.

A Kwanzaa Miracle, Sharon S. Gayle, illustrated by Frank Norfleet (Troll/Whistlestop, 1996). This colorful book will help teach children about the fun, tradition, and principles of Kwanzaa, an African-American celebration of community.

Miz Fannie Mae's Fine New Easter Hat, Melissa Milich, illustrated by Yong Cher (Little, Brown and Company, 1997). This is the story of a family trying to surprise their friend with a special gift.

Pass It On: African American Poetry for Children, Wade Hudson, ed., illustrated by Floyd Cooper (Scholastic Press, 1993). This collection features excellent illustrations and easy-to-understand poems by some of the greatest African-American poets.

Sunday, Synthia Saint James (Albert Whitman and Company, 1996). A celebration of friends and family in the black church and the community. The big print and bold colors in this book make it ideal for even the youngest children.

Support Groups and Organizations

Congress of National Black Churches, 1225 Eye St., NW, Suite 750, Washington, D.C. 20005–3914, (202) 371–1091, fax: (202) 371–0908. CNBC is a nonprofit religious organization that services the eight leading historically black denominations. Their program Project SPIRIT is designed as an after-school program for young children, a parenting education and resource center, and counseling service for families. For information on a SPIRIT center near you, contact Black Family Program director Jewell Dassance.

Family Resource Coalition, 200 S. Michigan Ave., 16th floor, Chicago, IL 60604, (312) 341–0900. This is a national network of community-based programs that develop family strengths. The coalition offers guides on how to find family support programs that fit your needs. Call or write for more information.

Chapter

9

Black and Proud: Raising Our Children to Feel Good About Themselves

Children are not born with ideas about race. For better or worse, everything they learn about all cultures, including their own, comes from other sources—us, other children, other adults, the media, and many others. That means it's up to us as parents to teach them a number of important lessons about race: That all people are equal and no one should be judged by the color of her or his skin. That, unfortunately, racism exists. That despite racism, past and present, African Americans have thrived and many—from Colin Powell to Oprah Winfrey—have achieved unprecedented levels of success and acclaim. That some of the many achievements of African Americans and some of our painful history has been left out of history books. And, most important, that—racism and history aside—your child is a special person who must learn to love her or his beautiful, black self.

Baby

A baby spends the first year of life absorbing both concrete and abstract ideas. Not only is she learning how to put the spoon in her mouth, but she's also taking in all the subtleties around her: your pleasure or displeasure at her appearance, your reaction to her in relation to other siblings, and your reaction to those outside the family. Though she may not be consciously aware of these inputs, she is computing them and incorporating them into her sense of self. These experiences will shape not only her feelings about herself but also about other people. Experts say that during this crucial stage of development, children need as many positive messages—and as few negative—as they can get, particularly about skin color, hair texture, and other racial identifiers. Here are a few ways you can help them develop a good self image:

- *Let them know they're beautiful.* Jessica Henderson Daniel, Ph.D., psychologist with the Judge Baker Children's Center in Boston, advises parents to bombard their children with affirmations. "Explain that we have different kinds of skin tones and hair types," says Daniel. "Tell them how colorful and gorgeous we are as a people and as individuals." Statements that show preference for one color or hair texture over another can have devastating consequences for a child (see more on p. 208).
- *Give them brown dolls.* Both boys and girls need dolls for a variety of reasons: to imitate adult behavior, to work out their fears, to feel powerful within their own world, and to express their imagination. By giving (or making) your child a doll

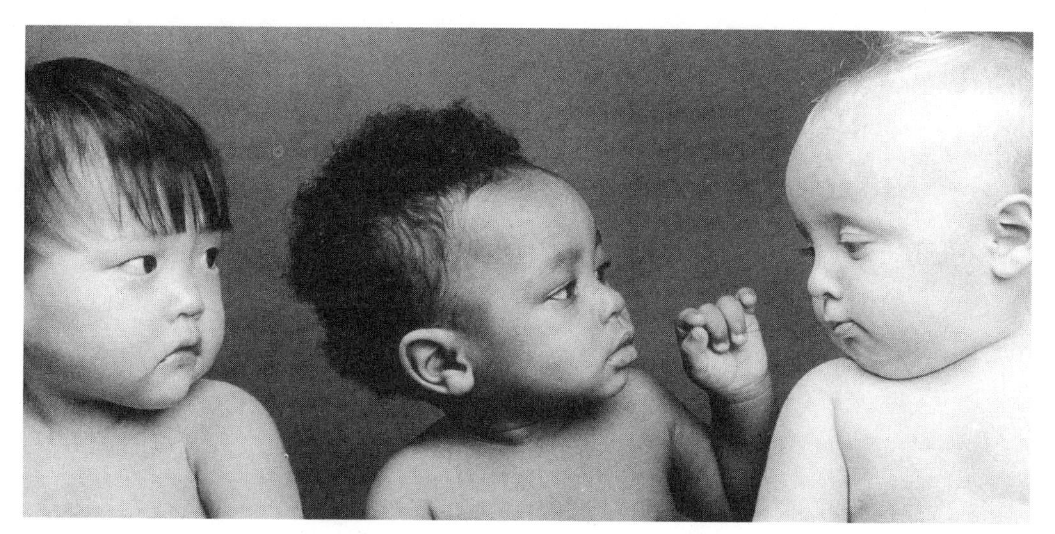

Encourage your child to have all kinds of friends.

that looks like him, he will see his hair texture and his eye and skin color as "normal" rather than different or "other." Dolls such as Baby So Beautiful or Cabbage Patch babies are ideal for little ones because they come in a wide variety of colors and features and are small enough for very little ones to handle.

- *Provide them with a safe and loving environment.* Dr. Daniel believes this will not only help your child feel secure and strong in general, but will also provide her with powerful role models in the face of future stereotypes that portray blacks as criminals or negligent parents.

Toddler

According to Joe R. Feagin, Ph.D., graduate research professor at the University of Florida's Department of Sociology, by the age of two or three children have already absorbed negative racial stereotypes that apply to themselves and others. "Television has some very negative images for African Americans," states Dr. Feagin. "Sitcoms, news shows, and crime shows teach a two-year-old to see blacks *only* as criminals, entertainers, athletes, and buffoons, instead of regular people." He asserts that while children's educational programming is better, it's still important to view it closely to make sure there are important black characters.

Another strong influence over small children's attitudes toward race is surprising:

Most researchers and parents believed that toddlers learned most of their racial concepts from adults, but Dr. Feagin's research has shown that other children are, in fact, the most potent teachers. "African-American children learn very early that they are 'different' or 'other' even in multicultural settings," says Dr. Feagin. "White children don't go through this. Children learn about white supremacy when a white child calls an African-American child a racist name and the black child runs away hurt and angry."

Good Hair and Bright Skin: Are We Still Color-Struck?

According to Dr. Daniel, we have a long way to go before we eliminate our own racist attitudes about ourselves and other black folks. We do ourselves a great injustice when we perpetuate the attitude that "brighter" (meaning lighter-skinned) is better and straight or "good" hair is more desirable than tightly curled hair. We create what Dr. Daniel calls the "pecking order of skin color," which fosters feelings of shame and self-hatred among those who don't fit into white mainstream standards of beauty. Among those who do, there can be other unfortunate consequences of feeling appreciated only for one's looks, not for what's on the inside. Both criticism and praise based on superficial traits can lead to feelings of insecurity.

Dr. Daniel suggests the following ways to avoid passing on *intra*racial prejudice to kids:

- ***Come to terms with your own beliefs.* If you were treated unkindly because of how you looked, make a promise to yourself that you will not do the same to your own child. If you were the center of attention based on your features, be careful not to treat your child this way. All children need and deserve to be loved for who they are, not their appearance.**
- ***Don't compare negatively.* If your family is like most, members come in a range of colors. Siblings and first cousins can range from chocolate to butterscotch, but don't put a value judgment on features. Instead point out each person's differences focusing on variety, uniqueness, and specialness. "Different doesn't have to mean better," says Dr. Daniel, "just interesting." The important point is to let all children feel it's OK to be whatever color they are.**
- ***Protect your children.* When friends or family make stinging remarks to your child about herself or others, stand up for your child by saying that she is beautiful just the way she is. "Furthermore, tell your child that though we love Nana, we don't agree with her," adds Dr. Daniel.**

"We have some concerns about Kiarra growing up in a predominately white enviroment."
—Diane Washington, mother of Kiarra, age 5; Evanston, Illinois

We are not the only African Americans in our neighborhood, but our town is only 15 percent black. The private school our daughter, Kiarra, attends is predominately white. Her life is very different from how my husband and I grew up in a neighboring city, which is still more than 70 percent African American. My husband's need to be close to his medical practice is what brought us to this predominately white suburb.

Still, we have some concerns about Kiarra growing up in this predominately white environment. We're afraid she may feel isolated, lonely, or that she doesn't really "belong." We want her to develop a strong sense of self and identity, and we don't want living in this situation to affect her negatively. There are a few things we do to ensure that she has frequent contact with other African Americans: We maintain close ties to our family members who live in the city. We visit our parents often and make sure Kiarra spends the night with her grandparents from time to time. We invite aunts, cousins, and other members of our extended family over for gatherings, and we get together with them at restaurants or area museums.

These occasions provide Kiarra with opportunities to be with black folks, and I believe they help reinforce her sense of belonging and racial identity. During these times, she gets to feel what it was like for us growing up, being around the sounds, smells, language, and texture of African-American life.

We also get together with our friends as frequently as possible. The majority of our friends are African American, and most are the parents of young children. In most cases, we share their values and interests, and we approach parenting in similar ways. Kiarra anticipates gatherings with our friends and their children with great enthusiasm. She spends more time with them and the neighborhood kids than she does with her white classmates. I also think her sense of self is reinforced by being with our close friends. She continues to learn about who she is and what behaviors are acceptable in our communities by interacting with other blacks.

Finally we try to convey to Kiarra that she, both as an individual and an African-American person, should be respected and cherished. We work on building her self-esteem, and we do this in many ways—by respecting her opinion, listening to her, and sharing information with her. We also teach her about her cultural heritage. I am always telling her things about the past and about why conditions are the way they are. My husband and I have always made comments to her about her pretty brown skin or her wonderful hair. She seems to have a healthy sense of herself as a result.

Dr. Daniel says that black psychologists have known for years that black children understand racial differences at an extremely early age, perhaps even before their second birthday. That's why it's critical to prepare our children early. Though our natural instinct may be to protect them by sheltering them from the idea of racism, it's best to deal with the reality of what exists. Says Dr. Daniel: "The most successful African Americans are those who are bicultural. They are steeped in their racial identity but know how to interact in our society's predominantly white culture." For toddlers, here are some tips:

- *Buy books featuring black main characters and children from different cultures.* The *What-A-Baby* board books, *Essence* Books for Children are good choices, and there are many others. Authors such as Ezra Jack Keats *(The Snowy Day)* and Daniel Freeman (the Corduroy series) have written classics that are available in board books. The new series by Bill Cosby entitled the Little Bill Books for Beginning Readers offers important lessons to children (and parents) on bullies, creative play, and expressing feelings. (See Recommended Reading for more suggestions.)
- *Instill racial pride early.* Mary Ann French, coauthor of *40 Ways to Raise a Nonracist Child* (HarperPerennial, 1996), says, "As long as he loves himself, you're giving your child the best start in life you can give him." At her house, French keeps an ancestor table with images of those relatives who are living, those who have died, and famous black heroes, such as Muhammad Ali. "Point to these people regularly to teach your child about triumph our people have had directly. This fosters a sense of pride especially for African-American children who are bombarded with images not like him." A powerful addition to any black home, French suggests, is having a black Bible and picking out stories that appeal to young children.
- *Introduce your child to different types of children and adults.* Drs. Daniel and French both believe that teaching your child about diversity helps her feel comfortable around different types of people and gives her the opportunity to see how you react in a similar setting. If you're relaxed and enjoying yourself, she will too. And you will have the ability to intervene should anything negative occur, racially or otherwise, and teach her how to handle these kinds of situations.

- *Limit TV viewing.* Unfortunately, most television producers aren't interested in a fair or balanced view of African-American life, but you should be. Although TV programs with black main characters have increased recently, the sitcom model is still based on making laughs and resolving simple problems. News and cop shows still show black people disproportionately as the "bad guys." These are damaging images for our children. Educational shows appropriate for children, such as *Sesame Street, The Puzzle Place,* or *Gullah Gullah Island* on Nickelodeon at least attempt to expose youngsters to different cultures and teach them positive values such as respect and cooperation. Regardless of whether your child watches educational or commercial TV, anything more than one hour of TV viewing per day is excessive for small children.

Handling Racist Incidents with Your Child

Both as a professional and a mother, Dr. Daniel has had many experiences helping children confront the pain of racism. "Our job as parents is to tell our children that, yes, there is racism but to keep working hard in your own lives. Let them know they can come back to you and you'll support them when they've been hurt."

Unfortunately, some parents don't prepare their children for what may lie ahead. "African Americans, especially upwardly mobile ones, really need to come to terms with this idea that they can function best if they deny their African culture and only accept the mainstream," says Janice Hale, Ph.D., professor of early childhood education at Wayne State University in Michigan. "These parents aren't creating an identity for their children, because they're afraid it will cause them to hate whites and not integrate well." Both Hale and Daniel agree that if parents don't deal with racism, their children will never understand how to deal with the unfair treatment they are sure to receive from mainstream society. Here are suggestions for a healthy defense against racism or racist attacks:

- *Talk to your child about racism.* "I began teaching my son about racism around age three, when he asked me why his hair didn't blow in the wind like the white children's hair at day care," remembers Dr. Hale. In *40 Ways to Raise a Nonracist Child,* French tells parents not to pretend we live in a colorblind society. "If your end goal is for your children to treat all people fairly, then say so, and be clear about it. . . . However, don't make the common mistake of

Teaching Children to Love Themselves

Dr. Beal's patients often worry about their children's self-esteem. Here is a typical question and her response:

Q: My eight-year-old daughter does not like herself at all. She hates her hair, her body, and her dark skin. I am having trouble persuading her to like herself as she is. Can you offer some solutions regarding her self-esteem? At what point should I consider getting help from a psychologist or psychiatrist?

A: Giving a child a sense of self-esteem is a unique challenge for African-American parents because our children often encounter negative images of black people. As a result, we have to be very conscientious and proactive about what they encounter and how it can affect their self-esteem.

First, when children are young, their sense of self-worth as individuals and as African Americans comes from their families. I caution parents to think about the words and statements they use in front of their children and how they might affect their images of themselves. Negative comments about skin color, hair texture, and facial features should not be made in front of children. As adults, we may laugh at certain comments made in jest, but children take such comments at their face value and will learn that it is bad or considered ugly to have certain features.

I also encourage parents to surround their children with beautiful images that look like them. Fortunately, parents now have a large selection of dolls and books to choose from. It is important to expose children to characters and images that are valued for their beauty and intelligence and look like our children. A nice video series entitled Happily Ever After: Fairy Tales for Every Child *was released by HBO. The series features traditional fairy tales that have been redone with characters from a variety of ethnic backgrounds, so your child will have a chance to see "Beauty and the Beast" or "Rapunzel" with African-American characters. There are also a number of books available for children. An excellent example is the award-winning* Amazing Grace *by Mary Hoffman and Caroline Binch (Dial Books for Young Readers). This book features the story of a young girl who will not be defined by either her race or gender.*

Finally, and most importantly, parents should praise their children and let them know that they are valued and loved. They should be reminded that their skin is smooth and beautiful and their hair is thick and strong. Parents should make time to spend with their children and tell them that their opinions matter, that they are intelligent, and that they are a gift and a blessing to their families. With this kind of

support and background, children will be better equipped to leave the home and face the challenges to their self-esteem.

As children grow older and enter school, strategies for instilling self-esteem must change. Parents need to make sure that they are not placing their children in environments where they may receive negative messages about themselves. According to Tami Benton, M.D., medical director of the Inpatient Child Psychiatry Unit at Children's Memorial Hospital and clinical instructor of Pediatrics and Child Psychiatry at Northwestern University Medical School, school-aged children want to conform with others and fit in. If your child is the only black child in her class, her self-esteem may be at risk unless her differences are recognized and associated with positive feedback. "A good example is the only blonde child in the class. She will be different from her peers but will be valued for her differences, which will help her self-esteem." African-American parents need to make sure the same thing happens for their own children. Teachers should recognize ethnic and cultural diversity in their classrooms and should encourage children to be proud of their differences while respecting the differences of others. If the school does not have a program or curriculum that embraces diversity, parents can work to enrich their schools or invite prominent guests from a variety of ethnic backgrounds.

Outside of the school, parents can expose their children to other African-American children who can serve as positive peers. Whether it be sports, dance, singing, or art, interactions with other children engaged in constructive activities will help African-American children develop a sense of belonging to a group whose members have a variety of talents and strengths.

Dr. Benton warns that it is important to address concerns about self-esteem in young children because these issues will be more problematic as children approach adolescence and become more focused on their bodies and the way they look. She also encourages parents to seek assistance from a mental health professional such as a psychologist or psychiatrist if their efforts do not help. "Low self-esteem can be the presentation of a more serious problem, such as depression, which would require professional intervention."

Again, this is one of the unique challenges facing African-American parents. However, there is information available to help guide our efforts. Two good sources are **Different and Wonderful: Raising Black Children in a Race-Conscious Society** ***by Darlene Powell Hopson and Derek S. Hopson (Fireside Books) and*** **Raising Black Children: Two Leading Psychiatrists Confront the Educational, Social, and Emotional Problems Facing Black Children** ***by James P. Comer and Alvin F. Poussaint (Plume).***

thinking we can solve our racial problems by [pretending we're all the same]." As your children get older, you can use books, museums, photo albums, and oral histories to share with them the truth of what it means to be black in America and how to cope successfully.

- *Arm your child with facts and good comebacks.* Dr. Daniel recalls a time when her daughter was told by a white child that she had big, ugly lips. "My daughter's brilliant reply was 'I can give bigger kisses,' " says Dr. Daniel.
- *Don't encourage violent responses to racism.* In Dr. Feagin's research, white children as young as three use terms like "nigger" and stereotypes like "you're smelly" in spite. Nonetheless, it's important for children to avoid hitting or punching an abusive peer. Reacting that way could lead to being punished and labeled as a "problem" (read: angry black child). Teach her to have truth and wit on her side so that when confronted with bigoted or ignorant people she can defend herself with the accomplishments of our people and know when to walk away from a belligerent bully.
- *Confront the authorities.* Your child has every right to a safe and suitable environment for her education. If any child or teacher makes a racist remark, or if there are even subtle signs of discrimination, your child should report them to you and to another teacher. After getting the facts, go to the school or day care yourself. "Tell them that this classroom is unsafe and your child is not able to learn," advises Dr. Daniel. "Explain that he's at a disadvantage because he's fearful, anxious, and angry. And furthermore, tell them it's wrong."
- *Most important, in the event of a racist event, encourage your child to share her feelings.* Dr. Daniel suggests that racist incidents can cause your child to feel very angry and insecure, so home should be where she can talk about her hurt feelings. Be an ally; let her know she's not alone, that she's not at fault, and that there is something she can do.

Preschoolers

By the time your child is in preschool, hopefully he will be armed with a strong sense of self-worth based, in part, on his racial heritage and family history. "What young children need most of all is to be in a nurturing setting where they learn that it's OK to be black," says Dr. Daniel. Family reunions, with relatives from all walks of life and a broad spectrum of colors and features—and, of course, who resemble each other—are a wonderful way for young children to learn how diverse and rich our folk really are. If your family is small, friends can stand in for relatives.

Another important learning tool is exposure to as many different experiences and cultures as possible. As Mary Ann French states in her book *40 Ways to Raise a Nonracist Child,* "Once your child has a solid sense of self and pride in her own people, it will be easier for her to find joy in the differences of others. . . . [Children will] begin to perceive, in very general terms, that people have different lots in life, often according to their color." Our job as parents is to help them broaden their view of themselves and others beyond the racist stereotypes to which people of color are often assigned. Here are some ways to help your preschooler understand how she fits into the world as an African American:

- *Praise diverse behavior.* For example, applaud your child for accomplishments that go against the stereotypes that tell our children they should only aspire to

"I told my son that skin color doesn't stop black people from doing anything."
—Judith King-Calnek, mother of Kimani, age 8, and Khemet, age 5; New Rochelle, New York

Not long ago my son, Khemet, developed a crush on a girl named Ashley (not her real name). He came home from school one day and said, "Ashley likes Daniel and Daniel said I can't marry Ashley."

"Why not?" I asked. Khemet said, "Because my skin is brown and hers isn't."

My son was very upset although he didn't quite know what to make of it. It didn't make sense to him. I gave him the whole nine yards: I told him we are black people but that skin color doesn't stop our people from doing what they want. That he could marry whomever he wanted to, that he could be friends with whomever he wanted.

I also called Daniel's mother. After introducing myself I told her I wanted to talk about something upsetting that Khemet told me concerning Daniel. I thought I did a pretty good job of being diplomatic. After I told her what Daniel had said, I said, "I just thought you should know because we don't raise our children like that." The mother was like, "Oh, uh, I don't know where he got that," you know, stammering and stuttering and stuff. But I had a pretty good idea.

Afterward, I told Khemet, we are black people—African American—and our skin is brown and we are free to do what we want. He just said OK and that was that.

be athletes, entertainers, or criminals. If your child shows an interest in science, nature, math, or reading, encourage it and introduce him to different ways he can use it in a future career. You can also introduce him to other African Americans in these fields. On the flip side, explain to him that if he's interested in sports or music that's wonderful too, but point out that these fields are very difficult to break into and that it's best to have other talents to fall back on.

- *Get involved in school.* When selecting a preschool, Dr. Janice Hale notes that "You must control the situation your child is in. Find a school where he won't be intimidated socially or feel out of place with other kids." Mary Ann French and coauthor Barbara Mathias advocate sending kids to multicultural schools so that they can learn at an early age how to interact successfully with other types of children. Dr. Hale, who chose such a school, learned that even in such settings, an African-American parent has to be persistent. She has made personal efforts to change her son's school curriculum to include more African-American storybooks and encourages other parents to help broaden their schools' views of African-American history. "For instance, during Black History Month, rather than looking at important Civil Rights leaders, focus on our accomplishments in science and technology."

RESOURCES

Recommended Reading for Parents

Black and White Racial Identity: Theory, Research and Practice, J. E. Helms, ed. (Greenwood Press, 1990). By presenting current research into racial identity, this book reveals the importance of a strong sense of self for healthy self-esteem.

Black Child: The African American Parenting 'Zine, P. O. Box 12048, Atlanta, GA 30355, (404) 350–7877, fax (404) 350–0819. This magazine addresses issues of concern to African-American parents.

Black Children: Their Roots, Culture, and Learning Styles, Janice E. Hale (Brigham Young University Press, 1982). This book explores the link between culture, learning, and identity.

Different and Wonderful: Raising Black Children in a Race-Conscious Society, Darlene and Derek Hopson (Fireside Books, 1992). The Hopsons discuss the challenges and joys of raising an African-American child.

Everyday Acts Against Racism: Raising Children in a Multicultural World, Maureen T. Reddy, ed. (Seal Press, 1996). This book of essays by mothers and teachers examines the effects of racism and suggests ways to eradicate prejudice.

40 Ways to Raise a Nonracist Child, Barbara Mathias and Mary Ann French (HarperPerennial, 1996). This book offers tips on how parents can avoid the pitfalls of racial bigotry in shaping their children's values and identity.

1001 Things Everyone Should Know About African American History, Jeffrey C. Stewart (Doubleday and Co., 1996). This is a comprehensive guide to significant events and individuals in African-American history.

Prejudice and Your Child, 2nd ed., Kenneth B. Clark (Wesleyan University Press, 1988). This classic book discusses the impact of racial prejudice on the self-perception of children.

Raising Black Children, James P. Comer, M.D., and Alvin F. Poussaint, M.D. (Plume, 1992). This guide focuses on helping African-American children cope with racism, develop a strong sense of self-esteem, and build academic skills.

Saving Our Sons: Raising Black Children in a Turbulent World, Marita Golden (Doubleday and Co., 1995). Golden shares her story of raising a black male child in challenging surroundings.

Recommended Reading for Children

Black, White, Just Right!, Marguerite W. Davol, illustrated by Irene Trivas (Tapestry Books, 1993). This picture book has a biracial girl as its main character (her father is white and mother is black). She explores her dual heritage and finds out it's "just right" for her.

Bright Eyes, Brown Skin, Cheryl Willis Hudson and Bernette G. Ford, illustrated by George Ford (Just Us Books, 1990). This is a story about the busy morning of four African-American preschoolers.

Kenya's Family Reunion, Juwanda G. Ford, illustrated by Cristina Ong (Scholastic Press, 1996). In a celebration of the ties that bind, this book follows a young African-American girl as she discovers the meaning of family love.

Look at You, Baby Face, Madeline Carter, illustrated by Keaf Holliday (Golden Books Publishing, 1995). This book depicts the antics and activities of beautiful, brown baby girls and boys.

Sweet Clara and the Freedom Quilt, Deborah Hopkinson, paintings by James Ransome (Alfred A. Knopf, 1993). This illustrated book tells the story of an enslaved girl who yearns for freedom.

Water Play, Margaret Miller (Little Simon/Simon & Schuster, 1997). This board book shows children of diverse backgrounds having fun with water.

When I Look in the Mirror, Sopoeia Greywolf, illustrated by Chris Hall (A & B Book Publishers, 1993). This picture book encourages a positive self-image through celebrating all the shades of African-American children.

Wild, Wild Hair, Nikki Grimes, illustrated by George Ford (Cartwheel Books/Scholastic Press, 1997). This is a story about a girl named Tisa and her attempts to avoid having her tender head of kinks tamed.

Support Groups and Organizations

African American Images, 1909 W. 95th St., Chicago, IL 60643, (312) 445–0322 or (800) 552–1991, fax (312) 445–9844.

Website: www.africanamericanimages.com

This organization conducts workshops and distributes information on developing positive self-images among African-American children.

The Association of Black Psychologists, P.O. Box 55999, Washington, D.C. 20040–5999, (202) 722–0808.

Website:www.abpsi.org

This national organization works to foster the mental health of African Americans by offering services, programs, training, and advocacy.

The Black Community Crusade for Children, 25 E Street NW, Washington, D.C. 20001, (202) 628–8787, (800) ASK–BCCC, fax (202) 662–3530, e-mail: cdinfo@childrensdefense.org

Website: www.childrensdefense.org

Coordinated nationally by the Children's Defense Fund, this organization works to strengthen black communities and ensure that no child is left behind. Programs include the Black Student Leadership Network, Freedom Schools, the Religious Action Network, and Celebrating Young People Who Beat the Odds.

I-Pride (Interacial/Intercultural Pride), P.O. Box 191752, San Francisco, CA 94119–1752. I-Pride is a nonprofit organization founded over twenty years ago to support the well-being and development of individuals and families who are of more than one racial/ethnic heritage.

Interracial Family & Social Alliance (IFSA), P.O. Box 35109, Dallas, TX 75235–0109, (214) 559–6929.

Website: www.flash.net/~mata9/ifsa.htm

IFSA is a nonprofit group where biracial families, individuals, and children can meet others like themselves.

National Black Child Development Institute, 1023 15th Street, NW, Suite 600, Washington, D.C. 20005, (202) 387–1281, fax (202) 234–1738, e-mail: moreinfo@hbcdi.org

Website: www.nbcdi.org

This organization works with communities and individuals to improve the quality of life for African-American children and their families. It publishes pamphlets and magazines on parenting, public policy child health, and other topics.

Project RACE, Inc., 1425 Market Blvd., Suite 330–E6, Roswell, GA 30076, (770) 433–6076, fax (770) 640–7101, e-mail: projrace@aol.com

Website: www.projectrace.mindspring.com

Project RACE advocates for multiracial children and adults through education, community awareness, and legislation.

Chapter

10

Who's Watching the Children? Child Care and Education

According to the U.S. Bureau of Labor Statistics, over 60 percent of black mothers with children under six work outside the home, and of those, 80 percent work full-time, making child care a primary concern for black women. But for most of us, this information isn't new; we've always worked, and for generations we've had to find ways—sometimes creative—to make sure our children are cared for while we are out in the world.

Statistics show that we tend to keep our child care "in the family." A 1995 report from the U.S. Department of Commerce called "Who's Minding Our Preschoolers?" indicates that at least half of all black children under five years old whose mothers work outside the home are left with family members. Grandparents play an especially important role in watching our young children, caring for 20 percent of all black preschoolers. Nineteen percent of black children under five are watched by other relatives, and about 9 percent are cared for by their fathers while their mothers work.

But today, more and more of us live apart from family members, so we aren't able to leave our children with grandparents or other relatives. That means that the other half of black mothers, as well as those who stay at home, are either paying to have a baby-sitter in the home or using group child care facilities, such as day care or family care centers. For parents wrestling with the problem of how to care for their children while they work, especially when family isn't available, this chapter will discuss different child care options based on need, cost, stimulating environments, and style.

Babies

Whether you are a working or stay-at-home mother, at some point within the first few weeks of your baby's life, you'll have to arrange for some type of child care so that you can return to work, go out for fun, or simply run errands that are easier to do without a baby in tow. For some mothers the idea of the first separation is very easy, and they welcome it. But for others, especially those without trusted relatives nearby, the notion of leaving their vulnerable infant in someone else's hands can be alarming. Finding honest, loving, reliable, and affordable caregivers is not always easy, but it's also not impossible. Despite the frightening hidden camera reports in the media over the past several years, there are many qualified caring professionals available. To help you decide what's right for your family's needs, we'll look at various types of paid child care arrangements, the average weekly costs, where and what to look for in good care, along with the pros and cons of each.

Baby-Sitters

Experts in human development now know that the most important factor in a baby's development is engaging with a loving adult, so having a caring sitter one-on-one can be a wonderful experience for your child. This is especially true during the first three years when developing close bonds is vital to your child's growth and intellectual development. There are several other advantages to having a one-on-one sitter, such as convenience, having close daily interaction with your child's caregiver, and not worrying about your child getting sick from other children. And if your sitter speaks another language it can be a great opportunity to introduce your baby to a second language.

Despite these advantages, having a one-on-one babysitter can be expensive, especially if the caregiver is living with you. But you can lower the cost by hiring someone part-time and juggling the rest of the time with relatives, sharing a sitter with another family, or taking your child to the caregiver's home. Finding a good sitter can also be stressful and time-consuming—or not. Before you start to look, clearly define for yourself what your needs and priorities are. For example, do you want someone black? A young person or someone who's older? Are you expecting the person to clean your house as well as care for the child?

Once you've decided what you want, it's time to start looking. The best ways to find a sitter are:

- *Recommendations from friends.* Parents whose lifestyles and parenting philosophies are similar to yours are great resources.
- *Recommendations from your pediatrician's office.* Staff members often know of good baby-sitters, and many offices have bulletin boards where sitters or families post notices advertising available caregivers.
- *Agencies.* Although agencies tend to cost a little more—they can charge a week's or even a month's salary as a finder's fee—a highly reputable one will prescreen, sometimes running background checks, and try to find experienced sitters who are appropriate to your needs and personality. Many will also train

The Pros and Cons of Day Care

When large numbers of women began entering the workplace in high numbers during the 1970s, experts on child development raised questions about the effect the mothers' working would have on their children. Women would have to choose, some experts and mothers thought, between career and family. Sending a young child to be cared for by someone else, the thinking went (and sometimes still does), would have devastating emotional effects on the child.

Fortunately, the worst fears are unfounded. For example, during their first two years, children are, in fact, safer at a day care center than in home settings (either at home or in home-based centers), according to a study published in the Brown University *Child and Adolescent Behavior Letter.* Children aged six months to two years fell while they were at home twice as often as children in day care facilities. (From age three to six, though, the gap lessened, with falls accounting for 65 percent of injuries at day care and 60 percent in home settings.) A long-term National Institutes of Health study showed that children cared for in settings with several other children have fewer behavior problems than those cared for by a full-time baby-sitter or in very small groups.

What's more, another recent national study compared three types of care—day care centers, home-based group day care, and home care (with or without the mother present). The study revealed that:

- *Children do not lose trust or have weakened emotional bonds with their mothers as a result of day care.* If the bond is secure, and the mother provides loving, sensitive, and attentive care at home, the child will be fine.
- *Children in high-quality day care tend to be more socially outgoing than home-reared children.* They are more cooperative, talkative, and comfortable meeting new people, and better able to participate in complex play.
- *Children from impoverished homes who are placed early benefit most from high-quality day care, showing greater intellectual development than children from the same backgrounds who don't attend day care.* However, children from affluent families gain the most cognitive advantages from staying home compared to their high-income peers who attended day care within their first year.
- *Children cared for at home and at home-based centers catch fewer flus, rashes, ear infections, and other childhood diseases than those at day care facilities.*

Do It Yourself: Forming Your Own Child Care Cooperative

Fed up with trying to find high-quality and affordable options for child care, many parents are finding innovative ways to share child care responsibilities.

Baby-sitting cooperatives, in which parents can bank baby-sitting time for their own children by baby-sitting other people's children, are a more organized version of what used to be dropping the kids off at a trusted neighbor's and returning the favor. If you know a group of parents nearby with children about the same age as yours, consider pooling your resources. This option works especially well for parents who work part-time or who need time alone, with a loved one, or simply to get things done. While one parent watches the kids for several hours, the other takes care of her business—and then they switch. This is a great way for you and your child to make friends and to expand your support network. As always, be sure to choose people you trust and who have similar parenting styles.

and provide support services for their child care workers. If you're looking for a live-in sitter, agencies tend to be the easiest and best bet for finding a match. Use only a licensed, highly recommended, or established agency.

- *Schools.* Often career centers or student information boards will allow you to post a notice of what you're looking for and get names of sitters.
- *Church.* This is a great resource because often the sitters are people in your community. You can find or place ads on bulletin boards or in newsletters.

Once you've gotten several candidates, begin setting up interviews with those who sound the best over the phone. Your baby needs to be present during the interview, because it's the interaction—how the sitter holds the baby, comforts him, and manages stressful crying—that's important. The best way to do this is to let them spend some time together in front of you.

Some qualities to look for are:

- *Experience.* Choose someone who has cared for a baby before—even if it was just her grandchildren. Ideally, find a sitter who has looked after babies your child's age. The more long-term (more than a year) jobs she's had, the better. Ask her to describe some particularly difficult situations and how she dealt with them, such as a colicky or sick baby. Ask her for references to verify her experience. Ask former employers to provide a balanced assessment of the candidate's personality and performance; responses can be revealing.

- *Enthusiasm.* It takes a lot of patience and caring to be responsible for an infant or young child. If your sitter comes to the job because she loves children and is eager to think of creative ways to pass the time, then you've found a good candidate. If, however, baby-sitting is only a job or a temporary gig, you may want to reconsider.
- *Compatibility.* Before you leave your baby in a sitter's hands, be sure you are in agreement about child care practices. Will the sitter pick up your baby when he starts to cry, or does she consider it "spoiling"? Will she discipline a child for being too messy? Does she believe in spanking? These are issues that can cause a great deal of friction, so it's best to discuss them early. You also need to consider the caregiver's personality and how it meshes with your own. If you want to maintain a formal relationship, but your baby-sitter is laid back, it may not work. Try to discern whether you are a good match in terms of age (do you want a young, energetic sitter, or more of a grandmotherly type?), temperament (is she too nervous for you?), and habits (is she frustrated by your messy apartment?).
- *Flexibility.* This is especially important if you work. You should discuss what would happen if you had to work late, if she's available on weekends, and any other situation that might come up that would affect her. As part of your agreement, you should work out some kind of a holiday, sick day, and vacation schedule so you can plan ahead of time when you'll need alternative care.
- *Honesty.* Don't be afraid to ask whether the person you are interviewing to watch your child has ever been arrested, used drugs, or abused a child. You may be uncomfortable with the way she responds. Even if you don't get a straight answer, at least you will have asked. And many agencies, surprisingly, do not have this kind of information on file. There are organizations that can run a criminal background check for you.
- *Responsibilities.* Be sure to spell out exactly what you want her to do. Perhaps all you need is child care. In other cases, you might want someone who will do light housekeeping, laundry, or run errands. Make sure your expectations match hers.
- *Cost.* You'll need to have a blunt, detailed conversation about how much the sitter costs. Some short-term sitters work for hourly wages from as little as $4 per

hour (for high school or college students generally) up to $10 per hour. Full-time sitters often work on a weekly wage from under $100 to $550, depending on if they are live-ins, hours, responsibilities, and location (major metropolitan areas, such as New York and Los Angeles, tend to be more expensive).

- *Training in CPR and other first aid procedures.* Many parents require that a baby-sitter have CPR baby training (which is different from CPR training for adults). If you find a sitter whom you like but who doesn't have training or needs a refresher course, you can offer to pay for a class. (You should take one, too!) They last a couple of hours and are generally held at local hospitals, nursery schools, community centers, or pediatrician offices.

Family-Based Care

This type of care is also called group home care because one baby-sitter looks after a small number of children in her home. Many parents like this situation, because it allows their children to be around peers and still get a lot of attention from one consistent caregiver. This can also be a cheaper alternative to a full-time baby-sitter, especially for those parents who work at home or only need child care on certain days.

The use of family day care has declined over the last decade, according to the report "Who's Minding Our Preschoolers?," in part because of "a growing uneasiness of parents to use a minimally regulated arrangement where there is a single provider" and reports of abuse and neglect by care providers. Because most group home centers aren't licensed, issues of safety, intellectual stimulation, and health often worry parents. Also, the informal nature of family care can mean a revolving door, where new children come and go.

The best way to find a family care center is either through word-of-mouth or a referral service. Ideally, look for a registered or licensed facility. Even if you know the caregiver, be sure to visit the home before committing yourself. Here are some things to look for and ask about:

- *How safe is the environment?* Just as you did when you baby-proofed your house, think of what your child could possibly hurt himself on or get into—electrical outlets, unprotected stoves, glass, table corners, or windows without guards. Studies indicate that group home care is the least safe of all child-care arrangements, so be on guard.

- *How many children are there?* Think of how much patience and vigilance it takes to watch your own child. When you add two, three, or even four small children, it gets infinitely more complicated regardless of how much experience a caregiver has. Be sure the sitter doesn't book too many children in one day or you'll run the risk of less supervision, less attention, and more accidents. The main advantage of family care is its low caregiver-to-child ratio.
- *What do the children do all day?* Some family care providers are highly organized and pride themselves on finding creative ways to interact with the children. However, many lack the money and education to implement a structured curriculum that emphasizes cognitive development. A good provider will have plenty of toys, allow for naps and some outdoor play, provide meals, and perhaps engage the children in arts and crafts. A poor one will rely on the television and confine children to a very limited indoor space.
- *What disciplinary measures does she use?* Find out how the caregiver handles physical disputes between children and what kinds of rules and expectations she has for the children. You need to be very up front about your limits as well (no spanking or time-outs longer than two minutes, for example). Putting a misbehaving youngster in an empty, dark, or locked room as punishment is both unacceptable and abusive.
- *What do they eat?* Many group care centers have children bring their own lunches and may provide a midday and mid-afternoon snack. Be sure to ask what they eat, when they eat, and if the caregiver has the equipment to heat food for a hot lunch.
- *How flexible are the hours?* Although it may cost you extra, many providers will let you drop off early and pick up late. Talk specifically about your needs and lifestyle to see how accommodating she can be and what costs extra.
- *What about illness?* Most family care providers don't want sick children to come in because they run the risk of infecting other children. Find out what her policy is on sick children as well as what arrangements she might make in case she becomes ill. Does she have backup or someone else to refer you to?
- *What are the costs?* Costs often vary according to your child's age, the number of hours, and location (major metropolitan areas are more expensive). Rates can be set by the hour, week, or a combination of the two for any extra sitting.

They can range from about $60 a week (for about six hours a day) to $300 per week.

Toddler and Preschooler

Now that your child is a bit older, she needs more stimulation and interaction with other children. That means it's time to look into day care centers, nursery schools, and preschools.

In the past, "day care" referred to a facility with extended hours meant mostly for working parents, nursery school was a program offered only a few mornings a week for children's enrichment, and preschool was a half-day program designed to ease young-

When Your Relatives Baby-Sit

Since almost half of us use our relatives as our primary means of child care, having clear-cut expectations and agreements are crucial to this type of arrangement. As with any baby-sitter, do a trial run for a week or even a month to see how things work out—or don't. Here are some issues to consider:

- ***Family doesn't always mean free.*** **Having a relative sit can take some of the worry out of child care, because nobody loves your children like family. However, don't forget that many family members baby-sit not only out of love, but also as a means of extra income. In the U.S. Department of Commerce report "What Does It Cost to Mind Our Preschoolers?" the average weekly cost of having a relative sit was $42 for about 28 hours. If you're considering asking a relative to sit, be sure to work out ahead of time whether and how much to pay.**
- ***Be clear about your philosophy.*** **If you have a family member whose disciplinary tactics or childrearing ideas are very different from yours, you should make your limits and values known. For example, you may not believe in spanking and prefer to avoid junk food. If your relative doesn't respect your beliefs, you may need to find an alternative.**
- ***Be considerate.*** **Don't take advantage of the kindness of your relatives—or start a family feud—by constantly showing up late or calling at the last minute. Treat your relative with the consideration and professionalism you would show a non-relative sitter.**

sters into kindergarten. These terms are more fluid now: Many day care centers now provide programs for cognitive development, nursery schools last all day, and preschools have designated toddler programs.

New research points to the many benefits of day care, preschool, and nursery school. "There is a long-standing myth that parents felt better having their children at home," says Melinda W. Green, past president of the National Association for Childcare Resource and Referral Agencies. "The latest research shows that children do as well or better in quality settings, because the social environment is a plus." She recommends that at about age four, if not before, children should be enrolled in some sort of group program to prepare them for school. "Children need to interact and learn to be social," she stresses. This should come as a relief to many working parents who don't have a choice about staying home with their children.

Picking a Program

Once you start to explore the many child care options, you will discover a seemingly endless array of schools, centers, and programs to send our children to. Some programs emphasize academics such as math and reading; others focus on a foreign language; others target gifted and talented children; and still others emphasize ethnicity, religion, or culture. Montessori schools are another option. Montessori trademarks include children learning at their own pace, placing children of different ages and abilities in the same classroom, and an emphasis on learning through hands-on experience.

From parents, personal experience, and media reports we know that not all of these choices are right for all children. To narrow the field, get recommendations from friends and relatives, or find a referral agency. The National Association for Childcare Resource and Referral Agencies is an excellent place to start. It can help you find local accredited (and nonaccredited) facilities as well as other resources based on your child's age and family needs. (The phone number is listed at the end of this chapter.) Don't rule out workplace options. Some large corporations—but not many—offer on-site child care for employees. Others provide referral services for local child care providers, or offer "emergency" child care for nights you have to work late or leave town. Ask the human resources department what your company provides.

When it's time to choose a day care center or preschool, visit at least three to five different schools (preferably without your child first) to assess each one's philosophy, space, and staff. Go during school hours and ask to see both the class that your child will be in and older classes, so you can see what his future classes will be like if he stays. Always call ahead for an appointment, but show up a little early or stay later so you can observe on your own how the center is run.

Once you've narrowed your options, weigh the pluses and minuses of each school by arranging for your child to visit and interact for part of a day. Then go with your instinct. If you get a bad feeling, even if you don't know why, take that strongly into consideration. If you have a sense that a place "feels right" for your child, it probably is. You may want to ask to contact parents whose children are enrolled in the program to hear about their experience and confirm any "hunches" you have.

Here's a checklist of important features to consider:

1. *Cost.* These days tot programs can cost almost as much as a college education! Depending on your geographic location, how many hours and days your child is in the program, and the center's reputation, tuition can vary greatly from a few thousand to over $10,000 a year, not necessarily including summer months. Tuition generally doesn't include transportation costs (which some schools offer), nor does it necessarily include prepared meals.

Don't let the price tag impress or deter you. High tuition doesn't necessarily mean a better education or experience for your child. Many less expensive programs are of very high quality. If it's out of your price range, check with the program director and referral agencies to see if you qualify for any tuition assistance programs, especially with programs that emphasize diversity.

2. *Safety.* The last thing you want to worry about is whether your child is safe. Check for the basics—outlet covers, safe outdoor equipment and flooring, fencing and safety from cars, and appropriate toys—and then look around for any other problems. Carelessness such as cleaning products not put away safely, plastic bags within reach, or unprotected sharp corners could all be signs of future trouble. All staff should be certified in CPR and first aid training and the facility should have emergency plans in case of fire.

3. *Nurturing environment.* During the early years especially, children need a sense of caring and security when away from their homes and families, often for the first time. This is more important than what they will actually learn during the day; in fact, without it, learning will be difficult. Watch how the staff interacts with the children. Look for lots of hugs, praise, smiles, interacting on the child's eye level, and extra cuddling for those dealing with separation. If you see caregivers reprimanding a lot, giving too many rules, yelling, or speaking harshly to the children, it could be a bad sign.

4. *Racial mix.* For African-American parents, this is perhaps one of the largest areas of concern. Early childhood education specialists, such as Louise Derman-Sparks, director of the Anti-Bias Education Leadership Project in Pasadena, California, believe that black children greatly benefit from a racially mixed or all-black setting. "Most kids aren't going to all-black schools," says Derman-Sparks. "So parents need to make sure that the programs they send their kids to can handle diversity issues and that all types are represented."

New research highlights the benefits of child care programs—good news for millions of working parents.

The "only one" syndrome can have a negative effect on a child, warns Derman-Sparks. "Although it depends on how strongly parents talk about ethnicity, most kids tend not to want to be different," she explains. "Even if they haven't experienced direct racism or rejection, they can feel invisible in the class and want to be like the others." Sensitive programs that may not be ethnically diverse can still honor different cultures every day through staff selection, posters, books, guest speakers, art projects, and theme days.

California psychologist and educator Thomas Parham, Ph.D., feels that the optimal setting for African-American children is one that clicks with the child's personality. "Kids need environments that are loving, stimulating, safe, supportive, and challenging," he says. "Many all-white environments are often not supportive to black children—though they could be. But it depends: If it's an all-white [program] and is very loving, it could be less traumatic than an all-black school with a bully."

Ideally, look for a balanced program that is nurturing, developmentally challenging, and racially mixed.

5. *Stimulating environment.* The room should be filled (but not overflowing) with a variety of activities geared toward different areas of interest. "If the class is very neat or too chaotic, it means that little creativity or active learning is taking place," says Derman-Sparks. "There should be artwork on the wall done by the children. You want to see the kids' impact on the environment but with some structure." Structured activities to promote reading and language could include children dictating stories, "writing" (scribbles at first that later develop into words) in diaries, or creating books. To help them understand math concepts, children should have access to scales, water tables for pouring, measuring cups, a calendar, and a play store.

6. *Flexible hours.* Many schools offer extended morning and afternoon hours for working parents. Discuss short-term (say, one evening that you may be running late) or long-term (if you have regular hours) arrangements and fees.

7. *Discipline.* Ask about the disciplinary measures caregivers take and under what circumstances. Hitting, biting, and fighting should call for some cooling off time or for a child to be reprimanded. But children younger than three, who aren't old enough to control their impulses or follow rules consistently, may not be ready for official time-outs. Beginning at about three or four, short time-outs, lasting no longer than a couple of minutes, may help a child calm down before rejoining the group. In all, discipline should mirror what you do at home and should always be geared toward teaching your child rather than simply punishing her. During your visit, observe how the staff handles incidents and ask questions about rules. Some schools' philosophies may not be to your liking, as they may be either too strict or too lax.

8. *Teaching style.* There are many different types of educational training, each with its own emphasis. Some schools and centers are more group oriented, while others emphasize independence. The program director often sets the tone, determining how the staff directs the children's activities, so note if these don't fit your child's learning style. For instance, if your child is very active and likes to learn by role-playing, be sure you cross off any programs that would expect her to sit through a lecture. A better choice might be one that's more interactive and encourages her personal learning style.

9. *Attitude toward parents.* A good program will allow you to visit your child

"My mother had raised two young children without daily help. What was wrong with me?" **—Allison's Story**

When Miles was born, I was under the false impression that I would be able to continue to work at home as a writer and care for him without needing extra help—at least for the first couple of years. Not only was I naïve, but I also underestimated just how complex life was with children, work or no work.

After Miles's first month, I put myself back on a strict at-home work schedule. I quickly discovered what should have been obvious: As Miles grew older, he slept less and needed more time and attention. Life was not getting easier, but harder. And with my extended family on the other side of the country, I knew I needed some extra help.

Fortunately, my husband and I were able to find a wonderful baby-sitter to come in every day for several hours. I soon realized how much I hadn't been able to do before. Working on my book had been nearly impossible, and simple errands like walking to the grocery store had been a major production with a baby in tow. I hadn't had a meal out, seen a movie, or visited with a friend in ages. Being relieved by Miles's sitter was a freeing experience, and, I soon realized, a necessary one.

As Miles got older and began to walk, I depended on his sitter more and more until she was eventually full-time. Without her, I couldn't keep the house picked up, cook dinner, make business calls, write, or have any time alone without interruption. At first I felt incompetent. My mother had raised two young children without daily help and she seemed to be able to function well. What was wrong with me that I needed so much extra assistance with just one child? Was I just lazy and not working hard enough, even though I was going to bed exhausted every night?

When I talked to my mother, she reminded me that she wasn't working at home while raising us. She also said that when Miles had stayed at her house, it was a complete wreck. I also discussed my feelings with a close friend, an experienced mother who was at home finishing her Ph.D. Although she was strapped for cash, she and her husband hired a baby-sitter for their daughter. Working at home was still working, and children of working mothers need care while their mothers are on the job.

Miles is now in nursery school, so I no longer need a baby-sitter to care for him while I work. However, I miss not having to juggle cooking dinner with supervising a toddler. Nevertheless, both of our needs are being met: He goes to a wonderful program where he can take part in organized activities with his peers, and I can be available for him when he's at home and continue to have a career that I enjoy when he's not.

"I needed to be less focused on teaching my children, and more directed toward exposing them to different experiences so they can learn what, when, and how they want." **—ANNE'S STORY**

I believe children are brilliant and are able to learn much more than adults. From the time my children were infants, I wanted to expose them to as many different experiences as possible. I wanted to take advantage of their natural curiosity and let them experiment and explore their interests. I also wanted them to understand that learning is not limited to school, and that they should be prepared to learn and explore their entire lives. So with these lofty goals, I set about reading, singing, playing music, dancing, and talking to my children, hoping they would take in some of the things I was trying to show them. Part of what I wanted them to learn was the basics they would need to know for school. The alphabet, counting, shapes, and colors were all things I taught and tried to incorporate into our daily lives.

After a while, it became clear that each of my daughters was learning, but each was learning in her own way. My oldest liked to please me and was delighted when I showed her how happy I was with her accomplishments. This made it easy to teach her. As she was learning her ABCs, my smiles, praise, and hugs were all that was needed to make her eager to learn. On the other hand, my youngest child was much less interested in pleasing me. All my attempts at the ABCs were met with frustration. She seemed more interested in other things, was bored with my attempts, and wasn't especially moved when I praised the efforts she did make. As time went on, my oldest daughter moved from ABC to C-A-T and started to read. At first, she was reading simple words from books I had taught her, but then she suddenly took off and was reading things I had never taught. When she started preschool, the teachers said it was too early to teach reading when I asked for their help. So I continued with my own efforts and found myself the proud mother of the only child in kindergarten who was able to read.

Without trying to push too hard, I encouraged my younger daughter to at least learn her letters, but she continued to refuse. Then one day she gave me a frustrated look when I asked her about letters in a book and blurted out "Mommy, that's an A-N-I-M-A-L, OK?!" I just sat there with my mouth open. It was as if she were telling me "Give me a break, I'm learning but I'm doing it in my own way, in my own time." Since then, I've stopped trying to get her to learn the way her sister did. I realized that my oldest daughter learned to read because it's what she really wanted to do; I just

helped. My youngest daughter, on the other hand, has great insight and can take things she understands, apply them to other situations, and come up with something new and wonderful. She is learning a lot, but feels less of a need to please me by showing what she knows. I also discovered she has learned to read some words—she spelled out the word EAT with spaghetti—she just doesn't see the purpose of letting me know. Finally, I realized that I needed to be less focused on teaching my children, and more directed toward exposing them to different experiences so they can learn what, when, and how they want.

unannounced at any time—a policy you should take advantage of, especially if you have any questions about your child's behavior or performance. The best schools encourage regular parental involvement. You and other parents could help with curriculum, offer suggestions, join parent groups, be a guest speaker, and attend parent-teacher conferences at least a few times a year. Many centers have parent lounges where you can informally talk and observe your children. Teachers should also have some system of communicating daily with parents about their children's progress, through informal talks or a diary.

10. *Community services.* As the demand for child care outside the home has increased, so have the needs of the families using them. In response to these needs, a different type of day care has evolved, one that moves beyond just taking care of the little ones to becoming more like community centers. For example, Parent Services Project in the Bay Area works with parents and staff members of day care centers to set up programs based on the needs of parents and children. Through extensive training, PSP provides family support through workshops and classes and has built a network of over five hundred centers. Because day care centers are a place that families go to daily, those affiliated with the project have expanded their outreach services to include drug abuse prevention, parenting workshops, access to health care, and other critical programs that help working parents.

11. *Sick child policy.* Some centers have sick-child rooms away from the main classrooms. These rooms are generally staffed with a separate caregiver, though not necessarily a medically trained staffer. Most children admitted to sick-child rooms aren't seriously ill, but are sick enough to be temporarily separated from other children where they can receive extra attention and rest. Be sure a physician is on call and readily available if you leave your child at a sickroom. This is a great feature for working parents who can't miss many days of work and who can't find or afford emergency child care.

12. *Staff ratio, qualifications, and longevity.* These factors, which are often ignored or overlooked when parents get sold on other aspects of a program, can reveal a lot about the quality of a program. For example, staff ratio (which should be no more than four or five children under three per staff member and eight to ten per staff member for preschoolers) can indicate how much attention your child will receive as well as how much control the staff has over the class. Staff qualifications, like a graduate degree or accreditation certificate, may predict how creative a teacher is, how she handles behavioral problems, and what she expects from the children. Finally, longevity is a good indicator of how happy the staff is (if they're treated well and paid well, they're less likely to leave), which can greatly affect how they treat the children. Look for programs with low child-to-caregiver ratios, teachers with advanced degrees in early childhood education or development, and staff who have been in the program for more than two years.

13. *Meals and snacks.* The most convenient programs provide snacks and lunches for free or include meals in the cost of tuition. Ideally, these will include hot lunches. However, many centers ask parents to pack lunches while they provide the snacks (usually juice and crackers). Find out if the school has a microwave so you can pack food that a staff member can heat for your child's lunch.

14. *Diaper policy.* Some programs screen out diaper-wearers after the age of three or four, so be sure to ask what the cut-off age is, if any. There should be a separate area away from food for diaper changing. Caregivers should wash their hands after diapering each child (some schools provide latex gloves and each child is required to bring his own diapering supplies), and diapers should be disposed of in a sanitary way. If you can smell dirty diapers, ask why.

15. *Nap times.* Some programs offer nap periods for children to sleep or just take an extended break. Ask when children nap and for how long. Some providers will let sleepyheads nap for as long as they need to, but others will insist on sticking to tighter schedules. Inquire about sleeping accommodations or bringing bedding for your child.

16. *Licensing and accreditation.* Most states or municipalities have codes and standards for child care operators that provide for the safety and health of the children (such as clearly marked fire exits, adequate ventilation, and acceptable number of people per classroom). Centers that pass these inspections are given a license or registration, and may be periodically reinspected. In some states, programs are not allowed to operate without this certificate. However, if your city or state doesn't require a license, you should carefully inspect and inquire about each facility yourself before sending your child there.

Many programs go beyond these local codes to meet higher standards set by independent national organizations. Programs that meet the rigorous requirements of an agency like the National Association for Family Child Care are issued accreditation certificates. These standards generally center on educational requirements and staff qualifications in many of the areas listed above (curriculum, child-to-staff ratio, staff-parent interaction, and staff training), though they often include health, nutrition, and safety as well. The Child Development Association (CDA, which trains and certifies teachers), National Association for the Education of Young Children (NAEYC, which sets standards for highly qualified care centers), and the National Association for Family Child Care (NAFCC, which awards certificates to family child care centers that pass 186 criteria) are three of the leading accreditation programs. Although certification from one of these programs is no guarantee that the program is of high quality, most good to excellent child care programs are accreditated.

Enrolling in a Program

Once you find a program you like and your child is enrolled, your active participation is crucial to how well your child does in that environment. Close communication with the program director and your child's teacher will help you to evaluate how well she is adjusting. Make a point to ask the teacher every day how your child is doing and ask your child the same. You will get a strong sense of whether or not your child is happy, being treated fairly, and is being challenged. If you aren't satisfied for any reason, approach the staff with your concerns. Be open to suggestions, their reasons for taking a course of action (even if your child doesn't like it, it still may be appropriate), and devise a plan together to improve matters.

If you and your child are still unhappy or the staff is not receptive, consider

"At Montessori, they're teaching Layla how to write and do math problems—plus she can count to eight in Swahili." **—Elijah Jones, father of Layla, age 4; Southfield, Michigan**

I had my daughter Layla in a day care that was about 60 to 70 percent white. At first I didn't think it was a problem, but soon I noticed that she was aware of racial issues, and they were affecting her self-esteem. She'd notice things like positive white cartoon characters and negative black ones. That worried me.

I decided to check out the Open Door Montessori Institute, which I had heard good things about. It was in Detroit, was black-owned, and stressed religion as well as mathematics. I walked through the school and talked to some of the teachers and was impressed. Layla would get to learn about black role models like Martin Luther King and see real African-American role models like the teachers and parents who were doing positive things.

When she enrolled at Montessori, I could see the effects right away. For one, at four, she knows things I didn't know at four. The other day she whipped off the fifty states. I can't even do that now! The day care provided activities for them, but they didn't really stress academics. At Montessori, they're teaching Layla how to write and do math problems—plus she can count to eight in Swahili, and she can tell you about Martin Luther King and Jesse Jackson.

Another thing I like is that the parents—many of them black—make presentations to the students about their lives and jobs. I hope these positive role models influence the students' characters as they go on to other grades and as they go on in life. These are the kinds of things that I don't think she'd get in other schools.

another program. But make this decision carefully, because too much change can be difficult, if not traumatic, for your child.

Making the Transition to Kindergarten

Because so many children spend at least part of their early years in a group program, the emphasis of kindergarten has shifted. Now kindergarten focuses less on helping children adjust to group and school environments and more on advancing their cognitive skills. In fact, many schools expect children to enter kindergarten knowing the following:

- colors, numbers, shapes, and sizes

- how to use pencil, crayons, and scissors
- how to work in a group, and independently as part of a larger group
- how to share, take turns, and respect other's property
- how to follow directions and rules and pay attention long enough for a short lesson
- how to identify common objects by sight and name, such as animals and household items
- how to use a wide variety of words in sentences, usually through an exposure to reading

If your child has spent all or most of his time at home or with relatives, don't worry. Studies show that once exposed to these concepts (which many children learn at home anyway), they quickly catch up to their peers without any disadvantages

Problems with the Program: Signs to Watch For

If your child isn't adjusting well to a particular program, any number of reasons could be causing the problem: He's being singled out by his teacher, his personality doesn't match the program, he isn't getting along with a particular child, or—at worst—he may be the victim of abuse. Dr. Thomas Parham suggests looking for the following signs:

- ***Changes in habits.*** **If your child isn't eating or sleeping well, or her toilet habits change (she starts soiling herself when she usually doesn't), take notice. She may be trying to communicate her distress through nonverbal cues.**
- ***Anxiety.*** **Fears about going to school or crying or clinging excessively when you leave her are signs that your child could be unhappy in her program. This is especially true if she liked it before.**

Signs of physical abuse include:

- ***Unexplained injuries.***
- ***Bruises, marks, burns, especially any that look suspicious.***
- ***Repeated injuries, regardless of explanation.***
- ***Genital injuries or infections.***
- ***Extreme focus on sexuality, sex games, or inappropriate sexual activities.*** **(For more on sexual abuse, see Chapter 4.)**

regardless of age. Keep in mind that your child's progress before, during, and after kindergarten will vary from the other kids in the class.

In many communities kindergarten is now considered part of primary school education, though in some cases it's not mandatory. Your child's current preschool program may have a kindergarten class, or you can check with your local public school, or another local program (such as a private or parochial school). Decide which program best meets your needs and your child's in terms of hours, ease of transition, location, and quality.

Children who haven't attended a group program before can get kindergarten "practice" a few weeks before school begins by participating in organized play groups, where they can learn about sharing, making friends, and following rules. Aside from making sure they learn how to socialize with other kids, you can prepare your kids for kindergarten by reading to them and establishing a daily schedule. Talk to your child about what's in store, and, if possible, go for a visit so he can see where his class will be, meet his teacher, and find his cubbyhole. Once your child is enrolled in school and he's established a regular routine, he'll soon adjust and be on his way to getting a formal education.

RESOURCES

Recommended Reading for Parents

America's Smallest School: The Family, Paul E. Barton and Richard J. Coley (Educational Testing Service, 1992). This book discusses the importance of parental involvement in educating children.

Black Teachers on Teaching, Michelle Foster (The New Press, 1997). This book documents the triumphs and struggles of twenty African-American teachers.

Critical Issues in Educating African American Youth, Jawanza Kunjufu (African American Images, 1989). This book tackles such questions as how a single, low-income parent can produce a successful student and how can blacks do well on standardized tests.

A Great Balancing Act: Equitable Education for Girls and Boys, National Association of Independent Schools, (202) 973–9749. This book discusses how parents and teachers can work to eradicate gender inequality in education.

The Hare Plan to Overhaul the Public Schools and Educate Every Black Man, Woman and Child, Julia and Nathan Hare (The Black Think Tank, 1991). The writers offer ten tips for helping your child get the most out of the educational process.

Kindergarten at Home, Cheryl Gorder (Blue Bird Publishing, 1977). This is a detailed guide on how to educate young children at home, written by an advocate of preschool and kindergarten home schooling.

Meeting at the Crossroads: Women's Psychology and Girl's Development, Carol Gilligan and Lyn Mikel Brown (Ballantine Books, 1993 [reprint]). This book provides insight into how girls learn to be silent and disconnected on their way to adulthood.

Multicultural Education Resource Guide, Cheryl Gorder (Blue Bird Publishing, 1995). This book assists parents and teachers in instructing children on cultural diversity.

Raising Lifelong Learners: A Parent's Guide, Lucy Calkins (Addison-Wesley Publishing, 1997). The authors of this book help parents become strong advocates for their children's educations. The book includes tips on everything from how to pick a preschool or kindergarten to building the foundations of literacy, math, and analytical skills.

Recommended Reading for Children

Afro-Bets Series is an Afrocentric series of books featuring black children in a variety of educational lessons. Titles include:

Afro-Bets ABC Book, Cheryl Willis Hudson, Culverson Blair (Just Us Books, 1991).

Afro-Bets 1, 2, 3 Book, Cheryl Willis Hudson (Just Us Books, 1988).

Afro-Bets: Book of Shapes, Margery Wheeler Brown (Just Us Books, 1991).

Afro-Bets: Book of Colors, Margery Wheeler Brown (Just Us Books, 1991).

Moja Means One: Swahili Counting Book, Muriel Feelings, illustrated by Tom Feelings (Dial Books for Young Readers, 1997). This is an award-winning book with illustrations of East African life.

My Little People School Bus, Doris Tomaselli, illustrated by Carolyn Bracken and the Paqui Team (Joshua Morris Publishing, 1997). This lift-the-flap board book, featuring the multiracial Fisher-Price kids, teaches young children about opposites, shapes, colors, feelings, and more.

Ten, Nine, Eight, Molly Bang (Tupelo Books, 1983). This book depicts a young girl of African descent as she counts her way to bedtime.

Support Groups and Organizations

Child Care

Child Care Aware Information Line, 2116 Campus Dr. SE, Rochester, MN 55904, (800) 424–2246, fax: (507) 287–7198, e-mail: HN6125@handsnet.org. This organization helps find child care resources and referral agencies.

National Association for Childcare Resources and Referral Agencies, 1313 F St., NW, Washington, D.C. 20004, (202) 393–5501. This organization assists parents across the country in locating child care facilities in their areas.

Parents Services Project, Inc., 199 Porteous Ave., Fairfax, CA 94930, (415) 454–1870, fax: (415) 454–1752. The Parents Services Project provides a wide range of activities and services to parents and families across the country, including leadership training, education workshops, parent support groups, and multicultural activities. Call to find out how you can open a parenting services project in your day care facility.

Education

Association for Childhood Education International, 17904 Georgia Ave., Suite 215, Olney, MD 20832, (800) 423–3563. This group designs programs and distributes publications on the education of children from infancy through middle school.

The Black Student Fund, 3636 16th St., NW, 4th floor, Washington, D.C. 20010, (202) 387–1414. BSF was established to desegregate elite, private schools in Maryland, Virginia, and the District of Columbia. It provides financial aid to students and distributes a directory of independent day and boarding schools in Maryland, Virginia, and D.C. ($3).

Council for Basic Education, 1319 F St., NW, Washington, D.C. 20005, (202) 374–4171. This organization makes available to members a newsletter, monthly magazine, and other information and services. The council also distributes a checklist of what to look for in a good school called "How Does Your School Measure Up?"

Educational Testing Service, ETS-Rosedale Rd., Princeton, NJ 08541, (609) 921–9000. ETS provides referral information and publications on education and the evaluation of children.

ERIC Clearinghouse on Urban Education, Institute for Urban and Minority Education, Teachers College, Box 40, Columbia University, New York, NY 10027, (212) 678–3000. The focus of this organization is on the education of urban residents and minorities, multicultural education, and racial, ethnic, and sex equity issues. The clearinghouse offers a national information service.

Family Math, Steve Jordan, Department of Mathematics, Computer Science and Statistics, University of Illinois at Chicago, 851 S. Morgan, Chicago, IL 60607–7054, (312) 996–7000, e-mail: Jordan@uic.edu. Family Math is a family-based program developed to encourage underrepresented groups (especially girls and students of color) to enter careers in mathematics.

Institute for Independent Education, 1313 N. Capital St., NE, Washington, D.C. 20002, (202) 745–0500. The institute distributes the Directory of Independent Schools ($6.50). This pamphlet lists names, numbers, and descriptions of African-American community-based schools across the United States.

National Association for the Education of Young Children, 1509 16th St., NW, Washington, D.C. 20036, (800) 424–2460, (202) 232–8777.

Website: www.nais-schools.org

This organization provides literature and other services to parents and educators.

National Association of Independent Schools, 1620 L St., NW, Washington, D.C. 20036, (202) 973–9700, e-mail: hhoerle@nais-schools.org

Website: www.nais-schools.org
Call to receive "The Family Guide to Financial Aid" and "Financing Private School Education," free pamphlets that provide important information on how to meet the financial demands of private school.

Toussaint Institute Fund, 20 Exchange Pl., 41st floor, New York, NY 10005–3201, (212) 422–5338. The institute provides a directory of historically independent black day and boarding schools in New York and New Jersey ($14.95 plus $1.50 shipping and handling).

African-American Schools

The following is a sampling from around the country of all-black schools with programs for young children.

Ivy Leaf Preschool, 629 E. Church Lane, Philadelphia, PA 19144, (215) 844–5440, Bettye Lighty, lead teacher. As one of the largest and oldest African-American schools in the country, Ivy Leaf offers nursery, pre-K, and kindergarten classes with additional kindergarten class at their lower school.

New Concept School, 7825 S. Ellis St., Chicago, IL 60619, (773) 651–9599, Taifa Daniels, director. New Concept School offers preschool to 4th grade classes.

Piney Woods School, Highway 49S and Piney Woods Road, Piney Woods, MS 39148–9989, (601) 845–2214, fax: (601) 845–2604. Piney Woods School offers preschool and kindergarten classes with boarding for grades 7–12.

Rottschafer Preschool (affiliated with Southern Normal School), 1787 Kirkland Rd., Brewton, AL 36426, (334) 809–0579, Frances Lewis, director. Rottschafer Preschool offers day care and preschool.

The Sheenway School and Culture Center, 10101 S. Broadway, Los Angeles, CA 90003, (213) 757–8359, fax: (213) 757–0955, Delores Sheen, director. The Sheenway School offers preschool through 12th grade.

Sister Clara Muhammad School, 102 W. 116th St., New York, NY 10026, (212) 622–2200, Abdul Rahaim Ali, principal. Affiliated with the Nation of Islam, this school offers religious instruction and an academic program for kindergarten to 8th grades.

Ujamaa School, 1554 8th St., NW, Washington, D.C. 20001, (202) 232–2997, Mr. Zulu, director. The Ujamaa School offers an academic orientation with integrated study of Nguzo Saba—the principles of Kwanzaa—for kindergarten through 8th grades.

Mentoring Programs

Big Brothers, Big Sisters, 230 N. 13th St., Philadelphia, PA 19107, (215) 567–7000, fax: (215) 567–0394.

Website: www.bbbsa.org

With 504 chapters across the country, this organization offers mentoring services and special events.

Girls, Inc., 30 E. 33rd St., New York, NY 10016, (212) 689–3700, fax: (212) 683–1253. This organization runs girls' clubs and mentoring programs designed to help girls become smart, strong, and bold.

Chapter

11

Learning and Play

As parents, we need to remember how much joy we took as children learning about life and how the world works. Although life was not always easy, even as tots, we could spend hours playing "house," building with blocks, or in a secret hideout with a best friend. Some of our favorite childhood memories are of our parents getting down on their knees to have a tea party or tucking us into bed with a favorite stuffed animal. As parents ourselves, we now understand that play is really learning disguised as fun. The more we can help our children enjoy learning about new subjects, the more curious and excited they will become. In this chapter we will discuss how children learn, the importance of play in learning, and how we can foster our children's creativity, imagination, and friendships. This chapter will also provide parents with toy suggestions and other resources for helping our children learn through play.

The Building Blocks of Play

We've all heard the saying "play is hard work," and for children this couldn't be more true. In our community, though, we often frown on those who are "trifling" or those who seem to play and get no work done. Negative stereotypes about our laziness and the fear that our children will have to work twice as hard to get half as far in life have prompted many African-American parents to emphasize hard work over play.

Sherry C. Deane, who has helped create the Successful Parenting Program with the National Black Child Development Institute, says that many parents aren't convinced of the value of play for our children. "They have to learn that play is a child's work, and we try to encourage parents and children to play together," she says. Because play is inherently fun, we often assume learning isn't taking place. However, it's usually easier for us to recall information when the situation is pleasurable and fun rather than boring or rote. The same is true for our children. And keeping them excited about learning is the key to success in school, as long as we balance play with the expectation of hard work and discipline when it's called for. Parents who can learn how to leave their adult lives behind and immerse themselves in their child's world occasionally will come to see how important it is for all of us to let go. It's during these times that we are most creative, imaginative, and in touch with our true selves.

Baby

During the first year of life, the human brain makes an amazing leap of growth both in size and in the information it absorbs. Contrary to old beliefs that babies are just "vegetables" or that "nothing's going on inside," infants are processing more information and putting the brain to work more than they ever will in their lives. Because the first year is a time for tremendous growth and opportunity, knowing the best ways to interact with your baby will go a long way.

How Learning Happens

New research indicates that before a baby is born, his brain is making connections that will establish his ability to learn and function after birth. This activity continues during infancy, when each experience your baby has makes a connection in the brain's circuitry. While your child's inherited genes have helped build the brain and keep his body growing and functioning, his experiences after birth will shape what he will learn. Connections within the brain are made by stimulating experiences (playing peek-a-boo, listening to music, and handling a rattle, for instance). In fact, researchers have discovered that positive parental interaction and basic toys (forget baby computers, flash cards, and highly technical toys) have the greatest effect on a baby's brain. This is especially true if the experiences are fun and become part of the way a baby plays. Repeated experiences reinforce the connections and make them permanent.

Most researchers agree that this time of immense learning and growth sharply declines after the first year and continues to decline as a child grows. Babies who are exposed to a variety of rich and stimulating experiences will develop language skills, visual coordination, muscle control, and emotional attachments. The more a baby, and later a toddler, is allowed to explore in a loving and safe environment, the more skills (and talents) she will be likely to acquire later.

Our elders, who felt that children should be "seen and not heard" or demanded that as young children we "sit still and don't touch anything," may have been trying to protect us from a disapproving, sometimes hostile, society but that attitude may inhibit learning and exploring. Research bears this out: Studies show that depriving a baby or small child of learning experiences by confining her to a playpen for hours, or not allowing her to pick up, play with, and touch (or taste) a variety of objects can in-

The Blocks: Five Stages of Play

Stage 1: Infants learn to experiment with and then master motor skills through repetitive actions like pushing, grasping, sucking, and hitting. They learn that their actions can make things happen: by holding a rattle and moving her arm, she can make the rattle shake and make noise.

Stage 2: Toddlers build on their infant experience to play in a more deliberate and complex way. For instance, they will pick up a bottle and throw it to see what happens. They then will crawl after the bottle and repeat the same action, generally with several different kinds of objects, to see what effect throwing (or hitting or pushing) will have.

Stage 3: Once they have learned to distinguish between objects and how they work (if you push a ball it rolls, if you pull a drawer it opens), toddlers can then apply this knowledge to their ability to use objects and play with them in a different way. For example, they know a cup is for drinking and they serve you a cup of pretend tea.

Stage 4: Make-believe play combines the use of objects and children's emotional and social worlds. They transform themselves into characters (doctor, fireman, or daddy) and use props, or the props (a block, doll, or paper bag) will prompt the direction of play. Because they are more aware of their social surroundings, other people, especially their peers, become an important part of play.

Stage 5: By age five, children are playing games with clear rules and ways to determine winners. Playing becomes more organized, competitive, and purposeful, and can foster other learning or social skills. For instance, team sports encourage friendship and motor skills, while chess requires children to think strategically and intellectually.

hibit vital brain development. Says Madge Willis, Ph.D., assistant professor of psychology at Moorehouse College in Atlanta: "Too often, our overstressed lives leave us with little energy and patience to devote to picking up and supervising a curious baby." Still, while we parents should—and must—tend to our own needs, we must also try to continually find something interesting for our children to do.

Likewise, being raised in a traumatic household can also damage a young child's development. Studies show that abused children's brains have less activity in the areas that are responsible for emotional attachment and memory. Abused children also experience more stress, and may develop trauma-related developmental problems, such as hyperactivity, anxiety, learning disabilities, and lack of impulse

Recognizing Your Child's Gifts

"Gifted" is a term that some child development experts believe has been misused. It used to mean any child who scored in the top 5 percent of all IQ test takers. This limited vision of intelligence shortchanged all but a few children who were very good at verbal and mathematical test taking. Historically, black children have been stigmatized by biased IQ testing and placed in learning environments that discouraged them from discovering or developing their talents.

A new way of thinking about giftedness defines the term in a broader way. Rather than simply focusing on IQ, some experts now believe that every child—in fact every person—is gifted in one or more areas, and they begin expressing their gifts early on, even in infancy. By recognizing your child's gifts, you can help make learning easier. To understand the different gifts that your child may possess—and learn how to nurture them—study the categories below, adapted from the book *Frames of Mind* by Dr. Howard Gardner:

- *Linguistic or verbal skills.* Children with this gift learn to speak and read early, and enjoy word games and writing. Parents can help verbal children by giving them books, introducing new words and meanings, and providing writing opportunities (such as helping your child keep a journal or make her own books).
- *Spatial or visual skills.* These children like to look at pictures and play visual games. They learn best with images, pictures, three-dimensional games, and learning tools. Parents can provide visual children with a variety of visual materials (maps, charts, graphs) as well as ways for them to construct their own creations with clay, blocks, or making collages.
- *Kinesthetic or physical skills.* These children learn by "doing" with their bodies, such as dancing, athletic activities, or active fantasy play. They often learn to walk early—before age one. Parents can help by providing opportunities and space for these active children to play dress-up, dance to different kinds of music, or learn new physical games (such as tag, catch, or trike riding).
- *Musical skills.* Children with this gift like to sing, dance, and listen to music, and they learn best through rhythm and melodies or songs. Parents can help musical children by exposing them to all types of music, providing educational materials taught through songs or rhymes, toy instruments, or beginning instruction in a musical instrument.
- *Interpersonal or social skills.* These children are "people persons," and they thrive when interacting with others in groups. Parents can help by providing opportunities for children to socialize with peers, work on group activities,

or contribute to the community through volunteering for church-sponsored activities, for instance.

- ***Logical or mathematical skills.*** **These children learn through developing abstract concepts and patterns. This is a skill you may not notice in a toddler; it may become apparent later, when the child is a few years older or starting school. Parents can help by exposing children to basic math concepts (such as counting and measuring), science concepts (such as cooking and astronomy), and a variety of puzzles.**
- ***Intrapersonal skills.*** **Children with this skill are often creative, thoughtful, and prefer playing alone, and that's how they learn best. Parents can help by giving children the time and space to explore solitary endeavors alone, such as reading, drawing, or fantasy play.**

In his book *Awakening Your Child's Natural Genius* (Tarcher/Putnam Books, 1991), Thomas Armstrong, Ph.D., suggests that you look at your child when she is most happy and excited during an activity, notice what types of activities she's drawn to, and be led by your child's interests. He warns, however, that once a child shows interest or promise in a particular area, don't put too much emphasis on the one area or your child may not develop in areas she's not as strong in.

control. Fortunately, new research demonstrates that even in instances of severe trauma, such as living with a drug-abusing parent, the damage may be lessened greatly if a child is exposed to enriching and loving experiences early on.

Most child development experts agree that there is no strict distinction between our children's genetic gifts and what a lifetime of rich experiences may provide them. Whatever your baby's gifts may be, the most powerful ingredient for her growth and learning is your loving attention.

Learning Language

When you look at your baby in all his brown chubbiness, do you feel an irresistible urge to speak baby talk to him? Scientists now know that speaking "parentese," that high-pitched, singsong voice with lots of pauses that we use with babies, actually helps your baby listen and learn. In fact, babies learn language most effectively from caretakers who are loving and talkative. Research indicates that speaking to your baby a lot, making eye contact, and maintaining a close emotional bond are the three most important factors in shaping your baby's intelligence, creativity, and abstract reasoning.

In one long-term study at the University of Kansas, babies whose parents spoke often, in parentese or regular adult conversation with lots of new words, became high academic achievers compared to those parents who talked to them less.

Reading Helps, But There's More

According to the U.S. Department of Education, in 1996 only 44 percent of African-American children were read to every day. Just as speaking to young children helps them acquire language, so does reading. Studies also show that reading to children is directly related to school readiness and academic success.

Reading, even to infants, is important. It helps them learn new words and associate them with images on the page. Board books with pictures of other babies or objects can help teach your baby new words and introduce her to concepts such as counting, colors, shapes, and what objects are used for. But don't bother pulling out your old college textbooks in hopes that you can teach her calculus or intensive Spanish by bombarding her with dull and complicated words. Dr. Willis warns parents against overdoing it. "More critical than reading bedtime stories every night is supporting language development in a variety of ways," she says. She suggests spending time talking to your baby, at least fifteen to twenty minutes each day. Singing is good, too. Through music, babies learn about tone and melodies—training ground for being introduced to many different new voices and ways of talking as his world expands. Music also allows children to express themselves physically and verbally while learning, making these experiences the most powerful and long lasting.

Toddler

After a child's first birthday, most parents are filled with both excitement and dread about what's in store for them. Because ages one and two are marked by a baby's increased independence—he's learning to walk, is generally finished breast-feeding, and has learned his new favorite word, "no"—parents often find themselves in a battle between their child's natural curiosity and need to play through exploration and keeping him safe.

Learning Through You

Small children are like living mirrors of our own behavior. At this stage, imaginative play becomes an important way in which toddlers experiment with language, work out feelings, and develop their creativity. She may put on a tie and declare, "Go to work now," gently caress her stuffed dog, or talk on her play phone.

Charles Flatter, Ph.D., professor of human development at the Institute for Child Study in Maryland, maintains, "We are as creative and imaginative as we will ever be in our lives when we are children." For this reason, he believes parents should support their children's desire for make-believe play rather than discourage it. "Parents often try to knock the fantasy play out, but through it, children learn new concepts about being a man and a woman, who they are, and how the world works," says Flatter.

The toddler period is filled with opportunities to help your child begin to understand his world by interacting with you or his caretaker. Here are some suggestions for taking advantage of teaching opportunities:

- *Show how to sort and count while performing household chores.* When you do the laundry or the dishes, take time to explain that you're separating the clothes by color. ("These colors are dark: green, blue, and black. These are bright: pink, yellow, and orange. And these are white.") Or count as you stack the plates, fold pairs of socks, or cook.
- *Give your child a doll.* A wonderful way to understand how your child feels and thinks is to give him a doll or animal and ask him questions about it while he cares for it. Washing and feeding a baby doll will help him with coordination and motor skills while he practices his parenting skills. Sometimes parents are surprised (or alarmed) by their children's behavior and may learn a few things about themselves. Seeing a child hit or yell at his baby can prompt a parent to modify behavior that has clearly hurt him. And seeing him lovingly cradle it can help a parent feel she's on the right track.
- *Give mini versions of everyday items.* Toy kitchens, dishes, cash registers, stores, clothes, makeup, doctor kits, cars, briefcases, purses, brooms, mops, or whatever you use in daily life are wonderful toys for children. Buying items from the store, being served lunch at a restaurant, or getting dressed to go out are all exciting situations for your child. Although you should let her be the

Why Johnny Can't Read . . . Yet

The inclination of black parents to make our children the best and brightest by having them read everything in sight by age four is laudable. After all, as our parents have always told us, "A black person has to be three times smarter to get the same job as a white person." Experts note that children who read regularly and maintain high reading levels through adulthood usually developed a strong passion for reading early on.

However, this passion should not be hurried by an overeager parent, and studies show that it doesn't work anyway. *Don't Push Your Preschooler* (Harper & Row, 1980) by Louise Bates Ames, Ph.D., and Joan Ames Chase, Ph.D., notes that "To date, efforts to push preschoolers toward behaving in an either more mature or more intelligent manner than they might otherwise have done have been singularly unsuccessful." So if your child seems resistant to reading, check yourself and make sure you're not pushing him too hard. He will not learn every word, number, color, or shape by your constantly drilling him every time you read him a story. For children at this age, the motto is, "If it ain't fun, it don't get done."

To make it fun, and help him learn, try the following:

- *Teach him the love of reading and encourage his natural inclination by doing it yourself and reading to him enthusiastically and often.* This is the best way to get a child to read. Make reading a relaxed, daily ritual.
- *Introduce the letters of the alphabet and numbers to a toddler.* Many books feature them, and you should begin to say them and have her repeat them early on.
- *Don't rush.* Your child may want to stare at one page for a while, or she may not make it through the whole book. Or she may want to stop and ask questions, or even go off on a tangent about something. Let her set the pace, and then gently move her along. She'll eventually be able to sit through the entire book.
- *Exaggerate the words and use voice intonations, facial expressions, and body motions to help the child understand the meaning of a word.*
- *Though you want varied reading materials, understand that children often like to read the same book over and over.* Memorizing the words to say when they see the picture is an important first step to actually reading.
- *Move beyond commercial, widely available books.* Though it's easy to pick up Dr. Seuss or Sesame Street children's books, make sure your collection is varied. With this in mind, visit an African-American bookstore or stop by the library and pick up several titles by lesser known authors. Look for bright, eye-pleasing artwork and rich language rather than familiar images.

leader in these games, you can offer up suggestions and introduce new words and concepts as part of the game.

Preschooler

As children develop, their physical, cognitive, and social skills enable them to play more complex games. Their burgeoning independence pushes them away from family members and toward making friendships with peers, a necessary stage of development. Play with friends and alone is often filled with imaginative scenarios that range from pure fantasy to imitation of the adult world. Having mastered the art of taking turns and following directions, preschoolers are also great at playing games with clear rules.

Learning Through Early Friendships

Before the preschool years, children's friendships and play are limited to brief interactions and side-by-side play, where each child is engrossed in her own toy. Though they may occasionally talk, run, and scream with each other, most children still aren't capable of sharing toys and taking turns before three years old. In order for friendships to develop, these rudimentary skills need to be mastered.

As your child develops, friendships become important.

As your child matures in his language and social abilities, you'll notice him having more direct interaction with other children and becoming more attached to one or two playmates. These are the buddings of friendship and important milestones. They signify children's ability to begin the process of separating from parents and feel comfortable outside the family; see that there are other ways of doing things; empathize with another person; seek out others like him with the same interests, temperament, and maturity level; and interact cooperatively with a peer. Like adult relationships, childhood friendships are crucial to a preschooler's well-being. Feeling close to another person makes it easier for children to be away from their parents. And friendships provide wonderful learning opportunities. They allow children to discover new interests, new ways of solving problems, and how to resolve conflict. Friends provide the only opportunity children have to interact with another equal, a rewarding experience for little ones who often feel outsized and overpowered in an adult world.

As your child makes and maintains friendships, you will remain her best source of guidance and comfort. Here are some tips to help your child develop healthy friendships:

- *Give your child opportunities to make friends.* Children in preschool have more of a chance to build friendships with their classmates. Even if your child attends a day program, he may be able to meet children with the same interests in an after-school program. Encourage bonds by setting up play dates for your child.

How Does Ebonics Affect Our Children's Ability to Learn Language?

The 1996 controversy in an Oakland school district over whether or not to acknowledge Ebonics (or "black" English) as the "native" language of the African-American students, and, with this understanding, teach English as a second language, sparked much debate. One issue that surfaced was whether or not Ebonics affects black children's ability to learn Standard English.

According to Dr. Willis, who is considered an expert in this area, the answer is no. Ebonics, which is considered by many experts to be a separate language and not "slang" or "broken" English, is widely spoken in most African-American homes and communities. Dr. Willis believes that we should "accept and embrace it as our own, as a way to celebrate our culture. But, like immigrants who speak their native language at home, we should tell our kids there's a time and place for everything, so that when they are in the classroom or outside the community, they should use Standard English."

Like most bilingual children, our children know by experience when to speak Ebonics and when to speak Standard English. Contrary to what some skeptics believe, this does not confuse our children any more than does learning that there are different ways to dress for play and for church. Dr. Willis contends that as long as our children are exposed to Standard English and the appropriate times to use it, they will adjust to school and social situations just fine.

Worst Toy Warning: Walkers Are Dangerous and Developmentally Harmful

Despite parents' best intentions to provide their babies with a chance to explore on their own and "learn" to walk at the same time, safety and child development experts are strongly advising against infant walkers for three important reasons:

1. Infant walkers are responsible for about 25,000 serious injuries (including skull fractures, broken bones, broken necks, and burns) each year. Children in infant walkers are at risk of falling down stairs, wandering unsupervised into dangerous situations, or tipping over.

2. Researchers at Case Western Reserve University in Cleveland have discovered that children who use walkers actually learn to walk later than those who don't use them. Because walkers have large trays that don't allow babies to see their feet, they can't visualize how their feet and legs are moving through space. Furthermore, the way babies move their feet and legs in a walker is different from how they use them when they actually walk.

3. Using walkers not only affects physical development, but also mental skills. Babies who used walkers scored on average ten points lower on infant development tests than babies who didn't use them. The lower scores reflect how confining a walker can be to a child who should explore by crawling and picking objects up off the floor. In a walker, a baby can't pick up dropped toys, pull herself to a standing position, or roll over on her back, exercises necessary for exploration and cognitive development.

A safer spin-off of the walker is Evenflo's Exersaucer, a stationary upright seat that allows your baby to jump, spin, rock from side to side, or sit and play with many toys fastened to the tray. But do not keep your baby in it for extended periods. Give her a chance to get on the floor and exercise.

- *Help him resolve conflicts on his own.* Without interfering too much in your child's interaction with his friends, use conflicts to help him understand other people's feelings, how his actions impact on others, and positive ways to work out problems. Ask questions like, "Why do you think Keisha is crying?" "How do you think that makes Tyler feel?" or "Is there another way you can work this out?" Also, suggest reasons why children may behave a certain way, such as "He's having a hard time today," and teach him to walk away from situations before they get out of control.

Playing When *You're* Pooped

No matter how much you love your child and want to play with her, some days you're worn out—tired to the bone and not up to entertaining a rambunctious toddler or preschooler. Or you're too brain dead to think of any new activities for your child to do alone. Rather than turning on the TV, try these tips for the tired. Most will work for children aged two to five, but you'll have to see for yourself.

- ***Give a young toddler three pots with water, and let him pour water from one to the other.*** **(This is best done outside because of the mess.) It's surprising how long children can be entertained by this. If he's old enough to not put things in his mouth, let him play with shaving cream.**
- ***Create a bag of "secret things," filled with dimestore toys, little books, juice, and snacks and set it aside.*** **Then use it to surprise your child, who'll be excited to discover new items.**
- ***Let her put on a puppet show or play for you.***
- ***Ask him to read his books to you.*** **Children can improvise—or memorize—so this will work even if he doesn't know how to read yet.**
- ***Create a beauty shop.*** **You be the client while she fixes your hair. Even better, invent a spa, so she can give you "pampering" services like massages, facials, and manicures.**
- ***Let him set up a restaurant with dishes and pretend food—or the real thing if you keep it simple.*** **He can be the host, chef, and waiter.**
- ***Have her build a fort using pillows or a tent by draping sheets over chairs or a clothesline.***
- ***Let him create a large outdoor art project by using colored chalk to draw on the sidewalk.*** **Use a hose to clean up afterward.**
- ***Ask your child to wash your car (so what if it doesn't really get clean?), or her toys or trike using soap and a hose.***
- ***Put aside old clothes, wigs, and jewelry for a game of dress-up.***
- ***Buy old or broken clocks or cameras at a yard sale or flea market for your child to take apart and try to put back together.***

For more activities, see the resource list at the end of this chapter.

- *Teach him helpful social skills.* In a study at George Mason University, researchers discovered that children who were well-liked were those who better understood and responded to their peers' communication, an important skill in making friendships. Popular children made eye contact, used their peer's name, and responded to the subject at hand. These are all strategies that you can help your child incorporate into his interaction with peers.

- *Close parenting makes for close friendships.* A recent study from Kent State University revealed that children with strong parental attachments played more cooperatively with their peers. Researchers believe this is because children with strong ties to their parents are more secure and confident, which spills over into peer friendships as well.
- *Respect your child's choices.* It's tempting to steer your child toward the children in the class whom you like or whose parents you might like. Unfortu-

Toys Just for Our Children

Many of us remember the "old days" when Mom had to make us a rag doll so we could have a culturally reaffirming toy, one that had our brown skin, curly hair, and gentle features. Today, savvy toy manufacturers understand the importance of dolls with realistic skin tones and facial features for African-American parents and children. Many have designed special lines aimed at our children, while black-owned toy companies specialize exclusively in African-American toys. Here are some that may interest you:

- **Hairplay Fun Kenya by Tyco Toys. This doll comes with hairstyling accessories like beads, hair lotion, and rubber bands. Other Kenya dolls include Bedtime Kenya, who comes complete with a book of poems.**
- **Imani Crimp and Bead by Olmec Toys. This black-owned toy company makes toys geared toward black children, such as the Imani doll. She has bendable dreadlocks and beads.**
- **Penda Kids by Cultural Toys/Hallmark Cards. This doll sports bright, ethnic clothing and facial features with a West Indian twist.**
- **Sun Man and Spawn by Olmec. These are poseable black superhero action figures.**
- **Black by Design Game by Olmec. This is a quiz game to help teach children about black inventors and other accomplishments within our culture.**
- **African Animals by On Your Mark. These are stuffed animals decked out in kente cloth.**
- **Portraits of African-American History Jigsaw Puzzle by WB Adams Puzzles and Games. This is a three-hundred-piece puzzle that celebrates our historical heroes.**

nately for your child, the friends you might choose for yourself aren't necessarily the ones he would pick for himself. Unless you notice an unpleasant or unacceptable quality in your child's choice of friends, it's best to let him make up his own mind. Exceptions would be:

*If your child's friend plays too aggressively, fights, or dominates most of the play time

*If your child is clearly uncomfortable playing with another child but doesn't know how to stop playing

*If another child insults your child, or repeatedly hurts her feelings

In any of these circumstances, it's time to intervene. If the situation doesn't get better by talking it out with both children and parents, maybe this is a friendship that wasn't meant to be.

Our Children in the Computer Age

How early should you start your child on a computer? That's a topic of endless debate. On one hand, too many blacks have missed the ramp onto the information superhighway, and you don't want your child to be among them. According to a 1998 study published in the journal *Science,* less than one-third of blacks own a home computer, compared to almost one-half of whites. And we are much less likely than whites to use the Internet. It's critical in this digital age that our children understand how to use computers and that they have access to the Internet, which is becoming a must-have tool for communicating, gathering data, and doing business.

Though you don't want your children to be left behind, you also may not want her to miss out on other kinds of childhood fun because she's spending all of her time hunched over a computer. And how do you monitor what your child sees, given the wide variety of content—including pornography and violence—that's out there? And finally, how young is too young? How do you know when to start and what's appropriate for each age group?

To help you sort through these issues, follow the suggestions below:

- *First, bring yourself up to speed.* Do you know how to use a computer and get on the Internet? If not, you can learn about computers through community centers, the library, local college or evening courses, or in the workplace. If you're ready to buy a computer, pick up any number of computer magazines or check

Girls and Boys: Do They Play Differently?

The following are three of the most commonly asked questions about gender, answered by a leading child development researcher, Dr. Charles Flatter. Some of the answers might surprise you.

1. ***Are boys and girls really so different?*** **Yes and no. Gender differences in behavior and play are probably more nurture than nature. When a parent gives a boy a truck and says "This is what boys play with"—and everyone around him, as well as advertising and television are saying the same thing—he'll want a truck. And though energy levels are not gender specific, we generally encourage and expect girls to be quiet.**

Rather than reinforcing rigid gender stereotyping, your goal should be to raise self-assured children. This is especially important for girls who exhibit passive behavior, which can lead to poor academic achievement or, worse, involvement in an abusive relationship later in life. Likewise, boys need to develop their emotions so that they can learn how to express their feelings (including frustration and disappointment) and feel empathetic toward others. Without these expressions, boys learn to push their feelings down, which can lead to inappropriate anger, drug abuse, and alcoholism.

2. ***Which toys are the best to give to boys, and which are the best for girls?*** **There is no such thing as a best toy for a boy or a girl. Some research shows that girls may prefer dolls and boys like to make roaring car noises, but experts are now trying to get parents to steer away from gender stereotypes, for reasons mentioned above.**

3. ***Should boys and girls play together?*** **Of course, if they want to. Friendships made with the opposite sex can be extremely valuable. More important than being concerned about the gender of your child's playmates is to help her find peers who have the same interests and play style. Ideally, children can have both male and female friends.**

out recommendations from Consumer Reports to determine which models best suit your needs.

- *Introduce your child to computers when both of you are ready.* Toddlers and preschoolers often become interested when they see you or others using a computer. It's OK to start children as young as eighteen months or two years old, as long as you monitor them very carefully.

- *Teach your child to respect the equipment.* Computers are expensive, and though they can be fun, they aren't toys.
- *Use the computer together.* It's best to check out a website or program first to make sure it's appropriate for your child. (For one, make sure there are positive images of African Americans.) Then introduce new features slowly to make sure he understands what he's doing. On the Internet, try kid-friendly websites such as www.pbs.org/kids/ which features Arthur, Mister Rogers, Sesame Street, and other public television favorites. Other suggestions: www.kids-space.org/and www.kidsdomain.com/ These are appropriate for preschoolers and precocious toddlers. Watch out for commercial sites sponsored by companies like McDonald's and Chuck E. Cheese, which are more advertising-driven than educationally based.
- *Sort through the software.* Software for toddlers and preschoolers is a booming, million-dollar industry, and choices are abundant. Some top-selling options are: Sesame Street Elmo's Preschool, Ready to Read with Pooh, Jumpstart Preschool, and Jumpstart Toddler. Two Afrocentric software titles: Imo & the King: An African Folk Tale (ages 3–9; 800–545–7677, website: www.davd.com) and Orley's Draw-A-Story (ages 5–10; 415–382–4745).

For more information on and reviews of websites and software, read *Family PC* magazine.

- *Encourage good posture.* Your child should sit sixteen to twenty inches from the screen. And adjust the chair for her, rather than placing her on top of piled phone books.
- *Limit computer time.* Don't let the computer become an "electronic baby-sitter." Allow a toddler or preschooler only fifteen to twenty minutes per day. Make sure you and your child continue to talk, think up activities that use creativity and imagination, play noncomputer games together, and spend lots of time outside and engaged in physical activities.

RESOURCES

Recommended Reading for Parents

Age-Right Play: Playful Learning for Infants, Toddlers, and Preschoolers, Susan Lingo (Group Publishing, 1997). This book offers tips on enhancing the relationship between you and your young child through play.

Awaken the Hidden Storyteller: How to Build a Storytelling Tradition in Your Family, Robin Moore (Shambhala Publishing, 1991). This book teaches how to tell stories and build the imagination.

Beyond the Bean Seed: Gardening Activities for Grades K–6, Nancy Allen Jurenka and Rosanne J. Blass (Libraries Unlimited, 1966). This book offers introduces gardening to young children.

Big Book of Fun: Creative Learning Activities for Home and School, Ages 4–12, Carolyn Buhai Haas, illustrated by Jane Bennett Phillips (Chicago Review Press, 1987). This book lists creative projects you can do with your child.

Bright Ideas for Creative Parents, Alice Chapin (Walker and Co., 1987). This book provides useful, simple tips on how to have fun with your children.

The Cooperative Sports and Games Book: Challenge Without Competition, Terry Orlick (Random House, 1995). This book explains how to use sports to build your child's confidence and encourage him to have cooperative relationships with his peers.

Discovery Play: Loving and Learning with Your Baby, Art Ulene and Steven Shelov (Ulysses Press, 1994). This book offers tips on engaging your baby in developmentally enhancing play.

Fun and Games for Family Gatherings, Adrienne E. Anderson (Reunion Publishing, 1996). This book lists numerous activities for having fun with groups of children.

101 Dance Games for Children: Fun and Creativity with Movement, Paul Rooyackers, illustrated by Cecilia Hurd (Hunter House, 1996). This book provides collection of games and activities which encourage children to use their imaginations while building social skills and coordination.

365 Outdoor Activities You Can Do with Your Child, Steve and Ruth Bennett (Bob Adams Inc., 1993). Games, experiments, and art projects are among the activities listed.

365 TV-Free Activities You Can Do with Your Child, 2nd ed., Steven J. Bennett, Ruth Bennett, and Steve Bennett (Adams Media Corporation, 1996). Increase family fun with these alternatives to television.

What to Do When Kids Are Mean to Your Child, Elin McCoy (Reader's Digest, 1997). This book helps parents "bully-proof" their kids with tips on teaching children coping skills and assertiveness training, as well as how to choose good friends.

Recommended Reading for Children

These books celebrate friends and cooperation.

A Kaleidescope of Kids, Emma Damon (Dial Books for Young Readers, 1995). This lift-the-flap-book celebrates diversity among children with humor and warmth.

Being with You This Way, W. Nikola-Lisa, illustrated by Michael Bryant (Scholastic Press, 1996). This book depicts friendship and fun among a multiracial group of children.

The Frog Prince, story adapted by Naomi Fox, illustrations by Neal Fox (The Confetti Company, 1993). This adaptation of a classic children's story depicts a fictional, multiracial children's drama club acting out the story. *Little Red Riding Hood* and *Sleeping Beauty* are other stories produced in this book and cassette tape series.

Mirandy and Brother Wind, Patricia C. McKissack, illustrated by Jerry Pinkney (Alfred A. Knopf, 1988). This a colorfully textured story about a southern girl's attempts to capture the wind and win the "cake walk" dance contest. It includes a cassette tape.

My Best Friend, Pat Hutchins (Greenwillow Books, 1993). Acceptance and appreciation are the themes in this story of a sleep-over between two friends.

Playtime 1-2-3., Jenny Williams (Dial Books for Young Reader, 1992). Playing and counting are the themes of this book which features multiracial groupings of children.

A Rainbow of Friends, P. K. Hallinan (Ideals Children's Books, 1994). This book celebrates the differences which make a group of young friends so special.

Shaina's Garden, Denise Lewis Patrick, illustrated by Stacey Schuett (Aladdin Paperbacks, 1996). Shaina and the family from Nickelodean television's "Gullah, Gullah Island" grow a vegetable garden.

Values 1-2-3, Sally Masteller (Modern Publishing, 1988). Friendship and cooperation among a multiracial group of children are the focus of this book.

Websites for Parents that List Activities for Children

www.family.com

This website has activities, educational programs, travel information, games, and chat rooms for families with kids.

Toys

Clutch Ball, $12.99. Call International Playthings, (800) 445–8347. This colorful ball with a rattle ring holds an additional surprise inside for your infant or toddler.

"Just Like Me" coloring book $5.00 (plus $1.95 for shipping and handling). Call (202) 526–1725 or send check/money order to DBW Create-A-Book, Inc., P.O. Box 4492, Washington, D.C. 20017 to order this coloring book which features African-American inventors.

Let's Pretend Restaurant, $16.00. Call Creativity for Kids, (800) 311–8684, extension 3037. This set, which includes menus, an order pad, a chef's hat, and plastic food, will foster a child's imagination.

Pretend & Play Puppets, $24.95. Call Learning Resources, (800) 222–3909. This set includes a washable cast of multiracial puppets with a storage box which also serves as a theater.

SunSensory teether, $9.00. Call Manhattan Baby, (800) 747–2454. This soft squeaking rattle is also useful for easing the discomfort of teething.

Chapter

12

Giving Strength: Helping Our Children Cope During Stressful Times

Most of us can rattle off a list of all the factors in our lives that stress us: work, other people, too much to do in too little time, money problems—the list goes on. And although it may not seem obvious, our children also have long lists of stresses in their lives. While their stresses may not be as complex as ours, they are just as real to them and require attention and relief.

In this chapter, we will discuss some of the major stress-causing events for young children and provide strategies to help your child cope. We will also discuss ways you can teach your child to cope with stress on her own—useful lessons she can take with her into adulthood.

Stress: What You Need to Know and Do

Stress is a word that we use to describe anything that challenges us. It can be something as minor as a broken nail to as serious as the death of a loved one, job loss, or

Signs of Stress

It's important that you know how to spot symptoms of stress in your child. According to Bob Pianta, Ph.D., professor in the school of education at the University of Virginia, signs of stress might include:

- **Not communicating or talking as he used to**
- **More easily distracted than usual**
- **More tantrums and mood swings than usual**
- **More negative behavior than usual, especially around activities that he used to like**
- **Very clingy and baby-like behavior**
- **Overly aggressive behavior**
- **Reverts in his toilet training**
- **Frequent nightmares**
- **Unexplained vomiting**
- **Lack of appetite**

Pianta suggests that children's habits that provide comfort to them, such as thumb sucking or hair twisting, shouldn't be cause for alarm. However, if your child displays these behaviors at very specific times (such as on the way to day care or to visit a relative) and nowhere else, begin to question the setting and caretakers more closely.

When It's Your Turn to Stress Out

Many times experts focus on children's stress and how parents can help their kids cope. But many parents wonder, "What about me?" Indeed, your stress needs to be addressed, because your feelings directly affect your child—ask any parent who is stressed and she'll tell you that's when her child decides to act out the most! When you feel yourself reaching overload, it's time to take action. Here are some tips for helping yourself.

- ***Anticipate stressful situations.*** **If you know that a certain time of the day (for example, when you arrive home from work or when you have to cook dinner) is more hectic or stress-provoking than others, try to head it off through careful planning. Tell your child you want his help while you are tied up. Involve him in other activities which you can supervise while you unwind, cook, or whatever.**
- ***Pinpoint the source of your stress and attempt to alleviate it.*** **Whether it's cash-flow problems, trouble on the job, or family tension, try to isolate what you're stressed about. This will enable you to focus on finding a solution, or at the very least get you talking about your problem with friends or family, who can also offer resolutions.**
- ***If you feel yourself losing control, leave.*** **Put your child in a safe environment while you go somewhere else to cool down. Take deep breaths and relax until your body feels calm again. Then think about a solution to the situation at hand before you reenter.**
- ***Tell your child how you're feeling.*** **If you're having a bad day, explain it to her so she doesn't feel that your mood is her fault. Let her know that, like her, you get frustrated and angry about things and need time to feel better again. You might ask her to help you by being quiet or playing alone. If you do slip and say something that hurts her feelings, be sure to apologize.**
- ***Take time for yourself to avoid stress.*** **Pampering yourself with a hot soak, hanging out with your crew, or enjoying a hobby are ways you can feel you've nourished yourself. Often parents get stressed when they feel they're deprived of having fun, so think of what would allow you to have fun and do it!**
- ***Break your routine.*** **Being spontaneous (with or without your child) can be a great relief from the usual daily grind. Take in a family movie, have a barbecue in the park, or visit an unusual museum exhibit.**

other life crisis. In children, stress can be difficult to recognize, especially if your child's stress is tied to your own. That is most often the case, says Dr. Pianta, who notes that "stress in children most often involves the primary adult figures in their lives or their homes."

At the most basic level, disorganization may trigger stress in a child. Children thrive on routine and order; they need it as much as they need love and discipline. Even a loving family that lives in a lot of chaos can relieve stress simply by establishing a daily routine. And by ordering your child's life in a predictable way, you may find yourself saying "no" much less—which will relieve any stress that a "misbehaving" child may be causing *you.*

Of course, Dr. Pianta acknowledges, all these stress relievers may be easier to talk about than to do, especially for single parents. But by following three important tips, Pianta believes you can avoid a lot of headaches and free yourself to have more fun with your child instead of living moment to moment:

1. *Have a morning routine.* One of the worst stressors for families is a hurried, chaotic morning. To avoid this, get organized the night before by setting out clothes to wear, packing lunches, and so on. Make breakfast quick and nutritious (instant oatmeal, cold cereals, or breakfast bars work), and spend the morning talking about what there is to look forward to that day instead of rushing frantically to get out the door.

2. *Establish regular mealtimes.* Studies show that children who are part of a family that eats regular family meals together are more successful in several areas—including academics and sociability—than those whose families don't eat together. "For small children, this is just another point of predictability in their day," says Pianta, "and it gives them more personal contact with you."

3. *Set a consistent bedtime.* This is one of the most important ways parents can help their children lead less stressed, more healthy lives. Sleep affects a child's behavior, learning, and eating patterns. Setting clear limits about where and when children sleep is one of the most loving acts of a parent. Plus, it will also help regulate your child's wake-up time. (See more on sleep and bedtimes in Chapter 6.)

Some types of stress are unavoidable because, as the saying goes, "stuff happens." Even in the most organized of homes, children can suffer from inner turmoil or anxiety. In these instances, parents can provide much-needed comfort and help children get through the rough spots that come up in everyday life. Try the following:

- *Talk honestly with your child.* Whether your child's being picked on by a bully in day care or her best friend has moved away, try to get her to talk about her feelings. Then explain that her feelings are natural and appropriate. You should also discuss family events or crises openly and simply enough for your child to grasp the true meaning of the event. A child as young as fifteen months can understand that you are upset now but that you will be OK soon.
- *Be empathetic.* Give your child's feelings as much regard as you would those of an adult. Even if you think he's making a "big deal" out of an event, validate your child's feelings by saying that you know he's going through a tough time and you understand.
- *Comfort her.* Your child relies on you for support and guidance, and your reactions now will set the stage for how she deals with stress later in life. Help her to see that things can be worked out and help her come up with ways to address her problems on her own. Be sure to provide lots of hugs and cuddles.
- *Boost his confidence.* Remind your child of ways he has dealt with a stressful event previously to reinforce that he has the ability to cope effectively with these situations when they occur. But always let him know he can come to you to talk things out.

Stressful Situations and How to Handle Them

As adults, we have more resources and experience dealing with difficult situations and are better able than children to put them in context, understand them, and cope. Small children are often shielded from stressful events because of their limited grasp on what significance the events may have. Nonetheless, they rely on our reactions to lead them through an event and teach them how to cope, so that our ability to deal with adversity greatly affects them.

The following is a brief discussion of significant life stressors that many young children are likely to encounter, along with some advice on how to handle them.

Death

When a family member or friend dies, it deeply affects both children and adults. Confusion, grief, anger, and guilt are just some of the intense emotions that surround death, making it a difficult subject to talk about with our children. When a death

"No matter how much we're going through, my husband and I still try to give Brianna all the love in the world." **—SAUNDRA FREEMAN, MOTHER OF BRIANNA, AGE 2; WISCONSIN**

Our family has been under a tremendous amount of stress recently. My mother was diagnosed with gastric lymphoma several months ago. At one point, we were told she only had two weeks to live. There was no one else to care for her, so one weekend, my husband, Charles, my daughter, Brianna, and I packed all our things into a U-Haul and moved from Virginia to Wisconsin.

Fortunately, my husband was able to find a job, but he has to work really hard. He has four ten-hour days per week, but he also works many more hours and weekends to get overtime. That keeps him away a lot, and more of the responsibility for our daughter's care falls on me—although one of the many things I love about him is that he doesn't mind cooking, cleaning, and taking care of Brianna when he's able to. Adding to the problem, my mother and I don't get along all that well. Though I must care for her, our relationship is strained. Fortunately, she is doing better now, but I still have to be caregiver, nurse, chauffeur, cook, housekeeper, and take care of my daughter, my husband, and myself.

Despite my own problems, fear, and frustrations, I've tried to watch Brianna carefully, to see how all of the changes and stress are affecting her. Kids are so resilient. The only thing I've noticed is that she's started biting her nails, which could be a nervous habit or could be teething. Other than that, she is oblivious to the whole thing. No matter how much we're going through, my husband and I still try to give Brianna all the love in the world. She also sees my relatives more often, since we're nearby so she gets a lot of love from them. And she likes being with my mother, getting into bed with her and wearing her hats.

During this transition, my husband and I have tried very hard to keep things consistent for Brianna. We tried not to make a big deal of what was going on, to shield her as best we could. When she gets older we will tell her that she is from Virginia and explain why we had to move here. In the meantime, we are just trying to keep things calm and balanced.

occurs, we need to remember that as we are affected, so are our children. Children's responses to death may be immediate or delayed, strong or moderate, and they may range from sadness to intense frustration. If your family has experienced a death, here are some suggestions to keep in mind:

- *Be honest, clear, and direct about what has happened to the deceased.* Use phrases that won't confuse a child, and tell him what it means to be dead. "He won't be back," "We'll never see him again," "She's gone forever," or "We'll always miss her" are phrases that you can use to explain the finality of death. You will only confuse your child if you say that his loved one "went to sleep" or "went away." Your child will expect his relative or friend to return or awaken. If you believe in an afterlife, discuss what has happened in a manner that won't frighten your child.
- *Use books to help.* There are many good children's books on the subject of death available, though some may be beyond your child's understanding if she's younger than three years old. (See Resources.)
- *Play with your child.* Play offers a wonderful window into your child's feelings. Drawing, playing with dolls or puppets, or playing "house" are all activities that let your child act out her feelings. Let her lead the play and ask her questions, especially about what she feels.
- *Answer repeated questions consistently.* More than likely your child will ask you the same questions over and over because he's trying to comprehend what "dead" means. It's hard for adults to imagine a state of not being, and equally so for children, so be patient. Brief, consistent, and direct answers will make it easier for your child to conceptualize the situation.
- *Maintain a normal routine.* When a change as big as a death occurs, children naturally feel insecure. Regardless of who passed in your child's life (parent, grandparent, or sibling), it's vital that his life remain stable. This will not only help him recover sooner and see that "life goes on," but will keep him from feeling as though his life is out of control.
- *Don't hide family grief.* Feeling intense sadness is natural for both adults and children. Parents should allow themselves to feel sad around their children, provided that they aren't frightening them. Showing your grief is an appropriate way to demonstrate to your child how much you loved and will miss your loved one, and gives your child permission to feel sadness and other emotions.
- *Let your child say good-bye.* Find some activity that helps your child say good-bye to her loved one. Putting together a small photo album with photos of your child and the deceased, planting a tree, or saying a special prayer are all good ideas.

"As I began to accept my father's death as a regular part of my life, and the grief began to subside, Miles's moods calmed, too." —ALLISON'S STORY

The morning after my father died, I told Miles to look me in the face while I said, "Miles, Poppy died last night while you were sleeping." "Poppy's dead?" he asked. Then he asked me if that was why I was so sad, and I told him yes.

Months before my dad died, we had gotten bad news from his doctor. We began to "put things in order" and come to terms with his approaching death. We bought books about the death of a loved one that were easy enough for Miles to understand. And I began to explain that Poppy's cough was due to an illness that would one day take him. "Poppy's very sick and very old," I explained, hoping he would make the connection between being sick, old, and dying and not fear for my death or his own.

The morning after my father died, I brought home the finality of what it means to be "dead." "Your body stops working, you don't breathe anymore, and you don't get better," I said. "Poppy's gone forever, Miles. We'll never be with him again." Miles naturally wanted to know where he went. I explained that his body was at the hospital now but would soon be gone. "But his spirit, the love we felt for him, and our memories of him will live on in our hearts and minds forever," I said, trying to avoid the details of exactly what would happen to my father's body and sticking to what was important for Miles to know. To offer him some comfort, I told him that I would be sad for a little while, but that I would feel better with time.

During the next few days, my husband, Mark, took charge of Miles's care. I spent my days helping my mother and brother with the details of the funeral and cremation, and all the other matters to be handled. I wasn't emotionally available to Miles for several days, as I was hardly able to care for myself. Miles was happy to be with his father, but I could tell he was clearly affected by our grief, the many people coming in and out of his Nana's house, and the silence that often filled the rooms.

In the aftermath of the funeral, Miles's aunts noticed he was much more quiet than usual. He seemed to be traumatized by the experience of Poppy being there one day and gone the next. I asked him questions constantly about his feelings. He admitted that he was sad, that he had mostly missed Mommy not being around as much, and he was angry at all the people coming over. He has never accepted change easily, and my father's death caused a huge transformation of our family.

After several weeks, Miles started talking and laughing again. His play involved a lot of death and sickness, so I knew he was working out his confusion and insecurities. The upheaval caused him to have more frequent and intense tantrums, turning

any small transition (going to day care, taking a bath, or sitting down for dinner) into a world war. As I began to accept my father's death as a regular part of my life, and the grief began to subside, Miles's moods calmed, too. As extra reassurance, I cut back on his day care and spent one entire day a week with him doing what he wanted. Several months later, I now see the results.

- *Include your child in family rituals.* As long as your child can sit without being too disruptive or you have someone else who can care for him while you mourn, you can bring your child to a funeral or memorial service. Some parents have strong objections about whether their children can "handle" a funeral service, and in many cases, their feelings are clearly justified (many youngsters have nightmares long after an open-casket wake). However, children also need a way to mourn and find closure, particularly if the person who died was an immediate member of the family. Whenever possible, think of appropriate ways to bring your child into family rituals.
- *Consider family therapy.* Especially in the case of a caregiver's or sibling's death, or if your child is having trouble recovering from a loved one's death, you should strongly consider at least a couple of sessions with a family therapist to help you and your child come to terms with the family's feelings surrounding the loss.

Divorce

Nearly half of all first marriages in America end in divorce, and African Americans divorce at a slightly higher rate. For young children, divorce can be earth shattering. Fearing change and not having both parents under one roof can fuel a child's desperate attempts and fantasies to bring her parents back together, no matter how many arguments she has overheard. Children old enough to understand what divorce means but not mature enough to know that they don't control all the events in their lives often blame themselves for their parents' break-up.

The best way to help your child deal with divorce is by talking to him as much as he's willing. Here are some other coping strategies that can help ease this difficult transition:

- *Tell your child what's happening.* As soon as you and your mate decide to separate or divorce, the two of you should sit down and explain the situation to your child so she's prepared to deal with it, too. Tell her that things have been tense and upsetting, but that both of you are trying hard to work out what's best for everyone. After speaking the first time, establish a regular time to talk with your child about her feelings and update her on any new developments or decisions you've made that concern her.
- *Explain, but don't overexplain.* Don't go into detail about why your marriage isn't working. It's enough to say that you aren't getting along anymore, or that you don't love each other the same way any longer. Don't discuss extramarital affairs, substance abuse problems, or any other problems that aren't necessary for your child to know about right now.
- *Assure and reassure him that your love for him won't change.* One of the biggest concerns a child has is that the divorce will change the way you or his other parent feel about him. Emphasize that the divorce is not his fault, that it's your decision, and that both parents love him the same as before, even if the circumstances are different now.
- *Don't make your child choose.* Wanting your child to take sides in the divorce will only put her under more pressure and stress. No matter how mad you are, restrain from talking badly about your ex to your child. Children shouldn't be made to love one parent more than the other or feel it's disloyal to continue having both their parents.
- *Work together in the best interests of your child.* You will probably have to muster all the maturity and strength you can to keep your child's interests in the forefront. As amicably as possible (and this may take a few trips to the family counselor), co-parent in ways that keep your child's life as uninterrupted and stable as possible.
- *Maintain a close relationship.* Because children need both parents, you should work at staying in close daily contact with your child and arrange for your child to continue his relationship with his other parent. By encouraging your child to spend time with your ex, you will help him see that his relationship with his parent is separate from your relationship and that he still has the love of both parents, even if they don't live together anymore.

Moving

Relocating is one of the most stressful events to occur in a family. All members must establish themselves in a new and unfamiliar environment, make new friends, and get acquainted with new community members in a number of settings, including at day care or school. For parents who must plan and execute the move, this is also a hectic and often frustrating time. For children, moving is especially difficult because it uproots them from all that they know. As Dr. Pianta explains, "Children largely define themselves by their surroundings, which is what makes transitions very hard."

During and after the move, expect your child to express signs of stress in many different forms, including mood swings, nightmares, or reverting in toilet training. Also expect lots of questions, often repeated, such as, "Is my bed going, too?" The best advice: Be patient.

Here are some other ways to make a move easier for your child:

- *Tell him well in advance.* Children make transitions more easily when they have plenty of time to prepare themselves.
- *Explain what the move will mean to her.* She needs to know that her life will change, that she'll be sleeping in a new room and have to make new friends. But also reassure her that many things will be the same, such as her bed, her toys, and all your furniture. Try to be as positive and enthusiastic as possible, but be clear that she will have to start saying good-bye to her old home and friends.
- *Encourage your child to talk about relocating.* Be honest and open about your sense of fear, loss, and excitement surrounding the move and talk about whether he might be feeling the same. Explain why you might be having a difficult time ("I'll be far away from my friends," for instance) and why you're also looking forward to moving ("I'm starting a new job I really like" or "We'll be closer to our family now.") By going over the pros and cons of the move, your child will understand that his conflicting feelings are normal and that with any change there's sadness and excitement.
- *Plan a going-away event.* A party with her old pals, a visit to the neighborhood park, or a one-on-one play date with her special friend will help her understand that although she's moving away, she can still keep in touch with the people she cares for. Photos of this event and the old neighborhood can be

"I learned a lesson about the importance of friends and family, and that I had more support in this new city than I ever thought possible." **—ANNE'S STORY**

After living in New York, I thought life in another city could only be easier. I wanted to leave to find a better quality of life for my children as well as better professional opportunities. My job search led me to a great position in Boston, a smaller and more manageable city. So, with a lot of anxiety and excitement over new beginnings, I decided to pack up my children and myself and move to Boston.

Moving is a stressful time. Moving to another city, where you have little support, adds another (thick) layer of stress. I tried to get things into place well in advance. One month before the move, I went to Boston for four days to find a place to live and child care—my two biggest concerns. With the help of realtors and child care placement agencies, I was able to set up home visits and baby-sitter interviews, and actually found a home and a great baby-sitter. The home was being fixed up and would be ready by the time we arrived, and the sitter was experienced and warm and seemed to love children. Once those issues were in place, I felt free to concentrate on settling things in New York, which included leaving my job, packing, and selling my home.

I spent each day running around, taking care of details, and trying to pack up my home. I had talked with my kids about moving, and how excited I was about this new beginning. We talked about keeping in touch with family and friends, and the great time they would have making new friends. Since I couldn't imagine having the girls around while I was unpacking, I arranged to have them visit their grandparents for a few days—and they were also excited about that trip. When the movers came to take our things, I felt like I had coordinated troop movements, but I had been organized, so I was able to pull it off. We left our home, said good-bye to our friends, and drove off to Grandma's house, where the girls would stay for a few days. Then disaster struck.

In the weeks before I left, I had called to make sure our house would be ready, and was told that it definitely would be. Imagine how I felt when I drove up with the moving van to find a home that was far from finished and filled with workers. What was I going to do? Where was I going to stay? Where was I going to put my belongings? Fortunately, my children were with their grandparents, so I only had to worry about myself. I had a long talk with the landlord who assured me everything would be ready in one week. My belongings were put into storage, and I stayed with a friend from college. However, after a few days, Grandma and Grandpa had to get back to their jobs and brought the girls to be with me.

There was not enough room to stay with my friend, so I took my girls and went to

a hotel, and spent every day on the landlord's back to get the house together. At the same time, I was worried that all this chaos was going to affect my girls and struggled to not let them know how desperate I felt. Although the house was not ready, it was too expensive to stay in the hotel, so we had to move in. Trying to make the best of it, I tried to settle in and had a chance to get to know the workers (they were my unofficial roommates). It was then that I found out they had slowed work because the landlord hadn't paid them, and that the house had failed lead inspection. LEAD!! IN MY HOUSE!! WITH MY YOUNG CHILDREN!! I had to get out immediately, but had no place to go—I was desperate.

My grandmother has seven brothers and sisters, some of whom live around Boston. As a child, I thought of them as "those distant relatives who live far away." Fortunately, they remembered me better than I remembered them. My grandmother had told them I was moving to Boston and had given them my number. The day I discovered lead in my house, my phone rang and I heard a voice say "Hi, Anne, remember me? It's your Great Aunt Mary. Welcome to Boston." I had been to her house once as a child, and I remembered her kindness. Hearing her voice, I burst into tears and told her everything that had happened to me. Once my relatives found out what was happening, they pulled together and were able to help us.

We ended up staying with a cousin whom I hadn't seen in over ten years. She had plenty of room and welcomed us, and it gave me such relief to know my children were safe. With my family's help, I was able to find another home (as well as a lawyer to deal with the landlord). This move proved to be one of the most stressful experiences of my life and caused a real crisis. However, I learned a lesson about the importance of friends and family, and that I had more support in this new city than I ever thought possible.

helpful if she starts to feel homesick later on. Also, create a small address book for her so that she can send postcards and letters from her new home.

- *Make a moving packet.* Show your child a map of his new neighborhood or a state or country map with a highlighted route from the old house to the new. On a neighborhood map, use crayons or markers to point out local children's attractions such as zoos, amusement parks, or nature centers. Show him where his school or day care is so he can be familiar with what he will be doing at his new home.

- *Pack a special box.* Set aside special items for your child, like a blanket, doll, stuffed animal, truck, a few changes of clothes, and other favorite toys to be packed the last day. This should be the first box opened on the other side.
- *Return to a normal schedule as soon as possible.* Sticking to the same regular bedtime and wake-up time, and eating, bathing, and going to day care at the same times can help your child feel secure. This is key to establishing a routine in a new home.
- *Remind her of other scary or exciting transitions, such as starting day care, that she dealt with successfully and which turned out to be good experiences.* Emphasize that the move is a chance for her to make new friends.

New Siblings

Many psychologists describe a child's reaction to a new sibling like this: Suppose your husband or partner came home and said, "Baby, I'm going to bring home another woman to live with us forever." Imagine how angry, betrayed, and jealous you'd feel that you had to share your partner's attention, time, and love with someone else. Few of us could handle this situation gracefully, so think of how hard it must be for a child when a new brother or sister comes home.

Help your children develop their own special relationship.

Most experts agree that having two children within two years of each other creates a difficult situation for both parents and siblings. Both children are still very dependent and vying for attention to get their needs met. And the parents are pulled in different directions and can feel overwhelmed by the responsibility and time required to handle both an infant and a toddler. If you're in this situation, then you are probably experiencing more stress than other families with children spaced further apart.

But no matter what the difference in age between your children, having another child changes the family dynamic and creates stress on all members getting used to a new situation. Preparation for this life-altering change is key to creating positive feelings between siblings. So before your new baby is born, use some of these suggestions to help your older child get accustomed to the idea of a new baby:

- *During your pregnancy, talk often with your child about what the change will mean for her.* She may be afraid she won't have any more time with you, or she may fear that the baby will take over all of her belongings. Comfort her by explaining that you will love her just as much as before, and that nobody can replace her. Also let her begin to understand the concept of sharing while at the same time allowing her to maintain some of her own private belongings.
- *Explain the birth as a family event for everyone to share.* If your child feels included, he will begin to get caught up in the excitement of the upcoming event. Involve him in plans and discuss ways that he can be helpful when the baby comes home. For instance, tell him that you'll need him to get the bottles of milk from the refrigerator, help stack diapers, or play with the baby while you cook dinner.
- *Have your child make a welcoming gift for the baby.* Putting together a book or collage to express things she wants to share with her little brother or sister can help her start to build her own special relationship with the new sibling.
- *Carve time out of your day to spend alone with each child.* All caretakers should make plans to spend extra time with the older child. This will help him feel that he's still important and will allow other adults to spend time alone with the baby.
- *Celebrate each child's special gifts.* All children are different, so be sure you respect their talents and personal quirks. Having separate activities you do with each child will help him or her feel unique.

The Legacy of Domestic Violence: Helping Your Child and Yourself

More than 2 million women are abused by their partners every year, making domestic abuse the number-one cause of injuries to all women ages fifteen to forty-four. Researchers estimate that at least 40 percent of these abusers go on to physically or sexually abuse the children as well. Domestic violence experts note that while public awareness about these crimes is greater than before, too many families still put off getting out of abusive situations. Below is information that will help you understand why it's vital for you and your children to receive help immediately. In saving yourself, you are also saving your child.

If you are a battered spouse or partner, you must understand that what's happening to you also affects your children. Studies show that witnessing a parent being abused is actually more harmful to children than being abused themselves. Experts speculate that a child's sense of powerlessness to help her parent and her inability to make sense of why her parent is being hurt make the event more traumatic than receiving the abuse themselves. The longer the abuse continues without intervention (and domestic violence experts note that most abusive situations get worse over time) and the more isolated you and your family are from outside help, the more lasting and damaging the abuse is to your child.

Domestic violence leaves a lasting impression that follows young children into adulthood. More than 80 percent of women in battered women's shelters and 40 percent of adults who abuse grew up in abusive homes. Women who witnessed abuse as children learn erroneously that part of womanhood involves being battered; males are more likely to grow up to batter because they believe that frustration and anger is relieved through violence.

Children exposed to violence in the home have a greater risk of behavioral problems now and in the future. Brain scans of abused children show that trauma and physical and sexual abuse early in life can affect a child's brain interactions and leave him vulnerable to developmental delays, memory lapses, behavior disorders, and attention deficit disorder. When a child suffers from an abusive event, he experiences stress that, over time, can result in long-term damage and make him more vulnerable to drug abuse and mental illness later on.

Even if your child seems "fine" despite living in an atmosphere of threats and violence, understand that young children observe situations closely and often have delayed reactions to their circumstances. Young children who are abused or who have witnessed abuse are also less able to express their emotions. You may begin to see your child's sense of frustration, helplessness, and fear in the following reactions:

- Discipline problems, especially aggressive behavior and constant defiance
- Problems relating to or getting along with other children, including fighting
- Refusal to go to bed
- Trouble learning or functioning at school or day care

- Displaying low self-esteem and/or withdrawal
- Depression
- Abusing other children, siblings, or animals

If you are currently in an abusive relationship with a partner or your children, here are some suggestions for you:

- *Help yourself today.* Shame, helplessness, and rationalizations are the main reasons parents don't seek help in abusive situations. But one phone call can change your life. Begin with your local police station if the situation is dire. Otherwise, domestic abuse hotlines or local shelters listed in the yellow or blue pages of your phone book can be a first step if you need to leave a batterer. Shelters provide a safe place for families, access to counseling and support groups, and, often, help in job placement. Parenting hotlines are good resources for child abuse, and attendants can direct you toward counseling services and parenting classes that will help you. Abuse is too complex and severe to resolve by yourself. Professional intervention is the most effective means of ending domestic violence of any kind.
- *Help your child.* If you feel overwhelmed by your situation, seek additional help for your children. Studies show that positive experiences with a caring adult can alleviate some of the damage abused children have suffered. Get the support of an organization that will provide referrals to child development therapists and parental support groups, such as the National Council on Child Abuse and Family Violence (800–222–2000).

Teaching Resiliency

For African Americans there's nothing new about learning how to bounce back from adversity. Our cultural history is one of survival and the ability to thrive in the face of extreme difficulty from slavery to the present day. Through the generations, our parents have taught us how to use our wit, optimism, determination, and faith to "keep our eyes on the prize," and when we get to the other side, to reach back for our sisters and brothers.

Recently, researchers have been able to demonstrate that humor, intelligence, faith, will, and community involvement are key elements to a phenomenon called resilience. Resilience, or succeeding in the face of difficulty, comes naturally to many of

Before the Hitting Starts: Early Warning Signs of an Abuser

Experts in domestic abuse have devised a profile of an abuser and what early abuse looks like. Emotional abuse is the precursor to physical abuse, and from there the problems can escalate into serious injury. Most women are caught off guard once physical abuse begins, not understanding that emotional abuse has been taking place all along. Here are some clues to detect an abusive partner:

- ***He's very controlling.*** **For instance, he tells you what to wear, whom to be friends with, what to eat. If you don't comply, he gets angry.**
- ***He is easily jealous.*** **He gets furious if you talk to another man and doesn't even want you to spend time with your friends or family.**
- ***He puts you down.*** **He criticizes or insults you or your appearance, ideas, or behavior and uses words like "stupid," "disgusting," or "trampy" to refer to you.**
- ***He has a "bad temper."*** **For instance, he scares you when you don't do things his way, he gets in fights or arguments often, he threatens you or others (sometimes with weapons or physical punishment), and acts in a generally intimidating manner.**
- ***He blames others.*** **He doesn't take responsibility for his behavior, including when he has hurt you or your feelings, saying it was your fault.**
- ***He doesn't respect women.*** **He believes men should be in control and women should do what he says. He puts women down (calls them "bitches" and "hos") and treats them as inferior.**
- ***He has pressured or forced you to have sex.*** **He says you "owe" it to him, tries to make you feel guilty if you don't have sex, or threatens you into having sex.**
- ***He abuses drugs or alcohol.*** **He pressures you to join him in substance abuse.**
- ***He shows early signs of abuse.*** **He has pushed, shoved, pinched, or kicked you, or otherwise tried to scare or physically hurt you.**
- ***He was abused as a child or saw his parents in an abusive relationship.***

us, but experts are discovering that it can also be taught. According to Saundra Murray Nettles, Ph.D., program co-director at Johns Hopkins University's Center for Research on Education for Students Placed at Risk, resilience is a process that begins very early in life. "Parents can foster resilience in their young children by staying involved in early education, providing structure and rules, and by being a caring, loving parent."

Our children especially can benefit from learning ways to recover from negative situations, because the alternatives are too devastating. "African-American kids who aren't resilient reach trouble in adolescence with risky sexual behavior, delinquency, substance abuse, teen pregnancy, and dropping out of school," says Dr. Nettles, who is also a leading researcher in resiliency in African-American children. She notes that early signs point to potential problems in a adolescence: the failure to read, difficulty making friends, a pessimistic attitude, and a difficult temperament. Fortunately, according to Dr. Nettles, resiliency isn't predetermined. "We can foster resiliency [in troubled children] and help them."

Helping Our Children Be Resilient

Over the past decade, leading experts in the field of resiliency, like Emmy Werner, Ph.D., at University of California at Davis, and Ann Masten, Ph.D., at the University of Minnesota, have been compiling studies of children who have been raised in high-risk situations—from being raised by a teen or unemployed parent to being exposed to a catastrophic event, like an earthquake or war. These researchers followed young children into adulthood and discovered that those who were most successful had personal, family, and community resources that helped them grow up into well-functioning adults. Based on her studies and the research of her colleagues, Dr. Nettles has compiled a list of ways we can teach our children to more effectively deal with the adversity that will inevitably arise in their lives:

1. *Accentuate the positive.* Children with a positive attitude don't feel overwhelmed or doomed easily. This attitude allows them to have hope and find ways to deal with troubling situations so they can continue to function.

2. *Keep expectations high.* Parents who praise their children while providing them with new challenges add to their self-esteem, a key component in resiliency. Young children will eventually internalize your expectations and turn them into their own aspirations.

3. *Teach independence.* Children who have a sense of control over their environment or situation also feel they have the ability to influence or change it for the better. Providing your child with opportunities for independence also helps her learn problem-solving skills even on the most basic levels, and will add to a feeling of accomplishment.

4. *Stress that getting help is OK.* Research shows that competent children learn how to balance independence with the ability to seek help when necessary. Communicating needs and getting help are forms of problem solving, and eventually lead to mastery of a skill.

5. *Find a talent.* Help your child find his talents or interests and then encourage him to seek friends with whom he can share them. The pride he'll feel will give him a confidence booster and an outlet.

6. *Give your child responsibilities.* Giving children responsibilities (helping out with chores, caring for an elderly relative or young sibling, or participating in community activities that benefit others) provides a sense of independence, pride, and purpose.

7. *Provide mentors.* Even the best parents can't do it all alone. Single parents especially need to call on trusted, loving adults to act as positive role models for their young children. Interestingly, research shows that boys do well with men who encourage them to express their emotions, and girls thrive with women who encourage independence and positive risk taking while providing support. Teachers, parents of close friends from stable families, and other family members are excellent resources.

8. *Spirituality helps.* Belonging to a church or having another kind of religious affiliation provides young children with emotional support outside of the family. The church community can be a place for your child to discover talents, participate in extracurricular activities, gain a sense of responsibility within his community, and call upon a spiritual power for comfort.

9. *Stay close.* A close parental attachment is the best safeguard for your child's future. A loving, warm, consistent, and respectful approach to childrearing allows for a healthy bond, which helps your child feel worthy, lovable, and secure. Additionally, your involvement in her daily life at day care, with a caregiver, or at home will strengthen those bonds even when you aren't around. Your open arms and loving attention will help guide her through failures and stressful events, until she's old enough to do so herself.

RESOURCES

Recommended Reading for Parents

Coping

The Optimistic Child, Martin Seligman, Karen Reivich, Lisa Jaycox, and Jane Gillham (HarperPerennial, 1996). In this book, the author of *Learned Optimism* and his colleagues offer parents and educators a clinically proven program to help children approach life with confidence.

Death

Children and Grief: When a Parent Dies, J. William Worden (Guilford Press, 1996). This book discusses how children respond to death and provides information on counseling services.

Divorce

Be a Great Divorced Dad, Dr. Kenneth N. Condress and Linda Lee Small (St. Martin's Press, 1998). This handbook covers practical and emotional issues facing divorced fathers today.

Good Men: A Practical Handbook for Divorced Dads, Jack Feuer (Avon Books, 1997). This book provides practical information on a wide variety of concerns to divorced fathers.

Talking About Divorce and Separation: A Dialogue Between Parent and Child, Earl A. Grollman (Beacon Press, 1989). This book provides information for both children and adults about the process of divorce.

The Good Divorce: Keeping Your Family Together When Your Marriage Falls Apart, Constance R. Ahrons, Ph.D. (HarperCollins, 1994). This book is based on solid research about the effects of divorce on children and tells parents how to help their children during this transition.

Moving

Moving Without Madness: A Guide to Handling the Stresses and Emotions of Moving, Arlene Alpert (Gemini Press, 1997). This book provides information on how to help your child negotiate the difficulties of moving.

Moving with Children: A Parent's Guide to Moving with Children, Thomas T. Olkowski, Ph.D., and Lynn Parker, LCSW (Gylantic Publishing Co., 1993). This guide offers tips on alleviating the stresses of moving with children.

Siblings

Siblings Without Rivalry: How to Help Your Children Live Together So You Can Live Too, Adele Faber (Bantam Books, 1996). This bestseller teaches you and your children how to problem solve and successfully resolve sibling conflicts.

Your Second Child, Joan Solomon Weiss (Summit Books, 1981). The author cites studies on birth order and parenting to help parents decide whether to have additional children.

Recommended Reading for Children

Death

Geranium Morning, E. Sandy Powell, illustrated by Renée Graef (Carolrhoda Books, 1990). Two friends who lose a parent learn to deal with their grief.

Gran-Gran's Best Trick: A Story for Children Who Have Lost Someone They Love, L. Dwight Holden, illustrated by Michael Chesworth (Magination Press, 1989). After his grandfather's death, a child recounts their special relationship.

Divorce

At Daddy's on Saturdays, Linda Walvoord Girard, illustrated by Judith Friedman (Albert Whitman and Company, 1991). This is a warm story of divorce told from the point of view of a young girl.

Mom and Dad Don't Live Together Anymore, Nancy Lou Reynolds, illustrated by Kathy Stinson (Firefly Books, 1988). This book discusses positive ways children can think and feel about divorce.

Dinosaurs Divorce: A Guide for Changing Families, Marc Brown, illustrated by Laurene Kransy Brown (Atlantic Monthly Press, 1986). This book addresses the range of feelings divorce produces in children by depicting the experience with dinosaur characters.

Moving

Moving Day, Harriet Margolin (Goldencraft/Good Day Bunnies Books, 1987). This book takes us through the feelings of a child when her family moves.

Moving Time for Kelly, Phyllis Martin, illustrated by Susan Yodert (Standard Publishing/Happy Day Books, 1998). This book discusses moving from the perspective of a child.

Siblings

Me Too!, Mercer Mayer (Western Publishing Company, 1983). This book depicts the compromises a big brother must make to accommodate his little sister.

Domestic Abuse Hotlines

National Domestic Violence Hotline, (800) 799–SAFE (7233). This agency provides emergency and nonemergency services in your area.

National Resource Center on Domestic Violence, (800) 537–2238. This center provides information and resources to help prevention of domestic abuse.

Organizations and Support Groups

American Psychological Association, 750 1st St., NE, Washington, D.C. 20002, (202) 336–5500. This organization helps families find counseling services and therapists who specialize in family transitions, such as divorce, abuse, new siblings, and death.

The Association of Black Psychologists, P.O. Box 55999, Washington, D.C. 20040–5999, (202) 722–0808

Website: abpsi.org

Families in crisis can call to obtain information on black therapists and programs to help black family members cope with stressful transitions.

Center for the Family in Transition, P.O. Box 157, Corte Madeira, CA 94976, (415) 924–5750, fax: (415) 388–1225. This organization provides counseling services for families in need.

Compassionate Friends, P.O. Box 3696, Oak Brook, IL 60522–3696, (630) 990–0010, fax: (630) 990–0246. With the chapters across the country, this organization provides friendship, literature, and support to the parents, grandparents, and siblings of a deceased child.

Effective Black Parenting Program, Center for the Improvement of Child Caring, 11331 Ventura Blvd., Suite 103, Studio City, CA 91604, (818) 980–0903. Recognizing the special stresses African-American families can experience, this program is designed to foster effective family communication, healthy black identity, extended family values, and proper child growth and development.

MELD (Minnesota Early Learning Design), 123 N. 3rd St., Suite 507, Minneapolis, MN 55401, (612) 332–7563, fax: (612) 337–5468. This organization sponsors parent support groups and provides literature for parents. These programs are designed to prevent instances of emotional or physical abuse by creating a healthy family atmosphere.

National Black Child Development Institute, 1023 15th St., NW, Suite 600, Washington, D.C. 20005, (202) 387–1281, fax: (202) 234–1738, e-mail: moreinfo@nbcdi.org

Website: nbcdi.org

This organization works to improve the quality of life for African-American children and their families by publishing literature and providing health programs which foster well-being.

Single and Custodial Fathers Network, 1700 E. Carson St., Pittsburgh, PA 15203, (412) 381–4800. This organization provides single fathers with educational materials and information about support groups.

Chapter

13

Our Family and Community

Throughout our history, many of us have not had the luxury of growing up in a traditional nuclear family: mother, father, and children in the same home. During slavery, our families were literally ripped apart. Plantations operated on the "stud system" whereby a strong, healthy male was "bred" with a strong, healthy female to produce strong, healthy "stock." Many men never knew which children they had fathered because they were quickly shipped off to another area to repeat the breeding process with another woman, and another. As depicted so vividly in Alex Haley's epic *Roots,* the babies themselves were often sold from their mothers to other plantations. Black people weren't even allowed to legally marry until the late 1800s. As renowned African-American speaker Reverend Tom Skinner has pointed out, the nuclear black family in America is only about 140 years old.

We have done a remarkable job for having undergone such atrocities. Fatherless men have learned how to be good husbands and fathers. Young, single women from "broken" homes have learned how to raise healthy, even brilliant, children. Teenagers have successfully raised children, with the assistance of grandparents and other caring folks. Somewhere along the way, aunts, uncles, cousins, and friends have all been called upon to make their contribution to our family structure. In this chapter, we'll discuss the different kinds of families that exist in our community and will offer resources to help each one thrive.

Single mothers can enlist male friends to provide positive role models.

Single Parenting

Chances are that one of every two mothers reading this book is a solo parent. If that's you, we applaud you for carving out the time to read this! As one recent advertisement proclaimed, you are a "Juggler," that is, a single woman who strives to maintain a balance between family, work, and other responsibilities. There was a time when a single mother, whether divorced, widowed, or "caught out there," as they say, could have relied on the support of her family and friends, most of whom lived nearby and were able and willing to lend a hand. But, as many of us migrated north to find a "better" life, we often left behind our support systems.

Our (Extended) Family

One privilege of being part of a black family is that you usually inherit a colorful array of "aunties," "uncles," "cousins," and "poppas"—people who nurture us but who often aren't blood relatives. Often, these women and men helped raise us—took care of us after school, made sure we went to church, showed up at every major family event with ten dollars tucked in a card, and offered a shoulder to cry on. In many homes, these adopted family members were friends of our parents who needed a place to stay, for whatever reason: loss of a job, or a spouse, or just needing some time to settle in after relocating from another state or country. From this eclectic mix of people who streamed through our lives, we discovered the world beyond our parents and often found security, love, and support.

Today, few of us have blood relatives who live next door. And the tradition of taking in strangers and friends of friends seems to have declined, possibly due to tighter pockets, less space, increased stress, and fear of crime. But the need for a support system has not gone away. In fact, there's probably more of a need for family network support than ever, as single mothers are saddled with the responsibility of supporting and raising a family on their own, and employment opportunities tighten for all African Americans. New parents especially must develop a network of reliable, accessible folks whom they like and trust, if they hope to raise a healthy family (and keep their sanity). Here are some ways to build and maintain supportive relationships with family members and close friends:

- *Keep in touch.* Attend family reunions and make efforts to maintain contact after the event via telephone, e-mail, letters, and visits.
- *Share stories.* Ask visiting family members and friends to share their histories and anecdotes with your children. This will create special family stories that your family will remember and feel connected to.
- *Move closer.* If you are in need of support, consider moving nearer to close relatives or friends who can enhance your family life. Family members can offer their time and experience in child care, and provide important loving support.
- *Give back.* Building a support network works two ways. Look for opportunities to offer your family and friends your time, your talent, or your money as a form of family cooperation. Family and friends will be more likely to pitch in and help when they feel you have done the same for them.

"It has been my pleasure to be a mother and a grandmother. . . . I've definitely gained more than I have lost."

—Belinda Robbins, grandmother to twin boys, age 4; Charlotte, North Carolina

I offer my daughter and grandsons any kind of support they need, be it emotional, financial, or physical. I just like to be in their company so I will visit them even when they don't need any baby-sitting. I'll also provide for them financially, and my daughter can bounce ideas off me about the boys' development. I give advice, when it is asked for. Unfortunately, I also give it when it is not asked for. She knows me well so, even when it is not asked for, she doesn't say much. She knows I don't mean any harm, but I try very hard to control it.

The boys were born three months premature and that was terrifying. I am thankful that I had the energy and the strength to be there with them when my daughter could not. I saw them nearly every day they were in the ICU, and when they came out of the incubator, I held them and talked to them and sang to them. It was frightening, though, and I hope I never have to go through that again. It was very taxing emotionally, particularly with the eldest one because he had so many episodes of breathing problems.

My daughter also went through a period of severe depression. I was very supportive during this time, trying to get her to go to the doctor and making sure she took her medicine. Mostly I just wanted to be there for her. It was a pretty bad period for her, and I think she suffered a lot because of the prematurity of the boys, as well as how their biological father responded to her and the babies. It wasn't just me, the whole family supported her. It was a wonderful thing the way the family came together.

The boys are so fascinating and loving. They are so innocent, and their minds are so open to learning new experiences. They have a delightful sense of humor and they make it clear that they love me. It has been my pleasure to be a mother and a grandmother. It has been a wonderful thing, even with all the problems and so forth. I've definitely gained more than I have lost.

Single mothers are often blamed for their situation instead of being understood and helped, and are sometimes frowned upon by the larger society—and that includes other black folks. But successfully raising a family as one person, sometimes on one income, is nothing short of phenomenal. For many mothers it takes its toll emotionally, mentally, and physically. Yet, as poet Maya Angelou says, "Still we rise."

One of the factors keeping many single moms "rising" is a commitment to staying

Don't Leave Us Out: Helping Fathers Stay Involved with Their Children

Despite the negative media images of black fathers who abandon their children, there are many concerned and responsible African-American men who want to be involved with their children but need help. Obstacles including society's fear of black men, persistent employment and housing discrimination, and the lack of positive male role models in many black men's lives all conspire to undo their good intentions as fathers. Fortunately, there are many community organizations run by black men to help others like themselves learn how to parent.

Organizations such as the Institute for Responsible Fatherhood and Family Revitalization in Washington, D.C., work one-on-one with fathers to break the cycle of abandonment by teaching them to resolve difficult and painful issues with their own fathers, with the mothers of their children, and within themselves. In addition, men are assisted with job training, employment, and establishing paternity.

There are a number of programs for fathers hoping to reconnect with their families. Many exist on grassroots levels across the country, and some innovative approaches are being taken, such as the one at Hartford Housing Authority's Family Reunification Program. This program seeks to knock down every possible barrier keeping fathers away from their families. And the barriers can be complex. For example, a family can be disqualified for assistance if the father is present in the home, even if he is making only minimum wage; the family could also lose their housing subsidy. Many fathers are reluctant to join programs because of back child support that they cannot pay. The Hartford program addresses this by significantly reducing the amount owed for fathers who commit to the program. The men must agree to be drug free, pledge to be an active role model for their children, and to move their families off of welfare once they are employed. In exchange, the fathers are taught the construction trade and offered well-paying jobs upon completion.

grounded, spiritually and emotionally. Despite what others may believe, most single mothers have very high expectations for their children and work incredibly hard to see them achieve. Dr. Rebecca Lee is a surgeon and the mother of a precocious daughter, Rachel. When Rebecca got pregnant and made the decision to see the pregnancy through, her then-boyfriend disappeared for a while after she told him she was pregnant. Today, Rachel and her father have a good relationship, which Rebecca

"There will always be something missing if a child has to wonder or ask 'Where is my father?' or 'Where is my mother?' "

—Damu Smith, father of Asha, age 5; Washington, D.C.

I don't consider myself a part-time parent. I am totally involved in my child's life. Her mother and I have had joint discussions about every aspect Asha's life as if we were married and living in the same house. We don't make any major decisions unless we consult each other. This pertains to her medical care, education, her recreational activities, birthdays and holidays, even her diet. We may not be married but we are the parents of a beautiful, wonderful gift from God and we have the responsibility to do everything we can to ensure she is healthy, happy, and emotionally well-balanced.

A lot of times people will see me with Asha and say, "Oh you are baby-sitting today." I will say, "No I am not baby-sitting. This is my daughter and I am raising my daughter." But this reflects the mentality that people have: If people see a man with a child they think that you just have her for the day, just for a couple of hours, that you are basically baby-sitting. That is not my situation at all. When Asha was born, I took three months paternity leave from my job. When Asha was one, she spent a month in the hospital and I lived in her hospital room the whole time. Her mother was sick with the flu during Asha's illness so I spent most of the time with her while she was in the hospital. I know Asha remembers that because I went out of the country for a month after that and when I returned she grabbed my neck and squeezed me and I just got the feeling she remembered Daddy was with her during her hospitalization.

A number of times I have had to rush her to the hospital with asthma attacks. One time in the middle of the winter I was thinking how so many women have had to do this by themselves and with other children in the house. This experience has really made me think about how hard it is for so many women without the man there. Being a parent has made this really very vivid. We are dealing with life and death matters when it comes to our children, and it must be devastating not to have the support of the other person. Children have emotional needs also. A friend may say something bad about them, they may get into a fight, or a teacher may say something they don't understand. You have to talk to them and help them through this. If you are not involved in the emotional and spiritual development of your child, they could have some serious problems as a result. They could be off center and off balance if you do not help explain things to them and offer support, not only through words but through

hugs and kisses. All these things are big, huge things in the life of a child. Parenting is being committed to the total development of your child.

It is important that both parents make sure their children are emotionally, spiritually, and materially taken care of. Mothers and fathers provide different and unique forms of support in our children's lives. There are little things that men do. We pick up our children more and hold them up in the sky. I am the one who is going to put Asha on my shoulder and let her touch the ceiling. It is important for children to know both their parents because it contributes to their emotional stability. There will always be something missing if a child has to wonder or ask "Where is my father?" or "Where is my mother?"

I am involved in every aspect of my daughter's life. Occasionally her mother and I will have dinner together or do something together so she can see us getting along. That is very unusual but, basically, we are united for our daughter. There are a lot of brothers like me, but the media never reports on that. There are also a lot who are not involved, but I don't want to be counted among that group.

facilitates. Rebecca finds spiritual guidance, social outlets, and male role models for Rachel at her local church. "The men in my family have good hearts but bad habits," notes Lee, "so I feel that having other male influences is very important." On Sundays, Rachel helps out in the church nursery and has been able to nurture her acting talent in both church productions and in local pageants. "These activities have really built her self-esteem and confidence." During the week Rebecca attends a church-based support group where she is able to both minister to others and have her needs ministered to.

Brenda Wade, family psychologist, *Essence* columnist, and author of *Love Lessons,* knows the emotional challenges single moms face; she's one herself. "I see a high degree of depression among single mothers, which often manifests itself in hyperirritability," says Wade. She strongly advocates that mothers maintain an "inner life" by taking daily quiet time, for their own sake and that of their children.

Other tips for single moms include:

1. *Include Dad.* Make every attempt to speak positively to your child about his father, and facilitate visits with him as much as is feasible. Sharing parenting responsibilities with your child's father is as important for you as it is for your child.

2. *Talk to friends and family*. Keep people who care about you informed as to how things are going and make a real effort to stay in touch with close friends regularly.

3. *Don't be shy about asking for help.* When you feel overwhelmed, exhausted, or just in need of a change, ask for help. Most friends and family will be happy to take your little one off your hands for a couple of hours. Or call a baby-sitter, even if you're working around the house or just want to take a nap.

4. *Talk openly with your child.* You and your child are less likely to get into conflicts if you discuss how you're both feeling. Ask her about her day, what good or bad events happened, or allow her to lead the conversation. She'll feel heard, understood, and that she got your attention. Most often children act out if they don't feel they have your attention.

5. *Have a date with yourself.* More than any other suggestion that experts have for single moms, this one seems to get ignored the most. Most moms—single or not—get caught up in what they "should" be doing. But taking breaks to have fun or just do nothing can be one of the best ways to be productive. Rest refreshes your body and mind, so if you don't have time, make time.

6. *Pay yourself first.* Take a set amount (however small) out of each paycheck and put it directly into a savings plan. Use the money to start a retirement fund, to take a trip, or to buy a new home.

7. *Get with other single moms.* Join a support group at your local church or community center. Nobody else understands your situation better than another single parent. You will find many opportunities to make lasting friendships.

8. *Plan your future.* Write down your specific hopes for the next few years and make small steps to achieve them each month. Keep reviewing your plan to see how you're doing.

9. *Understand child support regulations.* New federal laws have been passed that require state welfare agencies to identify fathers and force them to pay child support. In instances where the a man's paternity is in question, states may require him to take a blood test to determine his obligations. And, if you are owed child support from your child's parent, a new federal database has made it easier to receive that money. For more information regarding your right to identify your child's father and receive child support, contact the Department of Health and Human Services listed in the blue section of your local phone book.

10. *Surround yourself with as many good people who affirm you as possible,* so you can stay positive about the future.

Adoptive Parents

More than 30 percent of the children who enter the foster care system are black, according to statistics gathered by the North American Council on Adoptable Children. While about 100,000 live in actual foster homes with adoptive families, according to the Census Bureau, many more in reside in state-run group homes, and an inestimable number of black children are in informal adoption arrangements with family and friends.

Betty Hinton, family/parent advocate for the Administration for Children's Services, is an expert on "kinship placement." She elected to adopt five family members' children who would otherwise be lost in the state foster care system. Hinton has a total of eight foster children—seven boys and one girl—and is a single mother. "A family member calls and says, 'They're taking my child away, Betty,' 'they' being Child Welfare, 'Could you please take him?' " A former schoolteacher, she couldn't resist the opportunity to help save another child. "I said I was stopping at three, but . . ."

Professionally, Hinton helps families that are having problems finalizing adoption or working out personality problems, and she leads them to legal advice. She is currently working on a manual for adoptive parents. "Many parents have a hard time knowing what to do next, how to get evaluations and services for their children, knowing their rights as a parent," says Hinton. "It's hard to make the transition from being supported by an agency and a caseworker to a position where, after the adoption, no one is obligated to give you any help." Most agencies are only legally required to help get children adopted, not maintain their care after adoption. This presents a difficult position for parents who choose to adopt one of the many "special needs" children, those with developmental or physical disabilities. Within the system, a child can be labeled "special needs" just because of his age. "Children who are over eight years old and those who are part of a sibling group are labeled 'special needs,' " adds Hinton. "It means that it is harder to find adoptive parents for them, and if there are any mental, emotional, or physical disabilities, it's even more difficult."

The fact that 400,000 children in the foster care system currently with no immediate hope for formal adoption forces us to reexamine the question of who is an appropriate parent for a black child. "My opinion is that children should be placed with people they can identify with first," says Hinton. "Whoever the adoptive family is though, they should be people who are culturally sensitive. All children should have a loving, consistent, and affirming home environment." Hinton takes the issue of white parents adopting black children in stride. "It's not that white adoptive parents are being hateful or racist, they just don't know some things about caring for a black child." She laughs. "I have taken some of these adopted children aside at conferences and rubbed some Vaseline in their hair because they weren't looking quite right." Hinton says it's a rare case when a white adoptive parent is given any guidelines or advice about caring for their black child. This is one of the problems with cross-cultural adoption that could be easily solved with a diversity training component for white parents, like the one Hinton provides informally. "A black or Hispanic worker should go over with white adoptive parents what needs to be done. They don't know things like the fact that black children's hair doesn't need to be washed every day and that their skin gets ashy." Hinton notes that many white parents are afraid to ask these questions for fear blacks will ask why they adopted the child in the first place if they "didn't know what to do with her." Two of Hinton's own adopted children are of Hispanic descent, thus, she has gotten quite familiar with Spanish television, music, and cuisine.

Here are some of Hinton's tips for adoptive parents:

1. *Give your newly adopted child space.* You are both still strangers and need lots of time to adjust and bond. Respect your child's need to adjust and allow her to feel her way in her new family.

2. *Offer the child honest explanations about why she is now living with you.* "Children wonder whether they did something wrong to be taken away from their former home." Understandably, foster children are likely to have grown skeptical of adults and their promises. They will wonder if you too will "get rid of them" when you're tired. Honesty will build much needed trust between you.

3. *Consider family therapy.* Many children have been in multiple group or foster care homes in their young lives. Even children as young as two or three bring a lot of emotional baggage. There must be a safe place where everyone can regularly express their feelings and receive counseling, preferably together. The children's counseling may be covered by Medicaid, though yours may not.

4. *Be tolerant of "bad" behavior at first.* It's natural for all children to misbehave when entering an unfamiliar, even frightening, situation. Don't assume your child knows or understands any of your household rules until you explain them to her. If you notice her behavior isn't improving after a couple of weeks, discuss family counseling with your social worker or adoption agency.

5. *Don't overcompensate with material gifts or too much attention.* Spoiling an adopted child cannot make up for whatever hurt he has experienced in his life. Just like other children, adopted children need love, understanding, and your time to feel special. Focusing your entire attention on your child could make him very uncomfortable and make his adjustment harder. Instead, help him carve out a niche in your family routine. Begin by setting limits and boundaries in a loving way.

6. *Join a support group for adoptive parents, if there's one in your city.* Hinton notes that this will take some digging. "Many agencies don't offer them because they don't get any reimbursement from the state to offer postadoptive services." Often families create support groups themselves and the word spreads.

7. *Make an appointment to have your child evaluated by a psychologist* so he can be placed in an appropriate educational setting.

Children Having Children: Teen Parenting

The birthrate for teenagers has been steadily decreasing according to the latest data (1996) from the U.S. Department of Health and Human Services. Among older black teenagers, age fifteen to seventeen, the rate of birth has decreased about 5 percent each year since 1991. And black teens age ten to fourteen show some of the largest reductions of any ethnic group. Unfortunately, black teenage mothers still have a harder time finishing their education, getting well-paying jobs, and achieving parity with their older or married counterparts. And with welfare reform, things will only get tougher for those who need public assistance.

The bottom line is that too many of our teens are still "lookin' for love in all the wrong places." Many are suffering from poor self-esteem and are relying on others, often a boyfriend, to affirm them. "A lot of it comes from the lack of family time in these kids' lives," says Zola Allen, a youth pastor in Queens, New York. "Too often, even functional black families neglect to sit down and have dinner together, hug each other, and affirm their children. In many homes, parenting is more about administering discipline than offering love. This does not provide a good balance." She notes

"My mother really helps me out a lot. . . . She stuck by me and she really believes in me. That's what makes me able to do what I do."

—Tanisha, mother of a two-week-old daughter; Brooklyn, New York

I am sixteen and my daughter is two weeks old. I am in the eleventh grade and having her has really affected my education because now I have to rush through my homework. I don't have enough time to sit down and think about it if she starts crying; I have to stop and tend to her. I go to bed really late at night. For the past week she has kept me up until 4:00 or 5:00 in the morning. Then I have to get up by 7:00 and be at school by 8:30 A.M. I am kind of getting used to it but sometimes I fall asleep in school. But I do my work and try my best.

I am doing this because I don't want to live with my mother for the rest of my life. I want to be responsible and independent and be able to go out on my own. I want to make sure I have the money to give my daughter what she needs when she is older. I don't want to be dependent on her father or my mother. The better the education I get, the better the job I can get and the more money I will eventually make. If I don't do it now, I never will.

I would like to go to college, to be a nutritionist or physical therapist.

The father of my baby is eighteen and also still in school. Before he goes to school, he comes over and takes care of the baby. This lets me get my work done or get some more sleep. My aunt also helps, as well as my sister and my father. I also turn to my friends for help. My mother really helps me out a lot. I appreciate that because most mothers wouldn't. She stuck by me and she really believes in me. That's what makes me able to do what I do.

that some black parents are so strict that their teenagers are frightened of them and may have sex as a way of getting away from the tight control. Boredom, loneliness, poor grades in school, and lack of other constructive outlets (such as sports, art, or dance) are other reasons girls turn to boys to provide them with a way to fill their lives.

Several of the teenage girls in Allen's program recently gave birth. "Some of them are under the delusion that having a baby will give them something to love and who will love them," says Allen. "When the baby arrives, then they realize how serious it is. They are then forced to mature."

But teens who receive the proper guidance and nurturance through their pregnancies and after the birth of the baby can emerge with a new sense of maturity. "I just want to make something of myself now, for my child's sake," said one teen mother who recently enrolled in a community college. Allen helps the girls dig deep into their pasts and examine why they go to guys for affirmation in the first place. "We encourage them to be really honest with themselves. We explain that it's OK to have feelings and needs, but it's what they do with them that matters." Looking into their feelings and behavior will hopefully prompt these young women to understand how their actions will affect their futures.

Despite the obstacles they face, teen mothers aren't "doomed for life." Black teenagers are more likely than white teens to finish a high school education or equivalent, according to a 1990 study of teen parents in the labor market. Obtaining child care is key to finishing an education, and fortunately, many African-American teen mothers are able to take advantage of relatives' assistance or other affordable day care alternatives.

Here are some other suggestions for teen mothers:

- *Seek assistance.* Your local department of social services should be able to direct you to ways you can obtain aid for your education, your child's day care, and any help you may need in feeding or caring for your baby. Individual day care centers offer scholarships or other financial aid, so be sure to ask.
- *Network early on.* Find mentors or enroll in a mentoring program to help you seek out successful mothers who can help you with child care tips, offer support, and generally provide a good role model.
- *Set goals.* Map out what you want to do with your life and all the steps in between to get there. Understand that having a baby makes reaching goals more complicated, but not impossible.
- *Put your education first.* The sooner you finish your education, the sooner you can qualify for a high-paying job. Talk to your school counselor about your career and educational goals and see if she can help you find a way to reach them. Many school districts offer special programs for teen mothers in high school, but be sure their educational goals are the same as yours (some are geared toward helping moms get their GED but not to go on to college). Some schools are willing to work out a home-study situation if you show strong motivation and the ability to complete assignments.

- *Get creative when it comes to child care.* There are more options in child care than just day care or help from your mother. Think of other ways to get the help you need: Enlist the support of friends with experience baby-sitting, have younger relatives play with your child while you do your schoolwork, or barter baby-sitting time for one of your talents (for instance, fixing hair or tutoring).

Parents of Children with Disabilities

Parenting a young child with disabilities can be extremely challenging. Identifying and then negotiating the maze of services, treatments, and entitlements for their children's disabilities can be a full-time job for many parents. Black parents are confronted with other issues, such as single parenting, feeling isolated by a predominately white disability support system, and battling feelings of guilt and the social stigma associated with parenting a disabled child.

Whether your child is learning disabled or living with cerebral palsy, it's important for you to build the support network you need to care for and educate her. Both parents' and children's lives are enriched with the help of social services that provide you with the financial and medical aid your family is entitled to, family support groups in which parents learn how to give the best to their children, and educational services that provide ways to help your child integrate into society and connect with other children.

Elaine Fleishman, a social worker at the Office of Mental Retardation and Developmental Disability (OMRDD), works to empower families so they can advocate for the services their children are entitled to receive. Services this agency and similar ones provide include in-home care, counseling, recreation programs such as special camps, behavior management, and housing assistance such as home modification to accommodate a disabled child.

As provided in the Individuals with Disabilities Act, each state has established a parent training program to assist parents in understanding and coping with their children's disability. There are also many grassroots programs within the African-American community, such as Parents of Watts in Los Angeles, that speak to the specific needs of black parents with disabled children. To locate these and other services in your state or community, look in the blue pages of your local phone book for People with Disabilities.

Gay Parents

It's estimated that one in every ten African Americans is gay or a lesbian, and many are parents of young children. Unfortunately, while on the one hand we insist that racism be abolished, some of us are very intolerant of gays and lesbians in our own community. This hypocrisy is especially troubling when it comes to our children. They get the message that it's not fair to discriminate against people based on ethnicity, but acceptable to hurt others based on their sexual orientation. This belief implies that some of us are less equal than others, the same belief white racists used to keep us from exercising our civil rights. Homophobia (fear or hatred of gays and lesbians) only serves to further divide our community and teaches our children another form of prejudice.

African-American gay parents have even more challenges to face than other parents because they must constantly negotiate negative stereotypes about their ability to parent. Fortunately, many gay parenting groups have sprouted up around the nation to help gay and lesbian mothers and fathers support each other in the many issues they face: societal discrimination, family rejection, finding a place of religious worship, living in a safe and accepting community, and finding supportive child care. While these issues aren't always resolved easily, they aren't insurmountable. Many gay and lesbian parents believe the key to a healthy family life is to be honest and understanding.

Here are more suggestions to help black gays and lesbians navigate parenthood with small children:

- *Come to terms with your own feelings.* If you have any feelings of shame or guilt about being gay, it will come through when talking to your child. If you feel secure and confident about being gay or lesbian, your child will also feel secure and confident. If you have unresolved feelings, consider talking with a professional counselor who specializes in gay and lesbian issues.
- *Be open about what "gay" or "lesbian" means.* Once your child is old enough to ask or understand, discuss what being gay or lesbian means (loving someone of your same gender), that just because this is what you are doesn't mean your child will be too, and that it's different from most people.
- *Help your child learn how to talk about having gay parents.* Many parents believe it's best for their families to be discreet about having gay or lesbian

***"Let your child know that your family is normal although it may be* different *from others."* —JOI RHONE, MOTHER OF A 2 1/2-YEAR-OLD DAUGHTER; OAKLAND, CALIFORNIA**

When I decided I wanted to adopt, I knew there would be twice the usual barriers. Not only would I be a single mother, but I am also a lesbian.

I had been thinking about adopting for a while, but when I turned forty, I decided to go ahead. Through another gay friend who had also adopted, I learned of a local black adoption agency that was very open to gay adoption. They were more concerned with whether I would be a good parent than about my sexuality. When my daughter was ready for day care, I again turned to references from friends and other gay parents in the area. I found a center that already had one gay couple participating.

Now that my daughter is two-and-a-half-years old, I'm dealing with the terrible twos and searching for a good pre-K school. I have been visiting schools during open house and asking the teachers and administrators lots of questions: If they have other gay parents, how they would deal with issues concerning children of gay parents, and how problems in the past were resolved. I ask to talk with other gay parents who have children at the school to find out how they found the school.

Even if a school is gay-friendly, I know my daughter will have to deal with other kids. It's only natural for kids to ask where your daddy is. Prepare your child early on. Let your child know that your family is normal although it may be *different* from others. Help build your child's self-esteem. They have to be able to come back when other kids are cruel. You also have to have a strong support system around you and your child.

I still live in the area I grew up in and worship at a church I've been with for years. My community has always been very open to my sexuality and that hasn't changed since I've had my daughter.

parents until their children's friends are old enough to be sensitive about these issues. Other parents feel it's better to be up front and teach their children how to discuss their family situation. Either way, explain what your family situation is ("You have two daddies," for example) so that she can be clear herself.

- *Explain that some children and their parents are uncomfortable with the idea of gay parents, generally because they haven't been exposed to gay people.* If someone says something hurtful to your child about having gay parents, tell her that people are afraid of things they don't understand and can be cruel. Tell your child she can respond by ignoring the comments or discussing the incident with a teacher. Help her think of ways to deal with negative comments and teasing.

- *Find other gay parents.* Isolation, especially among black lesbian and gay parents, can be devastating. Other gay parents can help you find schools, child care, and play groups and can be an important source of inspiration, information, and empathy. (See Resources for more information.)

Starting All Over: Stepfamilies

When parents get remarried, it can be very difficult for young children. They often still have fantasies that their parents will get back together, and seeing their parents with new partners can be devastating. Fitting into a new family, whether a child lives in that home or not, takes a lot of time and a lot of love.

Parents and stepparents often don't realize just how affected their young children are by these family transformations. Unfortunately, many parents find themselves in the middle of a battle, with an angry, sad child unable to articulate her feelings on one side and a hurt, frustrated stepparent on the other. Like Rodney King, parents wonder, "Can't we all just get along?" Here are some ideas to help you ease your child into a new stepfamily:

- *Talk about the new situation openly.* Don't assume your child has a clear understanding of what's going on in your new life. Be honest and explain what your new spouse means to you. Let your child talk about his feelings. Young children most often feel confused, angry, jealous, betrayed, or left out. Tell him that whatever he feels is all right, and that he should talk about why, so the feelings can be resolved.
- *Have the stepparent engage in a one-on-one activity with your child.* Allow your new spouse and your child to devise an activity they can do together. It should be something both can agree on and that your child can look forward to.
- *Be sure to spend special time with your child too.* This is one of the most important ways to help your child accept your new family. He will see that even if you are with someone new, he still has a special relationship with you that can't be "taken away."

"I get a lot of pleasure watching my husband interact with my kids. They talk with one another and have developed their own way of interacting that is based on love and has nothing to do with me." **—ANNE'S STORY**

As a single parent, I had a lot of anxiety about dating. Knowing that relationships can come and go in adult lives, I didn't want my girls to see a series of "uncles" coming through our lives. After much reflection and advice from other single mothers, I decided to keep my relationships with men platonic in the eyes of my children. That way, they wouldn't differentiate between men who were my friends and those I was dating. I was confident that I had come up with the right approach to this situation when I met someone, fell in love, and we decided to get married. I couldn't pretend that he was "just a friend," but how was I going to let my children know that he would be a permanent presence in our lives, would live with us, and would be their parent as well?

Fortunately, my fiancé shared my concerns and we were able to discuss these issues and think about ways to deal with them. The first step was to let my girls know that he was more than just a friend. They understood the concept of "boyfriend" and we let them see us expressing affection toward one another. There were times when my children were jealous if we hugged, but they had gotten angry when I hugged my own sister, so I wasn't surprised when this happened. I kept reassuring them that I loved them just as much and had just as many hugs and "loving" saved for them, and I asked if it was OK for Mommy to get hugs from both him and them. Of course they agreed, which allowed them to get used to sharing my attention and affection.

Once we got over that hurdle, we began to spend time together as a family. Going to the park, skating, and going to the movies were fun and gave us all a chance to become comfortable with each other. As my children became comfortable, they began to act like real kids, which meant they needed to be disciplined from time to time. Very early on, I sat down with my fiancé and had a discussion about discipline. I laid out my concepts of discipline, how I wanted the girls to be treated, and what roles I did, and did not, want him to play. Fortunately, we agreed. If we had had radically different views about how the children should be disciplined I don't think it would have worked for us. But when it became clear that the relationship was moving toward marriage, we had several discussions about disciplining children so I knew we shared the same views and was confident we would develop an approach that worked for all of us.

After we told the girls we were getting married, they began to ask a lot of questions about their relationship with their birth father. We assured them that they would

still have a relationship with their father, that he would not be replaced, and that it was OK to love both their new stepfather and their father. We have had countless discussions about the differences between a biological and a step dad, and have told the girls that both are "real" dads who love their children.

Since the children are so young, I know they cannot express or fully understand some of their feelings. I know they have dealt with feelings of sadness since they know I will never reunite with their father. I know they sometimes feel guilty about caring for both their stepfather and their biological father. But overall, they are excited and happy about the relationship they are building with their stepfather. I get a lot of pleasure watching my husband interact with my kids. They talk with one another and have developed their own way of interacting that is based on love and has nothing to do with me.

We are still in the first year of our new lives together. As time has passed, our family's relationships have grown and our interactions have changed but I do not feel settled yet. I know there is more work to do to make sure everyone is feeling secure and cared for. But I think the groundwork has been laid and the girls are comfortable talking about their feelings as they try to sort out the changes in our family. I know we will revisit a lot of issues as the girls grow up and gain a greater understanding of relationships, family, and the experiences we have gone through. I definitely feel like we are making this up as we go along but I plan to keep talking to my children and answering their questions as we work together on becoming a family.

- *Decide how discipline will be handled and discuss it with your child and your spouse.* Be clear about the rules of your house and how they will be administered.
- *Be patient and compassionate.* Imagine how it must feel for your young child to see you with a new person in your life. It will take her awhile to get used to the idea that this person will be around for a long time. Allow for your child's disappointment, and help her find ways to fit into your new arrangement.

Both Worlds: Biracial Families

There are an estimated 4 million mixed-race children in this country, although these estimates are sketchy since many biracial children identify with the parent of color. Recent debates about whether mixed-race children should be identified in a separate category on the U.S. Census for the year 2000 have called attention to the complexity of race and identity. Tiger Woods, who is of both Asian- and African-American descent, believes in a multiethnic approach. He and other children from mixed families want to honor both cultural heritages and feel angry at having to denounce one ethnicity in order to be accepted by another. Unfortunately, many biracial children feel caught between two worlds, and often don't feel as though they belong to any.

Being the parent of a mixed-race child can present many unique challenges. Black parents who have Latino, white, or Asian children have not had the same experience as their children, but know the reality of growing up African American in this country. Being light skinned or different can mean favorable treatment from some people and hostility from others. White, Asian, or Latino parents with a black child must be sensitive to the complexities of race in a new way. They must teach their children about racism, comfort them when they are treated unfairly, and find ways for them to gain a sense of pride about who they are.

Here are some suggestions in meeting the needs of your biracial child:

- *Help your child gain a strong sense of self.* Regardless of race, children first need a strong foundation based on their talents, abilities, and personalities. With this base, children are more able to respect and appreciate how they are racially different from and similar to others.
- *Ground your child in racial reality.* Teach your child the history of both cultures. Provide books, family stories, dolls, or other culturally specific rituals (for example, celebrate El Dia De Los Muertos if she's Mexican or the Chinese New Year if she's Chinese). Exposure to her culture as well as others will help her understand how rich her heritage is. Also, be honest about the reality of being a person of color in America and that sometimes people will judge her without knowing her based on her appearance. (See Chapter 9 on ways to discuss racist incidents.)
- *Teach your child to appreciate being different.* Most likely your child will look different from, and in some ways hold different beliefs from, her peers because of her racially diverse background. Teach her that her uniqueness is something to be proud of, that being different isn't shameful but special. Many parents tell their children that it's wonderful to have parents from two different cultures because you get to eat twice as many different kinds of

foods, celebrate lots of different holidays, and have a rich array of family histories.

- *Join a support group.* Many mixed-race couples must choose which community to live in—predominately black, Latino, Asian, or white. While one person feels at home, the other may feel alienated. It helps all family members to befriend other mixed-race parents and children to avoid feeling isolated.

RESOURCES

Recommended Reading for Parents

Adoptive Parents

Adopting the Hurt Child: Hope for Families with Special Needs Kids, Gregory Keck and Regina Kupecky (Pinon Press, 1995). The authors cover adoptions that involve emotionally wounded children and spell out issues and solutions.

The Adoption Resource Book, Lois Gilman (HarperCollins, 1992). This book provides detailed information for adoption and families with adopted children.

The Complete Idiot's Guide to Adoption, Christine Adamee and William Pierce (Macmillian, 1997). Here is a complete guide to every step of adoption, including a section on nontraditional families.

Fatherhood

Black Fatherhood: The Guide to Male Parenting, Earl Ofari Hutchinson (Impact Publishers, 1995). This book is an insightful guide to the challenges and joys of fatherhood.

Faith of Our Fathers: African-American Men Reflect on Fatherhood, Andre C. Willis, ed. (Dutton, 1996). With essays from Cornel West, John Edgar Wideman, and Charles Ogletree, Jr., this book surveys the range and challenges of African-American fathers.

Lesbian and Gay Parenting

The Lesbian and Gay Parenting Handbook: Creating and Raising Our Families, April Martin (HarperPerennial, 1993). Here is a valuable resource from a lesbian parent to help gays and lesbians with general and specific parenting issues.

The Lesbian Parenting Book: A Guide to Creating and Raising Children, D. Merilee Clunis and G. Doresy Green (Seal Press, 1995). This is a guide by lesbian parents and therapists filled with advice and humor on parenting.

Parents of Children with Disabilities

The Child with Special Needs, Stanley I. Greenspan, Robin Simon, and Serena Weider (Addison-Wesley Publishing, 1998). Covers all types of disabilities, such as cerebral palsy, attention deficit disorder, and retardation, and helps parents find ways to help their disabled child.

Children with Disabilities, Mark Batshaw, ed. (PH Brooke Publishing, 1997). This book discusses various types of disabilities and the family's role in helping a disabled child. It also lists new medications and therapies.

Exceptional Parent. This magazine is published monthly. A one-year subscription is $32. It provides a forum for advice on issues faced by families of the disabled, and publishes the "Resource Guide for Parents" for $9.95 with over 1,000 organizations, services, and support groups. Phone: (800) 535–1910, website: www.cparent.com.

The Learning Differences Source Book, Nancy S. Boyles and Darlene Contadino (Lowell House, 1997). Here is a guide to help parents identify various learning disorders and list of resources for aid.

Single Parenting

Raising Sons Without Fathers: A Woman's Guide to Parenting Strong, Successful Boys, Lief Terdal and Patricia Kennedy (Carol Publishing, 1996). This book discusses ways that mothers can incorporate healthy role models and relationships into their sons' lives.

Single Mothers by Choice, Jane Matters (Random House, 1997). This book, written by the national director of Single Mothers by Choice, discusses options and rewards of single mothers.

The Single Mother's Companion: Essays and Stories by Women, Marsha Leslie, ed. (Seal Press, 1994). This is an anthology of various well-known women, like Senator Carol Mosely-Braun, and nonfamous single mothers sharing stories.

The Solo Parent, Diane Chambers (Fairview Press, 1997). The author offers advice on single-parenting topics like discipline, health, and meeting everyone's needs.

Recommended Reading for Children

Adoptive Parents

Tell Me Again About the Night I Was Born, Jamie Lee Curtis and Laura Cornell (HarperCollins, 1996). A girl wants her parents to recount the night she was adopted. This book explains the difference between adoptive and birth mothers in a sensitive and honest way.

Children with Disabilities

Just Kids, Ellen B. Senisi (E.P. Dutton, 1998). In this book, a girl spends time in a class for special needs children and learns ways she is different from and similar to them.

Someone Special, Just Like You, Tricia Brown (Henry Holt, 1984). This book introduces children to the idea that disabled children may look different but are actually the same.

We Can Do It, Laura Dwight (Checkerboard Press, 1992). This book shows children with a variety of disabilities and their families.

Fatherhood

Always My Dad, Sharon Dennis Wyeth and Raul Colon (Alfred A. Knopf, 1997). This is about an African-American girl who bonds with her mostly absent father.

A Lullaby for Daddy, Edward Biko Smith and Susan Anderson (Africa World Press, 1994). In this book, a girl makes up a lullaby for her father as a symbol of the love and caring she receives from him.

One Round Moon and a Star for Me, Ingrid Mennen and Niki Daly (Orchard Books, 1994). In this book, an African boy learns how special he is to his father despite the birth of his new baby brother.

Lesbian and Gay Parenting

Daddy's Roommate, Michael Willhoite (Alyson Publications, 1991). Here is a warm and straightforward story about a father's new partner.

Heather Has Two Mommies, Leslae Newman and Diana Souza (Alyson Publications, 1991). This is a classic book about a young child's acceptance of her two mothers.

Single Parenting

When Mama Gets Home, Marisabina Russo (Greenwillow, 1998). In this book, a working single mother comes home to three responsible children and shares housework and stories of the day.

Teen Mothers

Everything You Need to Know About Living with Your Baby and Your Parents Under One Roof, Carolyn Simpson (Rosen Publishing Group, 1995). This book provides useful and realistic advice for teen moms still living at home.

Finding Our Way: The Teen Girls' Survival Guide, Allison Abner and Linda Villarosa (HarperPerennial, 1995). This book discusses teen motherhood in a comprehensive chapter and lists resources.

Not Our Kind of Girl: Unraveling the Myths of Black Teenage Motherhood, Elaine Bell Kaplan (University of California, 1997). This former teen mother explores factors that influence young women to become mothers and dispels myths.

Organizations

Adoption

Adoption Resource Exchange for Single Parents, P.O. Box 5782, Springfield, VA 22150, (703) 866–5577.

Website: www.adopting.org/aresp

This organization offers information for single people considering adoption and publishes a newsletter. It provides more comprehensive services for parents in the Washington, D.C., area.

National Council for Adoption, 1930 17th St., NW, Washington, D.C. 20009, (800) 333–NCFA. This organization provides information about adoption and local referrals for adoption agencies in callers' state.

Pact, An Adoption Alliance, 3450 Sacramento St., Suite 239, San Francisco, CA 94418, (415) 221–6957. This is a nonprofit adoption service specializing in children of color.

Counseling Services

American Psychiatric Association, DPA Dept., 1400 K Street NW, Washington, D.C. 20005, (202) 682–6220. This association will locate a referral for a psychiatrist who treats adult or childhood disorders, and provides a series of pamphlets.

American Psychological Association, 750 1st St., NE, Washington, D.C. 20002, (202) 336–5700. This organization provides brochures on a variety of topics, including depression and anxiety, and has a referral agency for local therapists, including African-American therapists or those specializing in children.

The Association of Black Psychologists, P.O. Box 55999, Washington, D.C. 20040. Write for a referral in your area.

Gay and Lesbian Parents

Gay and Lesbian Parents Coalition International, P.O. Box 50360, Washington, D.C. 20091, (202) 583–8029. This organization publishes a newsletter and establishes local parenting groups that act as support and activity coordinators for gay and lesbian parents. There is a $25 annual membership fee.

Lavender Family Resource Network, P.O. Box 21567, Seattle, WA 98111, (206) 325–2643. This group offers legal advice for lesbian parents concerning child custody. It also provides information on parenting issues for lesbian parents.

Parents and Friends of Lesbians and Gays (P-FLAG), 1101 14th St., NW, Suite 1030, Washington, D.C. 20005, (202) 638–4200

Website: www.pflag.org

This organization offers a multitude of support services for gays and lesbians, including parenting groups. Call for a local chapter near you.

Single Parents

Single Mothers' Information Network, P.O. Box 68, Midland, NC 28107, (704) 888–KIDS. This organization issues a newsletter and information packet for single mothers for $2.

Parents Without Partners, 8807 Colesville Rd., Silver Spring, MD, (800) 637–7974, (301) 588–9354 in Maryland.

Website: www.parentswithoutpartners.org

This is the largest international nonprofit single parenting organization. Local chapters provide educational activities, family outings, and other services like cooperative babysitting. Go to the web page for the chapter nearest you.

Teen Parents

March of Dimes, 1275 Mamaroneck Ave., White Plains, NY 10605, (914) 428–7100. This organization provides pregnant teens with information and referrals to promote a healthy pregnancy and newborn health, such as immunizations.

MELD for Young Moms, 123 N. Third St., Suite 507, Minneapolis, MN 55401, (612) 332–7563. MELD offers information and support groups to young parents around the country.

Chapter

14

Safe and Sound: Safety and Emergency Procedures

As parents, it's our job to keep our children safe. And safety is especially critical for black parents given that unintentional injuries—such as accidents related to car crashes, falls, burns, suffocation, and drowning—are the number-one cause of death for African-American children under the age of six. The key word here is *unintentional:* Experts stress that 90 percent of accidents can be prevented.

PREVENTING ACCIDENTS AND INJURIES

Take Care in the Car

Children ages four and under account for 40 percent of all childhood motor vehicle accident deaths, and car accidents are the number-one cause of death in black children of this age group. The majority of these deaths occur when children are not wearing seatbelts or not restrained properly in a car seat. The following is a list of crucial suggestions for avoiding injuries and accidents in the car:

- *Always use car seats and seatbelts correctly.* Children under age six should never sit in the front seat and must always be strapped into an appropriate car seat. Infants who weigh 20 pounds or less must be placed in a rear-facing car seat in the middle of your backseat. Toddlers weighing between 20 and 40 pounds should use a forward-facing car seat and, again, be strapped in your backseat. Children weighing more than 40 pounds should be strapped into the backseat in a booster seat.
- *Make sure your car seat meets Federal Motor Vehicle Safety Standards.* If you're buying a used seat, check to see if the model has been recalled. Call the Auto Safety Hotline (800–424–9393) for more information.
- *Lock your doors when you're in the car.* Curious toddlers often pull on door handles and can open the door while you're driving. Activate child locks if they are available on your car.

Infant, toddler and preschooler correctly positioned in car seats.

- *Never leave a child unattended in the car.* There have been too many stories of parents who left their children in the car for just a minute only to return to find the car—and the child—stolen, or the car wrecked.
- *Follow the rules of the road.* The phrase "baby on board" should mean something to you. Don't speed or take unnecessary chances. Because you can't control the way others drive, be alert and stay on the defensive. It helps to keep distractions such as talking on the phone or screaming at other drivers to a minimum.
- *Never, ever drive while under the influence of alcohol or drugs.*

Prevent Falls, Watch the Head

Far too many African-American children are injured falling from windows; in fact, the rate is double that of white children under age fourteen. Children living in apartments are highly susceptible, and boys tend to be at a higher risk than girls. Other serious injuries can occur when children fall from bunk beds, down stairs, off bicycles, and off playground equipment.

To prevent accidents from falls:

- *Place guards on all windows.* In many states, window guards are mandated by law in apartments with children age ten and under. From the ground up, all windows should have guards unless they are designated emergency exits. Windows used for emergency exits should have removable gates that can be screwed into the window frame. You can buy guards at hardware stores or through mail-order companies that sell baby products. Keep furniture away from windows to prevent little ones from having easy access to window ledges.
- *Children under six shouldn't sleep in bunk beds.* That's the word from the Consumer Products Safety Commission. But if space is very tight in your home and bunk beds are a must, have your older child (she should be school age) sleep on the top bunk with a guard rail, and the younger on the bottom.
- *Install safety gates at the tops and bottoms of stairs.* They can ruin the décor, but they're a must to prevent injury. Place netting on the railings of decks and balconies.
- *Avoid baby walkers.* They inhibit children's physical development and can lead to falls. (For more on this topic, see Chapter 11.)

- *Keep a sharp eye on kids at the playground.* And try to steer them away from concrete and asphalt surfaces.
- *Have your child wear a helmet.* When riding bikes, rollerblading, skating, skateboarding, or even riding trikes, children must wear a helmet and other safety gear, like knee pads and wrist guards. Also, make sure your child plays in an area away from traffic.

Be Safe in the Water

Each year, hundreds of children die from drowning, 80 percent of them age four and under. And it's not just folks with pools who have to worry: A child can drown in only two inches of water.

To prevent accidents in the water:

- *Take extra care in the tub.* Never, ever leave a child alone in the tub, even in an infant seat designed for the bath. It may be tempting to run and answer the phone or check food on the stove, but an unsupervised child can drown very quickly. Put skidproof decals on the bottom of your tub to prevent slips.
- *Watch the toilet.* As farfetched as it may seem, children can drown in the toilet. Babies and toddlers have large heads compared to their bodies, and the weight can pull their heads down into the toilet or even a bucket of water. Purchase toilet locks, available in many toy and baby stores and catalogues, to keep toilets closed to curious explorers.
- *Teach your child to swim.* Even a baby can learn to get used to the water, and toddlers can take group or private lessons. (Don't be the teacher unless you are a strong swimmer and have experience teaching!) However, it's important to be clear about your child's abilities: Make sure your child can really swim before letting her go off on her own. Some parents who introduce their children to swimming lessons have a false sense of security that their kids can swim.
- *Don't overestimate your own swimming abilities.* If you can't swim, don't take a child in deep water or rough, unpredictable water at the beach. Take swimming lessons yourself, and learn CPR.
- *If you have a pool—even a wading pool—or you're visiting someone who does, take precautions.* Put gates or a fence around the pool, and don't allow adults who can't swim—or who are drinking or distracted—to supervise kids.

Child-Proofing Checklist

The goal of child-proofing your home is twofold. The first objective is to make her environment safe, and the second is to allow her to explore freely. Child-proofing allows children to safely satisfy their natural curiosity while not breaking any of your prized possessions (don't expect a child under the age of four to truly understand the value of a glass vase, even if you tell him repeatedly). Although you can't completely eliminate all sources of accidents (beginning walkers will often fall!), a baby-proofed home will enable your child to toddle freely without your having to hover and worry. Here are some ways to make your home more child-friendly (many of these suggestions are discussed in more detail throughout this chapter):

- ***Put up window guards to keep children from falling out of windows, even on the first floor.*** **Also, blind and drape cords should be wound up tightly and attached to the wall if possible so that your child doesn't get caught on them and choke.**
- ***Use safety plugs in electrical outlets and hide and secure electrical cords away from your child's reach.*** **Not only can she unplug things and potentially shock herself, she could pull a large appliance, like the TV, right off its stand.**
- ***Put all houseplants out of children's reach.*** **Many houseplants are poisonous and some are fatal in even small amounts.**
- ***Repair and clean up all chipped paint.*** **Small children have been known to eat paint chips, some of which contain hazardous amounts of lead.** **(See "Keep the Lead Out," p. 326.)**
- ***Make furniture safe.*** **Cover corners of tables with cushions; fasten bookcases (that children may try to scale) to the wall; stabilize any broken or tilting chairs, lamps, or couches; and remove tablecloths that, when pulled, could bring down valuables or heavy objects. Also, cover your furniture with washable slipcovers or fabrics so you don't have to worry about stains.**
- ***Use caution in the kitchen.*** **Close cupboards with childproof latches (but leave one available for your child, stocked with plastic and metal cookware he can play with). Protect the stove with knob covers or plastic barriers so your child can't turn it on, and when you cook, turn all pot handles toward the back of the stove. Knives, scissors, or other sharp objects should be far out of reach (as should step stools so kids can't reach them). Store all cleaners, detergents, plastic bags, and alcohol in high, locked shelves.**
- ***Use bathroom safety devices.*** **These include: a hot water indicator that shows when the water temperature is too hot for young skin (if you can, ad-**

just your water heater to 120 degrees); a tub spout protector so your child doesn't bump her head on the hard, sharp tub faucet; a tub skid mat to keep from falling; and a toilet seat lock. Store electrical appliances (hot combs, blow dryers, curling irons, electric toothbrushes) up high along with medications and cleaners.

- *Place safety gates at the top and bottom of stairs.* Some parents like to use them in kitchens or other rooms without doors because they want to keep their children out of them when the parents aren't present.
- *Cover or put away heaters, radiators, and fireplaces so your child won't get burned.* Unplug and store portable heaters when not in use.
- *Place skid pads under rugs to avoid slips, and don't let your child walk in socks on wood floors* (he should be barefoot or in shoes).
- *Never leave your child alone in an automatic swing or other rocking toy.*
- *Keep small objects safely stored.* This includes jewelry, beads, batteries, lightbulbs, mothballs, pins, or office supplies. Matches should be in a locked or latched cabinet. Cigarettes and ashtrays should also be stored safely out of reach.
- *Place all firearms in a locked and secure cabinet.* Be sure they are unloaded and have a safety latch employed. Put ammunition in a separate safe location.
- *Be aware of any objects or situations that could cause harm to your child and fix them as soon as possible.* Because your child is developing so quickly, you may not be aware of new skills that could place her in danger, such as pulling up on floor lamps, crawling up bookshelves, or opening up bottles.
- *Without harming your baby, teach him what happens if he touches a hot stove or an outlet, eats plants, or engages in any other harmful activity.* Do not teach him by placing his hand on the stove! Teaching should involve clear, simple explanations such as "Hot stove, burn, ouch!" or "Plant, yucky, makes baby's tummy hurt."

Protection from Guns

We live in a violent world, and more and more people are getting guns—or thinking about it—to protect themselves and their families. However, most people who own guns don't kill dangerous people but loved ones. And African-American children are more likely to die from unintentional shootings than children of other races.

To prevent shooting accidents:

- *The best way to prevent gun-related accidents in your home by far is to not keep a gun in your home.* Period.
- *If you feel you must have a gun, store it, unloaded and locked, and keep the ammunition in a separate location, away from a child's reach.* Be sure to use trigger locks and any other kind of safety devices.
- *Teach children the dangers of guns.* Let your child know that if she finds a gun, she's not to touch it—at all. Explain to her that she must tell an adult right away.

Keep Poisons Away

According to the U.S. Poison Control Centers, more than a million children are poisoned each year, and the risk for black children is twice that of their white counterparts.

To prevent accidents from poisons:

- *Put locks or childproof latches on cupboards containing cleaning supplies and cabinets that hold medications.* And don't forget to keep alcohol, cosmetics, and other toiletries (such as perfume, nail polish and remover, and hair relaxers) and commercial art supplies, like ammonia, paint, thinner, and glue, out of reach of children.
- *Use pesticides with care.* Roach "motels," insect strips, sticky mousetraps, bug spray, and boric acid are all hazardous to children. Use rodent traps at night when children are sleeping and clear them away in the daytime. Keep doors and windows closed and use screens to keep insects out. Ask about natural pest control at a health food store.
- *Buy products with childproof packaging.* When you dispose of a product, regardless of the packaging, don't throw it in an open container that a child can get into.
- *Don't forget that children can overdose on vitamins.* Don't get fooled into thinking that if one vitamin is good for your child, more is better. Vitamins should be treated as medicine, and both should be taken as indicated. Over the past decade, more than 150,000 cases of iron tablet poisoning of African-American children have been reported. Follow your doctor's or the label's directions when administering vitamins. Children under a year should only take iron if pre-

scribed by a physician, and older children should only take one vitamin a day. Don't coerce your child into taking vitamins or medicine by calling it candy. You run the risk of her accidentally misusing them, causing herself serious harm.

- *Know what to do in case of poisoning.* Keep ipecac syrup on hand to induce vomiting. Use it carefully and only as directed by a doctor or poison control center. Once your child does throw up, keep the vomited material for analysis. Always keep the number of the Poison Control Center posted somewhere visible; you can find it in your telephone directory.

On Guard Against Shocks and Burns

Each year about one thousand children die from burns and fires in the home, 70 percent of whom are aged four and under. And children must also be guarded from electric shocks.

To prevent accidents from shocks and burns:

- *Teach toddlers the meaning of "hot."* Let her touch something that's warm—like the outside of a bowl of food—and explain that touching something that's hot can lead to "ouch" or "boo-boo."
- *Supervise your child in the kitchen.* Never let a child operate the stove, and use safety devices on the stove, oven, and other appliances that prevent your child from reaching the control dials. It may be best to use a gate to block his access to the kitchen entirely.
- *Take plenty of precautions based on common sense.* Use radiator covers and fireguards, keep matches out of reach, avoid using space heaters, and keep electrical appliances away from water.
- *Be careful in the bath or at the sink.* Turn your hot water heater to 120 degrees or less to prevent burns, and, remember, never leave children in the tub unattended.
- *Install smoke detectors in every room.* Change the batteries twice a year (doing it when you switch the clocks because of daylight saving time is a good way to remember). If you have a woodstove or gas heat, invest in a carbon monoxide detector (usually under $40). This device can detect lethal levels of carbon monoxide, an odorless, deadly gas released from heating devices and automobiles.

Keep the Lead Out

The Centers for Disease Control (CDC) surveys indicate that poor, non-Hispanic black children who live in a city or older house are more likely to have elevated blood lead levels (BLL) than other children are. Children should have BLL's below 10 micrograms per deciliter of blood. Higher levels require close monitoring by a health professional and possibly treatment. Elevated levels of lead in a child's bloodstream can result in a whole host of problems related to the degree of lead poisoning. They include anemia, delayed mental development, low IQ, behavioral and coordination problems, and poor school performance. Most alarmingly, these effects are irreversible. In severe (but rare) cases, elevated lead levels cause convulsions, coma, and death.

While lead is also toxic to adults, children are more susceptible because they absorb it more than we do, which affects their newly developing brains. The tricky thing is that low levels of lead can be present in your child with no symptoms. This is why it is important to have your baby tested at around twelve months, especially if you live in an older building, or you know your paint contains lead.

How does lead get into a child's system? Mostly through the lead paint in houses or apartments. Any building built before 1978 probably used lead-based paint. Even if new paint has been applied many times since that first coat, when it peels off, the dust and chips from the original paint may be eaten by a curious child. The dust can also be on toys or anything that your child puts in her mouth.

Lead can also be present in drinking water that passes through lead pipes and certain types of earthenware, in soil, on playground equipment, and even in the air, though poisoning from these sources does not seem to be as common as from lead paint and dust. Most recently, the U.S. Consumer Products Safety Commission (USCPSC) found that vinyl miniblinds imported from Asia and Mexico posed a lead poisoning hazard. As the blinds deteriorate and lead dust forms on the surface, young children ingest the lead by wiping their hands on the blinds and then putting their hands in their mouths. (The CDC issued a recall and manufacturers complied.) How much lead exposure does it take to harm a child? Experts believe that even small amounts of lead in the body can diminish children's cognitive ability and learning skills.

Avoiding Lead

Based on tips from the Environmental Protection Agency and the USCPSC, here are some steps to take to protect your family from lead hazards:

- Wash children's hands, bottles, pacifiers, and toys often.

- **Have your home checked for lead hazards. (The National Lead Information Center can point you in the right direction to have this done properly. See Resources.)**
- **Clean floors, windowsills, and other surfaces regularly.**
- **Use a doormat to wipe soil off shoes before entering the house.**
- **Before you buy or rent, read the mandatory disclosures on lead-based paint hazards that landlords, sellers, and renovators are required by law to provide.**
- **Talk to your landlord about fixing any surfaces that have peeling or chipping paint.**
- **Take precautions to avoid exposure to lead dust when remodeling or renovating an older home (call 800–424–LEAD for guidelines). Fixer-uppers, be prepared: Guidelines will probably include hiring a professional to strip old paint off the walls using a special wet process (one that produces less dust) instead of doing it yourself.**
- **Ask your pediatrician to test your child's blood for lead content, even if he seems healthy. Lead testing is not mandatory, but if your child is at risk, it should be done at twelve months, twenty-four months, and annually after that until your child turns five. If your child has high lead levels and you need information on what to do, see Chapter 15.**

- *Devise and practice fire drills at home.* Teach your child how to exit a building safely in case of fire. (See p. 330.) And don't smoke, which will cut the risk of fires in your home significantly. Teach your child what firemen look like when wearing gas masks so he doesn't hide from one in a fire.
- *Prevent electric shock.* Cover all outlets with plastic safety covers and keep cords away from children's reach. If possible, hide outlets and cords with furniture. Explain to your toddler that electrical outlets and plugs can hurt her.

Breathe Easy

Every year, hundreds of children suffocate or die from choking and the vast majority are under age six. Most of these accidents happen at home.

To prevent accidents from choking and suffocation:

- *Keep small objects away from children.* Kids love to put things in their mouths, but they can choke on:

"Now I have poison control on my speed-dial; and advise parents to do the same."
—ANNE'S STORY

As a pediatrician, I always advise parents to keep the number of poison control posted near the phone. As a mother, I haven't always been able to keep my children safe but have been thankful that I had easy access to poison control.

When my kids were toddlers our house was thoroughly child-proofed and everything was locked, bolted, or put out of reach. I started to run into trouble when my children got older, three and four years to be exact. One night I had a friend come over to baby-sit. To make the evening easier for her, I thought I'd make a quick pizza for dinner and have the kids fed by the time she arrived. My kids love to help in the kitchen, but it takes time to watch them and slows me down when I'm trying to make a quick meal. So I sent them down to the basement (which I thought was child-proofed) to ride their scooters. Instead, they decided to make their own pizza. Their stove was my clothes dryer, and their ingredients were detergent, bleach, and fabric softener. I can imagine the fun they had pouring their ingredients in my dryer, and then mixing it up with a spoon.

I didn't find this mess until the next morning when I went to do laundry. As I walked down the stairs I could smell the bleach throughout the basement and it began to burn my eyes. I found they had taken a folded chair that was stored downstairs, dragged it across the basement, opened it, and used it to climb on top of the dryer to get the detergent and bleach. When I opened the dryer it was filled with toxic "pizza." Before I got angry, I got scared. My friend who had baby-sat had told me that my oldest daughter said her urine was red, but my friend never saw it. At this point, I was worried. I know that when you mix bleach and ammonia it gives off extremely toxic fumes and I thought the combination of detergent, softener, and bleach might have created fumes that had caused kidney damage, which was making my daughter urinate blood.

I immediately called the poison control center and spoke to a toxicologist who was extremely helpful. He accessed information on chemical interactions and was able to reassure me that it was not a dangerous combination. I was also thankful that he did not make me feel stupid or not in control of my kids. After that call I became a firm believer in the use of the poison control center. Now I have poison control on my speed-dial and advise parents to do the same.

Since I have very active kids, I really stepped up the child-proofing. Despite my efforts, I found myself calling poison control a few months later when they came into my room stinking of Vick's Vapor Rub . . . but that's another story.

*Coins
*Small toys or pieces broken off a toy
*Marbles
*Keys
*Christmas tree ornaments
*Jewelry
*Buttons, thimbles, and safety pins
*Small batteries
*And on and on

- *Serve food with care.* Many round foods, such as hot dogs, carrots, grapes, and peanuts, are the same size and diameter as your child's windpipe. Until your child has back teeth (which come in when a child is two to three years old), don't serve these foods without cutting them lengthwise. Grapes are especially dangerous and should be cut in half. Bite-size foods, like raisins and popcorn, should be avoided, as should foods with seeds, such as sesame seed bread.
- *Remove all plastic bags from your child's reach, and teach him that plastic should never go on his face or over his head.*
- *Pay attention to crib safety.* Make sure the slats on the crib are no more than 2¼ inches apart to prevent babies and toddlers from choking. (Kids choke when their bodies fall through the slats and their heads get stuck.) New cribs are up to standard, but you'll have to be more careful with old, used cribs and antiques. Remove large pillows and comforters from a baby's crib area and move the crib away from strings hanging from blinds.
- *Be careful with balloons, which can be dangerous.* Keep unfilled balloons away from children to prevent suffocation by swallowing. When a balloon pops, throw it out right away.
- *Tie up cords from the window blinds, and never let your child play with these cords or wrap them around her neck.* These are strangulation hazards for small children.
- *Place babies under six months old on their backs to sleep.* The American Academy of Pediatrics recommends this to avoid the risk of SIDS.
- *Attach pacifier ribbons and strings to your child's clothing, not around his neck.* Also, make sure the strings are short.

Fire Safety for Our Children

According to the National Fire Protection Association (NFPA), our nation leads all other Western industrialized countries in per capita fire deaths. In the United States, children receive three times as many burn injuries as any other age group, generally from kitchen accidents and playing with matches. Parents who smoke put their children at even greater risk.

With these statistics in mind, parents of small children should take extra precautions to avoid burns as well as carefully plan an emergency procedure in case there is a fire. Lt. Bill Premuroso, Town of Mamaroneck, NY, Fire Department, teaches fire safety to preschoolers called "Learn Not to Burn" (see the end of this sidebar for details). His suggestions, based on NFPA recommendations, could mean the difference between life and death:

- ***Go through the house to detect trouble.* Before there's an emergency, make sure you check for any fire hazards (for instance, using an extension cord for appliances instead of a surge protector, or placing newspaper or blankets near a fireplace or heater. Be sure to have a fire extinguisher in the kitchen and one near the bedroom. Smoke detectors should be in all bedrooms, in the hallways near bedrooms, and there should be at least one on every level of the house (including the basement, where many heating units are placed and many fires begin). Placing carbon monoxide (CO) detectors on every level of the house and near heating units is extremely important, too. Because this deadly gas is odorless and invisible, it can be present without your knowledge. During a fire, carbon monoxide levels are very high and can put you into an even deeper sleep, making it less likely you'll respond to a smoke detector in time. Smoke and carbon monoxide detectors can be purchased at hardware stores for about $40 each.**
- ***If your child can recognize numbers, teach her to call 911 if there is a fire (or other emergency) but in no other instance.* Teach her to call the fire department before trying to put out a fire herself. Fires get out of control very quickly and every second counts. Remind her that her safety comes first and that she should leave the house first and go to a neighbor's to call 911 rather than look for a phone in the house, especially if there's any smoke at all.**
- ***Devise a family plan of evacuation.* Teach your child that when a smoke detector goes off, she should leave the house *immediately.* Many children will hide in a closet or under the bed when hearing an alarm, but they need to know this is extremely dangerous. All family members should alert each**

other in the case of fire by yelling out "Fire!" so you can begin to evacuate. Here are the steps she should take to leave the dwelling:

1. ***Get out of bed and crawl on the floor to her bedroom door.* All bedroom doors should be closed at night for safety (closed doors give you more time and a fire less oxygen). Tell her that in a fire "bad air" or smoke rises to the ceiling and the "good air" is down low. Most people in fires die from breathing in smoke, not from the flames.**
2. ***Check the door to see if it's hot.* If so, leave through the second exit (a window or another door). All rooms should have two ways out, especially bedrooms, so that you can choose the safest route. Windows should have removable window guards and not be painted shut! Be sure all emergency windows are working. Teach your child ahead of time how to open these windows in case she must do so alone. Second-floor bedrooms should have escape ladders.**
3. ***Get out!* Based on your family plan, teach your child what to do after exiting the house. Families should have a safe meeting place outside so that all family members can be accounted for. Tell your child not to go back into the house for *anything,* not a favorite toy or pet, or she will risk her life.**
4. ***If your child catches on fire, she should "Stop, Drop, and Roll."* Children are more likely to run when their clothes catch fire, but this only feeds the flame. Teach your child first to cover her face, then to stop running, drop to the ground, and roll around until the flame is out.**

(For more information, contact your local fire department and the National Fire Protection Association. See Resources.)

In Case of Emergency

As your child explores her environment and tests her limits, it's inevitable that she will sometimes injure herself. As hard as you try to make her environment safe, you should also be prepared for those accidents that can't be avoided. All parents should be comfortable with basic first aid and should learn infant CPR (Cardiopulmonary Resuscitation). Both first aid and CPR classes are available through the American Red Cross or the American Heart Association and are held in local hospitals and medical centers, community centers, schools, and YMCAs/YWCAs. Training and practice in first aid and CPR will help you stay calm in an emergency while you take appropriate action. You should also keep important emergency numbers (such as

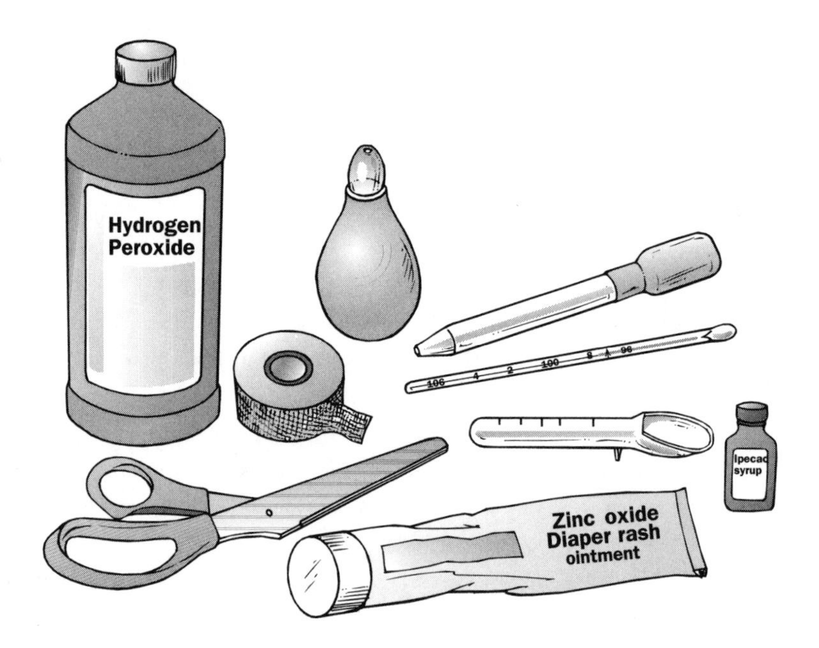

What you need in a home first-aid kit.

your doctor, the poison control center, the police department, fire department, and an ambulance service) posted in a convenient place.

In the meantime, if you become familiar with the following basic first aid techniques for common injuries you will either be able to take care of your child's problem completely or administer immediate care until professional medical help arrives. *In any emergency, be sure to call for help before tending to your child.*

Cuts

It's hard to see your child bleed, but remember: Kids sometimes bleed a lot, especially from a cut or laceration on the face, but the seriousness of a cut depends on how the injury occurred, its depth, and its location, not the amount of blood it produces. Do not be surprised when your child falls and you pick him up and find a face covered with blood. After you clean him up, you may discover only a small cut on his face. Small lacerations of the face or scalp can bleed profusely because the head has an abundant blood supply.

What to do:

1. Using any clean cloth or towel available—or your bare hand—control the bleeding by applying pressure to the wound. Apply constant pressure until the bleeding stops, which can take up to fifteen minutes if the cut is serious. (Do not apply a tourniquet unless you have been trained in their use. Tourniquets cut off the blood supply to the entire limb and could cause someone to lose that limb if not used properly.)

2. After the bleeding stops, clean the wound by rinsing it thoroughly with water. You do not need special soaps, sprays, or ointments; water can flush out any dirt and germs that may have been introduced into the wound. If the bleeding was difficult to control (took more than fifteen minutes to stop), don't wash the wound. Washing it could remove the bloodclot that is forming to stop the bleeding. Instead, take your child to the doctor who will clean the wound and control the bleeding.

3. You can apply a Band-Aid to a smaller cut to prevent further injury and keep it clean. However, when your child isn't active or is asleep, take the Band-Aid off to air the cut and help it form a scab.

When to call the doctor:

- If you cannot control the bleeding after applying pressure for fifteen minutes, or if blood is pumping from the wound
- If the edges of the wound are apart, because the child may need stitches
- If the wound is deep, about 1/4 of an inch
- If your child has not had all of his tetanus vaccines
- If the wound is in a very visible place, like the face. Stitches may help minimize the scar.
- If the wound is on a part that moves a lot like the knees or elbows. This may make healing and closing of the wound more difficult.

Burns

In most cases, children are burned by fire or hot water. Burns can also result from electricity and chemicals; these always require medical attention. First degree burns, such as sunburns, are the least serious. They cause redness, pain, and swelling of the skin. Second degree burns are deeper, more painful, and cause blisters. Third degree burns are most severe and go through all layers of the skin.

What to do:

1. Remove your child from the object that is burning her. If the burn is serious, don't remove clothing that may be stuck to the burn; that could cause more damage. If she has spilled something hot on herself and the burn is not serious, remove the clothes immediately to get the hot liquid off her skin. Take off any jewelry that may still be hot. For chemical burns, remove any clothing that may also be contaminated.

If it is an electrical burn, make sure she is not in contact with the electrical source before you touch her. If she is, break her contact using a nonconductive object—anything made of wood or rubber. If she's holding a wire or something in an outlet or socket, move her hand away with something nonconductive. (If you are anywhere near the fuse box and can think quickly, turn off the power there.) If you do not turn off the power or don't touch her with a nonconductive object, you could get shocked yourself and would be unable to take care of your child's injury.

2. Apply something cool to the burn such as cold water, a cool compress, or ice wrapped in a wet towel. (Be careful to avoid allowing an infant or young toddler to become too cold by placing her in cold water for too long.) Do not apply ice directly to the burn, because it may stick, causing more pain. For chemical burns, flush the skin with running water for at least fifteen minutes.

Any child with an electrical burn needs immediate emergency attention. These burns are very dangerous because they can cause damage to the internal organs, including the heart. After you've taken the child from the electrical source you should immediately check to see if she's breathing and her heart is beating. If not, begin CPR immediately (see p. 342). Even if your child is breathing normally, call 911 as soon as possible.

3. Uncomplicated first degree burns can be treated by letting them heal on their own. Only use ointments or salves on second degree burns, and then only use ones that have been recommended by a doctor. Never apply petroleum jelly or home remedies such as butter or toothpaste. To avoid infection, do not break open blisters that form.

When to call the doctor:

- If the burn is at least a second degree burn and covers a sizable part of the body

- For any burn that involves the eyes, hands, feet, or genitals
- For any third degree burns
- If the burn completely encircles or goes around a limb
- For all chemical and electrical burns
- If your child has not had all of his tetanus shots

Sprains and Fractures

Though children are very flexible and can withstand stretching or pulling injuries that would cause severe damage in an adult, they can still sprain ligaments—tissues that connect the bones of the ankles, wrists, knee, and other joints. They can also break their bones, especially their fingers, collarbones, arms, and legs. When fractures do occur—or even if you just suspect a bone is broken—seek medical care right away. The trickiest part is deciding whether your child has a fracture or a sprain.

Is it broken?

Your child probably has a break and not a sprain, and you should therefore seek medical help immediately, if:

- There was a snapping or popping sound at the time of the injury
- Your child is in severe pain and can't move or bear weight on the injured limb
- There is one very specific joint or small area that seems to really hurt. If your child has a sprain he will feel a general pain at the injury and in the surrounding area.
- The skin is broken and the bone is exposed
- You can see an obvious deformity under the skin and/or swelling and discoloration

Do not ignore complaints of pain or inability to use a joint. These are the best indicators of the seriousness of your child's injury. Do not allow your child to have significant pain for more than 24 hours without seeking medical attention. Once you have determined that you must get medical help, do not give your child any pain medications or any food or liquids (not even water) before going to see the doctor. Treatment of some fractures may involve anesthesia or putting your child to sleep, and this can be dangerous if his stomach is full.

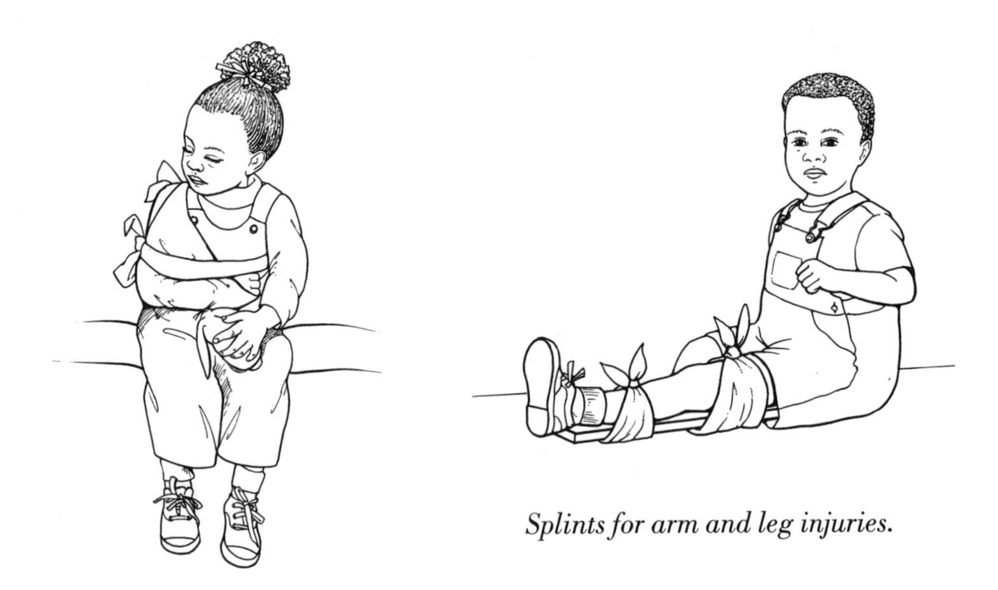

Splints for arm and leg injuries.

What to do if you suspect a fracture:

If you think the bone may be broken, stabilize the area by applying a splint, and let your child rest the injured limb. You can learn about splints in a first aid class. In general, a splint is made of any firm object such as a board, branch, or even a firm piece of plastic. It is applied to the area that has been injured and tied in place with a cloth or Ace bandage. Splints make it easier to get your child to emergency help without further injury. Also apply ice to the injury to help with pain and swelling.

What to do if you suspect a sprain:

Think RICE: Rest, Ice, Compression, Elevation.

- **R**est the injury. Keep the child off of it for at least a couple of days.
- Apply **I**ce or a cold compress right away for at least twenty minutes to reduce the swelling and relieve some pain.
- Use **C**ompression by wrapping the ice—or even a bag of frozen peas, which can mold nicely to the shape of your child's limb—to the injury, but not too tightly. Don't apply the ice directly to the skin as it can be very painful and damage delicate young skin. (Never use heat in the first 24 hours after an injury. You may be advised to later apply warm compresses alternating with cold compresses.)
- Keep the injury **E**levated as high as possible to help reduce swelling.

Drowning

In the event of a water accident at home, at the beach or lake, or in a pool, follow these steps below and then be sure to seek medical help—even if your child revives quickly and seems OK.

What to do:

1. Get your child out of the water immediately.

2. See if he is breathing on his own. If he is coughing or choking on water, that means he is moving air and clearing his airway. Do not interfere with that process.

3. If he isn't breathing on his own, start CPR. You should start CPR even if your

Kids-Only Fractures

There are several fractures that are unique to children. You and your health care provider should be especially concerned about a fracture through your child's growth plate, located at the end of his bones. This fracture is difficult to diagnose, and can greatly affect your child's growth. When your doctor first takes an X-ray, he may not see this type of fracture because there is no deformity of the bone, and will diagnose your child as having a sprain. However, if your child continues to have pain, return to the doctor for follow-up and get another X-ray. At this point, another X-ray may show some swelling around the fracture, which can occur when the bone is starting to heal. After this type of fracture, your health care provider should follow your child's progress closely to make sure there was no permanent damage to the growth plate.

Another common injury in young children is the Nursemaid's Elbow, which is caused by a sudden pull on the child's hand, trapping the ligaments between the bones at the elbow. The injury can occur when the child is picked up by her hands, swung by her arms, or suddenly pulled up by her hands (which might occur when she falls down while learning to walk). If she complains of pain in her arm and holds her bent arm close to her body after being pulled up by the hands, do not try to move the arm. She should be taken directly to the doctor who will determine if it is a Nursemaid's Elbow, and will move the joint with her hands to release the ligament. A cast is not required for this injury, but it may take thirty minutes before your child can move her arm again.

child has been submerged for a long time (up to forty-five minutes), especially if the drowning occurred in cold water. (See p. 342 for more on learning CPR.)

4. Call 911.

Choking

Choking is extremely common in children. It occurs when objects or food go down the wrong tube into the lungs instead of the stomach. If your child is coughing or able to make a sound with her voice, her airways are not blocked. However, if she cannot speak or vocalize, she cannot breathe. This is an emergency situation that requires you to call for medical assistance. (Before an emergency occurs, you should learn how to handle choking episodes in an infant CPR class. For instructions, see the following.)

What to do for a child younger than twelve months:

1. As calmly as you can, assess your child. If she is coughing or gagging that means she is moving air or is breathing and should cough up the item herself. If she cannot speak or cough or is turning dark red to blue, take immediate action.

2. Place her on your forearm facing downward and support her head and neck. Then give four quick back blows between her shoulder blades with the heel of your hand. She should cough up the item. (Do not attempt the Heimlich maneuver on a child this young.)

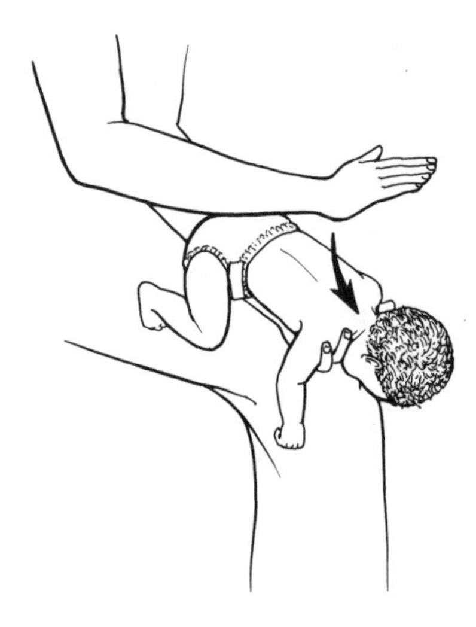

3. If this doesn't work, turn her over and lay her on her back on a flat surface. Then, with two fingers, give four quick chest thrusts on the lower part of her breastbone, pushing her breastbone down ½ to 1 inch.

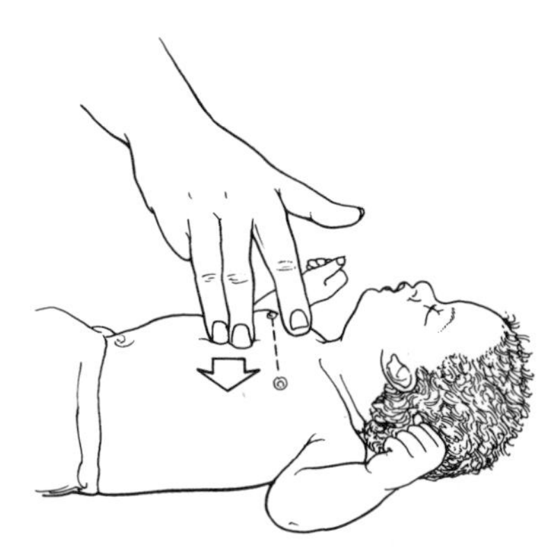

4. If she is still not breathing, open her airway by lifting her entire jaw and tongue. If you see the object, you can remove it *only if you are sure you can reach it safely. Otherwise you might push the object further back in her throat and worsen the situation.*

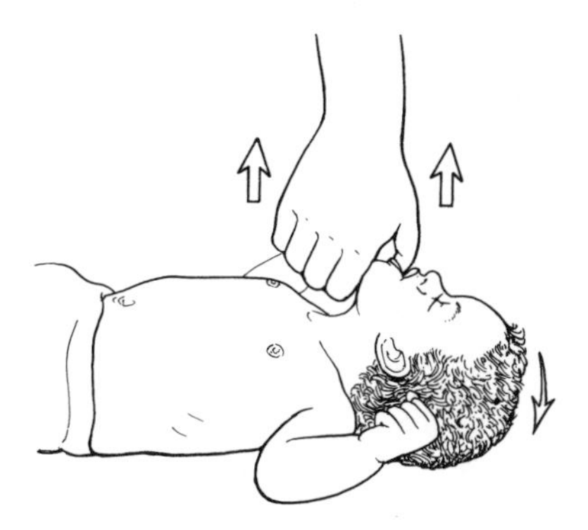

5. If she is still not breathing, give her two slow breaths using the CPR techniques explained and illustrated on pp. 343–345. If her chest doesn't rise as you breathe into her mouth, the air may not be going in. In this case, reposition her head by tilting it back and lifting the jaw to open her airway and give two more slow breaths.

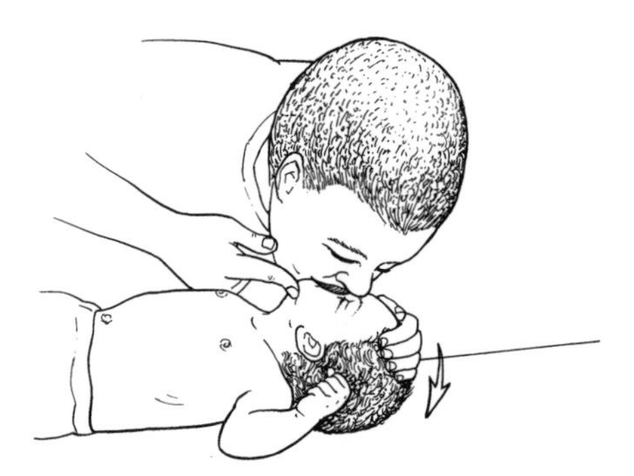

6. After one minute of CPR breathing (whether it works or not), call for emergency help and repeat these steps until medical assistance arrives.

What to do for a child older than one year:

1. Assess your child. If he is coughing or gagging, that means he can breathe and should cough up the item himself. If he cannot speak or cough or is turning dark red to blue, take immediate action.

2. Administer the Heimlich maneuver in one of two ways:

- Standing behind your child with your arms wrapped around his middle, apply six to ten upward abdominal thrusts with your fist placed between his navel and breastbone.

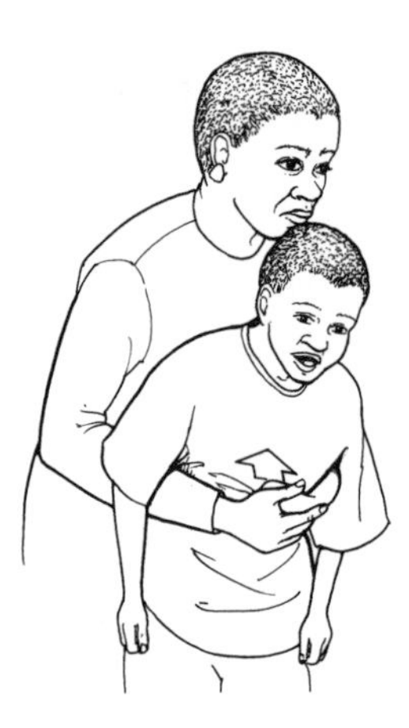

OR

- Lay him down and administer six to ten upward abdominal thrusts between his navel and breastbone as you straddle him.

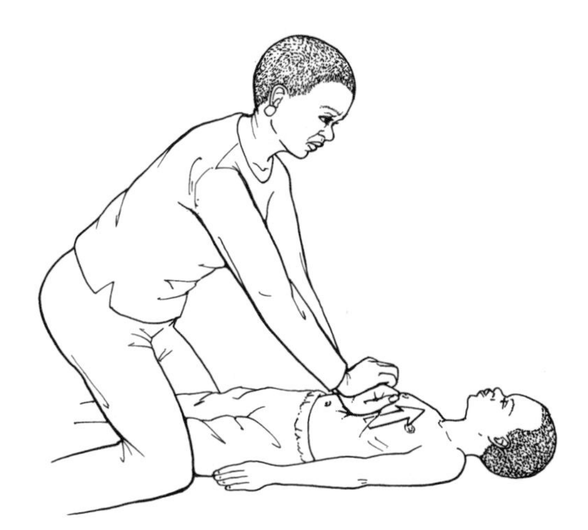

3. If this doesn't work, open his airway by lifting his entire jaw and tongue by tilting his head and lifting his jaw. If you see the object you can remove it, but *only if you are sure you can reach it safely. Otherwise, you might push the object further back in his throat and worsen the situation.*

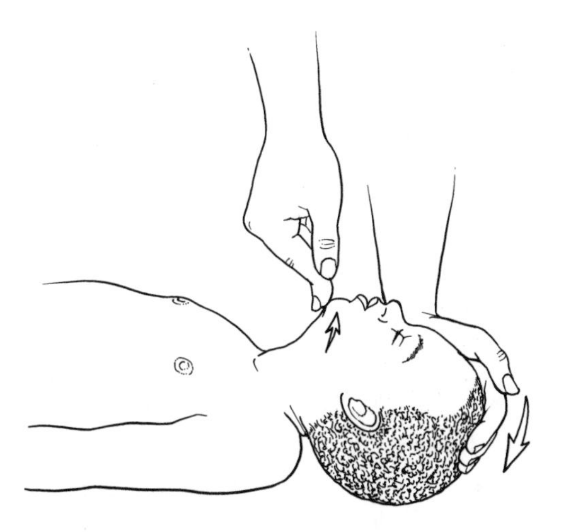

4. If he still is not breathing, give two slow breaths using CPR techniques. If his chest doesn't rise as you breathe into his mouth, the air may not be going in. In this case, reposition his head by tilting it back and lifting the jaw to open his airway and give two more slow breaths.

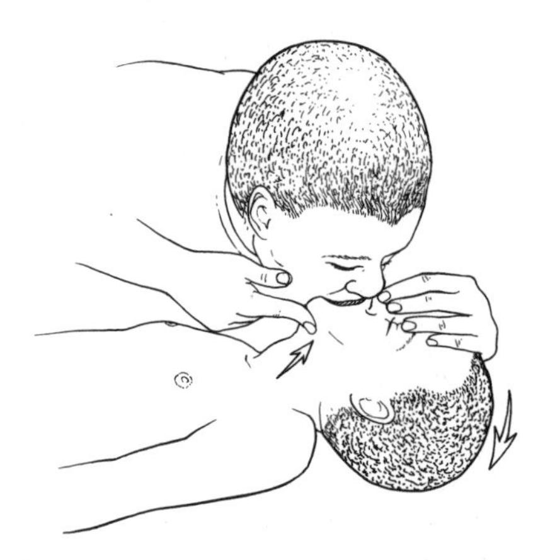

5. After one minute of CPR breathing (whether it works or not), call for emergency help and repeat these steps until medical assistance arrives.

When to call the doctor:

- If your child is in the process of choking
- Bring him to a doctor if you notice a persistent cough or wheezing. After a choking episode has occurred and the object has been removed, your child should suffer no permanent damage if the episode lasted less than two to three minutes. However, a child still may have a small piece of food trapped in his lungs even though he is able to breathe.
- If your child has ongoing gagging, increased salivation, or difficulty swallowing. The object may still be lodged in the throat.

CPR: What You Must Know

Every parent should learn cardiopulmonary resuscitation or CPR. Classes are available through the American Red Cross or the American Heart Association and are given in community settings across the country. The information offered here is not a substitute for proper training but can serve to refresh your memory after you've been fully trained in infant and child CPR. In a CPR class you will learn how to evaluate a patient; maintain the airway; perform CPR on an infant, child, and adult; care for choking victims of all ages who are either conscious or unconscious; the proper techniques for mouth-to-mouth resuscitation; and proper techniques for chest compres-

sions. CPR should only be administered by someone who has undergone training; improper technique can cause serious injury, especially to an infant or young child.

Before you begin CPR, assess the child to determine which CPR measures you will have to take, depending on whether or not she is breathing and has a pulse. To assess her, *check for consciousness first.* If she is not conscious, evaluate the ABCs: Airway, Breathing, and Circulation:

- ***Is the child's* Airway *open?* Make sure there are no foreign objects in her throat or mouth and that her head and neck are properly positioned to prevent obstruction of her airway.**
- ***Is she* B*reathing?* See if her chest is moving or if she is making an effort to move air. If she is, but there is no breath, her airway may be obstructed. If she is not breathing on her own you will have to administer mouth-to-mouth resuscitation.**
- ***Check her* C*irculation.* Is her heart beating? Does she have a pulse? If not, you will have to give chest compressions.**

Infant CPR (birth to 1 year)

1. Check for consciousness by tapping or gently shaking the baby's shoulder. If there is no response . . .

2. Call for help.

3. Roll the baby onto her back while supporting her head and neck. Place her on a firm surface.

4. Open her airway by gently tilting her head back with one hand while lifting her chin with the other. Check her breathing. Be careful not to overextend her head as this can block her airway. Look, listen, and feel for breathing for three to five seconds.

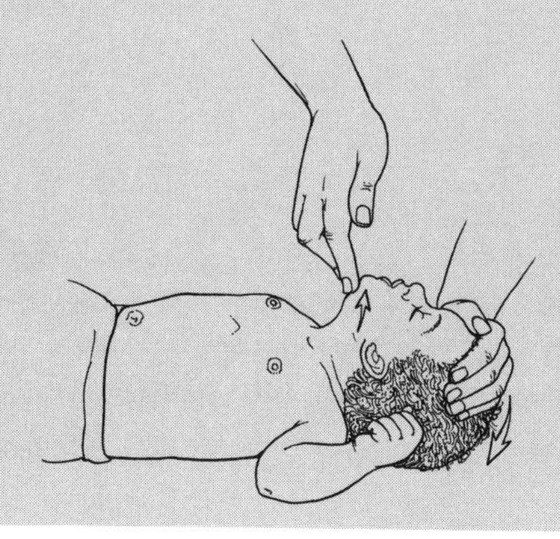

If she is not breathing . . .

5. **Form a seal around her nose and mouth with your lips, making sure they are placed tightly over the area. Give two slow (½ to 1 second) breaths. Make sure you see her chest rise as you give the breaths; if not, her airway may be blocked and you should reposition her head as described in step 4. Then, repeat this step.**

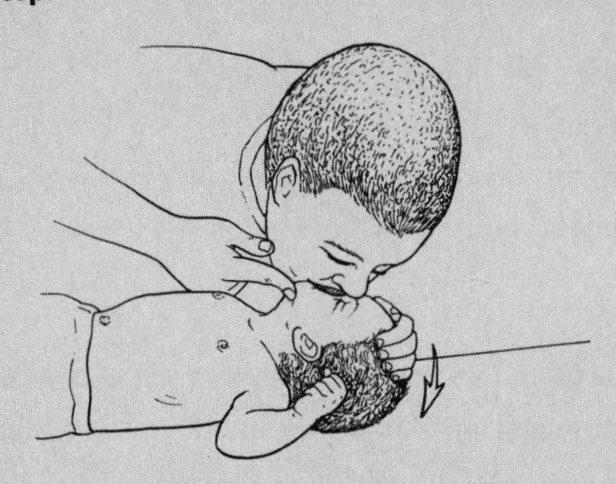

6. **Check her pulse either by feeling for her heart or by checking her pulse on the inside of her upper arm for five to ten seconds.**

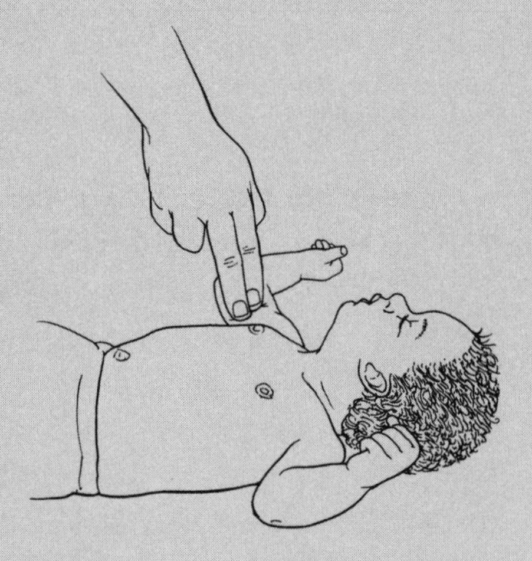

If she has no pulse or heartbeat . . .

7. **Start chest compressions. Place two to three fingers on her breastbone, just below nipple level, and give five quick chest compressions in three seconds. Depress the breastbone ½ to 1 inch by pushing straight down.**

8. **Give one slow breath using the same technique described in step 5.**

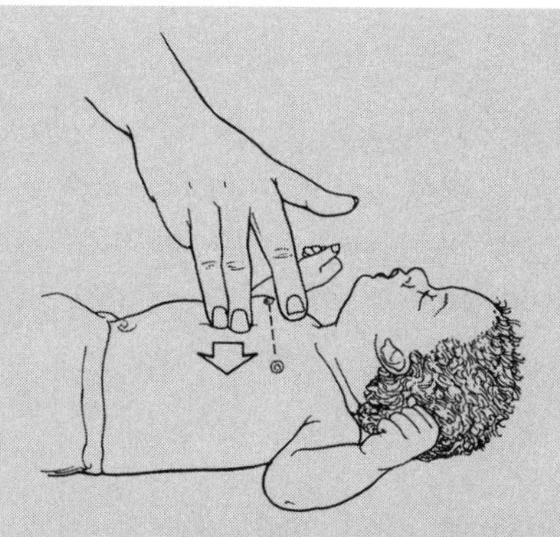

9. Repeat the above steps: one breath, then five chest compressions for one minute (twenty cycles). Then check her pulse.

If she has no pulse and the ambulance has not arrived . . .

10. Continue infant CPR giving one breath then five chest compressions until the baby responds or help arrives.

Child CPR (1 to 8 years)

1. Check for consciousness by tapping or gently shaking the child and asking, "Are you OK?"

If there is no response . . .

2. Call for help.

3. Roll the child onto his back while supporting his head and neck. Place him on a firm surface.

4. Open his airway by gently tilting his head back with one hand and lifting his chin with the other. Check his breathing. Look, listen, and feel for breathing for three to five seconds.

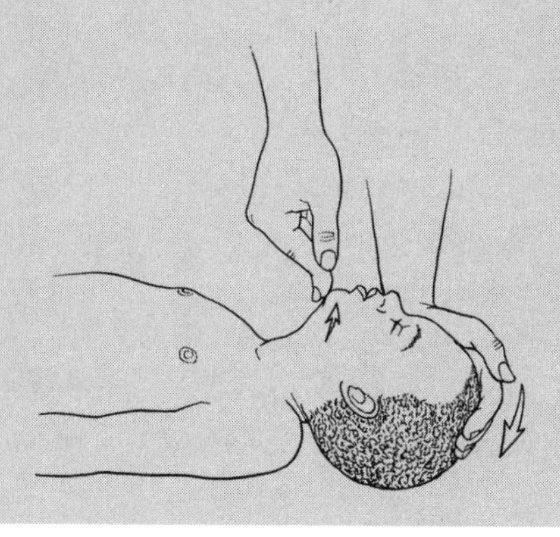

If he is not breathing . . .

5. **Give two slow (1 to $1^1/_2$ seconds) breaths by pinching his nose and forming a seal with your lips placed tightly around his mouth. Make sure you see his chest rise as you give the breaths. If not, his airway may be blocked and you should reposition his head as described in step 4 and then repeat step 5.**

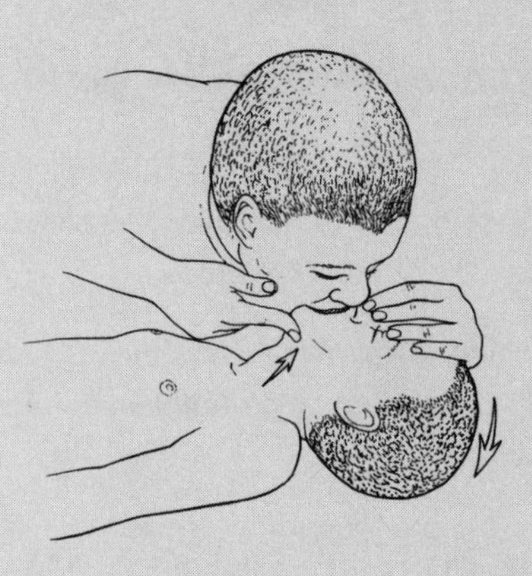

6. **Check his pulse either by feeling his heart or by checking his pulse on the side of his neck for five to ten seconds.**

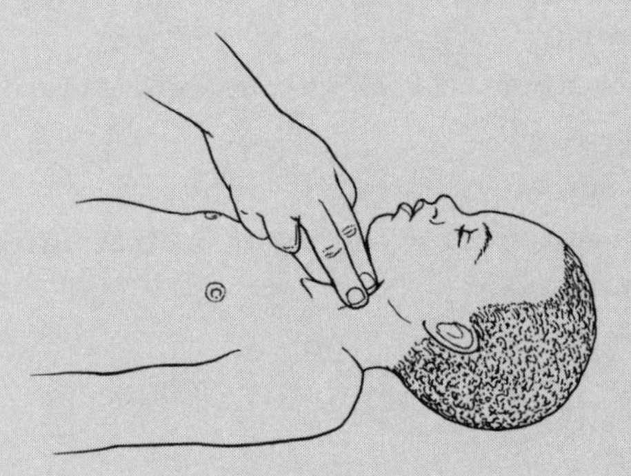

If he has no pulse or heartbeat . . .

7. **Start chest compressions. Place the heel of one hand over the lower third of the breastbone but two finger widths above the bottom notch. Keeping your fingers off the chest and your arms locked straight, give five quick chest com-**

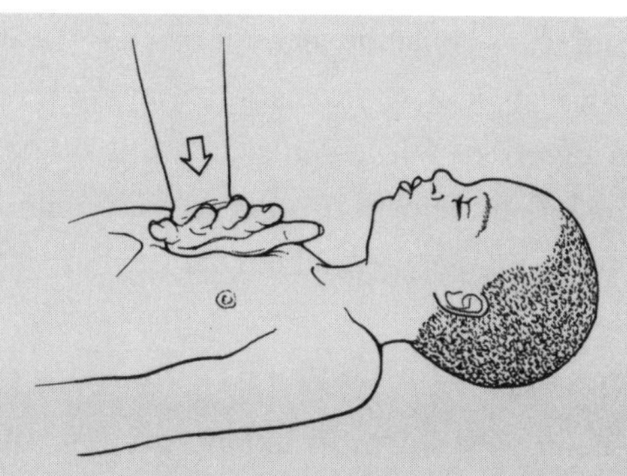

pressions in four seconds. Depress the breastbone 1 to $1^1/_2$ inches by pushing straight down.

8. Give one slow breath using the same technique described in step 5.

9. Repeat the above steps, one breath then five chest compressions, for one minute (twenty cycles). Then check his pulse.

***If he has no pulse and the ambulance has not arrived,* continue CPR, giving one breath then five chest compressions, until the child responds or help arrives.**

Head Injury

Though head injuries are extremely common among children, most are just small bumps that do not cause any serious problems or require medical attention. The skull can withstand significant impact without damaging the brain. However, after any kind of head injury, look for signs and symptoms listed below that may indicate brain injury.

What to do:

1. Do not give the child anything to eat or drink immediately after the injury. Wait to see whether your child needs emergency medical attention.

2. Apply ice and observe your child for the next 24 to 48 hours, watching for any changes. If he cries, he should be consolable and otherwise act normally. He may also complain of a mild headache and may vomit once or twice.

3. He may be sleepy, but should be easily awakened. Don't try to keep him awake. During the night, check on him every four hours to make sure he wakes up easily.

4. Call your doctor if you notice any significant changes or he has persistent vomiting.

Note: If your child loses consciousness or has a seizure as a result of a head injury, this may indicate a more severe injury or concussion and requires immediate medical attention. While you are waiting for help, move him as little as possible unless he's in immediate danger. (If he's undergone an injury to the spinal cord, movement could make it worse.)

When to call the doctor:

- If your child seems very sleepy or lethargic and is difficult to wake up
- If your child vomits more than twice
- If your child has a seizure or loses consciousness
- If you notice any drainage (either blood or clear fluid) from his ears or nose
- If he complains of a severe headache or seems especially irritable, confused, or not like himself
- If his movements seem uncoordinated, his vision is blurry, or his breathing is irregular

Poison

Poisons can be ingested, inhaled, or absorbed through the skin. Of course, you should be concerned about poisoning if you find your child playing with an open bottle of a toxic substance such as turpentine. However, you should also consider whether your child has been poisoned if he is inexplicably sleepy, unconscious; has seizures, stomach pain, nausea, or vomiting; is drooling, or having problems swallowing.

What to do if you suspect your child has been poisoned:

1. Assess your child. Is she conscious and fully awake? Does she have any burns in her mouth? Is she having trouble swallowing or breathing?

2. Call poison control immediately and follow their directions. (Always keep the number posted near the phone.) The operator will ask the age of your child, her approximate weight, the length of time since ingestion, the exact chemical names of the poison (these are usually listed on the bottle), the amount that was ingested, your child's current status, and if she has any other medical problems.

3. At this point, there are several things *not* to do:

- Do not induce vomiting or give ipecac unless directed by your doctor or the poison control center. Some poisons cause severe burns in the throat and mouth which can be worsened by vomiting.

- Do not give her anything to eat or drink unless directed by your doctor or the poison control center.
- Do not give her anything to eat or drink if she is having trouble remaining conscious.
- Do not follow the directions on the bottle; these instructions are sometimes out of date or inaccurate.

4. If you are told to go to the emergency room, take the poison with you so the staff can determine exactly which chemicals have poisoned your child.

5. If your child vomits, count the number of tablets in the vomit and keep them along with the vomit to show to the doctor. She will be able to estimate how much was ingested. This information is important in poisonings where an antidote or counteracting medication must be given.

6. For poisoning or burns of the skin, remove all clothing containing the poison. Flush the skin with lukewarm water for at least fifteen minutes. For poisonings or burns to the eyes, flush with water for at least fifteen minutes. Then take your child to the emergency room.

7. If your child has inhaled poisonous fumes, get him out of the area and into fresh air immediately. If he is not breathing, begin CPR. Call for an ambulance.

When to call the doctor:

- Call the poison control center whenever your child ingests something that is not food (such as houseplants, cosmetics, and vitamins); remember, many things can be poisonous. Depending on what was ingested, you'll receive instructions on the proper way to care for your child and be told if she needs to be seen in the emergency room or by your doctor.

Dental Injuries

Children often chip their teeth, push them in, or knock them out completely by falling down or running into objects. When evaluating the injury, it's important to consider if baby or permanent teeth are involved, the type of injury, and which teeth are hurt. Dental injuries are often accompanied by lacerations to the mouth, which bleed a lot and can be frightening to see. If your child does have an injury to her mouth and/or teeth requiring emergency care, make sure the emergency room has either dentists or oral surgeons who are familiar with the care of children. This is especially important because the placement of certain baby teeth is critical for the proper alignment of the permanent teeth, while other baby teeth are not so important.

What to do:

1. If a tooth is broken or completely knocked out, find the piece, rinse off any dirt (but don't scrub it), and put it in a glass of milk to take to the dentist.

2. If there is bleeding, control it by applying either pressure or ice.

3. Do not have your child hold a broken tooth in his mouth because he may choke on it. And don't try to put teeth back in their sockets.

When to call the doctor:

- If your child's teeth have been loosened or broken as a result of an injury

A Final Word

In any emergency, always remember to call for help. If your child is seriously injured, your instinct will be to take care of him, but remember to call for help *first.* Depending on the type of emergency, a delay of just a few minutes could make a big difference in how well he will recover. This is especially important if your child is not breathing. If that is the case, make sure someone has called for an ambulance or dialed 911 while you begin CPR. If you are alone, you should stop CPR after one minute to call for help.

RESOURCES

Recommended Reading for Parents

Caring for Your Baby and Young Child: Birth to Age 5, The American Academy of Pediatrics and Steven Patrick Shelov (Bantam Books, 1991). This book is a useful guide to recognizing and solving common childhood health problems and emergency medical situations. It includes basic care and safety guidelines and an encyclopedia of injuries, illnesses, and congenital diseases.

The Portable Pediatrician for Parents, Laura Nathanson Walther (HarperCollins, 1994). This book is a practical step-by-step guide to the first five years of life which includes information on medical emergencies and first aid.

The Practical Pediatrician: The A to Z Guide to Your Child's Health, Behavior, and Safety, Howard Markel, M.D., and Frank A. Oski, M.D. (W. H. Freeman & Co., 1996). This book focuses on the needs of children from birth to age eight and has a special section on child safety.

Protecting Children from Danger: Building Self-Reliance and Emergency Skills Without Fear/A Learning by Doing Book for Parents and Educators, Bob Bishop and Matt Thomas (North Atlantic Books, 1993). This book discusses such issues as fire safety, self-reliance, and what children should do when lost.

Raising Children Toxic Free: How to Keep Your Child Safe from Lead, Asbestos, Pesticides, and Other Environmental Hazards, Herbert L. Needleman and Philip J. Landrigan (Farrar, Straus & Giroux, 1994). This book is a practical guide for parents and physicians on how to evaluate risks and minimize children's exposure to hazardous substances.

Recommended Reading for Children

Barney Says, "Play Safely," Margie Larsen, M. Ed., and Mary Ann Dudko, illustrated by Bill Langley (Lyrick Studios, 1996). Barney helps B.J. remember to practice safety rules during a day of fun.

I Am Fire, Jean Marzollo, illustrated by Judith Moffatt (Cartwheel Books/ Scholastic Press, 1996). This book explains how fire can be used for good purposes, such as cooking or providing warmth, or can cause burns or destroy property.

We're Responsible: A Children's Guide to Fire Safety, Sandra J. Williams (Oceana, 1987). The Aware Bears discuss fire safety for children.

Organizations

American Red Cross, Health and Safety Department, 8111 Gatehouse Rd., Falls Church, VA 22042, (703) 206–7180.

Website: www.redcross.org

This organization offers health and safety education and literature on first aid, water safety, HIV and AIDS prevention, CPR training, and other programs.

Center for Injury Prevention, 5009 Coye Dr., Stevens Point, WI 54481, (800) 344–7580, fax: (715) 341–8400, e-mail: elain@cipsafe.org

Website: www.bucklebear.com

This organization works to prevent unintentional injuries and deaths to children by providing educational materials and safety equipment.

National Fire Protection Association, 11 Tracy Dr., Avon, MA 02322, (800) 344–3555. The NFPA sells the "Learn Not to Burn" kit for $9 (plus shipping and handling) as well as fire safety coloring books, removable tattoos, videos, and brochures.

National SAFE KIDS Campaign, 1301 Pennsylvania Ave., NW, Suite 1000, Washington, D.C. 20004–1704, (202) 662–0060, fax: (202) 393–2072, Heather Paul, Ph.D., executive director.

Website: www.safekids.org

The goal of this nationwide childhood injury–prevention organization is to raise awareness of health threats to children. SAFE KIDS works to make childhood safety a public policy priority, designs preventive strategies for low-income families, and builds grassroots coalitions.

National Lead Information Center, National Safety Council, 1025 Connecticut Ave., NW, Suite 1200, Washington, D.C. 20036, (800) LEAD–FYI

Website: www.NSC.org/ehc/lead.htm

The National Safety Council also provides guidelines and additional information on environmental health, air bags, and other safety concerns for children.

Chapter

15

What to Do When Your Child Gets Sick

Having a sick child can be a frightening experience. It can be especially distressing if your little patient is a baby or young toddler who isn't able to tell you what's the matter. But you can ease your own anxiety—and your child's—by arming yourself with a little knowledge about medical problems common in young children. While no book can substitute for sound medical care, including routine checkups and tests, you can avoid wasted time and needless visits to the doctor or emergency room by understanding when a symptom signals something serious, when it doesn't, and what to do.

The Most Common Illnesses

There are a number of illnesses that, no matter how hard you try to avoid them, your child *will* contract. It's hard to avoid common viruses that cause colds and flu, especially if your child is in a play group, day care, or has a lot of contact with other children. The best you can do to prevent these illnesses is give your child a healthy, balanced diet and plenty of rest, and teach her when to wash her hands. When she does catch an illness, you can treat her symptoms—and, of course, provide loads of TLC. In the case of common illnesses that are more serious—like strep throat—it's important to know the symptoms so you can take steps early and prevent complications.

Bronchiolitis

You've probably never heard of bronchiolitis—much less know how to pronounce it [bronk-EE-o-ly-tis]—but it is an extremely common viral infection in infants and children less than two years old. (Older children and adults are not susceptible.) Affecting the lungs and smaller breathing tubes leading to the lungs, bronchiolitis often leads to hospitalization. By age six, most children will have been exposed to the virus that causes it.

How Contracted: The germ that often causes bronchiolitis is called the respiratory syncytial virus (RSV). This germ is passed from person to person in airborne nasal droplets and in saliva.

Symptoms: Your child will first develop signs and symptoms of a cold with cough, congestion, and a runny nose, and she may also have a low-grade fever. She will develop some difficulty breathing and may have retractions and wheezing and her breathing rate may increase. When infants have bronchiolitis, their nasal congestion and increased rate of breathing make it difficult to nurse or take a bottle. In most cases, symptoms begin to subside in five to seven days, and should disappear in ten to fourteen days. But if your child has breathing difficulties that persist or progress, or she cannot take a bottle or nurse, she may require hospitalization.

What to Do: There is a drug available to treat the virus, but it is reserved for children who are hospitalized and have other medical conditions such as severe heart or lung disease. At home you can use mist and humidified air to help loosen the mucus, making it easier to cough up. Keep the humidifier running at all times, or place your child in a bathroom filled with steam from a hot shower for ten to fifteen minutes. Try saline drops to relieve nasal congestion and encourage her to drink a lot of fluids. Some doctors will treat bronchiolitis with albuterol (a medicine used for asthma) while others will not. You should discuss this possibility with your doctor to get her opinion.

Prevention: To prevent transmission of the virus that causes bronchiolitis, wash your child's hands frequently, and your own, too—especially after sneezing, coughing, or nose blowing. You should not allow anyone to kiss your child on her mouth. Children who were born prematurely or who have other illnesses affecting their hearts or lungs are more likely to have serious complications from bronchiolitis. If this is the case, your child may be eligible for monthly intravenous infusions of antibodies against the virus. Discuss this option with your doctor.

When to Call the Health Care Provider:

- If your child is not able to drink from her bottle or nurse
- If she has any difficulty breathing
- If you can hear her wheezing
- If the mist and fluids you give her do not alleviate her symptoms
- If you think she has an ear infection

When It Is an Emergency:

- If your child suddenly seems to be getting groggy
- If your child gets extremely agitated
- If your child has been working really hard at breathing and appears to be tiring out
- If your child looks pale or blue
- If your child seems especially ill

Colds and Flu

These common—and irritating—illnesses are caused by viruses that attack the lining of the nasal passages and throat.

How Contracted: The germs that cause colds and flus are passed from person to person in airborne nasal droplets and in saliva.

Symptoms: With both colds and the flu your child can have nasal congestion, runny nose, sore throat, cough, and fever. If these symptoms are accompanied by muscle aches and fatigue, it is more likely that your child has the flu.

What to Do: No medication can rid the body of the viruses that cause colds and flus. All you can do is focus on relieving the symptoms. Acetaminophen or ibuprofen for fever and body aches, saline drops or decongestants for nasal symptoms, warm mist or humidified air for cough, and plenty of fluids—water, soup, and juices—can help. While people will often treat their colds with natural remedies such as vitamin C, echinacea, or zinc, you should be cautious when giving them to children. Vitamin C is generally safe for children but there is not a lot of information on the safety, appropriate doses, or side effects of echinacea and zinc in children.

Prevention: To prevent transmission of viruses that cause colds and flus, wash your child's hands frequently—and yours, too—especially after sneezing, coughing, or nose blowing. Never allow anyone to kiss your child on the mouth. There is a vaccine available that is given every year to protect against the flu, but it isn't given to everyone. Children who were born prematurely or have asthma, sickle cell, or other conditions of the heart and lungs are candidates for this vaccine.

When to Call the Health Care Provider:

- If your child has a fever for more than 48 hours
- If your child has cold symptoms for more than a week
- If your child develops other troubling symptoms such as ear pain

When It Is an Emergency:

- If your child's cold symptoms progress and your child seems especially ill

Croup

This is a viral illness of the larynx (voice box) that leads to a harsh cough.

How Contracted: The germs that cause croup are the same that lead to colds. They are passed from person to person in airborne nasal droplets and in saliva.

Symptoms: Croup begins as a cold and then develops into a cough that sounds like a barking seal and worsens at night. It is often accompanied by fever. Symptoms generally continue for a week, though in some cases croup can progress to stridor, which is a high-pitched sound when your child breathes in.

What to Do: Since croup is caused by a virus, there are no over-the-counter medications you can use for treatment. Instead, focus on relieving the cough and discomfort in your child's chest using warm mist. Take your child into a steam-filled bathroom and let him breathe the moist air from a warm shower. After about fifteen minutes your child should be much more comfortable. You can also use a humidifier in your child's room. Give him plenty of fluids and acetaminophen or ibuprofen for his fever. *Do not* use cough medicine to treat croup because it may be harmful.

Prevention: The germs that cause croup are passed in the same manner as those that lead to colds and the flu. To prevent transmission, wash your child's hands frequently—and yours, too—especially after sneezing, coughing, or nose blowing. Never allow anyone to kiss your child on the mouth.

When to Call Your Health Care Provider:

- If giving your child mist does not relieve the symptoms
- If he has difficulty swallowing
- If he develops excessive drooling
- If he has not improved in one week
- If he has a very high fever

When It Is an Emergency:

- If your child suddenly seems to be getting groggy
- If your child gets extremely agitated
- If your child has been working really hard at breathing and appears to be tiring out
- If he looks pale or blue
- If your child seems especially ill
- If he develops severe stridor

Ear Infections

Ear infections are extremely common in children: Only one in three children reaches three years of age without having one. The infection occurs in the middle ear,

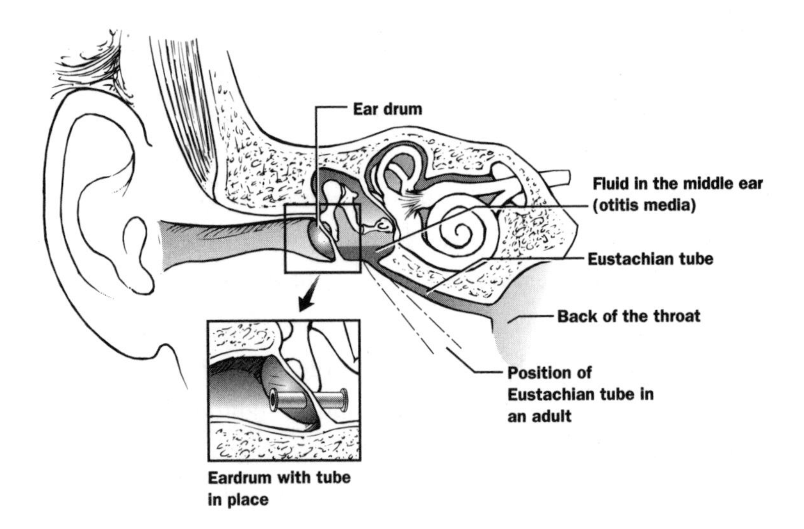

Chronic ear infections are sometimes treated with ear tubes to drain fluid.

which is connected to the back of the throat by the eustachian tube. The purpose of this tube is to keep normal pressure in your ears (it's what causes the "pop" when you swallow or yawn), and to drain fluid that collects in the middle ear. The eustachian tubes of children are shorter than those of adults, and they are less able to clear fluid from the middle ear. When children cough or sneeze, any germs in their throats can be pushed up into their middle ears and cause an infection in fluid that may have collected in the middle ear.

How Contracted: The germs that cause ear infections are the same as those that lead to colds and other infections. These are passed from person to person in airborne nasal droplets and saliva.

Symptoms: Your child will develop symptoms of a cold but will then develop ear pain. Fever is common, but doesn't happen all the time. Some children complain of decreased hearing or dizziness when they have an ear infection.

What to Do: Your doctor must look at your child's eardrum to diagnose an ear infection. If she does, your child will need antibiotics to treat the infection. Other medicines such as nasal decongestants have not been found to help ear infections.

Prevention: Your child can avoid an ear infection by avoiding colds—washing his hands frequently, especially after sneezing, coughing, or blowing his nose (you and others around you should wash your hands at these times too). Do not allow anyone to kiss your child on the mouth or smoke around your child.

Chronic Ear Infections

If your child has had three infections in the past six months, or four infections in the past year, your doctor may recommend a low-dose antibiotic every day to prevent recurrence. If this doesn't prevent infections, your doctor may send you to an ear, nose, and throat specialist to place tubes in the eardrums. These allow fluid to drain out and can prevent ear infections. Children will sometimes have fluid in their middle ears that stays after an ear infection. Tubes are also put into the ears of these children if they've had fluid for four to six months and their hearing is affected. Placement of the tubes requires general anesthesia. The surgery itself is very easy—a small slit is made in the eardrum and a tube is placed in the slit that allows fluid to drain out. These tubes are made of plastic and/or metal. After the surgery, your child will have very little pain. Most children are able to go home on the same day.

When to Call Your Health Care Provider:

- Whenever you suspect your child has an ear infection
- If your child is not better within 48 hours of starting antibiotics

When It Is an Emergency:

- If your child develops stiff neck or seems especially ill

Signs and Symptoms

Constipation

Description: Your child is constipated when he has hard stools that are difficult to pass; skipping a day or days without a bowel movement does not necessarily signal constipation—especially in breast-fed infants, who can go without a bowel movement for seven days.

What It Could Be: Infants often get constipated when solids, especially cereals high in iron, are introduced into their diets. Very inactive children are also prone to constipation. When older children are given vitamins with iron, they can become constipated. Once children are potty-trained and learn to control their bowels, they sometimes wait before going to the bathroom, because they are too busy playing, or

"Luckily, I found a reputable and highly experienced practitioner who could offer Miles a safe alternative therapy that worked when conventional medicine didn't."
—Allison's Story

Miles had his first ear infection soon after he was weaned from breast-feeding. Overnight, he changed from an affable, curious one-year-old into an inconsolable fuss-bucket. Understandably so, because when I took him to the pediatrician, she said he was suffering from acute ear infections in both ears. With a course of antibiotics and some Motrin, he was back to back to his sunny self within a week. But before long he was back where he started: stuffy nose, sleepless nights, lack of appetite, and prolonged tantrums. We received another course of antibiotics, but this time they weren't effective. His pediatrician chose a stronger antibiotic, which did work, but it also caused diarrhea and intestinal discomfort. All through the winter, with every new cold or flu, Miles's ears would become reinfected. By summer, his pediatrician assured us, the hot weather would help Miles get a break. In the meantime, she tested his hearing and cautioned that chronic ear infections could delay his speech development if he wasn't able to hear clearly.

Panicked by this new information, I made an appointment with an ear, nose, and throat specialist. He determined that Miles's hearing was normal and his speech development advanced, but he suggested that he surgically place small drainage tubes in Miles's ears at the onset of another infection. Confused by my limited options—the ineffectiveness of the antibiotics on the one hand, and the more serious measure of surgery on the other—I decided to wait until Miles's ear troubles began again.

I also began looking into alternative medical treatments on the web. One site recommended cranial manipulation ("neck cracking") by a chiropractor or doctor of osteopathy. Although I was still skeptical, not to mention nervous, about having anyone snap Miles's neck, I began making calls but I didn't have the nerve to make an appointment, even after an hour-long conversation with one specialist. Then I read in a national parenting magazine about a chiropractor who specialized in treating children's ear infections, and she was right in my neighborhood. Seeing that she had treated hundreds of children, I made an appointment immediately.

That summer day, Miles went to her with a runny nose that had begun in the winter and hadn't stopped. She talked to him, checked his ears, and demonstrated what she would be doing, using a teddy bear on the manipulation table. She explained that sometimes children are born with compressed bones near the backs of their ears and that these bones need straightening in order for the fluid in the eustachian tubes to

drain through the sinuses. After a few adjustments, she said, Miles's ear infections should improve dramatically. Placing Miles on the table, she felt around the back of his ears, distracted him with a little rhyme, and twisted his neck twice to the left and twice to the right. His little neck popped on each manipulation but he felt no discomfort. Over the next few days, Miles's sinuses cleared considerably and after only two more appointments, he was completely back to normal.

That winter, when he did have an ear infection, instead of using antibiotics I asked his chiropractor to treat him. Although he came down with several colds, Miles got only one other ear infection that winter. Because this infection had gone undetected for a while, it had become acute. I decided to employ both manipulation and antibiotics this time, a strategy that cleared Miles's ears within a week. Although I strongly believe in the merits of modern medicine, there are some obvious limitations. I was frustrated with the side effects and limited effectiveness of the antibiotics and nervous about subjecting my small son to major surgery. Luckily, I found a reputable and highly experienced practitioner who could offer him a safe alternative therapy that worked when conventional medicine didn't.

are in an unfamiliar place. When they finally go to the bathroom, it can be painful and they may bleed. This makes them less willing to go the next time they feel the urge. This pattern of holding stool and avoiding the bathroom is a common cause of constipation in young children.

What to Do: If your newborn is constipated, give him one to two ounces of water mixed with one to two teaspoons of sugar. When your baby reaches four months, offer apple juice; the sugar helps loosen his stool. Inserting a rectal thermometer stimulates the "ano-colic" reflex that makes the colon contract to help push out a stool. Feed older children plenty of fresh water, unpeeled fruit, vegetables, and high-fiber foods such as bran, oatmeal, graham crackers, and brown rice. If your child is constipated because he is holding his stool, have him sit on the potty at least once a day after either breakfast or dinner.

What to Avoid: Foods that cause constipation such as cheese, white rice, and starchy foods like crackers. Do not give your child laxatives without medical supervision. These can be habit forming and make your child dependent on them to have a bowel movement.

When to Call Your Health Care Provider:

- If the home remedies above don't work
- If constipation is a chronic and recurrent problem

When It Is an Emergency:

- If your child develops severe abdominal pain, a bloated belly, or vomiting

Coughing

What It Could Be: Coughing protects the body and clears the airway. An occasional cough is normal, but fever, or a severe or prolonged cough, may signal a larger problem. One cause of cough is croup, a viral infection of the larynx (voice box) that lasts for about a week. The cough sounds like a barking seal, is worse at night, and is accompanied by fever. Mild asthma can also trigger a dry cough that is usually worse at night and does not improve with cough medicine. Other things that cause cough are bronchiolitis and pneumonia—if your child has either of these illnesses, she will have a cough, difficulty breathing, and can have a fever.

What to Do: Since coughing is the body's way of getting rid of mucus, you do not want to stop that process. Rather than giving cough medicine, take steps to allow your child to cough more effectively. Keep your child under a cool mist humidifier to make mucus more watery and easier to cough up. Do not add medicines to the water or mist. You can also put your child into a steam-filled shower and let him breathe the warm, moist air for fifteen minutes to loosen his mucus. Give him plenty of liquids so that he's well hydrated. If the cough is keeping your child up at night and you feel cough medicine is necessary, select an expectorant, which loosens mucus. Never give a child under age two years of age cough medicine.

What to Avoid:

- Throat lozenges, which can choke your child
- Cough medicine that contains alcohol. Read labels carefully.
- People who smoke
- Cow's milk. Many people believe that cow's milk encourages mucus production. Studies have never proven this to be true unless your child is allergic to milk. If you want to avoid giving your child milk while she is sick that's fine as long as she is drinking other fluids such as juice.

When to Call Your Health Care Provider:

- If your child is wheezing as well as coughing
- If the cough lasts longer than one week without improving
- If your child develops an ongoing cough after having nearly choked on something

When It Is an Emergency:

- If your child has a coughing fit or spasm and turns blue or cannot catch his breath
- If your child is having difficulty breathing or seems to be breathing very quickly
- If he has difficulty swallowing or is drooling excessively
- If he develops a high-pitched sound when inhaling

Diarrhea

What It Could Be: Diarrhea functions as a way for the body to get rid of something that is irritating the intestines or colon. It is usually caused by a virus and is common in children, especially those in day care. Occasionally, diarrhea is caused by other germs such as bacteria or parasites.

What to Do: If the diarrhea is caused by a virus, there is no medication to treat it. You can keep your child well hydrated using oral rehydration solutions such as Pedialyte or Ricelyte. It's better to give her large amounts of fluids infrequently rather than small amounts frequently. If she is able to eat, offer her only bland foods such as rice and bread. In younger children, avoid diaper rash caused by diarrhea by changing diapers frequently and protecting the skin with an ointment containing zinc oxide (such as Desitin).

What to Avoid: Over-the-counter preparations like Kaopectate and Pepto-Bismol should not be given to young children. Do not give milk for two to three days after a child has had diarrhea. Children can have problems digesting the sugars in milk after being sick, and offering it too soon may cause gas or more diarrhea. Do not give sodas or juices with a lot of sugar to keep your child hydrated. The sugar can actually cause diarrhea and make the situation worse.

When to Call Your Health Care Provider:

- If your child has diarrhea with fever
- If you notice any blood in the diarrhea

- If your child is ill for more than 24 hours
- If your child's urine decreases or becomes darker, he's not able to make tears, or his mouth is dry. These signs indicate dehydration.
- If your child has severe stomach pains

When It Is an Emergency:

- If you cannot give your child enough fluids to prevent dehydration
- If your child appears especially ill

Difficulty Breathing/Wheezing

Description: There are several different ways your child can have difficulty breathing. When a child is in mild distress she will begin to breathe more quickly and have retractions. You will see her using her stomach muscles to breathe, and pulling in between her ribs. She may also have nasal flaring where her nostrils expand each time she inhales. Another sign of distress is stridor. This is a high-pitched, raspy sound made when your child breathes in. Finally, your child may have wheezing, a high-pitched whistling sound made when breathing out. Any of these signs mean your child is having difficulty breathing.

What It Could Be: An infection in any part of the respiratory system can cause difficulty breathing, including pneumonia and bronchiolitis. These illnesses generally begin as colds but as symptoms worsen, your child can develop mild respiratory distress. (You may notice that she is using her stomach muscles to breathe, her nostrils are flaring when she inhales, or breathing is accompanied by whistling or a raspy sound.) Asthma can also trigger breathing difficulty and wheezing. Another thing to consider is a foreign object. Even if your child inhales an object too small to block her larger airway, it may lodge in a smaller airway and cause a local pneumonia with mild respiratory distress.

What to Do: If your child is having difficulty breathing, seek medical attention immediately to determine the cause of your child's distress. If she has pneumonia, bronchiolitis, or another infection, she may be given antibiotics. Make sure she takes the antibiotics for the entire period prescribed by your doctor, even if your child seems better. Treatments for asthma will be covered later in this chapter.

What to Avoid: Do not expose your child to something that might aggravate her condition such as cigarette smoke, perfumes, or strong fumes from cleaning products.

When to Call Your Health Care Provider:

- Anytime your child is having difficulty breathing

When It Is an Emergency:

- If your child suddenly seems groggy
- If your child gets extremely agitated
- If your child looks pale, or blue, or seems especially ill

Earache

What It Could Be: Ear pain can be caused by an infection in the middle ear or ear canal (swimmer's ear), congestion, a scratch in the ear canal, excessive amounts of ear wax, or a foreign object stuck in the ear.

What to Do: Give your child pain-relieving medication such as acetaminophen or ibuprofen, and apply a warm compress to the ear to relieve the pain. If your child has an infection of the middle ear, your doctor will prescribe an antibiotic to be taken by mouth. Make sure your child takes the medicine for the entire period prescribed, even if he is better in just a few days. Infections of the outer ear can be treated with antibiotic ear drops. Treat excess wax by putting a few drops of hydrogen peroxide in your child's ear twice per day to dissolve the wax.

What to Avoid: Do not stick anything in the ear. The rule for putting something in the ear is: "nothing bigger than your elbow."

When to Call Your Health Care Provider:

- If the pain is severe or not relieved by over-the-counter pain medication
- If your child has pain for more than 24 hours
- If there is any drainage from the ear
- If your child develops any other symptoms such as fever

When It Is an Emergency:

- When the ear pain is associated with high fever
- If your child is not acting like himself or seems disoriented
- If your child develops a stiff neck; this might be a sign of meningitis

Fever

The best way to take your child's temperature is in his rectum with an old-fashioned mercury thermometer. Oral temperatures are hard to get in young children, axillary (armpit) temperatures are less accurate, and the readings from ear thermometers can be off by as much as a whole degree. Your child has a fever if his temperature is:

- Higher than 98.6°F, taken in the armpit
- Higher than 99.5°F, taken orally or with an ear thermometer
- Higher than 100.4°F, taken rectally

What It Could Be: Fever indicates infection; it is the body's way of responding to an illness and helps boost the immune system. Overdressing an infant or keeping her in an overheated room can also trigger a low-grade fever.

What to Do: Treat fever with acetaminophen or ibuprofen. They can also be given together; if one doesn't seem to bring down the fever, give the other. (For more on these medications, see pp. 378–379.) You can also try a sponge bath. Do not use cold water; a warm bath of 90.0°F can help a child with a fever of 100.0°F. Do not use rubbing alcohol to sponge your child. Make sure to give your child plenty of liquids.

What to Avoid: Don't let the fever get too high. High fever can cause seizures in young children. Do not use aspirin to bring down fever. In children, it has been associated with a rare but dangerous condition called Reye's Syndrome that causes liver and brain damage. Also, do not give your child Pepto-Bismol or Alka Seltzer when she has a fever. These contain medication similar to aspirin.

When to Call Your Health Care Provider:

- If your child seems especially ill, even with a low-grade temperature
- If your child has fever for more than 48 hours
- If your child has any evidence of serious infection such as ear pain or a stiff neck

When Is It an Emergency:

- Fever in an infant less than two months old, even low-grade
- If your child looks especially ill—seems lethargic, isn't reacting, or seems especially droopy, regardless of how high the fever
- If your child has a seizure

Itching

What It Could Be: Several conditions can cause itchy skin. The most basic explanation is dry skin, which is especially common in the winter. Hives, irregularly shaped red skin splotches, are triggered by an allergic reaction to foods, insect bites, and even medicines. Contact dermatitis is a reaction to something that has touched the skin, such as soaps, perfumes, lotions, detergents, and some jewelry. Poison ivy, poison oak, or poison sumac lead to severe reactions and are another type of contact dermatitis. Eczema, which is associated with allergies and asthma, is extremely common among children and causes dry, itchy skin. Some infections (like athlete's foot) and illnesses (like chicken pox) can also cause itching. Scabies, small insects that bury themselves under the skin, can cause itchy hands, and head lice can make the scalp itch.

What to Do: To heal dry skin, use plenty of hypoallergenic, hydrating lotion and don't bathe your child more often than every other day. Hives are treated with an over-the-counter antihistamine like Benadryl, and it's also important to try to determine what caused the reaction so you can avoid it in the future. If your child has contact dermatitis, avoid the products that are causing the itching. Hypoallergenic soaps, lotions, and detergents should be used on children with sensitive skin. Hydrocortisone cream or ointment, which you can buy at the drugstore, relieves the irritation but should only be used on your child after you have spoken with your doctor. If your child has poison ivy, wash the skin after exposure to remove the oils of the plant. Hydrocortisone is also helpful with this rash. Eczema is best treated by keeping the skin moist with lotions such as Aveeno or Eucerin. If there are areas that seem especially irritated or dry, talk to your health care provider about using hydrocortisone or another, stronger steroid ointment. You should also talk to your health care provider if you think itchy skin is the result of an infection.

What to Avoid: Do not let your child scratch. Cover her hands and keep her nails short to prevent infecting the itchy area.

When to Call Your Health Care Provider:

- If the above treatments don't work, your child's rash may be caused by an infection such as scabies.
- If the above measures do not relieve the itching
- If you are not sure of the cause of his itching
- If your child is scratching and his skin has become infected

When It Is an Emergency:

- If, during an allergic reaction, your child develops difficulty swallowing, a feeling of swelling in his mouth, tightening of his throat, wheezing, or difficulty breathing

Nasal Congestion

What It Could Be: Congestion is caused by swelling of the lining of the nasal cavity and is usually harmless in children, but can be a problem in infants. Most often, it is a result of an upper respiratory infection and can be accompanied by fever, sore throat, or cough. Clear nasal discharge, sneezing, and an itchy nose probably signal allergies, especially if you notice these symptoms at the same time each year, usually in the spring or fall. If your child has prolonged nasal congestion accompanied by thick, foul-smelling discharge, he may have something lodged in his nose or an infection of his sinuses.

What to Do: If your child has a cold, avoid decongestants; let his body fight the virus naturally. You can help by removing as much mucus as possible. If your child is too young to blow his nose, loosen mucus with saline nose drops and use a bulb syringe to remove the mucus. If your child has allergies, give him a decongestant to relieve his congestion and an antihistamine to control his allergic response. (Read more about safe ways to use these medications later in this chapter.)

What to Avoid: Do not give nasal decongestant sprays to your child. After prolonged use they can actually make your child's nasal congestion worse. Do not let anyone smoke around your child.

When to Call Your Health Care Provider:

- If your child has allergies and doesn't respond to the medications
- If congestion lasts for more than three weeks, or nasal discharge becomes thick and green, especially with fever or facial swelling, his sinuses may be infected.
- If you think your child has something stuck in his nose

Swollen Glands

What It Could Be: Swollen glands are usually swollen lymph nodes. Whenever the nodes swell, the body is fighting an infection. Swelling, which signals that the immune system is hard at work, occurs at different parts of the body, depending on the site of the infection. Colds and throat infections cause swelling under the jaw and in front of the neck, while cuts or scrapes in the scalp cause swelling along the nape of the neck. Occasionally, lymph nodes become infected, and they fill with pus and feel firm, warm, and tender. Mumps is a viral infection that doesn't attack lymph nodes but attacks the glands that make saliva, which are located in front of the ears. This infection is uncommon since children are protected by the mumps vaccine.

What to Do: In most cases there is nothing you should do for swollen glands. Just let your child's body handle the infection. If glands become infected, your child will need antibiotics.

What to Avoid: Do not bother the glands; if they are infected, do not try to squeeze them or remove any pus.

When to Call Your Health Care Provider:

- If you think the nodes are infected. They will be large, tender, warm, and the skin covering them will be red.

When It Is an Emergency:

- If your child is acting especially ill
- If the nodes become so enlarged that he has difficulty breathing or swallowing

Vomiting

What It Could Be: Vomiting is the stomach's way of getting rid of something causing irritation. Expect vomiting of small amounts of breast milk or formula in infants up to one year. In toddlers and preschoolers, vomiting generally signals a virus, such as "the stomach flu." With young children, you must always consider accidental poisonings, which induce vomiting as the body tries to get rid of the poison. Though less common, vomiting can also be caused by a food allergy.

What to Do: There are no medications to treat viruses, so all you can do is make sure your child doesn't get dehydrated by giving her fluids frequently (every fifteen minutes), in small amounts—one to four ounces depending on her age. Give your infant formula or breast-milk if he can keep it down. If she cannot tolerate formula, use an oral rehydration solution such as Pedialyte or Ricelyte. As children get older, they are less willing to drink these solutions, but Pedialyte is available as frozen ices, which older children are often more willing to take. After 24 hours of oral rehydration solution, offer your child solid bland food such as rice or bread.

What to Avoid: Do not give sugary drinks such as juice or soda, which contain too much sugar to be effective. If your child is absolutely unwilling to take an oral rehydration solution, a sports drink is better than juice or soda. Do not force your child to eat or drink anything if she seems sleepy, lethargic, or difficult to wake up.

When to Call Your Health Care Provider:

- If your infant is vomiting large amounts, or if the vomit is very forceful or projectile
- If your child's urine decreases or gets darker, his mouth becomes dry, or he is not making tears. These signs indicate dehydration.
- If your child has severe stomach pain

When It Is an Emergency:

- If the vomiting is associated with excessive sleepiness, lethargy, or difficulty staying awake. This may be a clue that he has taken something and poisoned himself.
- If you notice any pills or strange items in your child's vomit
- If your child vomits blood and hasn't had a nosebleed

What You Need to Know About Medications

An overwhelming number of medications are available to treat the common illnesses of childhood. They come in several different forms, and you can purchase several over-the-counter medications that are useful—though your doctor must prescribe antibiotics to treat infections. Once your child has finished his antibiotics, throw them out—do not keep them around to give the next time your child is sick. Because of the vast array of nonprescription children's drugs available, it's important for you to be well-informed before you walk into the drugstore to choose medication for your child. Always read labels carefully and use medication properly.

Giving Our Kids Antibiotics

The most common prescription medications for children are antibiotics. There are lots of different types which are given anywhere from once to four times per day, for one to fourteen days. If your doctor has prescribed an antibiotic for your child, there are certain things you should ask either your doctor or pharmacist:

- *How much should be given with each dose?* Have your doctor prescribe the dose in ccs (or mls); it is a more accurate way to give medicine to your child than using teaspoons. You can buy a medicine syringe at any pharmacy. Use it to administer your child's medicine in ccs.
- *How often does the medication need to be given?* If the prescription says three

times per day, does it have to be exactly every eight hours, which would probably mean having to wake your child in the night, or can it be three times during the day?

- *For how many days will your child need to take the medicine?*
- *What are the common side effects of the medicine?* Which side effects require a call or visit to the doctor?
- *What other medications are safe/not safe to give with the medicine?*
- *Can the medicine be given with foods?* Some should be given before your child eats, others after your child eats, and with others, it doesn't make a difference.
- *Can the medicine be mixed with food, milk, or juice to make it easier to give to your child?*
- *How should the medicine be stored?* Some need to be kept in the refrigerator and others can be kept at room temperature.
- *Does your doctor want to see your child when she has finished taking the antibiotic?*

Giving Your Child Medication

Follow these "Do's" and "Don'ts" as you choose medication and administer it to your child:

Do

- *Check labels carefully when using liquid medications.* They come in several forms: drops, which are generally for infants; elixirs, which means the medication has been mixed with another liquid to mask the taste; and suspensions, medication suspended in a liquid. These differ from one another and you should be cautious when substituting one for the other.
- *Watch for additives.* Some liquid preparations, including some colic medications and cough syrups, contain alcohol, which you wouldn't normally give to your child. Also, be careful of the amount of sugar in medications. Most are sweetened with sugars such as sorbitol so that children will take them. But if your child takes a large dose, or is on the medication for a long time, the sugars can cause diarrhea.
- *Measure liquid preparations accurately.* Kitchen teaspoons are not accurate.

Using Antibiotics Safely

If your child is under three years old, chances are two in three that she will have or has already developed an ear infection. Chances are also that to treat your child's ear infection her pediatrician prescribed an antibiotic, such as amoxicillin or erythromycin. In 1992, over 23 million prescriptions were written for middle ear infections (up from 15 million in 1985), according to the *Journal of the American Medical Association.*

Although these drugs have been highly effective in ridding children of ear and other bacterial infections, like urinary tract infections and strep throat, they have unfortunately also been overused. Overuse of antibiotics can cause antibiotic-resistant strains of bacteria to thrive in both the general population and in the children taking them. Many parents who are desperate to help their children recover from a viral infection or a lingering cold insist that the pediatrician prescribe antibiotics. What these parents do not realize is that antibiotics do not have any effect on viruses or other infections not caused by bacteria, and every exposure to antibiotics increases the bacteria's chance of becoming increasingly resistant to the drugs. This is why many children, after having used one antibiotic to treat previous ear infections, may have to switch to a new type to clear up future infections. With each course of antibiotics, any bacteria that has not been killed by the antibiotic survives, multiplies, and reinfects.

With antibiotic use so widespread now, the risk of drug-resistant bacteria has increased considerably. Although rare, children who have been exposed to many different and stronger types of antibiotics run the risk of contracting severe infections that only the strongest antibiotics can treat. For this reason, physicians are making the following recommendations when it comes to safely using antibiotics:

- *Take only if necessary.* Be sure that when you ask for, or when your child's health provider prescribes an antibiotic, that it will actually treat your child's infection. Viruses aren't treatable with antibiotics and using antibiotics to alleviate their symptoms can increase the likelihood your child will develop resistant infections. If there's any question about the effectiveness of antibiotic treatment, consider alternatives with your child's pediatrician.
- *Finish the entire course of treatment.* Many parents believe that their children can stop taking antibiotics as soon as they feel better. Of course it's a struggle to convince a protesting child that each dose is essential in wiping out the infection; however, the alternative of not finishing the entire amount prescribed can lead to more serious infections and complications. It takes about

five to ten days for an antibiotic to effectively kill the bacteria, depending on the brand. If your child does not finish her treatment, there is a great likelihood that the bacteria that hasn't been killed yet will quickly multiply and be a more drug-resistant strain. Your child will then have to be put on a stronger antibiotic and may have possibly passed the resistant strain on to another child in the meantime.

- ***If your child experiences side effects, call her pediatrician.*** **Side effects such as nausea, diarrhea, or other gastrointestinal problems are common with certain antibiotics. Nonetheless, always contact a physician when these occur. The doctor may want to prescribe an alternative. Signs of an allergic reaction, such as a rash, facial swelling, or difficulty breathing, should be reported to her pediatrician immediately.**
- ***Discuss alternative treatments.*** **The new consensus among physicians is that certain types of ear infections aren't best treated with antibiotics. In the past physicians liked to treat chronic ear infections with a long-term preventive dose of antibiotics. However, there is no real evidence that this treatment helps clear the infection, but it can cause your child to develop infections with drug-resistant bacteria. Many doctors have now adopted a wait-and-see approach to administering antibiotics, especially in the case of fluid in the ear, which causes chronic ear infections. Unless a bacterial infection develops, the best treatment is no treatment.**
- ***Practice prevention.*** **For babies, one of the best lines of defense is breastfeeding. Breast-fed babies have far fewer bacterial infections than bottle-fed babies because mother's milk has powerful antibodies that protect from infections. If your child attends a child care program, be sure she washes her hands frequently throughout the day, and keep her home when she's sick so that she doesn't infect other children.**

It's better to use a medicine syringe that can be bought at any pharmacy. One teaspoon equals 5cc (or 5ml).

- *Measure dosages based on weight rather than age.* It's more accurate.
- *Shake the bottle when giving your child a suspension to make sure the medicine is evenly distributed throughout the liquid and an accurate dose is given to your child.*

Tips to Get Children to Take Their Medicine

- **Put liquid medicines in a bottle nipple. By the time she realizes it isn't milk or juice she will have sucked it down.**
- **If you are using a medicine syringe, put the medicine on the side of your baby's mouth instead of on her tongue—it's harder to push the medicine out and it will go to the back of her mouth to be swallowed.**
- **Gently blow on your baby's face when she has medicine in her mouth; it makes her swallow.**
- **You can mix some medicines with a small amount of juice, milk, yogurt, or pudding to give to your child. Check with your pharmacist to make sure this is OK, and make sure your child gets the entire dose that was prescribed.**

- *Have your child use his front teeth to bite into a chewable tablet.* Otherwise, some of the medicine can get stuck in his back teeth and he will not get the proper dose of medication. If this is difficult, you can either break the chewables with the back of a spoon, or stick with liquids until your child is old enough to safely swallow tablets.
- *Use suppositories carefully.* These are medications administered by pushing them through your child's anus; they are then absorbed in the rectum. They are best used when your child is unable to take a medication by mouth, for example, when he is vomiting. The disadvantage of suppositories is that they come in premeasured form, making it difficult to adjust the dose to suit your child. If you need to cut the suppository to give an accurate dose, speak with your doctor, who can instruct you in the best way to do this.

Don't

- *Treat medication like candy.* Explain to your child that you are giving him medicine to make him feel better. You don't want to convince him that it is candy because he may find it later and think it is safe to eat and poison himself.
- *Give a child adult medication.* Giving a child half of an adult dose is not the way to give medicines. Use a preparation meant for children and give a dose that is based on his weight.

- *Interchange an infant product with one designed for older children.* Liquid formulations for infants and children have different concentrations of medicine even when it is the same type of medicine. Exchanging infant and children preparations could lead to underdosing in one case and overdosing in another.
- *Mix medications.* If your child is taking one medication—prescription or over-the-counter—ask your health care provider before giving her another drug.

Common Children's Medications

Every child gets sick with a cold or runny nose from time to time. Before this happens, you should talk with your doctor and ask her opinion about how to handle common ailments, and what over-the-counter medications she recommends. She should be able to tell you about several safe treatments you can give that do not include medication. When you are trying to decide what medications to give to your child you'll encounter a wide variety of decongestants, antihistamines, and antitussives. Below is information about commonly used medications that will help you sort through all the choices you'll find at your pharmacy. You will notice we give a range of weights when we suggest consulting with your doctor before giving the medication. This has to do with the different ages at which it is safe to give these medications. Overall, this list has conservative recommendations in terms of the weight your child should be before safely giving medicine. You can use it as a guideline and talk with your doctor if your child weighs less than the first weight listed under each medicine's dosage.

For Allergy, Nasal Congestion

Diphenhydramine—An antihistamine, medicine to relieve allergic reactions

Brand Names: Benadryl

When to Give: Use diphenhydramine to relieve allergic symptoms, such as sneezing and runny nose. It does *not* treat congestion associated with allergies. It can also be used for hives or eczema.

How to Give: Diphenhydramine is available as an elixir and caplets, and is given every 4 to 6 hours. It should not be given more than 4 times in a 24-hour period.

Dose:

Weight	Dose
<11 lbs.	Consult your doctor
11–16 lbs.	6.25mg or 1/2 tsp. elixir (12.5mg/5cc)
16–22 lbs.	9.4mg or 3/4 tsp. elixir (12.5mg/5cc)
22–33 lbs.	12.5mg or 1 tsp. elixir (12.5mg/5cc)
33–45 lbs.	18.75mg or 1 or 1/2 tsp. elixir (12.5mg/5cc)
45 lbs.	25mg or 2 tsp. elixir (12.5mg/5cc)

Caution: Diphenhydramine can cause drowsiness and should not be given to a child before going to day care or preschool. It can also cause agitation and nervousness in some children and should not be given before bed. Some parents have asked if it can be used to calm children while traveling, or on long road trips. Since some kids get nervous and agitated after taking the medication, diphenhydramine may be the last thing you want to give to a toddler who is about to be cooped up in a car for several hours.

Pseudoephedrine—A decongestant, medicine to relieve nasal congestion

Brand Names: Sudafed, PediaCare Infant Drops

When to Give: Pseudoephedrine is used to treat nasal congestion caused by colds and allergies.

How to Give: Pseudoephedrine is available as infant drops and elixir. It is often combined with other drugs in over-the-counter medications. For example, an allergy preparation might have an antihistamine for allergy symptoms combined with pseudoephedrine to treat the congestion caused by allergies. However, it is better to give it alone so you can give an accurate dose without worrying about under- or overdosing on another medication. Pseudoephedrine is given every 4 to 6 hours, but you should not give more than 4 doses in a 24-hour period.

Dose:

Weight	Dose
<16 lbs.	Consult your doctor
16–25 lbs.	0.8cc drops or 1/2 tsp. elixir (15mg/5cc)
25–33 lbs.	3/4 tsp. elixir (15mg/5cc)
33–50 lbs.	1 tsp. elixir (15mg/5cc)

Caution: Pseudoephedrine can cause agitation and jitteriness in children. If your child is taking another medication or has an ongoing illness, check with your doctor before giving this medication.

Saline Nose Drops

Brand Name: NaSal

When to Give: Saline or saltwater drops are excellent for clearing mucus and moistening the lining of your child's nose. They help relieve congestion, stuffy nose, and prevent dry nasal passages that can lead to bloody noses.

How to Give: Saline drops and nose sprays can be purchased at any pharmacy, but you can also make them at home. Take 8 oz. (1 cup) of warm water and add 1/4 teaspoon of table salt. Mix well, and store in a clean bottle for up to one week. To ease congestion in an infant, place 2 to 3 drops in each nostril with a dropper, wait 1 to 2 minutes, then remove any loosened mucus with a bulb syringe. Since this is only saltwater, you do not have to worry about overdosing your child, and can use saline drops safely in infants. You can also use the drops as often as needed.

Caution: Use only 2 to 3 drops at a time; you don't want to upset your child by pouring too much in his nose at one time.

For Cough

There is an astounding array of cough medicines that are manufactured and marketed to parents. However, most pediatricians advise against giving cough medicine to children. They do not help with colds and can hinder coughing, which helps to clear mucus from the body. However, the reality is many parents use cough medicines anyway, especially if the cough is waking the child at night. Should you decide to use cough medicine, you should know the ingredients contained in those preparations.

Dextromethorphan—An antitussive, medicine to stop coughs

Brand Names: Robitussin Pediatric

When to Give: This medication inhibits the body's urge to cough. You should use it only if your child has a dry, nonproductive cough.

How to Give: Dextromethorphan is available as a liquid, but is often combined with other drugs such as pseudoephedrine in cough and cold medicines. However, it is best to use one medicine at a time, to avoid under- or overdosing on different medications. It is given every 6 to 8 hours.

Dose: The doses below differ from those listed on the bottle. They are based on weight rather than age:

Weight	Dose
<12 lbs.	Consult your doctor
12–16 lbs.	5.6mg or or 3/4 tsp. elixir (7.5mg/5cc)
16–25 lbs.	7.5mg or 1 tsp. elixir (7.5mg/5cc)
25–33 lbs.	11mg or 1 or 1/2 tsp. elixir (7.5mg/5cc)
>33 lbs.	15mg or 2 tsp. elixir (7.5mg/5cc)

Caution: Do not use for chronic coughs or cough related to asthma. If your child is taking any other medication ask your doctor before giving dextromethorphan. Read the labels carefully; in some cough medicines dextromethorphan is combined with alcohol—an ingredient most parents want to avoid giving to their children.

Guaifenesin—An expectorant, medicine to loosen mucus

Brand Names: Robitussin Maximum Strength—A cough medicine for adults.

When to Give: Guaifenesin is an expectorant that works by thinning mucus, making it easier to cough up. Use for productive coughs to help it remove mucus.

Note: Guaifenesin is often found combined with other drugs such as antihistamines, pseudoephedrine, and dextromethorphan. Recommended doses vary depending on other drugs included in the medication. When bottled alone, make sure it isn't combined with alcohol, which you should avoid giving to children. Though guaifenesin is considered safe, we don't recommend giving it to children under age two years because it is often combined with other medications that can be dangerous for young children. Instead of using medication to loosen your child's cough, try warm mist (see the discussion on cough in this chapter).

For Fever, Pain

Acetaminophen—An analgesic/antipyretic, medicine for pain and fever

Brand Names: Tylenol, Tempra. Also known as paracetamol in other countries.

When to Give: Use acetaminophen for fever and mild pain.

How to Give: Acetaminophen is available as drops, elixir, suspension, chewable tablets, and suppository. It is given every 4 hours.

Dose:

Weight	Dose
<17 lbs.	Consult your doctor
17–26 lbs.	120mg or 3/4 tsp. elixir (160mg/5cc)
26–35 lbs.	160mg or 1 tsp. elixir (160mg/5cc)
35–53 lbs.	240mg or 1 or 1/2 tsp. elixir (160mg/5cc)

Caution: It should not be given to a child with a known allergy to acetaminophen. Taking too much can cause liver damage, so keep the medication in a safe place away from your child's reach.

Ibuprofen—An analgesic/antipyretic, medicine for pain and fever

Brand Names: Advil, Motrin

When to Give: Use ibuprofen for fever and pain, especially when pain is associated with inflammation such as muscle sprains.

How to Give: Ibuprofen is available as drops, as a suspension, or as caplets. It is given every 6 to 8 hours.

Dose:

Weight	Dose
<20 lbs.	Consult your doctor
20–30 lbs.	100mg or 1 tsp. suspension (100mg/5cc)
30–40 lbs.	150mg or 1 or 1/2 tsp. suspension (100mg/5cc)
40–55 lbs.	200mg or 2 tsp. suspension (100mg/5cc)

Caution: Do not give ibuprofen if your child has a history of stomach ulcers or gastritis, is allergic to aspirin, or has had a previous allergic reaction to ibuprofen. Do not give it if your child is dehydrated.

Alert: Diseases of Particular Note for Our Children

We have singled out five illnesses that, for various reasons, affect our children more often than they affect children of other races. As black parents, it is critical that we understand each of these problems—asthma, HIV, iron-deficiency anemia, lead poisoning, and sickle-cell anemia—and know what steps to take to prevent them when possible and how to treat them. It's also important that parents be aware of the latest information about treatment and prevention of these five illnesses. With that in mind, see the detailed resource list at the end of this chapter.

Asthma and Our Children

Asthma is a chronic condition that causes wheezing and inflammation of the smaller breathing tubes in the lungs. It is the most common ongoing illness in children and it has been increasing in recent years. Several studies have shown that it is twice as common among African-American children as it is among white children.

How Contracted: Children are born with asthma, but some outgrow it. Exposure to a number of "triggers" can bring on an attack. Common triggers of asthma are listed below. While not every child will react to every trigger, your child will react to at least one of these. Once you know what triggers your child's asthma, efforts to avoid these irritants will go a long way toward making him healthier.

Common asthma triggers include:

- *Pollen.* You will notice your child's asthma is worse during the spring and fall.
- *Molds.* These children tend to have chronic, ongoing symptoms that do not vary.
- *Dust.* These children also have chronic, ongoing symptoms that do not vary.
- *Pet hairs and feathers.* These children will wheeze whenever they have been near animals or in a house with animals.
- *Cockroaches.* This is a common source of allergens, especially for children living in cities.
- *Foods.* Certain foods like dairy and wheat products contribute to chronic asthma. These children benefit from having these foods removed from their diets.
- *Upper respiratory infections.* These are usually caused by viruses that irritate the airways and cause asthma attacks.
- *Tobacco smoke.* Several studies have shown that children living in homes with smokers have more problems with asthma. If your child has asthma, no one should ever be allowed to smoke around him.

- *Lung irritants.* These include perfumes, noxious fumes from cleaning products, pollution, and even cooking fumes.
- *Exercise.* Many children with asthma will wheeze after they have engaged in some type of strenuous activity, especially in cold weather.
- *Gastroesophageal reflux.* This condition occurs when the contents of the child's stomach pass back up the esophagus. It is thought that these children are constantly inhaling their own stomach acids, which irritates the lungs and causes asthma.
- *Drugs.* Many people with asthma wheeze after they have taken certain medications. Aspirin is a drug that sometimes triggers asthma.
- *Excitement/emotional upset.* Although stress does not cause asthma, it definitely affects the severity of the illness for many people.

Symptoms: The symptoms of asthma vary from mild with occasional episodes of wheezing (a high-pitched sound when exhaling) to severe with chronic wheezing and difficulty breathing that leads to panicked visits to the emergency room and hospitalization. The milder symptoms of asthma include a chronic, dry, hacking cough that is usually worse at night; a dry, hacking cough that occurs during exercise; a prolonged, harsh cough whenever your child has a cold; or a feeling of tightness or tickling in the chest without wheezing.

What to Do: The best way to treat asthma is to avoid the triggers that cause an episode. There are also several medications used to treat it. The exact therapy your child requires depends on the severity of his asthma, the triggers that cause it to get worse, and his age. Every child with asthma should have a regimen of medications that is tailored to his exact needs by a doctor who closely monitors his care.

The medications used to treat asthma in children ages birth to five include:

- *Bronchodilators* (Albuterol, Ventolin, Proventil), medicines that mimic adrenaline and help to open the lungs.
- *Cromolyn* (Intal), a medication that stops allergic responses before they happen and is used to prevent asthma.
- *Steroids* (Pediapred, Asthmacort, Beclovent), medications to stop the inflammation in the lungs.
- *Aminophyline* (Theophyline, Theodur), a medication that is similar to caffeine and opens the lungs.

Steps to Avoid Asthma Triggers

Asthmatics should:

- ***Avoid pollens.*** Don't take your child to places with a lot of pollen (areas with a lot of flowers and trees). Keep your windows closed and use air-conditioning. Do not let your child go out in the early part of the day when pollen counts are higher.
- ***Avoid molds.*** Your child should avoid damp areas such as places with wet leaves. To control mold indoors, keep wet areas like bathrooms and basements clean, dried, and aired out. Do not use humidifiers; they are nice wet environments where mold loves to grow.
- ***Avoid dust.*** Keep your house dust-free and control dust mites. Clean frequently and remove carpeting and heavy drapes, especially from your child's bedroom. Cover all your pillows, mattresses, and box springs in airtight covers. Remove all stuffed animals from your child's room.
- ***Avoid animal hairs and feathers.*** Sorry, no pets unless your child is cleared by an allergist. If you must have a pet, try to keep it outside and never let it go into your child's bedroom. If possible, shampoo the pet frequently. Do not use down pillows or comforters. If you do not have pets but your child is visiting someone who does, have him take his asthma medication (either a bronchodilator or cromolyn) before going to visit. Consider getting fish or a turtle instead of a dog or cat.
- ***Avoid roaches.*** Unfortunately, getting rid of cockroaches can be very difficult; they are a part of city life. Use insect sprays or bombs but make sure your child is not around when you spray, and let your home air out for a few hours before he returns. You may have to repeat spraying and/or bombing to get rid of roaches. Once the roaches are gone, use traps to keep them away.
- ***Avoid foods that bring on asthma.*** You may need to get your child tested by an allergist to find the foods that cause him problems. You can also remove suspected foods from his diet and see if there is a difference in his symptoms. Dairy and wheat products are common contributors to asthma.
- ***Prevent colds and upper respiratory infections.*** Make sure your child is rested, eats well, and gets exercise. Teach him to wash his hands before eating or touching his mouth, nose, or eyes. Avoid people with colds or the flu. Speak with your doctor about giving the flu vaccine to your child each fall.
- ***Avoid tobacco smoke.*** Don't smoke, don't let anyone smoke in your home, and don't take your child places where he will be exposed to smoke.

- ***Avoid lung irritants.*** **Don't wear perfume, don't use noxious fume-producing cleaning products while your child is home, and use an oven fan if you have one to reduce cooking odors. Don't let your child go outside on days when local pollution conditions are especially bad.**
- ***Prepare for exercise (don't avoid it).*** **Give your child a dose of his bronchodilator before he exerts himself. Avoid exercises that will take him outdoors in cold weather. Look for inside alternatives, such as swimming.**
- ***Have your child evaluated for gastroesophageal reflux.*** **If you think this is making his asthma worse, there are treatments available to reduce your child's symptoms.**
- ***Avoid any foods, medications, or situations that seem to trigger your child's asthma.***

Each of these medications comes in several forms: syrups, pills, inhaler pumps, and liquids for inhaling through a machine. You and your doctor should decide the exact medicines that are best for your child based upon his special needs. Never give cough medicine to a child with asthma as it will interact with his other medications. It also won't make your child feel better. If your child is taking asthma medicines, check with your doctor before giving any nonprescription medications.

Prevention: Once you know the triggers that cause your child's asthma, you must be vigilant to help your child avoid them. This will go a long way in relieving his asthma symptoms.

When to Call Your Health Care Provider:

- If your child has wheezing that doesn't improve with medications
- If his mild symptoms do not go away after one week of your treatments

When It Is an Emergency:

- If your child has severe wheezing or is unable to speak because of the wheezing
- If your child suddenly seems to be getting groggy
- If your child gets extremely agitated
- If your child has been working really hard at breathing and appears to be tiring out
- If your child looks pale or blue
- Anytime your child seems especially ill

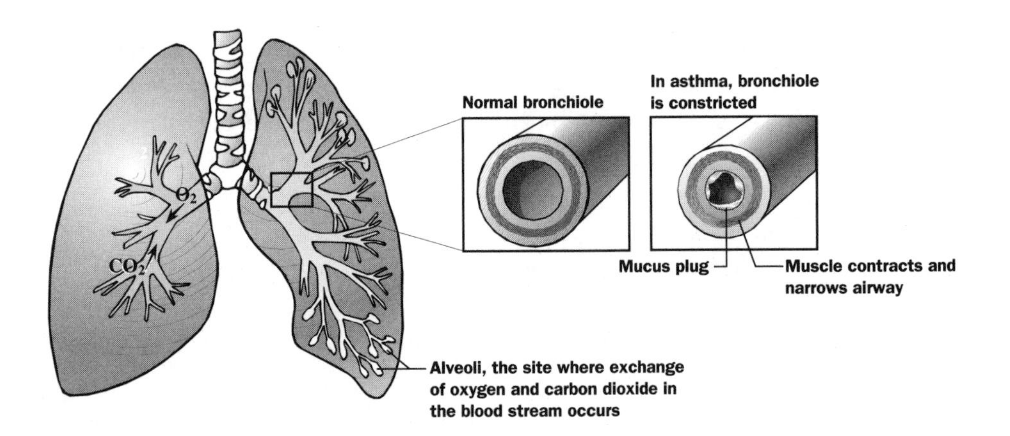

During an asthma attack, the airways of the lungs become constricted.

HIV (Human Immunodeficiency Virus) and Our Children

HIV is the virus that causes AIDS (Acquired Immune Deficiency Syndrome), which destroys the immune system and leaves sufferers susceptible to a variety of infections. Many of these illnesses are very serious if not deadly. HIV and AIDS disproportionately affect African Americans, especially women and their children; over 60 percent of newborn infants with HIV are black.

How Contracted: Infants most commonly contract HIV from mothers who are HIV positive.

Symptoms: The symptoms of AIDS vary and depend on the type of infections attacking the child. Symptoms can include recurrent "routine" childhood infections as well as pneumonia, developmental delay, poor growth and weight gain, chronic diarrhea, and severe anemia.

What to Do: A child with HIV should be in the care of a doctor specializing in HIV (either an infectious disease specialist or an immunologist) and a regular pediatrician. The therapies that are recommended for children with HIV change so rapidly that it is best to have a specialist who remains up to date on recent advances and will work with you to make sure you are aware of the latest forms of treatment as well.

Treatment of HIV requires the use of medications that attack the virus (such as AZT and 3TC), and giving medications to prevent infections commonly seen in children with AIDS (such as Bactrim). It also involves close monitoring so that any problems or infections can be treated immediately.

Prevention: In order to prevent transmitting HIV to a child, a pregnant woman who is infected must take AZT and her infant must take it immediately after birth. According to a nationwide study published in *The New England Journal of Medicine* in 1994, if pregnant women with HIV are treated with AZT during birth and pregnancy and their infants are treated for six weeks after birth, the rates of transmission to the infants can be reduced to less than 10 percent. Now that there is a therapy available to prevent transmission to infants, all women should seriously consider being tested for HIV when they are pregnant. If you request testing, any doctor can do it. At this point, this is the *only* way to prevent transmission of HIV to our children.

When to Call Your Health Care Provider:

- Any child with HIV or AIDS should have regular and routine contact with their doctor for checkups.
- Any evidence of an infection is a reason to call your doctor.

When It Is an Emergency:

- Anytime your child seems especially ill

Iron Deficiency Anemia and Our Children

This condition is extremely common among children and causes low levels of red blood cells which carry oxygen to all parts of the body. Anemia is especially serious in young children because it can be associated with lower IQ scores years later.

How Contracted: Iron deficiency anemia is caused by low levels of iron in the diet. Young children are prone to it because they grow very rapidly, which makes it difficult to supply enough iron in their diets. Certain foods, such as milk and dairy products, decrease the absorption of iron and can cause anemia.

Symptoms: There are no symptoms to indicate iron deficiency anemia. That is why testing in young children is very important.

What to Do: Once detected, iron deficiency anemia can be easily treated with dietary changes and vitamins or iron supplements. You will need to give your children more iron-rich foods such as lean beef, liver, whole grains, wheat germ, sardines, spinach and other leafy green vegetables, dried fruits, and beans. You should also cut down on your child's consumption of cow's milk and other dairy products; you can substitute soy products, which are available at health food stores. If your child takes iron supplements, be sure to give them to her with orange juice or other foods high in vitamin C to increase absorption.

Prevention: During pregnancy, make sure Mom gets enough iron. Then make sure your child has an iron-rich diet. Since infants and children are more susceptible to anemia, many foods such as formula, baby cereal, and Cream of Wheat are fortified with iron. Also, give your child soy milk rather than cow's milk once he is off formula.

When to Call Your Health Care Provider:

- If you have concerns that your child may be anemic or you would like advice about giving her high-iron foods

When It Is an Emergency:

- Iron deficiency anemia is rarely an emergency.

Lead Poisoning and Our Children

Lead poisoning occurs when lead from the environment gets into a child's body. This problem is more common among African-American children than other children and can cause developmental delays, lower IQ, and poor school performance.

How Contracted: Children can become lead poisoned in a number of ways. Older homes tend to have lead paint, which can chip off or peel. Children sometimes eat paint chips or ingest dust that settles on their toys. Lead poisoning is a problem in any home that is undergoing renovations. Children can also ingest lead when playing in soil that contains paint chips or dust around the home or in playgrounds. Less common sources of lead include lead pipes in the plumbing and certain ceramic glazes.

Symptoms: There are no symptoms to indicate early lead poisoning. That is why testing is very important in young children. Blood lead levels over 10 micrograms per deciliter of blood are considered elevated. A child who is at risk should be tested every year until he turns five.

What to Do: Treatment will depend on the level of lead in his blood. These recommendations have been developed by the Centers for Disease Control.

- *Blood lead level <10 mcg/dL.* This level is not considered to be lead poisoning and needs no further follow-up.
- *Blood lead level 10–14 mcg/dL.* This level is borderline. You should go through your home and your child's environment to check for any possible sources of

lead and remove them immediately. Your child should have a second lead test in three months to see if his lead level has improved or worsened over time.

- *Blood lead level 15–19 mcg/dL.* Children with blood lead levels in this range are at risk for reductions in their IQ. These children should be followed carefully by their physician and you should find ways to reduce lead in your child's environment. Then your doctor should repeat your child's lead level test in three months. If the levels are the same as before, the environment should be tested and cleared of lead. Several states have public health agencies that provide these services.
- *Blood lead level 20–69 mcg/dL.* Children with blood lead levels in this range should have complete evaluations that include a physical exam, assessments of their environment, and evaluations of their behavior and any impairments they may have. Children with blood lead levels greater than 45 mcg/dL should be referred to centers and physicians specializing in lead poisoning. These physicians have extensive experience in helping parents clear their homes of lead, getting state and/or city services to assist families when necessary, finding emergency housing if the child must be removed immediately, and determining if the child needs to be hospitalized to undergo chelation therapy. Chelation therapy is a process in which children are given medications that bind lead found in the blood so the kidneys can then filter it out of the body in the urine. Since lead is stored in children's bones, once it has been taken out of the blood, more lead will "leak" from the bones into the blood, causing the blood lead levels to rise again. Children who require chelation therapy can expect to undergo treatment several times until most of the lead has been removed.
- *Blood lead level>70 mcg/dL.* Children with levels this high are experiencing a medical emergency and need to be treated in the hospital by a specialist.

Prevention: Fortunately, lead poisoning is less common today because lead has been removed from paints and gasoline, which were major sources of poisoning in children. If your home is old or is being renovated and has paint that is more than twenty years old, you should have it tested for lead. You should also find out whether or not your drinking water comes through lead pipes. If it does, use bottled or filtered water. For a more detailed discussion of preventive measures, see Chapter 14.

When to Call Your Health Care Provider:

- If you have concerns that your child may be in an environment with lead

When It Is an Emergency:

- Extremely high levels of lead can cause brain damage, seizures, and coma. Your child's lead level should not get this high if you take precautions to keep his environment lead-free and have him tested at least once per year.

Sickle-Cell Anemia and Our Children

Sickle cell is one of the most common genetic disorders and affects 1 in 350 African-American children. People with sickle-cell anemia have red blood cells that change shape and get stuck in the smaller blood vessels, leading to severe complications.

How Contracted: Sickle-cell anemia is an inherited illness that is passed from parent to child and is most common in people of African descent, Middle Easterners, and Southern Europeans. Sickle-cell anemia should not be confused with sickle-cell trait, which affects one in ten African Americans but causes few symptoms. However, if you and your mate both have the trait, there is a one in four chance that your child will be born with the disease.

Symptoms: The problems caused by sickle-cell disease are related to the changed shapes of the red blood cells. Under certain conditions, they change from a smooth, round shape to a crescent, or sickle, shape. When sickled, the red blood cells cannot pass easily through the small blood vessels, get stuck, and block the blood flow to different parts of the body. Infants are protected from the symptoms of sickle cell for the first six months of life. As they get older, the blockages caused by sickle cell can cause a number of problems such as severe pain (known as a painful crisis), strokes and brain damage, lung damage, kidney damage, damage to the spleen and liver, and recurrent infections.

What to Do: In the past, children with sickle cell were not expected to live past the age of twenty. However, thanks to new therapies, people with sickle cell can survive well into adulthood. Any child with sickle cell should be in the care of a hematologist, a doctor specializing in blood disorders, as well as a regular pediatrician. There is no cure for sickle cell, but therapy to help children with this disease includes special vaccinations and daily antibiotics to prevent infections, vitamin supplements to help with the anemia, and even blood transfusions. When a child has a painful crisis she is usually hospitalized and treated with pain medications and a lot of fluids.

Prevention: Currently there is no way to prevent sickle-cell anemia but ongoing research in gene therapy may one day lead to a cure. At present, parents are tested for sickle trait, and if both test positive, they are counseled about the risks of having a child with sickle-cell disease. You can stay on top of the latest sickle-cell research by contacting the Sickle Cell Disease Association of America (see Resources).

When to Call Your Health Care Provider:

- Any child with sickle-cell disease should have regular and routine contact with their doctor for checkups.
- If your child has pain that is not handled by oral pain relievers and fluids
- If your child has an unexplained fever

When It Is an Emergency:

- If you think your child is having a stroke or has slurred speech, cannot move a limb, or seems disoriented

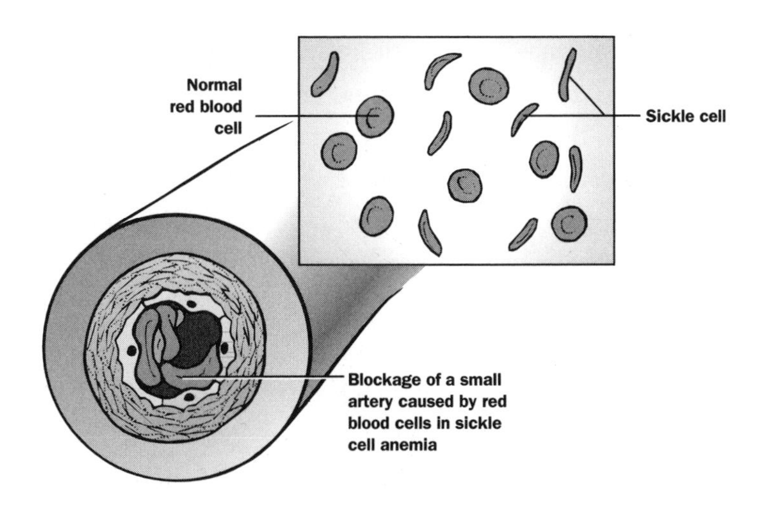

Sickled cells cannot pass through the blood vessels easily.

- If your child develops difficulty breathing
- Anytime your child seems especially ill

Childhood Diseases and Serious Illnesses

Chicken Pox (Varicella)

How Contracted: This viral illness is extremely common in children. It is highly contagious, passed from person to person through airborne nasal droplets from runny noses.

Symptoms: About fourteen days after being exposed to the virus, your child will become ill, developing fever and flu-like symptoms for about one day. You will then notice a rash over his entire body made of red, itchy bumps that will fill with clear fluid and become blisters. The rash will continue for about four days and will then heal, the bumps scabbing over within seven days. Once they are all crusted over, your child will no longer be contagious. A child who has had the chicken pox will be immune for life.

What to Do: In severe cases or if your child has problems with his immune system, your doctor will prescribe acyclovir, which is an antiviral medication that attacks the chicken pox virus, to reduce the severity and length of time your child will be ill. Otherwise, all you can do is manage the symptoms and wait for the virus to run its course. Give your child Tylenol for fever and soothe itchy skin with an oatmeal bath (e.g., Aveeno Oatmeal Bath Powder) and calamine lotion. You can also ask your doctor to prescribe diphenhydramine or hydroxizine liquid in cases where the itching is very severe. *Do not* give your child aspirin or products containing aspirin, such as Pepto-Bismol or Alka Seltzer. Aspirin can cause Reye's Syndrome, a condition that leads to severe liver and brain damage.

Prevention: There is now a vaccine available to prevent chicken pox. It is given when children are twelve months old, and it is 80 percent effective. This means that if 100 children get the vaccine and are exposed to chicken pox, 20 of them will still get the illness. Fortunately, children who catch chicken pox despite being vaccinated tend to have a very mild case. The chicken pox vaccine is currently not universally required for admission to day care, but many states will require it in the near future. Ask your doctor about day care and school vaccination requirements in your area.

When to Call Your Health Care Provider:

- If nonprescription medications do not provide enough comfort
- If you think any of the bumps have become infected

When It Is an Emergency:

- If your child seems especially ill, has personality changes, develops neck stiffness, has excessive bleeding from his rash, or develops difficulty breathing

Hepatitis A and B

How Contracted: Hepatitis, an infection of the liver, can be caused by several different viruses that are passed from person to person. The most common types in children are Hepatitis A and Hepatitis B. Hepatitis A is passed when someone has handled stool infected with the virus and does not wash his hands. This can occur when going to the bathroom or changing diapers. If that person then touches food, water, or something else your child puts in her mouth, the virus will be transferred and infect your child. Hepatitis B is the more severe disease of the two, but is more difficult to contract. It is carried in the blood and a person must have direct contact with the blood to become infected. In adults, this usually occurs through sexual intercourse or sharing needles. Children become infected when they are born to mothers who have Hepatitis B.

Symptoms: Both Hepatitis A and Hepatitis B are less severe in children than adults. In Hepatitis A your child will become ill four to six weeks after exposure; the symptoms of Hepatitis B develop two to five months after exposure. During the early part of a Hepatitis A infection, your child will have flu-like symptoms, fever, lack of energy, loss of appetite, and vomiting; some will develop jaundice. The symptoms of Hepatitis B come on slowly; in fact, many children born with it do not become ill until adulthood. Hepatitis B can cause complete liver failure and liver cancer when these children are older.

What to Do: There are no treatments for either Hepatitis A or Hepatitis B. Children with these infections are closely monitored by their physicians to make sure they do not develop liver failure. Since the liver metabolizes many drugs, ask your doctor before giving medications to a child with hepatitis. *Do not* give acetaminophen. It is metabolized by the liver and high doses can cause liver damage.

Prevention: Since there are no effective treatments, prevention is extremely important. There is a vaccine against Hepatitis A but it is not usually given to children. You can protect your child by demanding good handwashing habits from anyone who cares for her. This is especially important in day care centers where Hepatitis A can be easily passed. The vaccination against Hepatitis B is now given to all children in the first year of life. In addition, if you are pregnant you can make sure you are tested for Hepatitis B to avoid transmitting it to your child.

When to Call Your Health Care Provider:

- If he is unable to drink, is becoming dehydrated, or is unable to eat for a prolonged period
- If your child has been diagnosed with hepatitis you can expect him to not have much of an appetite. However, if your child shows any of the above conditions, seek medical attention.

When It Is an Emergency:

- If your child develops personality changes, extreme drowsiness, difficulty waking, or excessive bleeding

Measles (Rubeola)

How Contracted: Measles is caused by a virus that is passed from person to person through airborne nasal droplets. Though extremely contagious, it is not very common because most children have been vaccinated against it.

Symptoms: About ten to twelve days after exposure, your child will become ill, developing fever, conjunctivitis, runny nose, cough, and small white spots on the lining of her mouth. She will then develop a rash of small red blotches that start around the head, neck, and shoulders then spread, covering the entire body over two to three days. It will then begin to fade, again starting around the head and neck, then moving down the body. Children with measles are extremely irritable, miserable, and uncomfortable. Once your child has had measles, she will be immune for life.

What to Do: There are no medications to treat measles; you can only relieve the symptoms. Give your child acetaminophen for the fever, humidified air for the cough, and moisturizing drops for the eyes. Do not treat the rash; let it run its course.

Prevention: Make sure your child is vaccinated against the measles when she is twelve to fifteen months of age with the mumps/measles/rubella vaccine. (For a complete schedule of vaccinations, see the Appendix.)

When to Call Your Health Care Provider:

- If your child develops an ear infection or conjunctivitis while he has measles
- If you have any questions

When It Is an Emergency:

- If your child seems especially ill or develops difficulty breathing, personality changes, or a stiff neck

Meningitis

How Contracted: This infection of the fluid and lining covering the brain is caused by viruses or bacteria that enter the body through the mouth and nose and are passed from person to person in airborne nasal droplets and in saliva. Infants and toddlers are especially susceptible.

Symptoms: Viral meningitis is usually accompanied by mild flu-like symptoms and neck stiffness. Bacterial meningitis is more severe and can lead to serious complications such as loss of hearing and developmental delay, especially in infants. In the early stages of meningitis it will appear as if your child has the flu or a cold. The symptoms can then progress to include irritability, disorientation, seizures, vomiting, or neck stiffness.

What to Do: If you suspect your child has meningitis, you must see a doctor right away. It can be difficult to diagnose in infants and young children; the best way to determine if a child has meningitis is to obtain a sample of spinal fluid by performing a spinal tap. Bacterial meningitis is a very serious illness, especially in a young child, and it requires hospitalization, antibiotics, and close monitoring. Viral meningitis does not call for antibiotics and can be treated at home with rest and pain medications for the neck stiffness and discomfort.

Prevention: To prevent transmission of the germs that cause meningitis, make sure your child washes her hands frequently, especially after sneezing, coughing, or blowing her nose. You and others around you should, too. Do not allow anyone to kiss your child on the mouth. One type of bacterial meningitis in children is caused by a germ called Haemophilus influenzae type B (Hib). Children are now protected from this by the Hib vaccine which is given in the first eighteen months of life.

When to Call Your Health Care Provider:

- If your child has the flu or a cold and develops signs indicating meningitis

When It Is an Emergency:

- If your child is especially ill or develops a rash or excessive bleeding

Mumps

How Contracted: Mumps is caused by a virus that is passed from person to person through airborne nasal droplets and in saliva. It is not very common because most children have been vaccinated against it.

Symptoms: About seventeen to eighteen days after being exposed, your child will become ill, developing fever and swelling of the parotid gland. Located in front of his ears and along the jawline, this gland produces saliva and when it is swollen it is very painful and chewing is difficult. Mumps lasts about seven days, and your child is contagious until the swelling is gone. Once your child has had the mumps he will be immune for life.

What to Do: There are no medications to treat mumps, so all you can do is manage the symptoms. Give your child acetaminophen for fever, and avoid sour foods such as lemons and vinegar to prevent further swelling of the parotid gland.

Prevention: Your child will be vaccinated against mumps at twelve to fifteen months of age when he receives the mumps/measles/rubella vaccine. (For a complete schedule of vaccinations, see the Appendix.)

When to Call Your Health Care Provider:

- If you have any questions

When It Is an Emergency:

- If your child develops stiff neck, has personality changes, or seems especially ill

Pneumonia

How Contracted: Pneumonia is an infection of the lungs. There are several types of pneumonia, and most are caused by the same viruses that trigger colds. These germs are passed from person to person in airborne nasal droplets and in saliva. Pneumonia can also be caused by bacteria which are passed in the same way as viruses, but in these cases, the child tends to be sicker and have a higher fever.

Symptoms: Symptoms can range from very mild to severe depending on the type of germ causing the illness and your child's age. In general, pneumonia starts as a cold, then progresses to include a severe cough, a high fever, and some difficulty breathing.

What to Do: When pneumonia has been caused by a virus there is no medicine for treatment, and it can take seven to ten days for your child to begin to get better and three to four weeks for a full recovery. Bacterial pneumonia responds very well to antibiotics, and you will see an improvement within 24 to 48 hours of starting the medication and a full recovery in one to two weeks. Most cases of pneumonia can be treated at home, but if your child seems especially ill, is having trouble drinking fluids, or is having problems getting enough oxygen, he may need to be hospitalized.

Since it is difficult to tell the difference between viral and bacterial pneumonia, most children will be treated with antibiotics. You can also relieve the symptoms that accompany pneumonia. Give acetaminophen for the fever, humidified air or mist to loosen mucus, and make your child drink plenty of fluids. Do not give your child cough medicine. You want him to cough the mucus out of his lungs and cough medicine will inhibit that process.

Prevention: To prevent transmission of the germs that cause pneumonia, make sure your child washes his hands often, especially after sneezing, coughing, or blowing his nose. You and others around you should, too. Do not allow anyone to kiss your child on the mouth.

When to Call Your Health Care Provider:

- If your child is not able to drink fluids
- If he has any difficulty breathing
- If you can hear him wheezing
- If he has not improved in one week

When It Is an Emergency:

- If your child suddenly seems to be getting groggy
- If your child gets extremely agitated
- If your child has been working really hard at breathing and appears to be tiring out
- If your child looks pale or blue or seems especially ill

Rubella (German Measles)

How Contracted: Rubella is caused by a virus and is passed from person to person and in saliva. It causes only a mild illness in children, but is devastating to pregnant women who have not had rubella or been vaccinated against it. It can lead to birth defects such as deafness, heart problems, and mental retardation. Most pregnant women are tested to make sure they are not susceptible to rubella, but any child with rubella should be kept away from pregnant women just in case.

Symptoms: Two to three weeks after exposure, your child will become ill, developing a mild fever and a red, blotchy rash that starts around the head and neck and moves down the body. You may also notice swelling of the lymph nodes along the back of the neck. The illness is not severe, and most children are better within three to four days. Once your child has had rubella he will be immune for life.

What to Do: There is no medication to treat rubella; you can only relieve the symptoms. Give your child acetaminophen for fever, bed rest and fluids.

Prevention: Make sure your child is vaccinated against rubella at twelve to fifteen months of age when he receives the mumps/measles/rubella vaccine. (For a complete schedule of vaccinations, see the Appendix.)

When to Call Your Health Care Provider:

- If you have any questions

When It Is an Emergency:

- If your child seems especially ill
- If a pregnant woman has come into contact with a child with rubella

Scarlet Fever

How Contracted: Scarlet fever is an infection caused by the same germ that leads to strep throat (see p. 397). It enters the body through the mouth and nose and is passed from person to person in airborne nasal droplets and in saliva.

Symptoms: Your child will have a sore throat and fever for one to two days. She will then develop a rash that starts around her neck, groin, and armpits but then spreads over her entire body. Her skin will become red and she will develop small fine bumps that make her skin look like sandpaper. The rash is also darker red in the armpits and groin. Once your child has started antibiotics, the rash will clear. However, she may get some peeling of her skin including her fingertips and toes up to six weeks afterward. If it is treated, there are no long-term problems associated with scarlet fever.

What to Do: Your child must receive antibiotics to treat scarlet fever. Once she has been on medicine for 24 hours, she is no longer contagious. While scarlet fever is not extremely serious by itself, treatment is important to prevent the complications of scarlet fever such as rheumatic heart disease.

Prevention: To prevent transmission of the germs that cause scarlet fever, make sure your child washes her hands frequently, especially after sneezing, coughing, or blowing her nose. You and others around you should, too. Do not allow anyone to kiss your child on the mouth.

When to Call Your Health Care Provider:

- If your child is not better within 48 hours of starting antibiotics

When It Is an Emergency:

- If your child seems especially ill

Strep Throat

How Contracted: Strep is caused by a germ called streptococcus which enters the body through the mouth and nose and is passed from person to person in airborne nasal droplets and in saliva. Untreated, it can lead to complications such as heart disease and scarlet fever.

Symptoms: Strep begins with symptoms of a cold that progress to include sore throat, fever, swollen lymph nodes, and sometimes stomach pain. A child with strep will often have a red throat, and you may see pus on the tonsils. However, these symptoms can also be caused by a virus. Your child will need a throat culture to determine if he has a strep infection.

What to Do: Your child must receive antibiotics to treat strep throat. Once she has been on medicine for 24 hours, she is no longer contagious.

Prevention: To prevent transmission of the germ that causes strep, make sure your child washes her hands frequently, especially after sneezing, coughing, or blowing her nose. You and others around you should, too. Do not allow anyone to kiss your child on the mouth.

When to Call Your Health Care Provider:

- If your child is not better within 48 hours of starting antibiotics

When It Is an Emergency:

- If your child seems especially ill

RESOURCES

Recommended Reading for Parents

Asthma

American Lung Association Family Guide to Asthma and Allergies, Norman H. Edelman, M.D. (Little, Brown and Company, 1997). This book explains how to manage asthma and allergies, with special advice for parents of asthmatic children.

A Parent's Guide to Asthma: How You Can Help Your Child Control Asthma at Home, School, and Play, Nancy Sander (Plume, 1994). Written by the president of the National Allergy and Asthma Network, this book offers advice on allergy management, finding a specialist, and regulating children's activities.

Children's General Health

The American Academy of Pediatrics' Guide to Your Child's Symptoms, Steven P. Shelov, ed. (Random House, 1997). This is a comprehensive, accessible guide to 100 of the most common symptoms of children's illnesses from A-Z.

Dr. Spock's Baby and Child Care, Benjamin Spock, M.D. (Pocket Books, 1992). Here is a classic source book for parents, with an entire section on illnesses.

How to Raise a Healthy Child, Lundon H. Smith (M. Evans and Company, 1998). This book includes medical advice from a well-known pediatrician.

The Portable Pediatrician, Laura Walter Nathanson (HarperCollins, 1994). This is a guide to the first five years of a child's medical and behavioral health, with a special section on symptoms and their severity.

Raising Healthy Kids, Michio Kushi, Arline Kushi, Edward Esko, and Wendy Esko (Avery Publishing Group, 1994). This book presents a holistic approach to parenting and treating illnesses.

Your Child in the Hospital, Nancy Keene and Linda Lamb, eds. (Oreilly and Co., 1998). Here is a guide to help parents and children prepare for short- and long-term hospital stays. This book contains lots of practical and detailed information, from packing to billing.

HIV and AIDS

The Guide to Living with HIV Infection, John G. Barlett and Ann K. Finkbeiner (Johns Hopkins AIDS Clinic Staff, 1998). This is the most complete resource for people living with HIV/AIDS, with information on treatment, research, and family support resources.

HIV Infection in Children: A Guide to Practical Management, Jacqueline Y. Q. Mok and Marie-Louise Newell (Cambridge, 1995). A medically oriented book with detailed information on how children are specifically affected by HIV.

Pos magazine. Call 212–242–1900 for subscription information about this magazine, which offers timely information on research, treatments, and other HIV/AIDS issues.

Sickle Cell Anemia

Cell Anemia, Alvin Silverstein and Virginia B. Silverstein (Enslow Publishing, 1997). This book explains symptoms, treatment, and research and includes a Q and A section and website listings.

Sickle Cell Anemia, George Beshore (Franklin Watts, 1994). This book chronicles the history of the disease, describes its transmission, and discusses treatments.

Recommended Reading for Children

Asthma

Taking Asthma to School, Kim Gosselin, Barbara Mitchell, and Moss Freedman (JayJo Books, 1998). The authors talk to kids about how to manage asthma in a school setting.

Winning Over Asthma, Eileen Dolan (Pedipress, 1996). For children beginning to cope with asthma and its treatments, this book prepares young children for what to expect.

Children's General Health

Dinosaurs Alive and Well!: A Guide to Good Health, Vol. 1, Laurene Krasny Brown and Marc Brown (Little, Brown and Company, 1992). This book provides children with interesting and useful ways to maintain good health. It includes information on nutrition, illnesses, and stress.

Healthy Me, Angela Royston and Edwina Riddell (Barron's Educational Series, 1995). Children will learn about how the body recovers from minor infections and injuries (colds, scrapes, and ear infections) and the importance of doctor checkups.

When I'm Sick, JoAnne Nelson (Wright, 1995). This book tells the story of how three young children feel when sick with a cold, the flu, and the chicken pox.

HIV and AIDS: For Children

Be a Friend: Children Who Live with AIDS Speak, Lori S. Weiner and Phillip A. Pizzo (Aprille Best, 1994). In this book, children openly discuss the truth about living with AIDS.

Kids with AIDS, Anna Forbes (Rosen, 1996). Here is a clear, straightforward book that focuses on living with AIDS and accepting those who are infected.

You Can Call Me Willy: A Story for Children about AIDS, Judith C. Verniero and Vernon Flory (American Psychological Association, 1995). This is the story of an African-American girl with AIDS and how she bravely stands up to ignorance and discrimination.

Organizations

Asthma

Allergy and Asthma Network/Mothers of Asthmatics, Inc., 3554 Chain Bridge Rd., Suite 200, Fairfax, VA 22030–2709, (800) 878–4403. This organization helps parents of children with asthma learn about the most useful treatments and methods of management while also offering support.

American Lung Association, 1740 Broadway, New York, NY 10019–4374 (212) 315–8700.

Website: www.lungusa.org.

Call for a local chapter and information about your child and asthma.

Asthma and Allergy Foundation of America, 1125 15th Street NW, Suite 502, Washington, D.C. 20005, (800) 7–ASTHMA. This organization provides information on asthma management and treatments and publishes a newsletter and resource catalogue.

Children's General Health

American Medical Association, 515 N. State St., Chicago, IL 60610, (312) 464–5000. Call for referrals in your area for a physician specializing in your child's needs.

Website: www.asma-assn.org

National Medical Association, 1012 10th St., NW, Washington, D.C. 20001, (202) 347–1895. The NMA provides referrals to consumers for African-American physicians.

Website: www.natmed.org

Office of Minority Health, P.O. Box 37337, Washington, D.C. 20013–7337, (800) 444–6472. Call to locate organizations, community programs, experts, or educational material in your area for specific issues affecting your child.

HIV/AIDS

Just Kids Foundation, P.O. Box 42, Village Station, New York, NY 10014, (212) 627–3390. This organization provides advocacy and self-help strategies for parents and HIV positive children. It publishes newsletter and offers phone support.

Magic Johnson Foundation, 1888 Century Park East, Suite 1010, Los Angeles, CA 90067, (310) 785–0301. This foundation raises money to help organizations that care for people with AIDS and educates children about HIV and AIDS.

National Pediatric and Family HIV Resource Center, 15 S. 9th Street, Newark, NJ 07107, (800) 362–0071 or (201) 268–8251 for New Jersey residents. This organization provides consultations, technical assistance, and informational pamphlets such as "Jimmy and the Egg Virus" about a boy who learns he is HIV positive.

Pediatric AIDS Foundation, 1311 Colorado Ave., Santa Monica, CA 90404, (310) 395–9051. This is a national organization that funds pediatric HIV research and sponsors public education and school programs.

Positively Kids, P.O. Box 4512, Queensbury, NY 12804, (518) 798–0915. This organization provides education and support services for families and children living with HIV. It also publishes a newsletter.

Sickle Cell Anemia

SCARE (Sickle Cell Advocates for Research and Empowerment), P.O. Box 630127, Bronx, NY 10463, e-mail:scareemail@aol.com. This organization educates people with sickle cell anemia and their families.

The Sickle Cell Information Center, P.O. Box 109, Grady Memorial Hospital, 80 Butler Street, Atlanta, GA 30335, (404) 616–3572, fax: (404) 616–5998, e-mail:aplatt@emory.edu.

Website: www.emory.edu./PEDS/SICKLE

This center educates people with sickle cell disease and their families.

Video Resources

The Family Video Guide: Over Three Hundred Movies to Share with Your Children, Terry Catchpole and Catherine Catchpole (Williamson Publishing, 1992). This guide lists over three hundred movies to share with your children. It includes sections dealing with special concerns such as illness.

Appendix

Recommended Childhood Immunization Schedule United States, January - December 1998

Vaccines[1] are listed under the routinely recommended ages. Bars indicate range of acceptable ages for immunization. Catch-up immunization should be done during any visit when feasible. Shaded ovals indicate vaccines to be assessed and given if necessary during the early adolescent visit.

Age ► / Vaccine ▼	Birth	1 mo	2 mo	4 mo	6 mo	12 mo	15 mo	18 mo	4-6 yrs	11-12 yrs	14-16 yrs
Hepatitis B[2,3]	Hep B-1										
			Hep B-2		Hep B-3					Hep B[3]	
Diphtheria, Tetanus, Pertussis[4]			DTaP or DTP	DTaP or DTP	DTaP or DTP		DTaP or DTP[4]		DTaP or DTP	Td	
H influenzae type b[5]			Hib	Hib	Hib	Hib					
Polio[6]			Polio[6]	Polio		Polio[6]			Polio		
Measles, Mumps, Rubella[7]						MMR			MMR[7]	MMR[7]	
Varicella[8]							Var			Var[8]	

Approved by the Advisory Committee on Immunization Practices (ACIP), the American Academy of Pediatrics (AAP), and the American Academy of Family Physicians (AAFP).

[1] This schedule indicates the recommended age for routine administration of currently licensed childhood vaccines. Some combination vaccines are available and may be used whenever administration of all components of the vaccine is indicated. Providers should consult the manufacturer's package inserts for detailed recommendations.

[2] **Infants born to HBsAg-negative mothers** should receive 2.5μg of Merck vaccine (Recombivax HB) or 10 μg of SmithKline Beecham (SB) vaccine (Engerix-B). The 2nd dose should be administered at least 1 mo after the first dose. The 3rd dose should be given at least 2 mos after the second, but not before 6 mos of age.
Infants born to HBsAg-positive mothers should receive 0.5 mL of hepatitis B immune globulin (HBIG) within 12 hrs of birth, either 5μg of Merck vaccine (Recombivax HB) or 10μg of SB vaccine (Engerix-B) at a separate site. The 2nd dose is recommended at 1-2 mos of age and the 3rd dose at 6 mos of age.
Infants born to mothers whose HBsAg status is unknown should receive either 5μg of Merck vaccine (Recombivax HB) or 10μg of (SB) vaccine (Engerix-B) within 12 hrs of birth. The 2nd dose of vaccine is recommended at 1 mo of age and the 3rd dose at 6 mos of age. Blood should be drawn at time of delivery to determine the mother's HBsAG status; if it is positive, the infant should receive HBIG as soon as posible (no later than 1 wk of age). The dosage and timing of subsequent vaccine doses should be based upon the mother's HBsAG status.

[3] Children and adolescents who have not been vaccinated against Hepititis B in infancy may begin the series during any visit. Those who have not previously received 3 doses of hepatitis B vaccine should initiate or complete the series during the 11-12-year-old visit, and unvaccinated older adolescents should be vaccinated whenever possible. The 2nd dose should be administered at least 1 mo after the first dose, and the 3rd dose should be administered at least 4 mos after the first dose and at least 2 mos after the 2nd dose.

[4] DTaP (diphtheria and tetanous toxoids and acellular pertussis vaccine) is the preferred vaccine for all doses in the vaccination series, including completion of the series in the children who have received 1 or more doses of whole-cell DTP vaccine. Whole-cell DTP is an acceptable alternative to DTaP. The 4th dose (DTP or DTaP) may be administered as early as 12 months of age, provided 6 months have elapsed since the 3rd dose, and if the child is unlikely to return at 15-18 mos. Td (tetanus and diphtheria toxoids) is recommended at 11-12 years of age if at least 5 years have elapsed since the last dose of DTP, DTaP or DT. Subsequent routine Td boosters are recommended every 10 years.

[5] Three H influenzae type b (Hib) conjugate vaccines are licensed for infant use. If PRP-OMP (PedvaxHIB [Merck]) is administered at 2 and 4 mos of age, a dose at 6 mos is not required.

[6] Two poliovirus vaccines are currently licensed in the US: inactivated poliovirus vaccine (IPV) and oral poliovirus vaccine (OPV). The following schedules are acceptable to the ACIP, the AAP, and the AAFP. Parents and providers may choose among these options:

1) 2 doses of IPV followed by 2 doses of OPV.
2) 4 doses of IPV.
3) 4 doses of OPV.

The ACIP recommends 2 doses of IPV at 2 and 4 mos of age followed by 2 doses of OPV at 12-18 mos and 4-6 years of age. IPV is the only poliovirus vaccine recommended for immuno-compromised persons and their household contacts.

[7] The 2nd dose of MMR is recommended routinely at 4-6 yrs of age but may be administered during any visit, provided at least 1 mo has elapsed since receipt of the 1st dose and that both doses are administered at or after 12 mos of age. Those who have not previously received the second dose should complete the schedule no later than the 11-12 year visit.

[8] Susceptible children may receive varicella vaccine (Var) at any visit after the first birthday, and those who lack a reliable history of chickenpox should be immunized during the 11-12-year-old visit. Susceptible children 13 years of age or older should receive 2 doses, at least 1 month apart.

GIRLS: Birth to 36 Months
LENGTH FOR AGE & WEIGHT FOR AGE

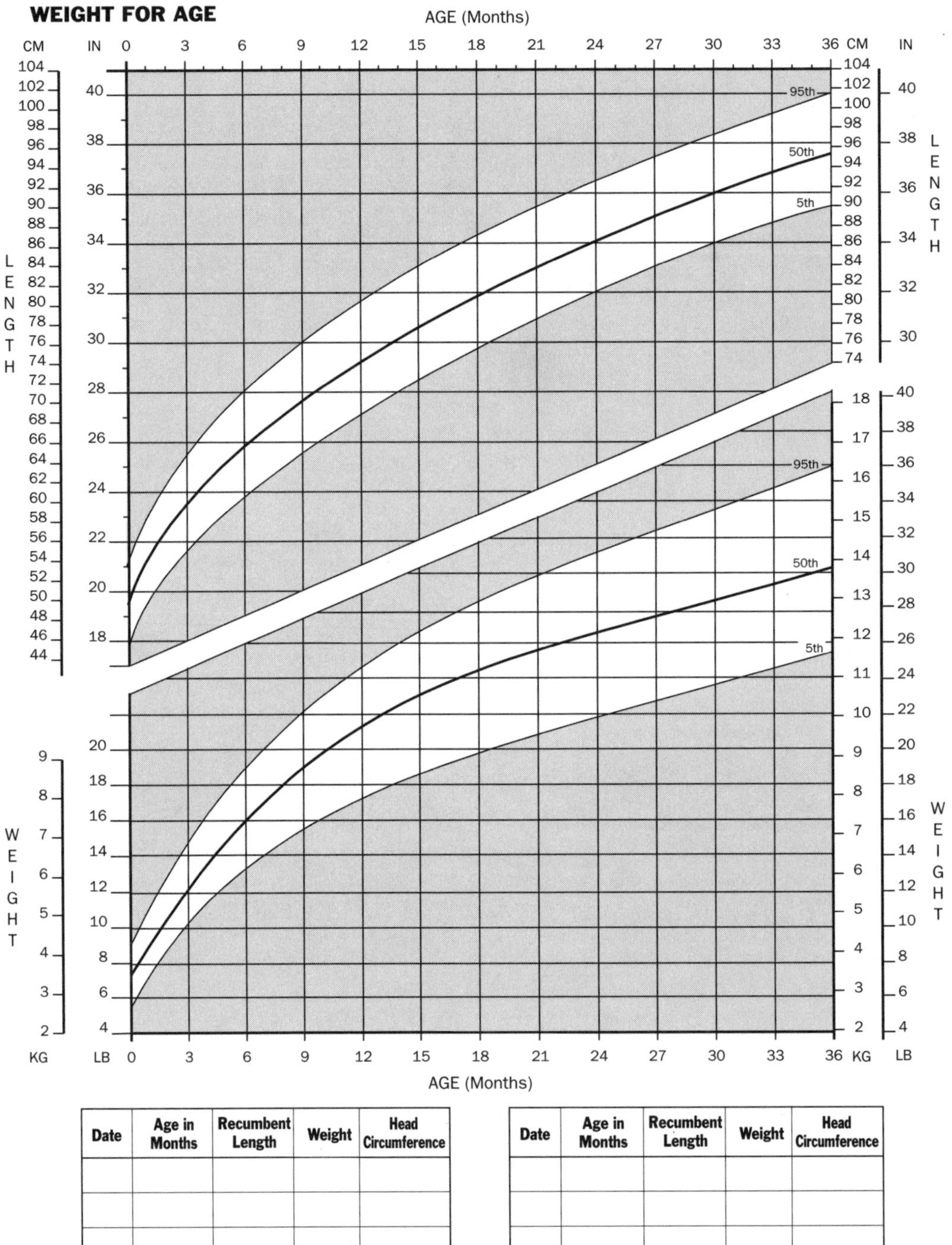

Date	Age in Months	Recumbent Length	Weight	Head Circumference

Date	Age in Months	Recumbent Length	Weight	Head Circumference

BOYS: Birth to 36 Months
LENGTH FOR AGE & WEIGHT FOR AGE

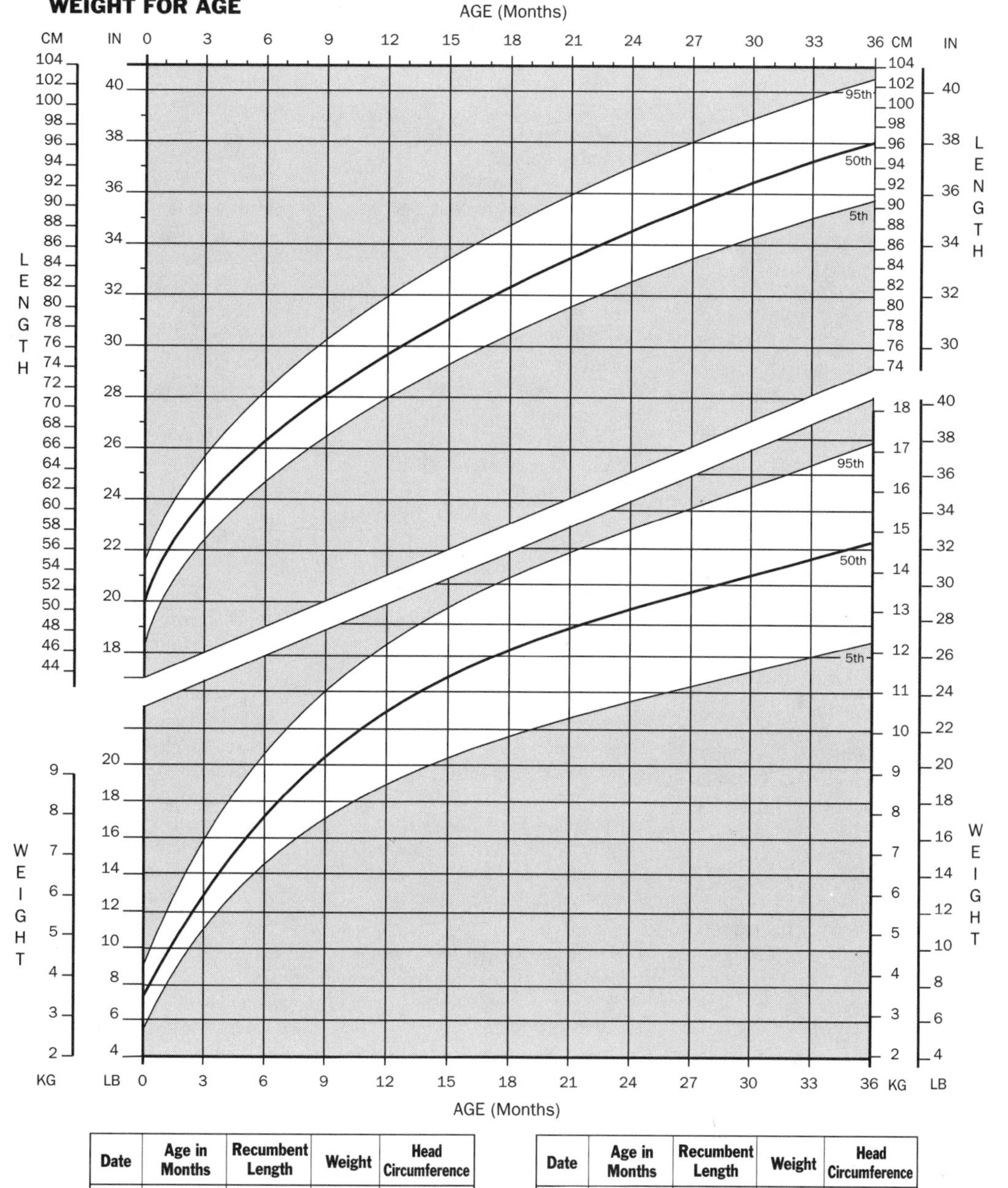

Date	Age in Months	Recumbent Length	Weight	Head Circumference

Date	Age in Months	Recumbent Length	Weight	Head Circumference

Index

Illustration/Photo Credits

INTRODUCTION
Page x: Steve Smith/FPG International LLC
Page xiii: Ron Chapple/FPG International LLC

CHAPTER 1
Page 1: Michael Kasowitz/FPG International LLC
Page 17: Mark French

CHAPTER 2
Page 24: Egan-Chin
Page 29: Mark French

CHAPTER 3
Page 42: Arthur Tilley/FPG International LLC
Page 53: Allford/ Trotman

CHAPTER 4
Page 59: Allford/Trotman
Page 74: Arleen Frasca
Page 80: Christian Michaels/FPG International LLC
Page 85: Egan-Chin
Pages 91, 97: Arleen Frasca

CHAPTER 5
Page 102: Vladimir Pcholkin/FPG International LLC
Pages 106, 117: Mark French

CHAPTER 6
Pages 131, 144: FPG International LLC

CHAPTER 7
Page 154: Allford/Trotman
Pages 160–161: Arleen Frasca
Page 178: Mark French

CHAPTER 8
Page 187: Mark French
Page 189: Allford/Trotman
Page 192: Mark French

CHAPTER 9
Page 205: Allford/Trotman
Page 207: Michele-Salmieri/FPG International LLC

CHAPTER 10
Page 220: Ron Chapple/FPG International LLC
Page 231: Mark French

CHAPTER 11
Page 246: Ron Chapple/FPG International LLC
Page 255: Egan-Chin

CHAPTER 12
Pages 267, 280: Egan-Chin

CHAPTER 13
Page 291: Vladimir Pcholkin/FPG International LLC
Page 292: Jill Sabella/FPG International LLC

CHAPTER 14
Page 318: Mark French
Pages 319, 322, 336, 338–347: Arleen Frasca

CHAPTER 15
Page 353: Allford/Trotman
Pages 358, 384, 389: Arleen Frasca

APPENDIX
Page 403 (Immunization Chart): American Academy of Pediatrics
Pages 404, 405 (Height and Growth Charts): Used with permission of Ross Products Division, Abbott Laboratories, Columbus, OH 43216 from "NCHS Growth Chart" © 1982 Ross Products Division, Abbott Laboratories